THE FIFTH
(AND PROBABLY LAST)
MORNINGSIDE PAPERS

THE FIFTH
(AND PROBABLY LAST)
MORNINGSIDE PAPERS

PETER GZOWSKI

M&S

Canadian Cataloguing in Publication Data
Gzowski, Peter
The fifth (and probably last) Morningside papers
Includes Index.
ISBN 0-7710-3716-3
1. Morningside (Radio program).   I. Title.   II. Title: Morningside (Radio program).

PN1991.3.C3G96 1994   791.44'72   C94-931966-x

The publishers acknowledge the support of the Canada Council, the Ontario Arts Council, and the Ontario Ministry of Culture, Tourism and Recreation for their publishing program.

Every effort has been made to secure permission from the authors of the letters, essays, poems, etc., included in this book. Further information would be welcomed by the publishers.

Typesetting by M&S
Printed and bound in Canada. The paper used in this book is acid-free.

McClelland & Stewart Inc.
The Canadian Publishers
481 University Avenue
Toronto, Ontario
M5G 2E9

1 2 3 4 5   98 97 96 95 94

CONTENTS

Paper Voices

A Preface by Peter Gzowski

It's been three years now since the last *Morningside Papers* were published — well, not the last, but the one before this one, which is *probably* the last, and not the latest, either, since the *Latest* came out a couple of years after the *New*, which *were* new at the time, just as the *Latest* were once the latest, if you know what I mean (the *Fourth* were always the fourth) — and nearly a decade since the first, which were just *The Morningside Papers* (who knew it would turn into a kind of intermittent Canadian *Chum's Annual?*), so even though (phew) there are a lot of copies of all of them around and lots of people are familiar with them, I thought it might be time for a bit of a refresher course on how to make your way through them, and how to figure out who's saying what.

Besides, as you'll see, this one's a bit different. The first voice, in place of mine, is Shelagh Rogers'. Nice idea, eh? Shelagh, after all, has been part of the *Morningside* mail for a long time now, and if you're going to open with a different voice, which I thought we should for once, is there a more pleasant one anywhere on the CBC — anywhere in the *world*, for that matter — than hers?

Voices are really what all the *Papers* have been about — the voices of Canadians speaking, and writing, from their minds and hearts. Once again, there are a number of people who write for a living in here. Some are writers we asked to contribute to the program over the years this collection represents — George "Whip" Bowering, for instance, or the five poets who came in one morning to read and ruminate about their art, or Martin O'Malley, or Silver Donald Cameron. Others — Susan Musgrave and her naughty tale of Leonard

Cohen, for example, or Tim Wynne-Jones and his memories of Kitimat — just heard something on the radio they wanted to respond to. In at least one case — there's a John Gray who wrote from Vancouver — I just don't know if the writer is a pro or not. As I wrote long ago, anyone who thinks that eloquent and literate writing in this country is practised only by those who've taken out a licence should join me any morning as I open the *Morningside* mail.

Also once again, we've made every effort to obtain the permission of all my fellow authors to reproduce or quote from their contributions. But, as I've said before, people move; we never have been able to find them all. I beg the forgiveness of anyone who is surprised to find his or her work here; I'd still rather chance that annoyance than risk the disappointment of leaving a deserving writer out.

Now, who's talking when? After Shelagh, there's a chapter — one of three — that's all mine, and elsewhere, the voice at the top, the one in the bolder type, is mine, as well. Other than that, a little ✉ indicates a new contributor or a new letter. The rest, I think, is self-evident.

And is this *really* the last *Morningside Papers*?

As the title says, probably. Nothing lasts forever, and it may well be time to turn this sort of project over to other anthologists. Along with all the other people who have shared the happy task of putting these books together, I'm very proud of what they've come to be; it would be nice to end with a bang.

Still, who knows? There was a time when I thought the *first* was the last.

Here's Shelagh.

Reading with Peter

An Introduction by Shelagh Rogers

I grew up with Peter Gzowski in the laundry room. He was the host of *This Country in the Morning*, which my mother always listened to while she was ironing. She thought he was groovy. I still associate that program with the fresh scent of newly washed linen and the sound of a steam iron puffing and belching. If you'd told me then that twenty years later I would be Peter Gzowski's most frequent guest, I would have said, "Get real. . . . The guy with the moustache and the horn-rimmed glasses who sits at a table somewhere and talks all the time in a smoky voice?" But, sure enough. And this is how it came to pass.

"Tell her if she giggles, I'll break her legs."

It was 1986. I was co-host of the local CBC morning show. Gloria Bishop, who was then the executive producer of *Morningside* (Patsy Pehleman succeeded her in 1989), asked me if I'd like to read the listener mail on air with Peter Gzowski. Eve McBride, who edited the *Morningside* letters and read them on air, was leaving the program to pursue a writing career. Gloria had called me a few years earlier to give me some advice: Get rid of the smile in your voice. I mean, if you had to report on an earthquake, who'd believe you? But it was Peter who said to Gloria, "Tell her if she giggles, I'll break her legs." I decided to give it a try. Eight years later, my legs are still intact.

I moved on from the morning show to co-host (with the versatile and buoyant Peter Tiefenbach) a national CBC Stereo program called *The Arts Tonight*. But I could never give up this gig.

Even before I presented the mail with Peter, I enjoyed eavesdropping on it. The *Morningside* mail is a CBC Radio — and a Canadian — phenomenon. It's radio's equivalent of a letters to the editor page, where people can vent their spleens or extend national debates or hurl invective at those who disagree with them. It's the original voice mail, if you think of it. But it's more than that, too — much more. Peter has called it a kind of village bulletin board for the nation. But it's more than *that*, too. People share their lives and record their experiences in their letters to *Morningside*. They write about who they are and what they do. They share their most intimate experiences. Sometimes, I think, they say things in their letters to Peter they might not ever say aloud. And sometimes, they're just very, very funny.

Reading the mail with Peter is an experience that, like this book, transcends the studio moment. Over the years I've been astonished and touched at how strangers recognize my voice. Seven years ago, I was hiking an old gold moilers' trail, the Chilcoot, and I sprained my ankle about two hundred feet from the summit. My hiking partners, Gordon and Gwennie Hooper, two wonderful seniors from Victoria whom I could barely keep up with — and two avid listeners — saw to it that I got medical attention. After the two-mile hike to the ranger's cabin, Gord and Gwennie left me in the hands of Marc Goudreau, park warden. He examined my swollen and by this time exotically bruised joint and got me to soak it in the glacier-fed stream out back.

In the course of our chat, he asked me if I was Shelagh Rogers. And I thought, Wow! You can get *The Arts Tonight* this far north? However, his next question was, "What's Peter Gzowski really like?" Well, my *Morningside* connection was an entrée to a meal of home-made bread, baked beans with maple syrup and an apple pie he'd made that afternoon. After dinner, I had a solar-heated shower. By the time I finished, Marc had pitched my tent. It was 10:30 and the sun was just going down behind the mountains, its last rays casting a coral haze on the glaciers. I count it as one of the best days of my life.

Another moment of recognition occurred when I was buying rainbow-striped condoms as an anonymous gift for a *Morningside* producer. (The *Morningside* "family" always draws names from a hat for the annual Christmas party.) After I said to the cashier, "Uh, they're for a friend," he said, "Hey, are you Shelagh Rogers?" I blushed and nodded. And, discreetly placing my purchase in a bag, he leaned closer to me and said, "So, what's Peter Gzowski really like?"

It's a question that's dogged me. After a speech about arts funding in Alberta, a talk about my years at Queen's for the alumni association, after a hog-calling contest at the Royal Winter Fair and during a couple of first (and subsequently last) dates, the question has come up. I have always answered it with, "He's just like he is on the radio." Which has some degree of truth to it. He looks like he sounds: at home, comfortable and maybe a little rumpled. He's the only person I know who gets runs in his sweaters. His socks are too short: when he crosses his legs there's the eerie fishbelly white of his calves.

Just as he is on the air, he's a peerless listener. He's taught me a lot about interviewing. He's a mentor who's given me the best career advice (which I've followed) and a friend who's given me the worst romantic advice (I've done the opposite). There are, of course, fascinating inconsistencies. He's naughtier and saucier off the air, and his language is bluer. (On the air, talk of lingerie makes him blush.) He's the man who has lent his name to literacy in Canada: his PG Invitational golf tournaments from coast to coast to coast have raised more than three million dollars. He's hosted roasts and galas for the cause. He's been out there in a very public way. But shortly after his own (1994 Leacock Medal-nominated) book *Canadian Living* came out, he was almost a no-show at his home-town launch party. We had to drag him to it. Yes, he's shy, too. What's Peter Gzowski really like? It's like asking how many surrealists it takes to change a light bulb. The answer is, "A fish." Hope that helps.

My side of the *Morningside* mail has a ritual. I drive in from the country to our corporate headquarters, the Canadian Broadcasting Centre, a building that takes up half a city block and still smells like a dentist's office. My partner, Charlie Cheffins, drops me off and I pray I can get a waiting elevator to the third floor. I head straight to the desk of Shelley Ambrose, who produces all the letters on *Morningside*. Shelley is a whirlwind of prairie energy who oversees every aspect of Peter's public life and without whom Peter could not be Peter. Over the past eight years, she's become my best friend. She orders me to read the letters over and fends off anyone who wants to talk to me. Marieke Meier, the studio director (and, by coincidence of our Ottawa roots, my friend since grade nine), calls Shelley to say they're ready for us. We head down the hall. I walk into Peter's softly lit studio with a mug of coffee and my ear-piece in one hand, the letters and a pencil (which I have to hold when I'm on the air or I cannot talk) in the other. I arrange myself in my chair, exchanging pleasantries with Peter. Or not. Sometimes he's incommunicado, perhaps just recovering from the previous interview, or gearing up for a later one. The music that's piping me in has fifteen seconds to go. Peter, who's been looking at his papers, looks up at the clock, beyond me, to the control room, to Shelley and Marieke. The music ends. We're live. And I, like all his guests at this moment, now have Peter's full attention. Peter looks at me and says, "Shelagh Rogers joins me now with some more *Morningside* mail. Morning, Shelagh." And we're launched.

There's a quickening thrill of not knowing exactly what is going to happen next. For example, we've had this thing about singing during the mail session. Sometimes a letter calls for it. On one occasion, after letters inspired by an hour-long hymn sing, I was all set to deliver an a capella version of an old stalwart, "From Greenland's Icy Mountains." Just as I was preparing to commence, Peter asked me if I'd like some piano accompaniment. "Peter," I said, "have you been hiding your musical talent from me all these years?" "Shelagh, I never said *I* was going to play the piano." And in walked John Fraser, then editor of

Saturday Night magazine and, like me, an old Anglican. He sat down at the piano, gave me a line of introduction and we performed it. Stirringly.

Now, I have always wanted to hear Peter sing because he so defiantly will not, and I've always thought he doth protest too much. Well, I've tried. For years. It took Lance Lindsay, the King of Karaoke, and Bobby Curtola — yes, the real Bobby Curtola — to get Peter to sing. He actually joined in on their rendition of "Bye Bye Love." A few days later, we had just finished reading the mail and Peter said, "Hold on . . . I've got one more and I want you to read it." He handed me a letter with the Toronto Mendelssohn Choir letterhead, a letter signed by Michael Ridout, manager of the choir. A choir I have always wanted to sing in. It was a letter asking *him* to audition for the choir! I could hardly contain my disbelief — and my jealousy! In my envious rage, I crumpled the letter up. (Peter had already made about a hundred copies, just in case, and one, as you'll see, appears in these pages.) But I have the last laugh. After the 10:00 news, at 10:05, 10:35 in Newfoundland — you can set your watch on it — Peter says, "Hello again, I'm Peter Gzowski and this is *Morningside*, hour two." If I could score it on the page it would look like this:

The "two" is about an octave higher than the "hour." I have the satisfaction of knowing that every morning while signing on the second hour, Peter sings.

The *Morningside* studio is a place of reckoning. I've always had the feeling that I know what I know. Until . . . Well, for instance, I always thought one said *indict* as it's spelled: *in-dicked*. And that's how I said it during the letters. Now I know, thanks to Peter — and after some public embarrassment. Then, a couple of seasons ago Peter had a number of discussions with people about logging. There was response from all over British Columbia. And I introduced a letter from Quess-nell, B.C. Peter tilted his head and said, "Where?" I responded with total authority: Quess-nell. He insisted I meant Kwuh-nell, which I most certainly did not. But deferring to his experience of the country, and his wide travels herein, I conceded. Then Peter read one from Vancouver. Then my turn with one from Clayoquot. I won't repeat here what I said instead of "Klack-wit." Occasionally, though, the score evens up. This season we had a letter from the Ottawa Valley, and Peter said the writer was from Man-*oh*-tick. Gotcha!

Aside from being iced in at home one Friday morning this winter, I've missed reading the mail only once in eight years, and that had something to do with a concussion. I've read the letters through some nasty colds and occasional laryngitis. One morning we were reading mail drawn from Peter's interview with a member of the Liver Lovers Club of Regina. The mail was about the various virtues and vices of the little organ of purification. Well, I was feeling the effects of a late-night party. I felt seasick. I was weaving, and the words were spinning in front of me. Then came the letter with the line, "The sight of the viscous red membrane sloshing about on a white Styrofoam tray." There now. As I write it, it's not so bad. But that morning, it very nearly caused a network first. I was green-faced, as Peter pointed out. I converted to vegetarianism. For at least a week.

Sometimes I wonder what people close to us would think were they to tune in randomly during our delivery of the mail and, say, hear me talk about my travels through the Himalayas (which I have never taken) or Peter's ultra-high Scrabble score (which he's never had). One morning we were reading letters about being gay in small towns. One impassioned letter began, "I am a radical feminist lesbian." This letter was read by Peter with great conviction. Later his daughter remarked, "Dad finally came out. And on network radio."

The letters draw us to each other and deepen the sense of ourselves and the country. They're a choral version of what Peter Gzowski does as a soloist. This book, like its four predecessors, is that chorus given permanence — a time capsule, in this case, of Canada in the early 1990s. Future readers will know we were enamoured of or flummoxed by technology, that some big women made the most of their size, that Leonard Cohen picked up his own socks. And what, I wonder, will those future readers make of the legendary poet Sarah Binks? Or Dennis Lee, Karen Connelly, Michael Redhill, Sharon Thesen and Julie Bruck, and their theory that Canadian poets share a collective landscape?

At the core, beyond the thousands of letter writers, there are four of us who put this collection together from the file folders the editor hands us. There's Peter, of course. There's Shelley Ambrose, there's me, and then there's the editor, Edna Barker, a pixie of a woman with huge editorial smarts. She loves the letters. She can quote by heart from all of them. Much of the passionate attention to detail in this volume is Edna's. The four of us meet face to face, on the phone or via fax and argue about what should go where, including out. The stuff of this book is what rose to the top. I think it's our finest *Papers* yet, and I would say that even if it wasn't the "probably last."

A letter from Marie Bremner, in Langley, British Columbia, puts it well. A number of years ago, Marie and her husband took a canoe trip across the Mackenzie River Delta and then west along the Arctic coast to Herschel Island. At a place called Shingle Point on the edge of the Beaufort Sea, they pulled in to an Inuit community. The women came out of their tents to invite Marie and her husband in for tea. ("Tea," Marie writes, "was tea or coffee, bread and jam or Spam, plus an invitation to put up our tent next to theirs.") A fearsome wind blew up, and one of the Inuit boats was being slapped by the waves and filling up with water. Marie and her husband and one of the women bailed like crazy and pulled the boat to safety. The Inuit woman led them out of the weather and to the cosy warmth of her family's tent. "The radio was on," Marie writes, "and as I wrapped my fingers around a steaming mug, my attention was caught by a few bars of music and then a familiar voice: 'Good morning. I'm Peter Gzowski and this is *Morningside*.' I was stunned to realize I was still in my own country, Canada."

Yes.

The 49-Second Essayist: Part One, 1991–92

The billboards, as we call them — the little pieces I speak at the top of each morning's program — have been a part of *Morningside* as long as I have, which is twelve years as I write this, and since I do them every working day of my life, that means I've written some 2,400 sets, give or take a few days off. Still, every day, and wherever we're originating from — and with whoever's typewriter I have borrowed — I begin by typing the same shorthand: Good morning ... (the number of dots varies — actually everything varies; I'm an old-fashioned four-fingered typist, fast but sloppy) ... I'm PG ... (even I can fill in the name from my initials) ... this is M'side, or occasionally, when I'm on a strange machine where the asterisk sits in place of the single quotation mark, M*side ...

How much I write after that can vary. The form was originally created to fit what radio people call a "doughnut" in our now-familiar theme, which David Thomson composed and recorded for us in 1982. There's a musical shimmer, then "Good morning, etc.," then a bit more music — doodle-dee-doo-doo, doodle-dee-doo-doo — and then, as I start talking, the music fades to a kind of neutrality. That's the doughnut. If I go precisely forty-nine seconds — hit the post, in radio-ese — the music swells back up just as I finish. Most days, I manage to do that (you have to learn *something* after twelve years of practice). I write my piece, and then read it aloud to Marieke Meier, our studio director. Marieke listens for both content and time — I actually think reading aloud helps *all* writing — and then I polish my draft as best I can and we head for the studio. If I miss the post by miles, there are some other choices. David

Thomson, bless his heart, recorded some different-sized doughnuts one year, and sometimes we just drop the music entirely and I read right up to the introduction of the first guests. But most days, for twelve years, that's how *Morningside* has begun.

As "billboards," of course, my little pieces are really supposed to be just advertisements for what's on the morning's line-up. I *try* to make them do that, or at least send some signal of our more enticing items, but, over the years, they've taken on a kind of format of their own — instant essays, as it were, in which I try somehow to reflect the mood of the day, or note some passing history.

Here are a few from the first of the three seasons that make up this book. There are some others later on. In each case I thought I'd show you what an original typist I really am, and how, working at the last minute, I try to hit the doughnut.

good morning.....i M P⁴....this is M'side, 91-92

One of these years, i'm sure, the Lord will open September in the part of Ontario where I hunker down ~~tear the summer~~ with ~~a~~ *sticky mugginess or a* ~~grind of thunder or some~~ cold, driving~~raint~~z rain.~~x.anyxxmpx lxxampaxazxithxaxtaxxaftapixitxxappingxhaxix~~ But not ~~xxgexhaxx t92xzxxxxxanxaxaaxxxxxxxxxaxxxhxaxxxxhxaxmaxmaxmahxmzm~~ t..is yea͡r, I can assure you--not September ~~92.~~ '91͡. A late-summer heat wave broke on Friday night, and for the last couple of days where I was, the air was like chilled chardonnay, and a ~~cool,~~ *warm,* friendly breeze ~~whipped~~ *stirred* white-caps onto the azure lake. ~~There's a touch of colour in the trees now, and the~~gypy~~mathxxxxxx oh the chamois-like evidence of gypsy moths on some of the trunks,~~ but ͡even to come back to this lovely job, it was not, yesterday afternoon, easy to leave.

What a ~~glorious~~ glorious summer this has been! I got

trapped, once, in the awesome power of a ~~torrential~~ thunderstorm

on the Manitoba prairie, and, on the Nova Scotia shore, played

one eerie round ~~ofgolf~~ of golf under ~~that~~ a sky stained grey *this summer*

by the forest fires of ~~the~~ Baie-Comeau. But when I remember ~~it~~--

and I will--the ~~sky~~ *sky* will be warm with sunshine and rich with

laughter, the corn will be ~~ripe~~ *ripe* again, the tomatoes juicy, and

I'll smell the ~~dark~~ nicotinia in the gentle evening air.

And so, however, to work. This is the tenth time I've

opened these proceedings. I think I'm right in ~~thinking~~ *pointing out* that

not a single ~~*incumbent*~~ politician I'll interview in the months to come

held office when I began; I know I'm right in saying that

two of the people in the car ~~that brought~~ that brought me in

from the country yesterday--my granddaughters--had not yet

~~been~~

been born. When, ~~I was~~ on Friday, I read the list of the

people who really make this program, only two of the names--

Janet Russell ~~xxxxxxxxxxxxxxxxx~~, our ~~script~~ *production* assistant

and Dave Amer, who picks our music-- ~~they~~ were there in

the fall of ~~xxxxx~~ '82.

But for all of that, I feel at home here. And for all

my nostalgia for summer, I'm anxious to get on with what lies

ahead.

So happy Labour Day, if you're still on holidays. Here,

once again, we go.

September 12, 1991

GOOD MORNING . . . I'M PG . . . THIS IS M'SIDE . . .

Someone I heard on Toronto radio much earlier this morning said
that on *his* way to work he'd seen three posties, waiting for the bus that
would take them, for today at least, to *their* work. Trouble was, of
course, there'd be no bus today. Strike. The person I'm supposed to
have dinner with tonight — the person I have dinner with most
nights — is in New York today, and though the planes have been flying (those whose crews haven't been laid off), who knows if she'll get

back? Strike. Outside the window where I typed these notes, half the street is under construction; traffic's snarled. The machine on which I'm typing — maybe the last of the old steam-driven manuals — now jams when you hit the question mark (which is a bit of a handicap in my business) and I can't find anyone who can fix it. But am I grumpy . . . I mean, am *I* grumpy (curse that faulty key). Heck no. Are you — I mean: are *you* (question mark).

Look. Stick around. We have a terrific program today — I think.

October 3, 1991
GOOD MORNING . . . I'M PG . . . THIS IS M'SIDE
That great noise that emanated from the SkyDome in Toronto last night — isn't it neat the way the television announcers just call it "SkyDome," as if it were a place, like Kamloops (it's actually not much smaller), or maybe a condition to be achieved, like Nirvana — the great noise that emanated from there last night may have sounded to some like the ecstasy of victory, but to my ears it was more like one giant, collective sigh of relief. A lot of non-fans, of course — and I know there are some — were just relieved to know that for a while at least they won't have to know the "magic number" any more, the figure that started appearing in the Toronto papers sometime in May and marked what the Blue Jays had to do to do what they finally did last night, which was to clinch the pennant of the American League East, or to smile sympathetically while otherwise rational people dissected ERAS, ribbies and on-base percentages. But for the fans — and there are lots of them — the relief was even more distinct. For even the staunchest of us (and yes, I confess, I've wasted more evenings than I ought to glued to the radio or the TV this summer), the season that sort of came to an end last night (they'll be playing at least till Thanksgiving now), has been one long, fingernail-biting session of alternating glimmers of tentative optimism and paroxysms of abject despair. Oh, no, not Jim Acker, we would say, or please, please, Joe, not this time too — the Jays, scrapping for every run this season with a team built on speed, defence and strategic bunting, actually struck out more than the boom-boom Detroit Tigers.

Forgive us this morning, will you? Those of us who've sweated through so many cliff-hangers all season — do you know that this champion team has in fact won only fifty-six percent of its games — have never, till now, or till about quarter past ten last night, really believed our heroes could do it, not in our hearts, and it's been tougher than you'll ever know managing them from our couches, or over our car radios or from our seats in — why not? — SkyDome. Today, we need a moment to collect our thoughts. The play-offs will be with us soon, and our plan — so far — is to play them one game at a time.

October 31, 1991

GOOD MORNING . . . I'M PG . . . THIS IS M'SIDE . . .

Heard a nice little story the other day and, although it's apropos of nothing on Morningside today, I thought I might pass it along. It took place about ten days ago, when Wayne Gretzky's father, Walter — a really nice guy, by the way — was fighting back from the brain aneurysm that's laid him low, and Wayne was away from hockey and at his bedside. Wayne, in fact, was alone with his dad saying, it's me, Wayne, if you recognize me, squeeze my hand. Suddenly, there *was* a response, and Wayne knew his father would pull through. "He knew me, he knew me," he said as he left the room. "Gee, Wayne," said someone outside, "I don't want to let you down . . . but *everybody* knows Wayne Gretzky."

November 28, 1991

GOOD MORNING . . . I'M PG . . . THIS IS M'SIDE . . .

Notes from a weekend of royal watching, with their, ahem, royal highnesses in Toronto.

Volume One: Friday afternoon. He is — this stands out over all my observations — *unbelievably* good at his job. I see this right away. I am standing, along with a number of other people more or less connected with the literacy movement, in the lobby of the seventh-floor head-quarters of an organization called YES Canada, which works — with remarkable success — with high school drop-outs. Because, inevit-ably, the royal party is a tad behind its minute-by-minute schedule (Diana is at an AIDS hospice, while Charles comes here), we are even more than usual on edge. Protocol Pooh-Bahs are squabbling with each other over who stands where, who says what, where cameras are

20

allowed, where they're not. A lot of people, some of them plain-clothesmen, wearing name tags that say "Police" (not my idea of undercover), are talking into cellular phones. One of the YES Canada kids, crowded into the tiny lobby behind a velvet rope, comes close to fainting.

But when the Prince of Wales himself arrives, looking for all the world like Madame Tussaud's come to life, everything calms down. He simply *relaxes* everyone. I remember, to my surprise, to call him Your Royal Highness. But when he asks me if I'll also be part of some of tomorrow's events, I blurt out something vacuous. Ah well, he's probably used to it.

Later, in an informal, sit-down conversation with the young people, he does it again. He would make, dare I say it, a first-rate guest host of *Morningside*. Once again, he puts everyone at ease, picking the nervous kids' names from their lapel badges, asking them intelligent questions, appearing at least to be truly interested in their answers. The kids, too, remember the proper honorifics — Your Royal Highness on first meeting, sir thereafter. The protocol Pooh-Bahs are relieved. But one of them — the Prince's press secretary, I believe — says quietly, "Actually, he doesn't take these things very seriously. If they called him Charles, I don't think he'd mind."

Volume Two: Saturday. The royal gala. Big bucks. Some of these tables — the ones closest to where Charles and Diana sit — have gone for $25,000. Not the one where I'm sitting. I'm emcee, nervous as a kitten, wearing a new dress shirt, my shoes freshly shined (the man who did it refused payment when he learned where I was going), my hair a rigid helmet of hair spray. At my table are a couple of people from Sec State, two guys who've worked non-stop for the past eighteen hours decorating the room, the Prince's head security chap and a man from the Ontario Provincial Police.

Desperately, I seek gossip. No luck. Best I can do is get a yarn from the OPP man, who tells me that this morning at a restaurant in Niagara Falls, young Prince Harry was delighted to see his granny's picture on the money.

Nice evening, though, pretty well stolen by a young man from Papua New Guinea, a student at Lester B. Pearson College of the Pacific, one of the beneficiaries (along with literacy) of this evening's largesse, who speaks eloquently on a live TV feed from Vancouver

Island. Says Your Royal Highness, by the way, even though, later, one of the officials of Pearson College says it was hard to stop him from saying "ma prince."

The prince's security man, by the way, fails to win the pool on when their RHS will leave. He bet on eleven-thirty. They stay till quarter past twelve. Diana — I cannot see this from my table — apparently did a bit of jitterbugging, with the Hon. Bob Rae.

Volume Three: Sunday morning. A final glimpse. The royals — all four of them — go to church across the street from my apartment building. People start lining up about seven o'clock, for their eleven o'clock appearance. I am — or pretend to be — working. But from time to time, I go to the window, just to . . . well, to look at all the royal watchers. When they finally emerge from the cathedral, Charles and the little princes in natty suits and blazers, Diana in a gay white hat and red-trimmed suit, I find myself pressed to the glass. Should I wave, I wonder. No, I decide the Prince is probably too busy today to greet old friends.

December 24, 1991
GOOD MORNING . . . I'M PG . . . THIS IS M'SIDE . . .
Notes — if that's the appropriate word — of a non-singer.
I wasn't always like this, you know. As a kid — is it a trick of memory that I think I was a boy alto? — I could belt it out with the best of them, not only in school concerts, but out on the landscape, where, when I wasn't being Teeder Kennedy, with Foster Hewitt announcing my every move, I was sometimes Bing Crosby. Ever hear an alto doing "White Christmas" at the top of a toboggan run?

Later on, working on travelling construction gangs — the alto was a baritone now — I sometimes did the boom-be-boom-be-boom-be-boom-be-boom-be-boom-be-boom-be-boom part to "Blue Moon" on Friday nights, and there was a time, during the early years of my marriage, when I learned the guitar-chords to "Tomorrow Is a Long Time" and was known to chime in on the chorus. One of my sons, by the way, unencumbered by heredity, picked up that old guitar and now, twenty or so years later, makes his living — not a great one, mind you, but a living — wringing magic out of one of its electronic successors.

Maybe, come to think of it, there *is* some heredity at work there.

My father, the musician's granddad, could sing like a cross between Cab Calloway and Mario Lanza, if that's possible. And my own career — my own *public* career — may well have come to an end when I was asked to audition for a choir he used to star in. I can still see the expression on the organist's face as he asked me for a scale or two. It is as if Bobby Hull's old hockey coach had just learned Brett couldn't skate.

At Christmas — along with the times I'm at someone's head table and the opening bars of "O Canada" blare from the speaker — I *wish* I could sing . . . or wish, perhaps, that the self-consciousness that blossomed before that kindly organist's disappointed eyes would disappear.

January 27, 1992
GOOD MORNING . . . I'M PG . . . THIS IS M'SIDE . . .
So was Walter Pidgeon, wasn't he? And Deanna Durbin — in Winnipeg? Glenn Ford, I know — I looked this up — was born in Montreal, and certainly Mary Pickford, in Toronto. Saul Bellow, I think, spent part of his boyhood in Canada and so, unless I'm wrong, did Mort Sahl. Art Linkletter — here's another one I'm sure of — grew up in Moose Jaw. Not to mention John Kenneth Galbraith, Michael J. Fox or — though he was *born* in Scotland (like Sir John A. himself) — Alexander Graham Bell.

And now, by golly, Mark Rypien who quarterbacked the Washington Redskins (that really is an offensive name, isn't it?) to a lopsided victory in the Super Bowl yesterday. This morning, Mark is a Canadian — Calgary-born, as one newspaper says in its very first sentence, even though he hightailed it to Spokane when he was five.

And why not, I say. We take 'em where we find 'em. How you doing, eh, Mark?

February 14, 1992
GOOD MORNING . . . I'M PG . . . THIS IS M'SIDE . . .
A note of sadness, this morning. The woman we called Nancy B. died last night in Quebec City. Even after her death — peaceful, and serene, we're told, surrounded by her family — we know so little about

23

her. Twenty-five. Immobilized. Needing mechanical aid even to breathe. Living what she described herself as "no longer a life." What made her laugh when life was good, I wonder; what did she like to read? Her death was proper. *Her* choice, duly considered, duly achieved. As Dennis Kaye — our own Incredible Shrinking Man, as he calls himself — wrote to *Morningside* on the day of the court decision that affirmed Nancy's right to choose, "life was meant to be lived, not frantically clutched like some last crust of bread." Still, it's sad; we mourn for her, I think, even as we salute her courage and her grace, and hope, at last, that she's found peace.

February 20, 1992
GOOD MORNING . . . I'M PG . . . THIS IS M'SIDE . . .
I am too much of a sceptic to think there was more than coincidence in this, but the truth is that the first thing that struck my mind when I heard this morning that A.J. Casson had died was the thought that, yes, yesterday evening, I had been looking at it again, and thinking of him.

"It" is a package of Buckingham cigarettes — long gone from the market now. It's a pouch pack, as they used to say, and I have kept it as it used to be, even to the now stale cigarette jutting up from its open top. It's mounted, behind glass, on the wall where I work at home, along with a couple of other souvenirs, and the story behind it is this.

Mr. Casson, who was a lovely man, used to drop by here from time to time. One day, in the early eighties, when Buckinghams were still around and when I used to smoke in the studio, he noticed my open pack on the table.

"Did you know I designed that?" he said, chuckling.

"Really?" I said.

"Sure."

It was, I suppose, not unexpected. As the news has reminded us this morning, A.J. Casson began his career doing seed catalogues and, over the years, he often supplemented the meagre living he earned from his early paintings with bits of commercial work. I treasured that moment and kept the package, which he was happy to sign for me, as a reminder of, among other things, the often very real connection between genius and the mundane. He was an artist who was *of us*.

And there I was last night, looking at that old Buckingham package, and thinking about him. He was ninety-three when he died. It's really nice to remember him.

March 16, 1992

GOOD MORNING . . . I'M PG . . . THIS IS M'SIDE . . .

"Before spring gets here," said Otte Rosenkrantz in an eloquent defence of winter we read here on Friday, "I have my fingers crossed for another foot or so of snow," and he went on to limn the pleasures of the season, of cross-country skiing across the tranquil wilderness, of returning, fresh-faced and skin a-tingle, to the warmth of a winter fire.

A moving plea, and though I don't know if nature heard it where Otte lives, which is near London, Ontario, up our way, over the weekend it tried. There was a fresh fall on Friday night, not a foot or so, but enough to cover the landscape, and the drive in to get the papers was through a wonderland of whipped cream, topping the evergreens, and a fresh white coat across the frozen lake. The columbines, which had sent up fresh yellow shoots the week before, had snuggled in again under the covers; the snowdrops were nowhere to be found.

It was, truly, lovely — fresh and clean and bracing. A postcard to cherish. I dug my boots out of the blanket box, blew on my fingers, and set out across the glistening countryside.

Half an hour later, I was home. The hell with it, Otte. I've had enough.

March 19, 1992

GOOD MORNING . . . I'M PG . . . THIS IS M'SIDE . . .

And, oh, dear, he made another error, this time throwing over the first baseman's head, to set up the only Kansas City run in yesterday's exhibition game against the Toronto Blue Jays. At the plate, he went one for four, which isn't bad, except that if he's going to hang on with the big club, as they say, he's got to do a little better.

He — I can't tell you how I love saying this — is a kid named Zoskey . . . Eddie Zoskey as it happens, who spells his name quite differently than mine, but Zoskey all the same, and all through the waning weeks of last season, and the spring training for this one, he's been the agent of my happiest fantasies. Zoskey's at the plate now, Zoskey hits one, Zoskey makes a diving catch. Yes. I take my baseball on the radio, you see — I never have been to the SkyDome — and every day, as young Eddie has struggled to earn a permanent promotion from the minors, my heart has gone out to him. My heart, nothing — he's been me. And Zoskey homers to win the World Series. But it is not to be, I'm afraid. Zoskey may languish in Syracuse again this year. Or, maybe, the Jays could get a taller first baseman. Name, anyone?

March 23, 1992
GOOD MORNING . . . POO-SHOO. . . . I'M PG . . . THIS IS M'SIDE FROM SIOUX LOOKOUT . . .
We're in north-western Ontario this morning, not much farther from Winnipeg, actually, about five hours by car to the west and a bit south, than from Thunder Bay, about four to the south-east. It's stunning country and very Canadian: lakes, rivers, hardrock, spruce. The weather's gentle today, and though there's still snow on the ground, and the ice on Pelican Lake across from where I sit is thick enough to ride a snowmobile across — more on that in a moment — there's spring in the air. The "poo-shoo" I assayed as we came on the air — so like the French *bonjour* that when someone said it to me yesterday I thought perhaps we'd gone astray — is in fact a local native greeting, part of the language they call "Oji-Cree," a blend of the two traditional ways of speaking here. I offer it in greeting to a number of new *Morningside* listeners who join us this morning, courtesy of the Wawatay Radio network, which stretches out from Sioux Lookout, a kind of regional capital of Ontario's first nations, as far as Sandy Lake, Big Trout Lake, Kasabonika Lake to the north — I watched the team from Kasabonika play a gallant game in the big hockey tournament here yesterday — and, to the north-east, to such places as Attawapiskat and Moose Factory on the edge of Hudson Bay. *Morningside* is honoured to be on this remarkable network this morning, and to work in the Wawatay facilities here at home base. From here, we'll reach out to a number of places — to Montreal for our Quebec report, and, in hour three (he said, crossing his technological fingers), to Austin, Texas, for a chat with Paulette Jiles, the American-born poet and

novelist who, over her varied career, has won a Governor General's Award for poetry and helped to start the institution we broadcast from today. But we'll do some snowmobiling, too. Our first report, in fact, was gathered by snowmobile. Yesterday afternoon, a gang of us mounted our machines — well, our borrowed machines, in my case — and rode across the lake and up the rise of land on the opposite shore. This is the hill — the mountain, as they call it here (forgive them, Alberta) — that gives this town its name. And at the summit, I talked with two long-time local residents: Garnet Angeconib, who'll join me later for some talk of Wawatay, where he now works, and Peggy Sanders, a local historian. With the wind blowing a few last flakes of snow across our faces and the buzz of the other snow machines sometimes audible in the background, we looked out across the land, and a bit back in time.

March 26, 1992

GOOD MORNING . . . I'M PG . . . THIS IS M'SIDE . . .

One time, a few years ago, I wrote Barbara Frum a fan letter. It was when Shirley MacLaine, the American actress and, uh, visionary was on tour, and as sometimes happens, she was both here one morning and on *The Journal* in the evening. My own interview had been frustrating. I'd *tried* to take Ms. MacLaine seriously, but, and even though (to tell you the truth) I was a bit glamour-struck, I'd had a bit of trouble not giggling. In short, I did a lousy job. Then, on *The Journal*, I'd watched Barbara. She just sat across the table, fixed Shirley MacLaine with that quizzical I-can-see-through-all-this-you-know look she had, and said something like, "I don't know what to make of you." It was the perfect question, the perfect approach, and though, like a lot of people in this business, Barbara relied on hard-working support staff in everything she did, it was pure Frum.

My *goodness* she was good, and, the next morning, I typed out a short note to say as much to her.

But know what? She came round that afternoon just to sort of check up — as if she couldn't quite believe what I'd said — as if she herself wasn't quite so sure. Maybe that was typical, too. She was, you know, as nice as she was good.

Barbara died last night, as I'm sure you know. She was fifty-four. We're all hit hard.

May 12, 1993

GOOD MORNING . . . I'M PG . . . THIS IS M'SIDE FROM CALGARY . . .

I was at a dinner last night that in almost every sense could not have been further removed from the tragic events of Plymouth, Nova Scotia. It was an awards ceremony — a gala, as its organizers dubbed it — and the people there were in a celebratory mood. Still, early in the evening, there was a reminder. The winners of various provincial and territorial awards — they were for work in education, if that matters, some remarkable partnerships between business and the schools — were introduced by region, and the first group to stand up came from Atlantic Canada. Newfoundland, New Brunswick, PEI, Nova Scotia.

Nova Scotia. Our gala mood was broken. Even as the name of the province was read out at the Calgary Convention Centre, you could feel the impact. The story grips us. We feel helpless. This morning, like a lot of other people, I flicked on the TV, just in the hope that there'd been a breakthrough. But there on the screen were the same grim faces, relaying still more of the same grim non-news. Still digging. Have to keep moving in their own fresh air. Ground falls. Diagrams. One of the mine managers, in tartan shirt and tweed jacket, patiently explaining where the crews were working now, how far they still had — maybe — to go. In the cold light of the Maritime dawn, a reporter reviewed what was known and held out once again the faint glimmer of hope.

We have nothing to add this morning — except to say that here, in Calgary, as everywhere else across this country, the tragedy of Plymouth is reality for us today.

Oh, Heck

All right, all right, it's a euphemism. I certainly said much worse (to myself) when I pulled the rock that started all this. But it was about as close as we could get on the radio to the only suitable reaction to something that has gone hopelessly and irreversibly wrong. Oh . . . heck. Or "heck" will do.

My goof was classic. It occurred in the billboards (you may notice I haven't included that little gem in the selections in this book) just after Bill Clinton was inaugurated as president. I wanted to make a point about his oratorical style, and how it seemed to lack the memorability of, say, John Kennedy. "'Ask not,'" I typed merrily, "'what you can do for your country . . .'" and I went on to pontificate about that unforgettable quotation. "Even now," I said, "thirty-two years later, we can all complete the almost biblical turn of phrase."

For once, even Marieke missed it as I did my read-through, and it was not until I had finished my forty-nine seconds, and the theme had returned and faded and I was half-way through welcoming our business columnists, that it hit me.

I had got it, of course, exactly backwards.

Ah, well, at least it inspired some sympathetic disaster stories in the mail.

✉ It was a sultry summer's night two years ago, and I had a wicked attack of insomnia. Finally around five o'clock I decided to try turning off an old, noisy electric fan. When I got up I noticed there was a van parked with its engine left running across the street in front of my friends' the Graces. Then, much to my horror, I noticed a man with a flashlight skulking up the front steps and poking around the front porch, where husband John Grace keeps his ten-speed.

"Quick, wake up! There's a burglar at John and Pam's!" I screamed at my snoring husband. He groped for the window and peered out.

"Yell at him. Scare him off!" I demanded, as I fumbled around in the dark, trying to plug in the bedroom phone.

"Should I call the police? No, I'll call the Graces! But what if I wake up the kids? Oh God, I'll have to anyway." I dialled their number.

"John — quick! There's a burglar on your porch — he's trying to steal your bike!"

Across the street, John dropped the phone and flew down the stairs stark naked — then mid-flight, decided he was in no condition to confront an intruder. So he ran back to get his wife's dressing gown.

In the meantime, my husband was obeying orders — yelling at the burglar to back off! Get lost!

The whole drama was over within three or four minutes, just long enough for a faint glimmer of light to appear on the horizon as dawn approached.

The intruder jumped into his van and started up the street. Much to my surprise he stopped again — to rob another neighbour.

"It's the milkman," my husband sighed as he deciphered the writing on the side of the van.

I collapsed back on the bed, pulled the covers over my head — and didn't sleep a wink for the rest of the night.

Oh, heck!

Margot Brunelle
Halifax

✉ When he was eleven years old, a young friend I know owned a model glider that had a three-foot wing-span. It was made of Styrofoam, with a hard black rubber nose like a hockey puck. One hot June evening, he launched the glider from the roof of his twelve-storey apartment building. He hoped it might fly as far as the street — perhaps fifty or sixty feet — but because he was pretty sure it would fall like a stone, he didn't aim it; he just let it go. Up, up and away! The craft soared beyond his wildest dreams. It flew over the lawn, over the driveway, over the four-lane street, over another lawn . . . Uh-oh! It was headed directly towards an apartment building across the street.

Now this happened to be a Friday evening, when observant Jewish families welcome the Sabbath with candles, sacramental wine and a festive dinner beautifully served. Indeed, Sabbath dinner is not an everyday event.

One such family lived in the building across the street. And when they sat down to dinner on this particularly hot evening, the sliding door to their balcony was wide open. Really wide open. Wide enough so that, suddenly, with no warning, in swooped the glider — just as the family raised their wine glasses for the traditional blessing. The timing couldn't have been better (or worse, depending on your point of view).

You know those tricks where the magician pulls a table-cloth off the table without disturbing any of the dishes? This was the opposite. In a surgical strike worthy of Desert Storm, that glider took out everything on the table, leaving only the cloth.

Oh, heck!

Joan Lee
North York, Ontario

✉ I was sixteen and madly in love with an older man (twenty-one and going to university, how too cool) whom I had met up at the cottage. Mike lived in Scarborough, I lived in Hamilton. I conceived the daring plan of phoning him up to ask him to come visit me. This precipitated an agony of approach-avoidance conflict — yes, I will; no, how could I?

Finally I picked up the phone and dialled, palms sweaty, heart pounding. For a *girl* to phone the *guy* was at that time a very daring act. Scraps of heavily rehearsed dialogue gibbered through my mind. Maybe he won't even be home . . . maybe he won't remember me . . . God, maybe he'll laugh at me . . . I could hear the ringing at the other end.

At last, Mike picked up. "Hello?"

And I answered sprightly, "Hello, Karen? This is Mike."

Stunned silence from him. Oh, heck! I blushed from the toes on up. Mike Adams, are you out there? Remember me?

Karen Wassenberg
Windsor Junction, Nova Scotia

✉ "You've got a good-sized baby here, Cathy, even though you're only thirty-eight weeks." This statement was made quite authoritatively as I tried to bolster my confidence while standing next to her bulging, be-sheeted abdomen. I was still wet behind the ears as a young family doc but keen to show the depths of my diagnostic acumen.

Cathy proceeded to push well over the next ten minutes as the excitement in her husband mounted, and unbeknownst to them, my anxiety climbed. My nervousness subsided and their joy peaked, when with one almighty heave Cathy delivered an apparently healthy boy. I got the cord clamped and cut and the squalling, pink, slippery babe wrapped up and into his mother's arms.

"Now you two enjoy this new guy while I get down to the business of delivering the placenta," I commanded. "It won't take a sec." After ten minutes of gently tugging on the cord, praying fervently that it wouldn't snap, I nonchalantly announced, "Placenta sure is reluctant to come. Never mind, though, I'll just busy myself repairing this small tear in your skin."

Cathy, meanwhile, seemed to be increasingly restless.

"Gee," she exclaimed between pants, "these after-cramps seem more like contractions!"

Ever the knowledgeable and reassuring doctor, I hastened to

remind her that this sort of thing had to be expected, seeing that she'd previously delivered two children.

As I finished my fine stitchery, she handed the baby to her husband saying, "George, you hold on to him for a minute, these pains are so bad I'm afraid I may drop him."

"Cathy, try to relax a bit. You've been through a lot but I'm almost done." Then again reassuringly, "These after-pains are nature's way of tightening down your uterus, so you won't bleed."

I returned to the reluctant placenta and began to pull hopefully on the cord.

"Doctor, you've got to do something about these pains. They're really bad!"

"Okay, Cathy, hold onto the nurse's hand, I'm going to reach in and see what's holding this thing up."

I carefully and slowly inserted my gloved hand, mindful of not disrupting my needlepoint.

Had it not been for the mask on my face, all present would have seen it blanch instantly. My hand had run into the source of her pain and the sluggish placenta. You guessed it: a chubby twin's bum! *Oops!*

Bob Lewis-Watts
Barrie, Ontario

✉ I worked for several years as a production planner for some of Vancouver's large commercial printers. Every few years the Workman's Compensation Board would reprint its safety guidebook for loggers. This handy little publication was titled *The Fallers and Buckers Handbook.* The ramifications of the title will be obvious to most. It was a constant source of amusement in production departments across town. Nonetheless, I always approached the book's name with a certain amount of trepidation. To alleviate this I would mentally pronounce the name several times before actually speaking it, a technique that seemed to work quite well. One sunny spring morning, with the new edition of *The Fallers and Buckers Handbook* hot off the presses and sent off to a local trade bindery, I decided to phone and check on its progress. As the receptionist connected me to the bindery owner, I ran through my little mental mantra: "Fallers and Buckers, Fallers and Buckers," I said to myself. I should pause here and mention that the bindery owner was a stern and devoutly religious man; nothing could slow your job down faster in his shop than to use the Lord's name in vain when talking to him on the phone. When we were finally connected, and with "Fallers and Buckers" firmly planted in my brain, I engaged my tongue. You guessed it. With a sense of total horror I heard the fateful spoonerism slip smoothly out of my mouth. Like a rabbit in front of a Kenworth, I completely froze. "What did you just say?" came a chilly voice back over the phone. Before I could stop it, my rogue tongue sprang into action and clearly and articulately repeated itself. Now to make things worse, I felt a rapidly rising urge to giggle and quickly bit my tongue, hard, both to stop the laughter and maybe to teach the thing a lesson. "Wednesday afternoon" were the two very icy words that came down the line, followed by a very distinct click. Next year our company lost the bid to reprint the handbook, and I heaved a great sigh of relief.

Neil McAllister
Vancouver

✉ As a college student, my father had taken a job at one of the CBC affiliates as a disc jockey. When he tells this story, he is quick to remind his listeners that in those days, disc jockeys were simply that. They were the guys responsible for flipping discs onto the turntable and taking them off. They were "back-room" boys whose voices were never heard over the air waves. One of their many responsibilities entailed providing appropriate fade-out music in the event a program was interrupted by a news bulletin.

One evening, the announcer received a news flash over the wire. The HMCS *Warrior* had gone aground in Liverpool Harbour. "Quick, Harold," he said, "I'm about to break in and read this bulletin. Get something!" "What?" said Dad. "I don't know," was the response. "How about a sea shanty?"

Dad ran into the small, dark room that served as the music library and scanned the shelves. There, in a far corner, he spied a small label marked "Sea Shanties." He grabbed one of the few records above the label and ran out. The announcer had already begun. "Ladies and gentlemen, we interrupt this program in order to report that HMCS *Warrior* has just run aground in Liverpool Harbour. No injuries have been reported. Stay tuned for further information later in this broadcast." The announcer nodded to my father, who slapped his record on the turntable and dropped the needle in place. I have always thought that I would pay a million dollars to see the look on their faces as they and their listeners were treated to a rousing rendition of "What shall we do with a drunken sailor?"

Oh, heck? You bet!

Anne Leavitt
Hamilton, Ontario

✉ So there I was, in 1967, cosily ensconced in a great job, nineteen floors high in Place Ville Marie, Montreal, driving my 3.8 Jag, a bachelor in Montreal during Expo 67, a neat little apartment (and they were hard to get during Expo), when the telegram arrived from Western Union advising me my Irish Hospital Sweepstakes ticket was a winner. Would I please present it to the bank within six weeks to collect my winnings? Yes I would and, indeed, did.

The top prize was £100,000, or $300,000. Yes! With no delay on my part, I quit my job, hopped a flight to Bermuda, spent about $6,000 in savings in three weeks ("Let me get this round, I'm rich") and returned to Montreal, broke, expectant of riches, and with a great tan.

I received a $900 consolation prize. The way it worked was, of those tickets initially selected from the barrel (mine was one), only a few would be matched up with a horse in the race for a chance at the grand prize. Mine was not one of those. All others (like mine) received the consolation prize of $900.

I'd quit my job, sold my Jag, sublet my apartment, spent all my money, and you guessed it, I said, oh, heck!

Ian Nicholson
Kanata, Ontario

35

✉ It was around fifteen years ago, when my children were aged two and four. Some friends had divorced and left us custody of their cat, Countess, who had just come to live with us and was not to be allowed outside for a few weeks until she was acclimatized. I had slipped into the bathroom for a very quick shower while the children played in their bedroom. I was lathering up my hair when the four-year-old came in and said, "Mummy, Ben spilled the paint." We were about to paint the spare bedroom, which had fitted seventies' dark shag carpet, and a large can of white paint was on the counter in the room. I leapt naked from the shower, hair foaming with shampoo, grabbed a towel and rushed to the bedroom, where I found an upended can of white paint emptying onto the carpet. I banished the kids to their room, flung off the towel and began scooping white paint back into the can. I quickly became coated with white paint, with shampoo dried in my hair, which stuck out all over my head. After the initial oh heck, I found myself yelling at the kids as I worked in a crazed manner. At some point I think my oldest son, Mark, must have looked around the corner of the bedroom door and seen his naked mother, coated in white paint, hair on end, yelling as she kneeled on the floor praying to the paint god, and decided it would be as good a time as any to leave home. I heard the front door slam and looked out to see him heading off down the street. I ran downstairs, opened the door to yell after his retreating body, and that was when the cat got out.

I phoned a neighbour, explained the situation in thirty seconds, and she agreed to grab Mark as he went past and hold him until things got back to normal at my place. This left the cat. I threw a raincoat over my naked paint-stained body, dried hair sticking up in spikes, and slipped out the front door and into the bushes at the front of the house. If I stayed on my hands and knees no one would see me. I crawled around in the bushes trying to lure Countess back and praying that the mailman, meter reader or anyone would not show up and make my day. No, they didn't, but while I was in those bushes and before I finally caught the cat, I did pause to utter the most heartfelt "oh, heck" of my life.

Ros Davies
Whitby, Ontario

✉ Prior to emigrating to Canada, I was working as an electrical design engineer with the United Kingdom Atomic Energy Authority. We were building a research facility at Winfrith Heath in Dorset. As part of my duties, I attended a regular monthly progress meeting held on the site. The chairman of the meeting was a senior executive of the company, well-known for his feisty demeanour and a stickler for getting work done on time and to a high standard.

At one such meeting, he soon made it known that during his habitual site inspection, he had noticed a particularly glaring error in construction. Company policy required all men's toilet doors to be coloured blue and all women's to be pink. Somehow or other the facilities in the administration building had their doors in reverse colours! The civil engineer was made well aware that this had better be put right promptly.

A month later, the chairman was in a noticeably foul mood. He had again inspected the site before the meeting and had found that the men's toilet doors were still pink and the women's still blue. The air itself was blue for at least five minutes while he informed the civil engineer in no uncertain terms that he was unaccustomed to having his clear and simple instructions blatantly ignored. The civil engineer said that he had given instructions to his staff to correct the problem and had been told that the necessary change had been made. Evidently he had failed, amongst other things, to include the doors on his own pre-meeting inspection. He was dispatched from the meeting to investigate and report back. He returned, looking very sheepish, about thirty minutes later. When the chairman demanded his explanation, he confirmed that he had indeed given instructions for the problem to be corrected. The doors had been repainted in the correct colours the day after the previous meeting. However, a week later the carpenters had then made their contribution by changing the doors. Oh, heck!

George W. Bowhay
Devon, England

✉ I was a young high school teacher in that big small town, Galt, Ontario; my wife, after teaching elementary school for one year, had quit to pursue her Master's degree at McMaster in Hamilton. As a result, she was out of town each day during normal office hours when one would ordinarily book routine appointments with a doctor, and so the task fell to me.

I grew up across the bay from San Francisco. At that time, most young people with pretensions to "culture" read the *San Francisco Chronicle*. I, too, read the *Chronicle*, including the work of such well-known columnists as Herb Caen and John Wassermann. Wassermann's column was titled "The Wassermann Test," a joke I thought I understood.

Back to my narrative: the usual common clues had indicated to us that my wife might be pregnant, and I agreed to call the local hospital and book an examination. In order to do this, I had to go into the main office of the high school, ask a secretary if I could use the phone and make my call with the secretaries, members of the administration and students listening in. I was somewhat concerned about this lack of privacy and so I determined that I would not use any terminology so crass as "rabbit test" or even "pregnancy test."

So I called the hospital, identified myself and asked the reception-ist to book a Wassermann test for my wife. There was a short pause at the other end of the line. The receptionist then asked if I would like one for myself, as well. I hung up immediately.

I can't tell you about the expressions on the faces of the secretaries, the vice-principal or the grade-thirteen girl who was standing at the counter getting an excuse slip so she could miss my class the following period; I fled the office without daring to look up and rushed to the library and Webster's Third International where my suspicions were confirmed: a Wassermann test is a test for syphilis.

Even now, twenty-two years later, I find that I have been wearing a silly, almost painful grin the entire time I have written this.

Jim Barnes
Brussels, Ontario

✉ It was a small new high school in the small community of Delhi deep in the heart of south-western Ontario's tobacco country. Those of us who had been part of the sixty students who made up the inaugural grade-nine classes in 1942 had, five years later, become a somewhat snobbish and élite two rows of grade thirteens who deigned to share a classroom with three rows of grade twelves. We saw ourselves as worldly wise, and it was "our school."

A general assembly had been impossible in the three-room Continuation School that had been the predecessor of the new, much larger and better-appointed high school. Now, besides Lit. Meetings once a month for the entire student body, there was a general assembly every morning for what was referred to as Opening Exercises. Each morning at nine o'clock the two hundred students and eight staff members gathered in the gymnatorium — a gymnasium with a stage at one end. There we all sang "God Save the King," listened to the daily Bible reading, said the Lord's Prayer and then heard the announcements of the day before trundling off to our first class.

When we leaders of the school graduated into grade thirteen it was decided that the senior students should be in charge of the morning assembly rather than the teachers. Finally our maturity could not be denied, could not go unnoticed. There was even a student accomplished enough as a pianist to accompany the rather ragged rendition of the national anthem.

The format was simple. After the low grades and our fellow seniors had paraded into the gym — the grade nines standing at the front, graduating to the grade thirteens at the back, teachers along the wall — the two in charge of the Opening Exercises would take their places. The first week one would stand stage right and read the Bible, the next week that same person would take the stage-left position and act as a kind of emcee. It would take about nine weeks for the complete rotation before a turn was repeated.

By the new year all of us in grade thirteen had become rather blasé and, before the word was coined, "cool" about appearing before the whole student body and staff.

It was my turn to read the Bible. My best girlfriend was emceeing the Opening Exercises.

That day the Bible reading was Matthew 19, verses 27 to 30. I was reading from the King James version, the only version I am aware of that could have led to what happened.

Peter tells Jesus that they have given up everything to follow Him and he, Peter, wants to know what shall be gained from this. Jesus answers that "when the Son of Man shall sit on the throne of his glory, ye also shall sit upon twelve thrones."

Oh, if only there hadn't been that second "shall sit"!

I think it is safe to say that what the students learned would happen to those twelve thrones from the way it was read to them that morning has never been so preached from any pulpit anywhere.

Also, they never did learn that while this dreadful desecration of the thrones was taking place, the disciples would be "judging the twelve tribes of Israel" because I slammed the Book shut, my friend bluffawed (that's a cross between a blurt and a guffaw), "Let us pray" . . . and I did, oh, I did.

My last recollection of this incident, which is indelibly burned in my memory, is the peek I took at the row of teachers. Eight pairs of shoulders were . . . shaking! I don't think they were crying.

Sharon Sproule
Espanola, Ontario

✉ In the fall of 1973 I was practising veterinary medicine with all the enthusiasm one would naturally have after fulfilling a dream I embraced since age twelve.

The small animal surgery was a tidy little room with all the latest in anaesthetic and surgical equipment, lights and a keen support staff.

In the interests of efficiency, the routine spays and castrations, or neuters, were prepped by the support staff after veterinary examination and anaesthetic induction. The candidates were wheeled into surgery already positioned, clipped, washed and draped. Surgical drapes covered the entire animal except for the rectangular area over the abdomen where I was to operate.

On the day in question, I was having some difficulty locating the ovaries on a young cat spay. This was quite unusual, but I diligently searched through the tiny opening, confident that another brilliant piece of work would soon be completed.

Just as I was considering a larger incision to see what mysterious anomaly lay within, my assistant looked under the drape covering the tail end of the cat. Her eyes slowly moved up to meet mine, and I knew. Oh, heck!

Pet owners often ask to have their animals spayed, or "spayeded," and consider the term to be synonymous with neuter, which it is not. Sometimes they will say "spay" because they have difficulty using the "other" word. For these reasons, we are supposed to verify the sex of the pet before surgery.

The responsibility for this *faux pas* rested squarely on my shoulders, and I could feel the flush of embarrassment permeating my surgical mask. I closed up the abdomen, dispatched the appropriate organs without delay and contemplated how much I should reveal to the owner.

Barry Heath
Saskatoon

✉ While my husband, a friend and I were driving from Cape Breton to Toronto one summer, we stopped for a coffee break in a small town in eastern Ontario. The restaurant had a lobby of sorts with stairs going down to washrooms and a door leading into the restaurant proper. My husband and friend scurried downstairs to the washrooms. I went in and ordered our coffee. While I waited for the coffee, to stretch my legs a little, I paced across the front of the room, which took me from the inside door across to the other side, and back. As I approached the door on one of my trips across the room, I noticed that the zipper of my very snug jeans (this was, after all, way back in the seventies) was wide open. As I was looking down, a little disgruntled at having just "exposed" myself in front of a room full of diners, I noticed out of the corner of my eye that the restaurant door was opening and someone was coming in. My friend, I thought. Without looking up I pointed angrily to my fly and gasped "Look!" When I looked up, I realized of course it wasn't my friend, but a complete stranger, a man whose entrance into the restaurant I was blocking while pointing obscenely to my open zipper. The restaurant patrons enjoyed it immensely. Double heck!

Pat O'Neil
Sydney, Nova Scotia

✉ I graduated from the Ryerson School of Journalism in Toronto last spring. A few months ago I started working in Saskatchewan as a reporter for the *Prince Albert Daily Herald*.

I worked summers at the *Globe and Mail* and the *Toronto Star*, so the move to a smaller newspaper was quite a shock. At the big papers, teams of copy editors scour stories to purge them of errors. I still thank God for the editor at the *Star* who caught this goof of mine: "The time capsule also contains a message from Prime Minister Brian Adams."

The Prince Albert Daily Herald has only one overworked editor to check for goofs. So reporters have to catch their own mistakes.

One afternoon last October, I read and re-read my story about Madonna's book, *Sex*. A local church gave me a press release asking people to boycott stores selling the book. I was determined to get it right.

But when the paper hit the streets the next day, I realized I hadn't read my story closely enough. Here's what more than ten thousand readers saw: the church "is appealing to all those *against* common decency to boycott" stores selling the book. Oh, heck!

Drew Hasselback
Prince Albert, Saskatchewan

✉ My wife's birthday was last week. The plan for the day was simple: pick up my wife's present from the store where it had arrived in the nick of time, and then my two sons and I would take Mom out for dinner. After dinner, we would put the kids to bed and settle back in front of a cosy fire.

This is what happened instead:

Our one-year-old son woke up with a temperature of 102°, so the dinner out was cancelled. I decided to make a steak dinner and a birthday cake instead. While I was icing the cake, the steaks burned to a crisp. While I was cooking hot dogs to replace the steaks, the cat licked the icing off the top of the cake. As we sat down to eat, I realized I had forgotten to pick up my wife's present. As we finished dinner, the phone rang. I'd forgotten about an important meeting and they'd been waiting half an hour already. By the time I arrived home my wife was already asleep. Oh, heck!

Alan Brown
Scarborough, Ontario

✉ For many years I was the writer and commentator for a CBC radio show, *Neighborly News from the Prairies*. My material was gleaned from the prairie weekly press. One story outranks the rest.

Two roofers were replacing the shingles on an old two-storey home. One of them drove to the scene, mounted to the roof and decided that the slope was too steep to permit him to work. He took a long rope and anchored one end to the bumper of his pick-up truck. He then ran the other end over the peak of the roof and tied it around his waist.

He was working away when — oh, heck — his partner walked into the yard and remembered that he had to pick up supplies at the lumber yard. He jumped into the pick-up and drove out of the yard. The partner on the roof put up valiant resistance. He took the TV aerial and part of the chimney with him when he was dragged over the peak. He bounced off the lawn and was being hauled down the street before the driver realized what was going on.

Happy ending — no serious injuries, although I suspect there was a little tension in the partnership.

Fred McGuinness
Brandon, Manitoba

✉ Some months ago I suffered an angina attack and was undergoing an angioplasty procedure at the Royal Victoria Hospital in Montreal.

Well, there I was, looking at my internal plumbing on the huge monitors; there was a cardiologist jiggling the controls with two specialist nurses assisting him; and there was this radio playing pop music.

Using my bargaining power as the principal actor, I pleaded with the heart specialist, "Would you mind if the radio were switched to an FM station carrying classical music?" He quickly did so and I felt a little calmer.

But hardly five minutes had elapsed before we all became aware of the fact that the composition being played was Chopin's "Funeral March"!

In all the hundreds of hours I have spent listening to FM music I have never once heard this work broadcast.

We all laughed (I hysterically).

Oh, heck!

Irving London
Westmount, Quebec

✉ During the summer of 1978 I took a course called Clinical Pastoral Education as part of my training for the ministry. It involved working as a chaplain intern in two hospitals in Hamilton, Ontario. One day I was at the Henderson Civic Hospital. The next day I was at the Hamilton General Hospital. This went on for three months.

One hospital had stainless-steel water jugs for each patient and plastic urinals for the men. The other hospital had plastic water jugs and stainless-steel urinals.

One particularly hot and humid day, I was working on a ward full of men. The rooms had four beds each. It was visiting hour. One of the men never had any visitors and his command of the English language was weak. What English he did have was mostly street language, which he didn't like to use with women or ministers. Language barriers don't normally bother me, and the nurses suggested I visit him during visiting hours to help his morale. So in I go — an eager, young, female, helpful chaplain intern.

The room was crowded. He seemed happy to see me and started gesturing towards the jugs on his bedside table.

"Oh," I said helpfully. "You want a (gasp from the watching crowd) drink." And I poured him a huge glass of urine.

Oh, heck!

The nurses were not amused. After I had disposed of it and washed up, I had to go back into that room. This time I poured him a glass of water. But he didn't want it. I had been almost right the first time. So I handed him what he wanted, closed the bed curtains and left. It was just too much to go back a third time.

Leslie-Elizabeth King
Swan Lake, Manitoba

✉ It is always difficult to verify the accuracy of good stories, since they are, of course, embellished by retelling and may only vaguely resemble the original event. So it is with the story our bull semen salesman told us about his neighbour who had just purchased a new four-wheel-drive John Deere tractor. (John Deere owners, like Cadillac owners, know there are no equals.) The very first job for this new tractor was to agitate the hog-manure lagoon, and since this process takes an hour before the pumping can begin, they decided to go for coffee. When they came back, however, the tractor had disappeared from view, except they could still hear it roaring at full throttle. Upon closer examination, the air-intake and muffler were just visible above the lagoon surface. The variations on "Oh, heck!" were numerous.

Wilf Buhler
Osler, Saskatchewan

✉ Seven years ago, I was a harried young mother of three children under the age of four. My husband was a salesman — off working about sixty hours a week — and I taught English as a Second Language for adults four evenings per week at the local high school. The schedule was very demanding — classes began promptly at six forty-five. This entailed a fair amount of organization on my part — organization that was often disrupted by the unforeseen intervention of three young children.

This particular week was the pre-Christmas season, and between running about for gifts, baking pies for the upcoming season and trying to prepare my home for six invited guests over the holidays, I was run ragged. Three nights in a row I had picked up my teen-aged baby-sitter and left her with the admonition to "leave the dirty dishes in the sink — I'll do them when I get back," and proceeded to outline the thousand and one things I'd had to do that day. I was determined to change things on Thursday, as I put away the dishes that had been so kindly washed for me once again the evening before. I did not count on the overactive artistic abilities of my son Pierre (four) and daughter Michelle (two).

About four o'clock I mounted the stairs to lay out pyjamas for the night, change the baby and then try to get supper on. I had been marking exams for the past half hour — and was grateful for how well the baby had slept and how quietly the other two had played. I should have known better! I walked into the playroom to find curtains, walls, dressers and children coated in what Pierre called "pretty paint." A large-sized jar of Zincofax cream had been smeared everywhere (if you don't know, this is an extremely thick cream used in diaper-rash protection). What a nightmare! I hustled the children into the bath, but it took a long time to clean them. The baby was screaming in her bed as the clock crept inexorably on towards six, when I must fetch the sitter. I managed to throw supper together and finish marking the rest of the exams. As I hurriedly dressed at five to six, I realized that once again I had a sinkful of dishes. I *couldn't* leave them again! So I did something I had sworn never to do — I threw all of the dishes into the oven, washed the table and countertops and fetched the sitter with a clear conscience.

When I returned at ten-thirty my parents were there! I was so excited that they had decided to surprise me by arriving a few days early. They would be in time to help us trim the tree on Saturday. Friday passed in a glorious haze of last-minute shopping and fond reminiscing. We ate out on Friday evening, and on Saturday I planned a wonderful roast beef dinner. At three o'clock, I began to pre-heat the oven to 350°. At three-fifteen the smoke began billowing into the living-room, where we were all trimming the tree.

"Oh my God — the dishes!" I screeched. I'm sure they all thought I was quite mad as I made a dash for the kitchen and yanked open the oven door. Black smoke formed a cloud about us as we gazed in horror at the disaster. Puddles of multi-coloured plastics formed beneath dripping oven racks in the fiery depths of my old electric oven. I said "Oh, heck!" (or words to that effect, you understand). My mother was in a state of shock. "Do you remember when you were fifteen — and I used to leave dishes in the oven — you used to preach at me about it, especially after I melted my best pot handles!"

No use telling her this was my first experience at harried housekeeping tricks — not when everyone was shaking with laughter at my expense.

Fran Asselin
Ste-Henedine, Quebec

FOUNTAINS OF USE

Although she does not appear in it directly, the person responsible for this chapter is Jill Porter. Jill, who lives in Winnipeg, where her husband is the headmaster of Balmoral Hall School, is a woman of both ferocious organizational energies and infectious enthusiasm. In the spring of 1994 her energies helped to lure me to a book fair at the school, which, among other things, raised some money for literacy. While I was there I noticed her enthusiasm for the old-fashioned classic fountain pen she was using to make notes — the same one, it turned out, she'd used to write her master's thesis. At the next *Morningside* story meeting (one of the side benefits of my occasional sojourns away from Toronto is the number of ideas I run into) I wondered about other such aficionados. We brought some together. We heard, as you'll see, from plenty more. Thanks, Jill.

B. A. Bauman
South Porcupine

Dear Peter:—

On your show this morning, 9:10 A.M., you were on the topic of the fountain pen, a writing instrument not often used anymore. The ballpoint has taken over, since the end of World War II.

When I started school in 1928, at age 7, we learned to write on a wood-bordered slate ▭ about 10×30 centimetres. A soft slate stylus shaped like a round wooden pencil was our writing instrument, | 15 cm. in length. Erasing was done with a damp sponge. Once we could form letters and words we moved on to pencil and paper, and errors could easily be corrected using an eraser.

✉ On my office wall I have a framed 1951 class photo showing form 3a at St. Gregory's Boys High School in Manchester, England. All of us are wearing school blazers and embarrassed smirks, and our breast pockets are crammed with Conway Stewart fountain pens and propelling pencils. We seem to be leaning to the left, no doubt because of the combined weight of ink, lead, metal and plastic, and the glitter from the massed clips makes us look like a gathering of South American generals.

Pete Garvey
Shallow Lake, Ontario

✉ I have used a fountain pen since I was a child at school in England in the mid-fifties (I seem to recall that there was a penalty of some sort for being in possession of a Biro, still the eponymous name for a ball-point in Britain), and currently write with a Montblanc Diplomat, the magnificent "Meisterstück #149." It was the first thing I purchased with my new, fresh-out-of-university Chargex card in 1972.

At that time, the pen shop in the Arcade on Toronto's Yonge Street sold them for $75, a substantial sum for me. The man in the shop, though, told me that they really needed to charge more, but people were used to seeing the slim ad which appeared in every issue of *The New Yorker* and would not pay more than the price quoted in that ad.

Today, the #149 costs about $500, a price even a passionate pen lover must find outrageous, and that brings me to the point of this letter. I am writing this morning with a computer because my Montblanc has had to go away for repairs. The great problem for all fountain pen devotees is where to get good parts and service these days. While the manufacturers are willing to offer service on their new products, they will tend, automatically, to replace (at great cost) rather than attempt to repair such things as that nib which has, over the years, bent perfectly to one's hand.

Tony Rees
Calgary

✉ I have used a fountain pen all my life — my first was a Parker 51, given to me when I was five in 1953 by my mother, with the admonition to *always* use bottled ink and *not* the frightful black goo dispensed from enamel teapots into debris-filled ink-wells by our primary school teachers — guaranteed to gum up any *respectable* pen.

For years I used it in schools all over the world — wherever my journalist stepfather's work for Reuters took us, but it disappeared from my life when I was at a convent boarding school in England, where the nuns required us to write in italics with a wedge-shaped nib, available then only in the Osmiroid range. I missed my old companion, but with the characteristic carelessness of youth neglected and finally mislaid it forever. I tried many substitutes over time, but could never find anything that felt as comfortable or that delivered the hand I intended to the paper. It seemed, alas, that the Parker 51 had become obsolete and unavailable for all time.

Imagine my delight when, many years afterwards in 1989, whilst sauntering through a junk-cum-antique shop where I had sought relief from the glare and heat of the streets of Pinang, Malaysia, I suddenly beheld a veritable treasure trove of battered Parker 51s encrusted with the dirt of ages, in a dusty glass case. After trying all the pens with the bottled ink provided, I found one in green Bakelite with a stainless steel cap and the nib worn as if destined for my use. Miraculously, the rubber bladder hadn't perished and didn't leak.

50

I paid the asking price equivalent of two dollars to the astonishment of the ancient Chinese shopkeeper who had done his best, all the while, to steer my attentions to a box of shiny new Japanese felt pens. He appeared to think he had taken a chance venturing such an astronomical price, but immediately set about polishing up the remaining pens and placing them prominently in the shop window, no doubt envisioning similar sales to tourists with "limited" discrimination like myself.

I like to think my "new" pen has a history. If only pens could speak — imagine what secrets they could divulge! Mine is probably the most precious personal possession I have, and my unwillingness to let others "borrow" it "for a minute" is the subject of much sardonic amusement to my friends, none of whom have possessed or used a fountain pen.

They simply *don't* understand.

Dorothy P. Rogers
Comox, British Columbia

✉ For the past fifteen years, I've been writing with a Parker given to me on my fortieth birthday. I occasionally use a huge and totally unreliable twenty-year-old Montblanc. I also own a Waterman, given to my father nearly seventy years ago as a graduation present; I don't use it much because, as is often the case for things and persons over fifty, it has bladder problems.

The Parker pen is by far the best, and I have owned at least two others in the course of my life. It does not blotch, mess or otherwise foul up the page or the hand that is using it. I might add that, as a purist, I do not use cartridges (I also object to the new play-off system in major league baseball and to a variety of other important disruptions of the social order); they are expensive and wasteful.

Charles S. Bourgeois
Beaconsfield, Quebec

✉ I have been using fountain pens for years — mostly Sheaffers and Osmiroids bought at the local Zellers store, except for the fourteen-carat gold-nib Sheaffer purchased in London ten years ago for forty-five pounds. An indulgence and an extravagance, sure enough, but when you go to England you have to return with something properly substantial.

My notes all through library school were inscribed in blue ink (the wet kind) with hardly a blotch among them. The ink flow made for fast note taking and when you got to the end of the page there was a *slight*, irresistible curl of the paper. Also, it was easy on the hand; you don't have to grip as hard as you do with a ball-point.

Though I don't use a fountain pen to the exclusion of anything else (I've been known to *type* personal letters), it seems that the fountain pen is the tool of choice when it comes to writing journals. I tried to keep a recent journal on the computer but after two dissatisfying weeks I took up my pen again. Of course you have to have the requisite paper too but that's another discussion.

Ink — the real flowing, staining, kind — is noble. There is little else that gives a letter importance than black ink. Fountain pens offer the right balance between uninterrupted flow and the luxury of time to think about your words. And, yes, my handwriting is different when there is a fountain pen in my hand.

Witness this and witness this.

Whenever I've brought my fountain pen to elementary classes in my travels as an occasional teacher, students are always intrigued by what they regard as something of an anachronism. Yet they're all curious to try it and they go away marvelling at its precision and grace. I sometimes wonder if fountain pens in school would lead to tidier script, but don't let a teacher hear me say that.

The fountain pen I currently use was given to me by my husband and daughter when my son was born four years ago. It's one of the tonier Sheaffers, weighty in hand, a rich dark burgundy. I remember well the delicious pleasure of filling it with permanent black ink from the well in the glass bottle (no cartridges for this purist!) and writing till my fingers ached. Somewhere in the Grey Bruce Regional Health Centre in Owen Sound there is a pillow case bearing the vestiges of my enthusiasm for fountain pens.

Sure, there are accidents and leaks and stains that look as if I've just been booked at the police station. And sure, you shouldn't bring anything written with a fountain pen near the bath-tub. But that's just part of the territory.

Rose Morley
Owen Sound, Ontario

✉ This letter is being written with a pen that, two hours ago, was the object of a frantic search. I had misplaced it the evening before, something a true owner seldom does, but I did, and had to pay the price through worrying.

To aggravate matters, I was scheduled to go on a one-day business trip early this morning and it appeared it would be done "penless." I was able to work through that crisis, but I knew all the while I would feel naked. As it turned out, my trip was cancelled at the last minute, giving me an opportunity to launch a more orderly search. The story has a happy ending and the pen is back where it belongs.

I have been a devotee of the instrument long before the current wave of interest began. There has always been something rich, warm and tactile about the smoothness of ink on fine paper. Remember that scene early in George Orwell's 1984 where Winston Smith uses his pen, safely hidden from Big Brother? That evokes the pleasures of the pen.

The process of using a fountain pen gives rise to certain rituals, and over the years, it becomes an extension of self.

This pen, a Sheaffer, is about four years old and I use it daily. It has developed its own character and personality, and I believe it helps me to be a better writer. I sign my cheques and business correspondence with it and use nothing else in personal letters or when writing in my journal.

A fountain pen is a way of life. It represents reason and moderation in an age of technology and impersonalization.

I love my pen.

Lyle Nicol
Kenora, Ontario

✉ I am writing this letter with a Parker Dufold which states on the clip quite distinctly "Patented Sept. 5th 1916." This pen was presented to my mother-in-law when she decided to emigrate to Canada in 1926, which incidentally was the year I was born. At the time she gave me the pen — quite a few years ago — it was in rather rough shape. It had not been used in years. The nib was bent almost backwards. I was very chuffed with the pen and decided to send it to the Parker Pen Company to be refurbished. They returned it to me stating, due to the age of the pen and unavailability of parts, they would be unable to repair it. I was disappointed and decided I would try to repair the pen myself. I soaked the barrel in hot olive oil then put it in ice water then back into the hot olive oil. I managed to separate the parts and on doing so found the original tube or ink sac had disintegrated. I then separated the nib and support from the holder. Then I straightened the nib and took out the dents. I then had to find a sac, or tube as we used to call it. Parker Pen did not have one — the local suppliers did not have one. The next time I was in Toronto I went to Eaton's College Street. The lady in the pen department at Eaton's said, "Oh, an old Parker Dufold." I thought I had struck pay dirt but no — she said unfortunately they did not have any tubes. However she said if I wanted to try the Arcade at 33 Yonge Street they might be able to help. Well, I went to the Arcade and a gentleman of about seventy-five was behind the counter. When I showed him the pen and asked if he had a tube, he said yes in a most matter-of-fact manner. Nothing special about asking for a tube for a pen of this vintage. He went to the back of the counter and came back with a tray of rubber tubes. He said, "These are a ridiculous price, twenty-five cents, used to sell them for two cents apiece." I said I would take two, which surprised him. I put the tube in the pen when I got home, stuck the nib in a bottle of ink and filled it. I put pen to paper — smooth as silk. My mother-in-law passed away a few years ago in her ninety-seventh year, but every time I take her pen in hand to write, she is with me.

Jervis Weir
Chelmsford, Ontario

✉ My pen is an Elysée; light, slim and a wonderfully deep, rich blue colour with gold accents. It was a Christmas gift from my mother about a dozen years ago.

My first fountain pen was a Sheaffer made of black plastic with a silver cap. It came with two spare plastic ink cartridges and beyond that more cartridges were bought in small yellow and blue boxes of five each. When the cartridge was empty it was thrown out or, more often than not, we would cut the ends off and they became great spitball shooters. Being so small they were easily concealed in small, grade-five hands and I was able to pepper classmates and the classroom ceiling with spitballs and never get caught. They also made realistic fake cigarettes, especially on cold days when our visible breath looked like cigarette smoke.

You know, I think my fountain pen has been too long in the desk drawer and I feel a sudden urge to make some spitballs.

Joel Luet
Calgary

✉ Of the millions of blotters that were produced annually, you can't find one today. I have one, found in my school *Roget's Thesaurus*, advertising a Tommy Fitzgerald running for Student Council, and this brings to mind the glories of the blotter.

You were really growing up when you arrived in grade five and had your own ink-well *in* your desk. The teacher handed out blotters and demonstrated how they were to be used. They were fascinating objects. By placing a corner in the ink-well, you could watch the ink flow up the paper fibres in a fanlike spider-web manner. If you wet the corner with your tongue before placing it in the ink, the upward flow was much faster. Also, by blotting the writing immediately, you got backward writing, and you needed a mirror to read the message.

Ah, the message! Just about every blotter carried a message on the back, mostly in the form of advertising. Local politicians favoured this method, as a blotter remained on the desk glossy side up with the message always in plain view. No junk mail, these blotters. The mailman or some local boy dropped them in your mailbox with the advertising printed on the back. They were useful and were kept handy as everyone used an ink pen, and a blotter was essential. Besides they came in all kinds of different colours and could be used for cutting and making various designs for Christmas and other festivities.

Do you remember those semi-circular pieces of finished wood with a nice knob on the top to use as a handle? The blotting paper was placed on the round part and clipped on at the ends and you rolled the blotting paper over the ink instead of patting the blotter on top of the still wet writing. Anyone who owned one of those rollers was classy and up-to-date.

Earl Dupuis
Ottawa

✉ The ink blotter that sits on my computer has a three-inch-wide, six-inch-long rocking-horse base on which sits a rectangular block with bevelled edges. A graceful knob sits atop and screws down through the other pieces. Unscrew the knob and you create a gap between the two pieces of wood, and I expect that the ends of the blotting paper would fold into that gap and be secured by tightening the knob.

I bought this lovely old blotter at a yard sale for less than five dollars. It had belonged to John Barrett, a sea captain (or Master Mariner, as his business card read) who sailed the Newfoundland–Portugal route around the turn of the century. I know this because John Barrett was my grandfather. The blotter was played with and abused by me and my siblings as we grew up, but that didn't dim my outrage when I found out that my dad had it up for grabs at his yard sale! I was eighteen, living on my own, but must have been suspicious that Mum and Dad were going to try to ditch some family treasures before they moved. I showed up for the sale and bought the blotter over my old pink pointe shoes from my ballet years. I've never used the blotter for its intended purpose (does blotting paper exist any more?) but sometimes I rock it on my hand or my desk and imagine the ledgers it has blotted and the swelling seas it sailed.

Years before the yard sale I brought that blotter in to show my grade-five class. Our teacher, Miss Smith, had just introduced us to cartridge pens and blotting paper (which didn't fit my blotter). My mother had told me that if you put blotting paper in your shoes, the paper would draw the blood down from your brain and you would faint! Easily a day off school, if you time it right, thought I, and I shared the secret with only my closest friends. But what if you fainted and no one thought to take your shoes off — would not all your precious bodily fluids end up pooling below knee level? And should the blotting paper go next to your bare soles inside your socks or just in your shoes? Although it was much discussed, none of us dared try it. And in grade six we graduated to ball-point pens. But I still wonder.

Cindy Barrett
Kemptville, Ontario

✉ I am writing this on a notebook computer, sitting in my wing chair, listening to some piano jazz. Art Tatum, I think. You can tell from the extended runs. Almost a surfeit of notes, cascading over one another, nearly getting caught in the net of melody and rhythm, but emerging as a clear, evocative structure with, unbelievably, each phrase perfect and self-contained.

But I'm getting off track. I always use a computer now. I used to use a pen and paper. It was actually a special pen. My father gave it to me when I was twelve. He got it when he left his job at the newspaper. Sort of a going-away present, although he never said at the time why he had to go. He used to complain about the paper but I knew he really liked it. He would go on at dinner about how they didn't pay enough and, if it wasn't for Max, the City Editor, he would have left long ago. Or they couldn't get along without him. Or — I liked this one the best — someone had to teach these college grads how to write. But we all knew that the paper was his life and he would never quit. I guess that made his leaving even more of a shock. Surprisingly, Mother didn't seem too upset. "I've seen it coming for years," she once said over breakfast. Dad didn't reply.

He introduced me to jazz. He had a collection of old 78s that he would listen to for hours. All by himself in the den, door closed, that scratchy old music all but obscured as it seeped out through the walls. You could still hear the rhythm, though, the bass line steady, rock hard, anchoring the rest of the band; the drums sharp and insistent, keeping the other musicians in line. One day I was standing outside the door when he opened it and said, "That's Count Basie. He plays piano. He's not a real count, of course, but they call him that because he's like royalty. He's so good that the other musicians look up to him like he was a king or a duke or a count."

He was leaning against the door and the music was loud now. The band was in full flight, all sections playing in unison, trumpets high above the rest, the sound surging through the doorway as if it would sweep away my father and everything else before it. Then it ended, suddenly, except for four short notes on the piano. "Plink, plink, plink, plink." And it was over. I thought those four notes the most wonderful sounds I had ever heard. They just hung there, complete in themselves yet an inseparable part of the whole piece. The music was finished but I could still hear those notes.

"Well, don't just stand there. Come on in," Dad said and backed out of the doorway, rather unsteadily. I entered the room while he removed a glass tumbler from the top of the desk, rummaged through his desk and brought forth a small cigar. "You don't mind if I smoke, do you?" he said. I grinned and nodded. He had never asked my permission for anything before. We sat in the acrid fumes for an hour and listened to the most wonderful music ever played: Duke Ellington, Benny Goodman, Tommy Dorsey, Glenn Miller. Most of all, I remember my father leaning back in his chair, eyes closed, fingers tapping out the simple rhythms on his knee or the top of the desk, stopping only to put on a new record. I don't think I said a word for a whole hour.

We had many sessions after that, and I came to appreciate what jazz meant to him, how it was a solace, a retreat where only he could go, a wall behind which he could shelter when the paper or Mother or something inside him made life too hard to face. We never talked about it but I knew.

About a week after he was fired, Dad called me into the den. He was sitting at his desk, turning something over and over in his hand. There was a bottle on the desk, half-filled with amber-coloured liquor. A glass was lying on its side next to it. No music was playing. It was very quiet. His record collection, which was normally stacked neatly on shelves beside the window, was scattered on the floor. Two records lay broken but he didn't seem to notice. He stared straight ahead and hardly seemed to see me when I started to enter the room.

"This is it," he muttered. "This is what twenty years of hard work and devotion are worth. One more chance. That's all I wanted. One more lousy chance. I could've done it. How many times did it happen? It would have been the last time. The bastards."

I looked up quickly. I had never heard him swear before. Really swear. Never in all those complaints and accusations had there ever been more than a "damn" or a "hell."

He stopped talking and looked down at the object in his hand. I saw it was a pen, a shiny black fountain pen, with a gold clip. His head waved slightly from side to side while he examined it. He picked up the glass, poured some of the liquor into it and drank the contents in one gulp. I recognized the sweet, sharp odour. I had smelled it in the room before. "What good is a pen, if they don't let you write? Am I just supposed to write letters with it? Goddamn it, I'm a newspaper man, not a bloody poet."

He was almost shouting now and totally oblivious of me.

"I give them my life and they give me a . . . a pen." He stopped suddenly and finally acknowledged me in the doorway. I had never seen him look so completely vulnerable. His body seemed barely to occupy his thin shirt. His eyes looked through, rather than at me, as if trying to locate me by reference to the objects in the room. His hands continued to play with the pen. He was drunk, of course, but I didn't know it.

"You take it. You take it. You can use it more than I can."

He leaned over the desk and pushed the pen towards me. I smelt the pungent odour again, only stronger. I didn't take the pen. I couldn't move.

"No, no. It's yours." I was almost crying now. "They gave it to you. I can't have it. It was meant for you."

He got up slowly and unsteadily. Grasping the edge of the desk with one hand, and holding the pen with the other, he made his way towards me. When he reached the end of the desk, he stopped, closed his eyes and pitched forward onto his knees. The pen dropped in front of him.

I ran forward to him. "Dad, Dad," I cried, "are you all right? I'll take the pen, if you want. I didn't mean it. Please, give it to me."

But he didn't. He opened his eyes, smiled and put both hands on my shoulders. The smell of the liquor was overpowering. His face, so close to mine, was pained yet comforting.

"Son," he said in a voice now soft and thick as syrup, "I'm sorry. I'm sorry. I'm sorry. I've had too much to drink and I'm feeling sorry for myself. It's a problem adults have when things get . . . get out of hand. I'd really like you to have the pen. It's important to me. When you write something, it might inspire you. You'll write something great and think of me. Okay? Promise?"

Still smiling, he took his hands from my shoulders, bent down, picked up the pen and handed it to me. It was a thick, shiny black cylinder, with a gold clasp like an arrow mounted on the cap. I unscrewed the cap and pushed it onto the other end of the pen. The nib was also gold. I took the pen in my right hand. It felt powerful in some strange way. I wouldn't use a pen like that for just anything. I hugged my father very tightly.

"Now go away and let your father drink in peace," he said with a smile on his face. As I turned to leave, he swayed, grinned at me again and passed out on the floor.

Dad was right. I did use the pen and it did seem to inspire me. Not for work, of course, but when I really wanted to say something. A love letter or a poem, for example. Then I would pick up the pen, get some sheets of really good bond paper, lock myself in the den and write. And, of course, put on some good jazz.

Dad died a year ago. I had moved to another city and we hadn't seen each other in a few years but we did write. I used my pen, of course. He didn't work steadily after the paper but managed to support Mother and himself with free-lance work. His last letter complained about rates for free-lancers and the fact that no one today can really write.

When Mother phoned me with the news of his death, I went into the den, put a Count Basie record on the machine, took the pen and sat down to write. I'm not sure what I wanted to do, an obituary perhaps, and maybe that was the problem. I couldn't find anything to say. The words just wouldn't come. I must have sat for an hour and the page was still totally blank. Finally, I got up, went to my desk, rolled the pen in a handkerchief and placed it in the bottom drawer at the back. I haven't used it since.

I guess there's no real difference between a pen and a computer. They're both just tools. In some way, though, it's like jazz. Some instruments, like some people, have more heart, and it's heart that makes music. Count Basie knew that. So did my father.

Lion J. Sharzer
Aylmer, Quebec

LIVING WITH CANCER: A WIFE'S STORY

When Kathleen Winter began to keep the honest and powerful journal — the notebook, as she calls it — that makes up this chapter, she and her husband, James, were living in St. John's, where James had been working, among other jobs (they are both freelance writers), as the art critic for the *Evening Telegraph*. They've moved since, as you'll see, though not from Newfoundland, whose lilting accent you could hear as Kathleen read her work on the air.

A word of acknowledgement here, too, if I may. Kathleen took her first offering to the CBC's St. John's office, thinking it might make for meaningful regional radio. The network producer there, Marie Wadden, recognized it at once as deserving a wider audience, and alerted Shelley Ambrose, my incomparable assistant, who produces many of *Morningside*'s written pieces, and in all the months ahead, helped Kathleen bring her words to the radio.

This is a slightly longer version than we were able to broadcast, and it includes a postscript that Kathleen faxed to us just before these pages went to press. But this is Kathleen's journal, as her story — and James's — unfolded.

July 3, 1992

I want to start a notebook now before too much else happens: if this is to be a long haul then too much can be forgotten. I wish this was the book on wildflowers I was going to write, but it isn't. James was diagnosed June 8 with cancer of the lung. Now he has had two bronchoscopies, two biopsies and a mediastinoscopy. The results of the last test will be ready, the surgeon says, on Monday. This is Friday.

The mediastinoscopy is what James had today. Dr. Gardiner said there was a small "risk." When he said this he parted his thumb and forefinger almost an inch. I did not say, "A small risk of what?" James asked Dr. Gardiner if he could eat after the operation, and Dr. Gardiner said he could probably eat his lunch.

At 11:30, three hours and fifteen minutes after the operation, which was said to take about an hour usually, I realized nobody was going to phone me and tell me anything. I did the usual round of busy signals and transfers and on holds that anybody does when they call a hospital, and finally found from his room-mate Mike that James could not talk. "Can he hear?" I asked him. Yes. I said tell him I'll be there in a few minutes.

I took a taxi there. I walked along the corridor of 5 East preparing myself visually. The books I have read, and the doctors, describe a mediastinoscopy as a very small procedure — hardly an operation at all. I hadn't been prepared to hear Mike say that James couldn't talk.

When I went in I saw that they had hurt my husband. He was pale and disoriented. He could not get up. His face was swollen. He was wearing a hospital johnny suit, but it had fallen off his back. His neck had a fat oblong bandage puffing out, and his whole chest and shoulders were uncovered. His chest and throat were painted with a smeared brown substance, and two dark ribbons of dried blood were snaking from beneath the bandage and down over his back. He could hardly speak and kept drifting to sleep. I kissed him and stroked him. The pillow had plastic under the cover, and it wasn't thick enough. J's hand had an IV needle in it; the dripping bag of salt water hung beside him. I kissed him and stroked him until I had to get Esther from the day care where she goes part-time. J looks after her in the afternoons — I have a day job, and I am wondering what is going to happen about that. I took today and yesterday off, but I can't take every day off and still keep the job.

I left him asleep and found the nursing station. I went in and said to two nurses, "Excuse me." They didn't turn around. I said to their backs, "I am James Wade's wife, and I was wondering if anyone is going to wash all the brown stuff off him" — they were looking at me by now — "and there's dried blood running down his back as well." The nurses smiled and were warm then. They said they would surely wash him — that they didn't do it right away because he was resting. Later on the phone J said two nurses came in and sponged him and told him they were doing it because his wife had expressed concern for him. That made me feel good. Later I went to the hospital again and he was so much better. His face was pink again and he was washed. He was my Jimmy again.

July 5

Before James went into the hospital, I wanted to shoot a roll of film of us — James, Esther and me. But I never got around to it. I saw a picture one morning that I will never forget.

He was taking her to the day-care centre; they were walking hand in hand down the driveway. I was watching them through the living-room window. They went down, the new maple leaves filling the air over their heads, sunshine falling in dapples on Esther's sun-hat, on J's browny-gold hair. Esther's sun-hat was new — white with a brim and red trim. I had put a blue corduroy pinafore dress on her, red tights and her big sneakers. Her legs were lovely and long. When they walked down the hill together I felt them precious and dear. James had just had his thirty-ninth birthday, and Esther had recently had her third. I told myself it didn't matter if there was no picture. Photographs don't always retain the whole love and tenderness of a moment, and memory, while it lives, is more sensitive to these things.

July 6

Esther cried in bed then said, "I'm crying because Daddy is sick." She spends a lot of time with her daddy when things are normal. This morning before we brushed our teeth, she was standing on the toilet the way she does so she can reach the sink, and I said give me a standing-up hug. She gave me a cuddly one and said, "Marry me! Marry me!" in a plaintive tone. I remembered her Beauty and the Beast cards, one of which has Beauty and the prince standing up,

64

hugging. "I'm the Beast," Esther said. "Yes, I'll marry you," I told her, hugging her. "Oh look — you're a handsome prince now!"

"Do handsome princes like cinnamon toast?" she asked me. "Yes," I said, "they love it. Do you want some now?" "Yes," she said.

This evening when the surgeon and interns entered room 5107, J and I were lying in his bed under the sheets reading a magazine. They laughed and we did, too. I got out of the bed and sat down. They told us Dr. Spurrell was right, it is cancer, and Dr. Gardiner thought surgery was really the only option, and with our permission it could proceed around the middle of this week, when he can get operating-room time. It looked like he wasn't going to elaborate on what type of cancer it was, so I asked. "It's called large cell cancer," he said, and I knew J felt relieved. I was glad of the books Nancy had sent, so we knew something about it. After they left, J danced around the hospital grinning, singing, "I've got cancer," to the tune of "Frère Jacques" — a tune we had used as a baby song about Esther. We both felt a great temporary relief, which came partly from being told something conclusive after this torture of waiting.

July 14

Things are not very good. The operation was not a success. Dr. Gardiner took me aside and told me that the cancer is more extensive than he had hoped. This was last night when I went to visit James, at around 7:30. What happened was that Dr. Gardiner told me this on the telephone as I was about to leave for the hospital. When I said I was coming he said he would elaborate in person. At the hospital I went to see James first. James told me, "They didn't take my lung out." I was hurt and shocked that James had to know this in his weakened condition, for he had been opened up . . . the whole surgical operation had been done, except for the removal of the lung.

Dr. Gardiner took me to a small room where we sat down. He told me that it had taken a long time in the O.R. to find the extent of the cancer, partly because the top lobe of the right lung had collapsed over the main part of the tumour. He told me they found that the cancer had spread beyond the lung to the trachea and the superior vena cava, and said there was extensive lymph node involvement. He wrote these things down for me. I asked him what stage the cancer had reached. Before, with the idea that it was confined to one lung and could be removed, it had been considered to be at what is termed stage I. Now Dr. Gardiner says the cancer is known to be at stage III B. I asked him if there was any such thing as a prognosis at this point, and he said he doesn't think Jim will live much more than a year. The big book Nancy sent confirms this. It gives the five-year survival rate for people with stage III B as less than five per cent.

Today James does not seem to be progressing well at all. He is very jaundiced, because of the liver's reaction to the extensive blood transfusions he has had during and since the surgery. He has a fever, and tonight he told me he needs oxygen almost continuously. He said, "I'm traumatized," and he repeated this; traumatized emotionally as well as physically, by the surgery and its futility.

July 17

Yesterday was a beautiful day studded in a long succession of cold, rainy days. At a bus stop on the way to the hospital I saw a rhododendron tree in bloom in Bannerman Park, surrounded by beds of pansies, marigolds and stocks. The formality of the garden, the misty green trees, and a pecking starling and black dog sniffing, were miraculously beautiful in the face of what is happening. I realize that God is giving me a greater capacity to appreciate beauty, and it is a gift, this capacity, that He is giving me because I need it. Daisies, clover and a waterfall at the river on a walk with Esther this week gave me the same pleasure. I only pray now that God will give James something to gladden his heart, too, and ease his pain and disappointment.

July 30

James is a lot better. The jaundice is gone, and he can do things for himself. Yesterday I bought a juicing machine and made carrot juice for him. I have read enough to convince me that more can be done to fight cancer than surgery and radiation. Nutrition, spirituality and the emotions have their part to play, too.

But we're having trouble with the emotional part. Our relationship has changed because for the past month I have been James's nurse, and because he may be dying. As his nurse, the role I've been given automatically is one of lifting him, cleaning his incision — which had become infected — making his bed, attending his toilet — all the things I used to do when I worked at one time looking after old people. Doing that and caring for three-year-old Esther, too, and dealing with the endless stream of visitors, all of whom require tea or coffee and some food and bright conversation. . . . Well, James wonders why I go to bed at 10:30, leaving him awake, alone.

It's true that I have a lot of new feelings. Things are not the same as they were before he was diagnosed with cancer. Before we can have a spontaneous kiss or hug each other out of joy, delight or the happiness of little things in life, we have to step over the abyss of death. This is how I feel, anyway. Maybe it will change.

There is also this thought: if he really is going to die in a year, it is going to be very hard to live as if we weren't just waiting for death. The way we are used to feeling about our life has to change if it isn't going to be horrible. The way we are used to feeling — the way everybody feels — is that we assume we are building our life, our family, our relationships. I didn't realize until now how strong that feeling is . . . and if the future is taken away from us, the whole point of the present is called into question. I have long heard that it is important to live in the present. I didn't know how very much my hopes were pinned on the future.

Most of the reason they are pinned on the future, I realize now, has to do with how dissatisfied I am about the present. I have been dissatisfied like this for some time — even before James's diagnosis. Now that I am writing this, my thoughts are sorting themselves out pretty fast. I would like to examine this, and then maybe — wonder of wonders — do something about it.

Both James and I have been having vivid dreams. Last night I dreamed there was a swan in the kitchen. I was busy, and I shooed it out the back door, where it stayed, pressing itself outside the kitchen window, pecking at the seam of the sill with its beak.

Now I feel that for me, as for others — because I have read it — a swan is the symbol of spiritual fulfilment. Graceful, mysterious, tall and beautiful, a swan can crown a pool with exquisite beauty. But this swan was out of the water; it was moving slowly and awkwardly across my kitchen floor, and its bottom feathers were dirty. Moreover I was much too busy to welcome this swan. I was answering a phone call, and someone was at the front door — a usual scenario these days. I told Jim of the dream at breakfast, just mentioning the swan's appearance and my herding it out the door, and he immediately said, "I would have kept it." That got me thinking about what the dream signified. I don't normally interpret dreams, but the meaning of this one seems pretty clear and simple.

A swan — symbol of spiritual fulfilment, and a creature I normally find beautiful — tried to come into my house. I noticed it was dingy and out of its element. I was too busy for it. I shooed it out. The dissatisfaction I referred to earlier has to do with just this. There is a certain person I need to become. I am not becoming her. I need to see the swan return to its magical pool and become fulfilled myself. The way is not clear yet, but it will become so.

September 27

Jim has tired easily and has been coughing ever since the last one or two radiation treatments. He is completely drained after any exertion and often has fits of a dry, hacking, itching cough. He came home today after visiting his family in Conception Harbour overnight, and I was struck by the fact that he looked unwell. The one-hour drive had drained him and he had to lie down immediately. He looked haggard and thin and drawn. I felt sad. He revived a little after he had a rest and I made him some food. I asked him if he thinks the fatigue and coughing are a result of the radiation or the cancer, and he said maybe it's both. Fatigue and coughing were symptoms he had before the operation or radiation.

Today was a perfect September day. Earlier, when Jim was still away, Michael and Gaile came to take Esther for a while, but their itinerary was so inviting I went with them. We went walking in the hills above Quidi Vidi and found a table-shaped rock where we sat and had a picnic. The seams of the rock had partridgeberries sewn all down them, and in front of us, down below, the little inlet sparkled and glowed a deep green, while gulls wheeled and cried in the chamber of the rock inlet. The air was warm and scented. Esther and I took our shoes off and felt the warm rock, with its lichen. Down below all around the water were people walking with babies, big-eared dogs, friends, each other. The whole town was celebrating a late September Sunday where the light struck trees' branches in a gold blaze and filtered through their leaves in a green haze. On a telephone wire six little birds sat up bright, watching. People who had fancy, old-fashioned cars paraded in them with the tops down. It seemed not a leaf anywhere dared to turn yellow; all was green, summer held in suspension. I came home, and Michael and Gaile took Esther with them.

I read on the verandah for a while, appreciating the trees draping the garden. Then I got out my new water-colours and did an ink and wash sketch of some fungus, which Esther with stunning accuracy says is like the dried apricots she likes to eat, growing out of the rotten old chopping block near the wood-horse. Then I decided to walk to the end of the driveway to look at the lovely light that was gilding the trees and the western side of the street. At the bottom of the driveway I found the street irresistible, and so with the next street, until I was down by the river, walking and raising my arms to the lovely sun, the day, Sunday, in the straw hat Gaile had given me, a fringed goldy-brown scarf tied around the hat, and my new sunset-coloured dress. No wonder Jim looked unwell when he came back, compared to the gold light singing in my veins.

September 29

James is very sick today; fever, chills, weakness and fatigue, and pain in his lower back and head. He took some of the morphine elixir left over from his surgery. His cough is still bad, as it has been ever since the radiation stopped. He is lying on the couch under a sleeping bag all the time, and his eyes look sunken and his expression down-hearted. At supper today he said, "I'm dying — my body is breaking down." I wonder how much of this is a reflection of his recent visit to relatives, where he said everyone treated him as doomed.

Deborah Clarke, with her husband, Len Penton, and son Joel, came and took me and Esther partridgeberry picking. We went to the meadow we visited earlier this summer, and the partridgeberries were wine-ripe, glowing like jewels amid the caribou moss and around the junipers. The barrens beyond the meadows were rolling and fragrant under a blue sky. Debbie and Len brought their Coleman stove and we had a cup of tea on the berry grounds. Across the rolling hills we could see St. John's spread out, and two pockets of limitless ocean.

Then Debbie and Len took us to the other side of town to a trail in the woods, where we gathered chanterelles. It was the first time anyone had shown me how to identify these wild mushrooms, and to have been shown this is one of the highlights of my life. To me it is a very, very special thing to gather chanterelles. Their name alone describes their loveliness, delicateness and rarity. With their apricot-coloured stems flaring upwards in the peat floors of coniferous woods, they are, I told Esther, like fairy skirts dancing. I will sauté them tomorrow in a little butter and share them with Michael and Gaile, as well as with my little family.

October 5

I'm at the Heritage Bakery Café. Jim is at home lying on the couch. Esther is at day care. I put her in all day today. I needed a break after the weekend. No day care on weekends. I realize, sitting here after eating a bowl of chili and bread and a muffin I didn't have to make myself or wash dishes after, that yesterday and today when I got out of the house and sat down somewhere, I was shaking. Yesterday I put it down to the nervousness of being a new driver — I'm driving to little sanctuaries now — but today I don't think it's just that. I've been out of the car for forty-five minutes now, and I'm still shaky. This morning I felt impatient with Jim and tried not to show it, but he felt it. He just kept asking me to do little things — get him an apple, turn on the heat, sew buttons on his shirt . . . all reasonable things that I should do for him, but it seemed I couldn't get to sit down for a second, and after getting Esther ready and taking her to day care I just wanted everyone's claims on me to stop.

I managed to refrain from saying something very unkind to him. I said a wretched little prayer in the bathroom then went out and smiled at him. He smiled back. Everything's all right but it's perhaps more of a strain than I realize if I'm shaking when I get away. Later this morning as I was sewing buttons on my coat — that's when he quite reasonably asked if I'd do the ones on his shirt — he began to cry. He sobbed, lying there on the couch under the green quilt I got out of payment from a poetry reading and a brown scratchy woollen monk's blanket, and when I asked him to talk to me about it, he said, "It's Esther, I'm going to die and leave Esther."

"Little Esther," I said cruelly. He sobbed more.

"Her daddy." I was relentless.

"Yes. And she's too young."

I felt unsympathetic, although I stroked and comforted him.

"Maybe you won't die," I said. "Have you thought of that?"

"Yes."

"Do you think you're going to?"

"Yes."

I felt that if he died I wouldn't marry another man. I would get strong, and with Esther do the best I could to have a good, strong life in a cabin somewhere. I'd keep my friends, and I might get lovers, but I wouldn't marry anyone else. Either men are too dependent or they are bossy and manipulative. Today I just look at them and they fit right into one class or another. Either you end up having to look after them, or you wind up realizing they neither need nor love you.

Of course this is one of those momentary statements that life doesn't permit to survive. Poor Jim. Sometimes I think he'd be better off with his mother. She'd sew his buttons on, fuss over him, make him meals that he liked, love him more than I do. She wouldn't have other things on her agenda; selfish things, young woman things, wild river walks, sketch-books and diaries. She wouldn't hurt him by having her own hidden, inner life.

October 6

Well, I'm at the Heritage Café again — for breakfast. Things are okay at home, but we are having some tense moments. Yesterday J said I never wanted to spend time at home. I said I just needed to get out and be alone sometimes, when Esther is in day care. It makes me feel good to sit over a coffee and write or read. At home it is too depressing if I have to stay there all the time. Jim does feel a little better this morning. I told him let's try not to let circumstances make our relationship deteriorate. I explained that I need time to recover, and that if I am not always solicitous to him it's because I find all this hard, too. Actually I'm quite horrible. I just feel such a need to escape, especially now all of a sudden I have my driver's licence.

I love driving the car. Yesterday I took her to get a rim sealed and marvelled at how quickly the mechanic does heavy work, all his machines able to perform big tasks. He sprinkled water around the rim and found the leak and found one on the valve, too. He replaced the valve for nothing, and the whole job, which included lifting the car, locating the problem, removing the tire, sanding the rim and daubing rim and tire with sealant, replacing the valve, replacing the tire, replacing the wheel on the care and lowering the car, cost me $5.99. I never saw anybody do that much work for $5.99 before. As he worked I thought of my brother, in Florida, doing the same thing, with black hands, overalls and a mind full of dreams — lifting a sunken sailing boat in the Bahamas, making enough money to own his own garage in the Codroy Valley; never saving any money, always getting into debt, trouble. Handsome to women and warm-hearted, dangerous. I nearly cried a little in the garage.

Driving a car. I love the car's privacy. You open the door and get in, like a woman in a movie. You are in your own little cubicle. The cubicle can move through the city, through the country. Yesterday after my downtown errands I sat in the car beside the parking meter and read a story in Gabrielle Roy's *The Fragile Lights of Earth*. The car is a sanctuary, a chariot of freedom, an escape vehicle. When I put the key in the ignition and press the pedals, adjust the shift — all these things are hard, mechanical, contrasted with my human and female softness, yet they do what I say. No wonder men are mad about cars. A car seals you off from the world, yet through the world you spin, protected, enclosed. Not vulnerable like a walker, the cold wind blowing up your fingernails, hurting the tender flesh inside your ears, torturing your face and hair. A car makes you feel powerful. Of course, one wrong move and you will see what a dangerous illusion this is.

November 20

I'm at Woolworth's coffee shop now, where Santas, Snoopies and presents are painted on the windows beyond which the year's third snowfall is lightly floating across the big downtown post office. A frowning woman with a short grey perm is drinking a huge soft drink in a paper cup, and her grandson takes it from her — it is his — and sucks so long and hard on the straw that his jawbone shakes.

Gradually Jim has come to the point where he goes outside only to do his weekly column or to have a rare outing. The last outing was to go to Holyrood, where Gerry is making a clay sculpture of his head and shoulders. He hasn't been out since, except to do the column, and today if he has strength enough he wants to go out and buy a new pair of winter boots. I couldn't possibly say, "What do you need boots for?"

I saw a mother, father and child walk past the decorated window in the snow of Water Street and felt a pang — will James, Esther and I ever walk like that again? Such a simple thing — as Paul says, people don't know what precious things they have.

February 12, 1993

I am not minding this February at all. The sun has come out many days in a row, and there is bright, soft, new, clean snow in a healthy thick coat everywhere. The trees are graceful in their spreading reaches and the roads are covered in a pale frost coat because the striking city workers have stopped mucking them up with salt and sand. To walk somewhere is to move briskly in dancing light, frost sparkles spiralling in the air, pure, fresh air washing one's breathing. Jim is like an Arctic explorer this morning in his Russian hat, fur-hooded parka and old green knapsack, dusty green corduroy trousers, as he heads off to class and the library.

Last night I dreamed he died. They took his body away somewhere before I had seen it. I travelled all over the hospital and the city, which had become unfamiliar, looking for the doctor, the room where Jim lay. I searched with Esther in my arms. We couldn't find him. I have never felt such a sense of loss as I did in that dream. No matter how much anybody — friends, family, hospital staff — cared or helped us, nobody loved us like Jim. Nobody understood us like Jim, and we didn't love or understand anyone like we loved him. I cried in the dream, and it was a deep, tragic, wailing cry from the soul. It was one of those dreams whose feelings are true when you are awake, too. I awoke and snuggled into him. I never told him about the dream.

73

March 12

I decided in these journals I was going to at least try not to apologize for my feelings. What would be the point? A big part of cancer is the uncertainty and slowness with which it does its work, and I have feelings about that. When he dies . . . if he dies . . . uncertainty. Meanwhile I am supposed to remain concerned about him only, happy to remain loyally at his side whether he dies, lives, fluctuates, dwindles, pines or thrives, all the while unconcerned about the eventual outcome, concerned not for myself, my sexual life, passions, youth, age, companionship — for it is a very certain kind of companionship I enjoy now; one in which Cancer comes to bed with us, sits in the apartment with us, laughs, hides coyly, doesn't come out with a statement of its intentions, expects me to ignore it, love it, console it, like being with it. Well, I don't like being with it, and I do feel that its slowness is a horrible thing, not a blessing. Today that is what I feel, and I make no apology about it.

March 21

I need this journal for healing tonight. It's funny; I got used to telling Jim everything, and now that he is dying he has become part of what confronts me; part of the "other," and I can no longer confide in him completely. I'm trying to get a grip on myself and "face it."

"Face it" is what I learned today at my old-time haunt, Ladies' Lookout on Signal Hill. Ladies' Lookout is a stone seat in a cleft in the cliff face at the top of Signal Hill. I drove up Signal Hill today and walked past the tourists to the lonely place. Today was a glorious day welcoming spring. The snow's crust surface had blue fire in it and flashing ruby crystals. In Ladies' Lookout I found some comfort in the cold cliff face. The rock had two streamlets of melting ice trickling from one crevice. Splotches of cheerful lichen adorned the stone seat, on which I sat looking out to sea. I gathered sticks, a dried flower star, soft yellow-brown grasses.

I regarded the stone face rising over me into the sky with comfort. The cold air, cold stone, cold me. I felt good. The stone was "facing it," and I must face it, too. The stone wasn't indulging in any illusions or delusions. I must be like that, too. The gifts of dry thistle and grasses, melting streamlets like tears down the rock, lonely bird calls;

all were strong, and I must be strong. Some tears glistened down my face, too.

I gathered my mosses and thistles and grasses (the grasses were laid low, hugging the earth), and I pressed my lips to the cliff face. I was surprised. It was the best kiss I've had in years. Who would have thought the rock of a cliff so passionate.

Tonight I went to the Cathedral with a friend, and the service was about the link between passion and suffering. I could relate to that. Lent is accompanying me with its beautiful story of fasting and barrenness, passion and suffering, cold rock and flesh pressing against each other in an embrace of love and agony.

April 30

A few things have happened to return to me the gift of being able to love my husband. The terrain of the heart is so mysterious, it is impossible to say with certainty what the things are exactly, or even if it is these things and not some mysterious wave or current. However I do love James today, and prize and cherish him, and I am grateful and relieved to be able to do so . . . to see him for his best, loveliest, most spiritual and poetic self. His soulful self, the one that I married. And of course to do that I have to become my soulful self, the one that married him.

First of all, Gerry gave James a portrait done as J sat in the class Gerry was instructing. The portrait is the nicest one, I think, that he has done of James. In it J's face, hair and expression are bathed in a soft light. Gerry has captured J's thoughtfulness, gentleness, his poetic and spiritual soul, and his feelings as he faces death: acceptance of it and sorrow about his youth, dying young and leaving a wife and Esther.

I have come into the other room to look at the portrait as I write about it. The head is filled with thoughts, and they have the strength and sadness I just mentioned. But there is also the feeling that Jim is not alone. The light that is coming, just small, but soft and strong, from the side he faces . . . and the vulnerable, accepting aloneness of his face . . . and the beautiful colours — dark blue-black and warm, deep purple — of his clothing . . . this is the beautiful Jim, the one whom God is with. One cannot doubt, in looking at the painting, that his God is with him. All the human problems, the petty things, fall away when faced with the ultimate eternal spirituality of the person. I can see that Gerry has put himself in the painting, too, because he also has, as Jim has sometimes, this beautiful, strong, pure quality about him — this clarity and transparent truthfulness, as a clear pond lets you see into its beauty — its fish, rocks, green underwater life. Gerry knows, best of all people perhaps, how to understand or at least to see this special duality Jim has — on the one hand this clear, striking quality, and on the other hand the muddied waters, the clouded view, the life clouded with cares that lead to sin, as the Bible calls our manifest weaknesses. But in this painting is the lovely quality of forgiveness — this is James with his forgiven soul, as Jesus sees him, as Jesus, saying "Judge not," would have all of us see each other.

Then Beth called this morning. She is one of the world's fairest natural objects, like a star, or a beautiful stone, a gem. She spoke about how I will speak to Jim after he dies, when I look up at the stars, and he will not seem far from me.

And there is the weather: soft, misty, rainy; forgiving and healing, mysterious and comforting in its dimness, no glare.

Then there are the tidal pulls, the moon's influence on my woman tides; as they change so do my inner oceanic waves . . . This whole experience between James and myself has taught me how influential these pulls beyond my will, my conscious control, are upon me. I humble myself before this knowledge, love it and forgive myself.

May 11

Last night Jim said something that revolutionized the way I've been looking at the cancer, at our marriage. He said that because of the cancer we are not the same couple we were before it happened; we are really a different couple. And he's right.

And it's because I've been looking at us as the same couple — injured and war-torn — that I've felt so miserable. Looking at us as the old us — with cancer — is not the same as looking at us as a whole new couple. If I look at us as a new couple altogether, I see new possibilities. No longer is the future a failed version of our hopes. The future does not begin with the old couple, the past. It begins with us the way we have become. Our old hopes might be dead. It's time to see that they are dead, and to bury them. To start from now, instead, presents us with a whole new set of possibilities. I merely begin to understand this now as I write.

Intuitively I feel our moving to the country fits in with this. Our old hopes, our old dreams, our old selves, each and together; buried. But Jim is still here, and I am still here, and Esther is just starting out, but even she faces this change. We are still here, and we have survived everything that has happened to us. If we continue with the tattered forms of our old selves, we will be pathetic and wounded and eternally sad. I don't understand this fully yet, but perhaps Jim is right, and we have changed, each of us and together, into someone, something, else. Somehow I feel this insight equips us for our new future, our different future, the one we never thought we would have.

June 16, 1994

Jim, Esther and I are in the kitchen. It's a sunny morning. The sounds are Vivaldi's Kyrie in G minor for double choir, a pineapple Popsicle being slurped, and songs of the white-throated sparrow and a cathedral of other songbirds in the woods beyond the open door.

Yesterday we planted chives, strawberry plants and thyme in the garden. Today all the plants are springy and upright; they've taken fine.

It's even more beautiful living here than it was when we moved in this time last year. Esther and I cut some alders and I made a love-seat out of twigs and sticks and bent roots. I planted a peony and the seat is slowly being shrouded in fireweed, scarlet-flowering bean vines, and leaves and flowers of a young mountain ash. The seat is a twisted network of arching roots and curling sticks. We sit on it and watch things grow: the peony, sage, sweet basil, tomatoes. Jim calls the seat a symbol of our love. It looks like something from Middle Earth; it has a strange orange root at the front, and its legs are masses of gnarled and knotted wood. Our nephew Ryan likes it; he explains to his parents that it's not really that uncomfortable — you just have to find a "sweet spot." Anyway, Jim and Esther like it, and so do I. Yesterday, as spring rain started to fall on the dandelion and wild strawberry and sorrel near the seat, a grosbeak couple alighted on the spray of roots that forms part of the back rest; the male with his plumage the colour of dried raspberries, and the female the greeny yellow of pineapple-weed.

The garden is starting to develop and soften around the edges. Today Jim is going to bring wooden scaffolds from his mother's so we can finish painting the house. Esther and I are going to a puddle near the pond to get some clay I found yesterday. We're going to make little mud confectionaries with stone cherries and currants in them, and let them bake in the sun, like I did when I was a little girl.

COLLECTED POETS

The person responsible for *this* chapter — in a very different way than Jill Porter must answer for fountain pens — is Ian Pearson.

Ian is our literary producer. A writer and a critic himself, he joined the *Morningside* unit in the fall of 1993, and his insights on both writers and writing helped to maintain — may well, in fact, have raised to new heights — the position we're proud to hold in the world of Canadian letters.

In early spring, when there was at last a brief gap in the parade of novelists and non-fiction authors who appear on the program at a rate not far below one a day (and Ian reads *all* their books), he arranged an event both of us had wanted to stage for some time. Here's how — in Ian's prose (for yes, producers often write the introductions you hear me read) — it began:

PETER GZOWSKI   Not long ago Leonard Cohen was on *Morningside*, recounting, among other things, the days when poets would read their stuff in Frank Scott's Montreal kitchen, putting their souls on the line, as he said, with their words. This morning we've convened our own gathering of poets. Perhaps we could recreate the spirit of Frank Scott's parties. In Fredericton is Karen Connelly, who recently won the Governor General's Award for *Touch the Dragon: A Thai Journal*. She'll read from her collection called *A Brighter Prison*. Julie Bruck is in Montreal. She'll read from her first collection, *The Woman Down-stairs*. Dennis Lee, the poet laureate of Canadian children, is with me in Toronto to read from his latest adult collection, *Riffs*. Also in Toronto is Michael Redhill, reading from *The Lake Nora Arms*, and in Vancouver, Sharon Thesen will read some new poems and maybe something from *The Pangs of Sunday*. Some of our poets may throw in other new poems, as well. Good morning to everyone.

Should I be concerned that Leonard Cohen said it sounded a little competitive at Frank Scott's place? I don't know. Dennis, should I be scared?

DENNIS LEE   Well, I have Redhill under the table here with me. Apart from that there's no competition at all.

MICHAEL REDHILL   I think Dennis Lee's foot on my head is a dream come true for me.

PETER   Let's just get right to a poem. Karen, do you want to go first in Fredericton?

KAREN CONNELLY   Sure, I'll go first from Fredericton, but this is not a poem about Fredericton. It's a poem about the place where I spent some time last year, on the island of Lesbos.

PETER   Before you do this, there's a house in this poem, right?

KAREN   There is a very small house in this poem. So small, in fact, that you can barely see it.

PETER   Now is this the house that you invested part of your Governor General's Award money in?

KAREN   Sh. That's supposed to be a big secret.

PETER   A big secret? You said it on *Morningside*.

KAREN   Well, I was hyper. You caught me at a really bad time. I would have told you anything you wanted to know that morning. Yes,

80

it is that very house, but more than the house I think it's the field and the olive tree that belong to the house I'm interested in.

PETER   The podium, such as it is, is yours.

KAREN   This is a new poem, and so far the only title I have for it is "April, on coming to the island."

> First morning, the white-haired shepherd
> wades through sheep to greet me
> So I taste the milk of a goat.
> Haul cool water at dawn.
> Dusk, crush green sage in a clean palm.
> The old man tells me the earth.
> *This is camomile*, he says, thick hands
> gentle-crushing the yellow flowers.
> *And this, peppermint*, he points with his stick.
> That's basil, *vacilico* in Greek.
> *And here, oregano*, sweetly ravished by bees.
>
> so much earth, so many waking rocks and flowers who grew
> beyond Eden, they are nameless and pure,
> like the first blood singing in the first child,
> splashed symphony of scarlet.
> I saw the field outside of Kalloni
> burst into a million burning poppies.
> I have seen sheep eat petals of fire.
>
> Words cannot embrace living flame
> I cannot tell the passion-whirl of butterflies by the well,
>   nor dusk's honey dripping from the olive trees,
>   nor the stone on the road hissing into a turtle.
>
> So many years sanding language smooth
> only to learn and relearn that mystery
> resists finished edges.
> My tongue is a tentacle of the octopus

groping in the sand, probing a ruin
of blue shadow.

These nights, I love the moon, patient sculptress
gathering light from a quarry of darkness.
Living whispers run over my shoulders
as mice pillage the stone house,
as mighty ants ransack the peaches.
When darkness frees the constellations,
    shining animals graze on heaven.

How to memorize the names for such brilliance
    When all I see here burns?

PETER   That's Karen Connelly reading in Fredericton. You have a
rapt audience here.

KAREN   Let's all go to Greece and write poetry.

DENNIS   I love that line, "mystery resists finished edges." That just
kind of stuck into my brain. Actually I like the way it's so hard to pronounce and yet that helps that sense of "mystery resisting finished
edges."

PETER   There was another word — what did you say after "he points
with his stick"?

KAREN   "That's basil, *vacilico* in Greek." It's everywhere in Greece.
They're always patting their *vacilico* so they can get the smell of it on
their hands.

PETER   Mmm, wonderful. Michael Redhill in Toronto, you're up
next. Your new collection is called *Lake Nora Arms*. Is that a real
place?

MICHAEL   Lake Nora is sort of an amalgam of different places,
but they're all in northern Ontario. Not northern-northern but

mid-northern, the Orillia area, Gravenhurst. We have a family cottage up there, so a lot of the memories are drawn from that place, but they're all sort of fictionalized, too.

PETER   Do you write there? Do you write of that place when you are there?

MICHAEL   Yeah, in fact my mother was threatening to sell the place I write in. I said, "Go ahead, sell the place if you don't want me to write another word for as long as I live." This is called "Happy Hour."

The chicken magnates sit
by the fireplace, spouting prices
in clipped dactyls, cigars glowing
like stars in the corner of the room.
Their wives circle the buffet,
loading up plates for them. Dogs
and children crowd underfoot, the din
is enormous. Outside,
incessant rain. Lake Nora is transfigured:
goose-flesh. All day my mother has prepared
for the gathering, poppy bagels, withered fish
with the eyes still in, a huge
anniversary cake.

Later, the grandparents stand
at the edge of the candles, chins glowing and
blow them out. A camera
grinds in someone's hands sucking up
the moment, freezing it in camera amber.
People navigate the thin hallway
to the bathroom, flat against the walls
like spies. A punch-line floats in the air
how should I know — I'm fourteen miles from home!
and my mother turns, laughing,
her mouth full of cake.

I look around. The chicken men are drunk,
their empty glasses tilt on their bellies.
A child has fallen asleep. A woman
I have never met thumbs up poppy seeds
from the table and eats them as she argues
with her neighbour. The crazy
aunt and uncle who still love each other
kiss in a corner. After this is all forgotten
we'll long for the background
where the unnamed visitor appears
in all the films, whose name
no one remembers. We'll watch those films
years from now, reviewing
the divorced and the dead,
that old ambient weather.
Someone will say, I wish I could go back
and someone else, No, never.

SEVERAL POETS   Wow, that's great.

PETER   I like the "thumbing up the poppy seeds."

A POET   I liked the "people pressed against the wall like spies."

MICHAEL   You guys should all come some night. At six every night
between July and September. See for yourselves.

PETER   We're having our next session at Lake Nora Arms.

SHARON THESEN   Sounds like a good place for it.

PETER   Now, Julie Bruck?

JULIE BRUCK   I grew up with a poet in the house and it was a nice
thing to have. When I was a kid my mother was always bouncing lines
off me. I wasn't too pleased with that but it was still a good thing to
have as a child. Okay. I think I'll read from the first poem from the

book. It's call "Car Alarm." It was written a couple of years ago when people were already stepping over the homeless on the street but the sound of a talking car was something that stopped them in their tracks. I had put my back out in an aerobics class and I was lying on the floor and I could really only move around on my knees, and I was lying there captive. The window was open and I heard this voice coming through the window. So I crawled over very slowly to see what was going on and this is the poem.

Outside the bank, a Mercedes-Benz tells one
in a group of teen-age boys he's *too close*
to the vehicle. Please step back. He does, and the car
says, *Thank you.* A bolder boy decides

to press things — rubs his thigh against the vehicle:
The car says, *You have stepped inside*
the perimeter. Step back — but some girls
have gathered, so the boy crosses his arms, stays
right where he is. The car starts to count down
from five. The boy doesn't move. *Thank you,*
says the car at zero, and the boy turns, gouges
the metallic finish with a key, while another

kicks the tires, and a third jumps on the hood.
All the while the car says, *You are too close*
to the vehicle. Please step back. The girls
scatter. The boys follow — a straggler twists

the antenna. *Thank you,* says the car. *Thank you.*
Thank you. A woman comes out of the bank
and looks crazily around. Someone she hasn't seen
in years, someone with a great patience, whom she may

have dreamed of last night or loved at seventeen;
someone she knows and can't quite place, has spoken.
Just now. Here in the street. This is the first thing
in a long time, of which she is certain.

KAREN   How it turns, huh? It's so strange. I read that, and I read it again and again and again, trying to know the woman and what she was thinking. The ending is just brilliant. I really like the ending.

JULIE   Thanks.

PETER   Who is the woman, Julie? Maybe we don't want to know.

JULIE   I don't think you do want to know, and I don't think I want to know. She's an amalgam, the way Lake Nora Arms is.

MICHAEL   I think I saw her up at Lake Nora, actually.

JULIE   Yeah, I hear she travels quite a bit, but just to places that she's very familiar with.

MICHAEL   She has a thing for poppy seed bagels.

JULIE   Yes.

PETER   Dennis Lee. Your new book *Riffs*. Very musical, right?

DENNIS   It is. Riffs is a jazz term, of course.

PETER   Now, have you just picked up the Dennis Lee of children's poetry and moved that part of you into adult? There must be a connection.

DENNIS   The sense of play in words that came out a lot in the children's poetry I found coming out in a way that I wasn't used to at all in these little pieces.

PETER   You write some of these some time ago, didn't you?

DENNIS   It took me twelve years. The manuscript was finally thirty-seven pages, so that's roughly three point one pages a year. There was a sense of play from the children's poetry that seemed to start coming out, in some way, for the first time in adult stuff while I was writing *Riffs*. It's the story of a love affair. Maybe I'll do some from

86

the beginning, where the couple is happily infatuated with each other. So these are four pieces from the early part of *Riffs*.

When I lurched like a rumour of want through the networks of
    plenty,
a me-shaped pang on the lam,
when I ghosted through lives like a headline, a scrap in the
    updraft,
and my mid-life wreckage was close & for keeps —

    when I watched the
    birches misting, pale spring
    voltage and
    not mine, nor mine, nor mine —

then: a
lady laid her touch a —
among me, gentle thing, for which I stand still
startled, gentle thing and feel the
ache begin again,
the onus of joy.

Wal, acey deucey
    trey divide —
I'm a guy
    with a fine wide-eyed
lady freckles too &
    squirms when she
feels good, I feel so
    good just
doin aw
    shucks
tricks and she's
    SOFISTIKATED!

Pen-
ultimate lady, alive-sweet
skin and sesame:

why do we ever rub con-
tours, if not to conjure
shapes of what we aren't and
crave to be? . . .
touching you I am
meat & pronto, I lounge in the chutzpah of
flesh; then woozy with
laughter and midnight and
caring, pure
carnal
panache—you, you, you in your frabjous parade—
how should I
reach for more?
Yet always behind you (this is
why I shy away), barely beyond you
is
nothing at all . . .
Lady,
do not be offended when I
go there.
When you're up to yr
homburg in
hopeless, & the

damsel is not here —
what merrie cheer? zip zip no goddam cheer:
just
DIT-DAT-DOTS of biological/
ontological urgency—

pages of empties . . .
late-night lady reprise.

MICHAEL   That's wonderful.

PETER   Would each of those be a riff? Would you think of them that
way?

DENNIS   Yes, I think of each as one as a riff. You know a riff in jazz —
it started off being one thing, but now it's understood to be the little
improvisational run a solo instrument will do, usually charged with a
lot of feeling and often very short. It's something that will never
appear again. It's improvisation, so each of these, the distance emotionally is about a sixteenth of a centimetre. There is no rumination
on things, no reflection on things. The experience itself is lodged in
the texture of the language. Actually, I didn't know what I was doing
with it. A lot of it was written intuitively, so I came to understand
afterwards how it was working.

SHARON   You know what is emerging here? There seems to be sesame and poppy seeds.

PETER   That's what we're serving at Lake Nora Arms.

MICHAEL   I have to tell you I read *Riffs* cover to cover in bed one
night, which I recommend to everyone

SHARON   So did I. That's exactly how I read it.

MICHAEL   We were not in the same bed. I want everyone across
Canada to know that. And I have to tell you for the next five days the
word "frabjous" was just in my head. I could not get it out. I don't even
know what the word means.

PETER   You didn't make it up, did you?

DENNIS   No, that's out of Lewis Carroll. Remember — "'Twas bril-
lig, and the slithy toves Did gyre and gimble in the wabe."

PETER   Sharon Thesen, you've been patient.

SHARON   Well, I've got onus from Dennis's poem.

JULIE   "The onus of joy."

SHARON   "The onus of joy," wow, what a phrase.

89

PETER   Well, the onus of performance is upon you, Sharon.

SHARON   Yes, indeed. I'm going to read a poem from *Pangs of Sunday* called "The Parrot." I went home and wrote this poem after coming out of Capilano College with a friend, who pointed out some people down at the bottom of an enormous tree. You don't realize how big the trees are here until you have to look up and try to find a parrot at the top of one. It's like an Emily Carr dark rainy landscape on the side of the mountain where I teach, and here was this parrot — red tail feathers way up there — and talk about out of place. Someone had let their parrot out to fly around. I guess that's the price of freedom. They were desperate. The parrot had been up there for hours. It was not going to come down. So I had to go home and wonder what had happened to this parrot.

> She flew, she was up
> & gone, they had let her out
> for a treat & were sorry now.
> Red tail feathers
> way, way up in a fir tree
> on the side of a mountain.
> It was north. Crows
> eyed her. Way, way down
> the people were making
> little pyramids of peanuts &
> calling her name: Isabel! Isabel!
> They clicked their tongues
> and whistled, they went away and
> came back later. The sun got large
> and red, turned the heat up
> under her vocabulary. Later
> they could hear her exhortations
> to the moonlight: Hey Sailor!
> Good Golly Miss Molly! Want
> A Cracker? So what!
> The crows backed off
> & stared, diamond bracelets dangling
> from their beaks. All that night

the parrot prayed & sang,
in the morning it was over.
She glided downward, branch
to spiky branch. The people
wept and applauded, rushed her
back to her cage exhausted,
and undisputed champion
of the air. She was never the same
after that. The vet said it was
a bit like the cave scene
in *A Passage to India* — something
to do with language, the dark &
existence. Stupendous!
the parrot kept saying for years
after & the crows invented a red dream.

DENNIS   Bravo. That's fantastic.

KAREN   That poem didn't mean much to me until I met people in
Calgary who have an infatuation with birds. They just love birds, and
they've always lived with a few birds in their house. I know they're listening today, and I was thinking of them when I found out you might
be reading it. It's so good.

PETER   That was the kid from Tisdale, Saskatchewan, giving us the
Capilano landscape there, too.

SHARON   That's right.

DENNIS   One of the things that's so much fun about that poem is
the way you can listen to it and assume there is a parrot that's flown
away, and that's great. It's lovely at that level.

PETER   Well, Sharon's parrot is apparent when she reads it.

DENNIS   Yeah, I believe it completely. And at the same time there
are all sorts of things about unlived life, getting free for a day, all those

things going on without having ghastly symbolic labels pasted on them. It's very sure-footed.

SHARON   Thanks.

PETER   Hearing each of you read in such different ways changes the texture of the poem that you might have explored before on the page. I know that's an old and tired thing to say to a poet, but it's just such a better experience. We should do this on radio all the time, and cancel books.

DENNIS   Such an interesting question — when you write, the voice you hear — how do you score it on the page to help the reader get close to it? In some ways you never can.

JULIE   You really can't. You can't. Once I've heard a poet read her or his work it changes absolutely and forever for me. I always hear that voice.

MICHAEL   I heard Derek Walcott read in Toronto about a month and a half ago, and I went back to his books that I used to hear in my own voice because I had never heard his before.

PETER   Do you read aloud when you read?

MICHAEL   No, I tend not to. They knock on the ceiling if I do.

SHARON   Who is that up there reading poetry?

PETER   Plastered against the ceiling like a spy.

MICHAEL   "No more culture."

PETER   Karen Connelly, you're up.

KAREN   Okay. Well, this is a poem about exotic animals — another kind of parrot. It is called "The Lesser Amazon."

Last night I dreamt
I was the salamander who does not burn in fire:
my lips welcomed saffron tongues of flame.
I scurried pliant through desert grass,
my amphibian memory algae-moist,
not with dragonflies.

In South America, tree frogs live
in the pooled water of bell-shaped leaves.
They never touch earth but make their choir
in a ripe canopy, serenading higher
than the skulls of hunters.

Those very frogs leap from my rhododendron
into the kitchen sink
Shreds of jungle dazzle this old house.
Where are all these vines growing from?
This morning a parrot torpedoed over the table.
Yesterday afternoon in the bathtub,
after a surge of curious hissing,
I found a nest of baby snakes beneath
the bathmat, living red leather,
tongues flicking an ancient orange.
They covered my feet in an exotic reptile weave,
wound up my shins and looped themselves
around my waist and neck and slid anxiously
through my slick hair.
It took me an hour to comb them out
and send them slithering to the garden.

It can't go on like this.
The neighbours gossip:
     Has she kidnapped orangutans?
     Has she given birth to panthers?
Birds of paradise have chased away
the sparrows and magpies and the problem
with peacocks is the potency of their screams.

Roses of dusk bloom to darkness.
Mesmerizing creatures watch from the trees
of these turquoise nights, listening
to me rush through the rainforest of my body,
searching for you.

Deep into cardinal soil I plunge my hands,
probing for the roots of the source,
hoping to plant you in this jungle
though I know you're not native to it.

Love, my throat is the lesser Amazon.
I want you to slide in.

Find a slim-ribbed canoe.
Learn how to swim.

All these hot poems. I realize that Canada really is the coldest country on earth, and I should be in Fiji right now.

SHARON   Or inside a Rousseau painting. That's where I was.

KAREN   Good.

PETER   I thought you were a Matisse painter, Sharon.

DENNIS   The lush green space, all that basil.

SHARON   And the surrealism. Wonderful. The snakes.

PETER   Yeah, we didn't have to really have the snakes, did we, Karen?

KAREN   Sorry, I couldn't resist that. I know it's really obvious. It's embarrassingly obvious, but I couldn't help it.

PETER   Michael Redhill.

MICHAEL   This is a poem from near the end of the book. It's called "Two Meditations," and it's based in part on a long day hike around a lake I know. It rained on that day and it was bright on that day and so the whole season was on that day. "Two Meditations."

i

A red-furred dog melts underground. A fine rain falls, soaking the soil. In puddles above the place it's buried, concentric eyes open over each other. Some of the dog rises up into the puddle and parts of the dog touch the air and slide in the water down to the lake. Then the dog becomes fish and lily-pad. On some mornings when it's very hot, the lake steams and some of the red-furred dog becomes air that rises and becomes part of a warm wall of air. Then it rains, a fine rain like hair.

ii

We're walking along with the field-guide, finding dogwood with its "head of small flowers." The book says nothing about its bark. I want to tell you about this place. I grew up here. Some years everything that lives vanishes from the lake, and in other years it's choked with fish. It's just inscrutable nature — not a mystical cycle. I can't stand those new religions — inventing magical order to stave off terror. If we let it happen, this place'll be overrun with suburban gurus quipping their mono-syllabic negations. Sometimes when I walk here alone, I can't feel anything and I call that awestruck. I think that this place feels nothing for itself, not even *just is*. Ah — feel that? Look at that pool of water there: rain. O's opening — that's not awe, that's shock. OH. *So this is what I am.*

PETER   The gasps of delight, the sounds of delight that come down that electronic highway as a poet appreciates what he or she hears. A well-turned phrase. It's practically like going to the ballet with a dancer.

SHARON   I really love the way all the poems we're reading are connected. It's the magic of poetry itself. For me it's the magic of composition in my own mind when I'm moving around inside a poem and picking things out in association, and things will come and then show up in another poem. For example, I've got diamond bracelets again in a poem I wrote recently. It's fun to follow all the transitions and connections. The colour red moving into Michael's poem. As Julie pointed out, the bagels and poppy seeds. I've got nachos coming up.

PETER   We're going to have a feast, apparently.

MICHAEL   There is also the sense of the five of us being a slice of what is going on in Canada right now. We are all writing in the same time and we're writing from the same imagery, despite the fact that Karen's first poem was drawn from Greece and my poems are drawn from northern Ontario and Sharon's poem is drawn from some inner landscape. I'm not sure where that was, but I wish I could go there. Poetry, I think, is in some ways an apprenticeship in language, and some of the most exciting novelists I have read have done this intensive work earlier in their careers. I think it shows in their novels — there is an incredible attention to detail in Michael Ondaatje's novels and in Margaret Atwood's novels.

PETER   But you say apprenticeship. Doesn't that point diminish the value of the poetry?

MICHAEL   I don't think so, because I don't think the apprenticeship ends — I mean it goes on. You keep learning and you keep growing. There's a certain quality to writers who started as poets, and I think it has to do with the atomization of the experience and the attention to detail.

DENNIS   It can be good or bad. The classic poet's novel, the classic bad poet's novel is one that tries to do everything with language. There might be two characters on a collision course, or whatever it may be, and something has to resolve itself one way or another in action, and you get there, and suddenly there is this great smokescreen of language coming up, and you've got all of this glorious imagery, and then the person has scooted out the other end and is racing ahead in the book as if they had actually written that scene — but it was never there.

KAREN   And you're left standing there yelling, Story, please, story.

DENNIS   So poets can be real cheaters when it comes to writing fiction.

PETER   Julie Bruck?

JULIE   Poem.

PETER   Is this also from *The Woman Downstairs*?

JULIE   Yeah. I'm going to change what I was going to read because I'm going to start consciously to pick up on things people have been touching on. I'm going to do the poem that has a lake, and animals, as well. It's called "Summer on Rewind." The poem began with the experience of driving into New York City from the country and stopping just across from Penn Station in the middle of those absolutely leaden heat waves in the middle of the summer and getting out of the car after being in the country for a week and our feet sinking in what I can only describe as New York's own primordial ooze in the gutter. The poem was an attempt to write my way out of that moment. "Summer on Rewind."

A man and a woman walk backwards
from opposite directions, turn and meet
on a corner, while emergency vehicles scream
across 34th Street, against the one-way signs.
Their embrace lasts so long the homeless
back off, withdraw their cracked palms.
A small car takes them up the Thruway,
trunk-first. Although she appears
to be driving, both stare at the receding
skyline like riders in a caboose.
They shimmy from the car, lunch hurtles
from their mouths, rearranges itself
on plates; wine flows into a bottle,
sealed with original cork, metal closure.
A waitress takes everything away.
In the middle of a lake, they tread water,
laughing and kissing, lips losing their blue.

They swim in feet-first on their stomachs;
toes begin a perfect are and they're upright
on the dock, towels reattached to dry bodies.
Sleep ends in exhaustion, figures weaving
on a narrow bed; buttons are fastened
with pleasure. They're bright-eyed, shot
through with energy as a second man stands
between them holding a drink, indicating
one to the other. Each withdraws a hand,
each toddles backwards. She goes to her
parked car, repacks a suitcase. A friend's
sedan swallows him, backs down the road.
It is morning. It is night. It is the day
before and the lake is a pane of glass.
Then, a small disturbance by the dock:
A circle of ripples contracts, as a hawk
drops its small fish and travels tail-first,
up into the clear blue on a backwards path
so clean, so purposeful it seems each talon,
each muscle, each fragile bone wants
nothing but to hunger, higher, alone.

KAREN   Wow, we're out, we're out of New York.

PETER   Dennis Lee.

DENNIS   Well, here is an unpublished poem. It's from a sequence
called "Blue Psalms." So this is a Blue Psalm, and it's about trying to
love things in the world without having to possess them completely.

That creatures are not enough.
Hawkmoth and tanager snag me, muskies recall me, though alien in weedkill, raccoons
with their savvy instinctual poise haul me back to earth and
wired in their unwitting circuits, bobtail and carapace all
species invade me,
tangling my reified soul once more in the bone fraternity

98

of things that are born and die —
yet though I crave it,
kinship and diastole the
creatures are not enough.

And roots are not enough. Such
bounty I came to! heart residence on earth and I have loved
a patch of ground too well: confess, confess at
dusk each summer long how a boy stood
claimed by the hush of the Shield — the slow dark
blotting the pines, and across the fretted
lake the loons re-echoed, and the excellent chill of infinity
entered my blood to stay as I went on listening, went on
listening. I was practising my life among
rocky companions, but the
place is gone.

People, I hear we are catastrophe.
I hear we are strangers here. For though we
re-fashion earth in our image,
though in our hunger to nest we disnify the real,
I hear we have no home: no
home but hunger

And precious, precious the dear ones — but also, that
dear ones are not enough. What man has been
lucky in love like me? raised in a warm, in a
principled sprawl of a family; gifted with luminous
friends, who make low-rent jokes and live their lives nobly;
and quickened by eros — hard in its seasons, but holy and
gracias, rare woman; and children who fasten my heart.
Yet what will endure in time? and whom do I own?
Was I not given such
peerless companions that I might learn to say, in love, *Not
you, dear heart; nor you; nor you* —
go by?

PETER   Sharon Thesen.

SHARON   Well, boy, what a hard act to follow. There is a wonderful graciousness to that poem, Dennis.

DENNIS   Well, that's a gracious thing to say, Sharon.

SHARON   I'm going to read "Eating Smarties in the Truck," which is a poem about . . . Well, it's an oh, no, alone again poem. I'm often on the road or in traffic in my poems, and in this one I'm coming up from Seattle, so some of the references here are quite local to Vancouver. Anyway, I'm coming up from the south and I'm stopped. I've got some Smarties and I'm listening to the radio and driving and I felt a pang because this person who used to sit beside me in the truck had these knees. There's something about men's knees that are a total give-away. If they wear dresses and try to get away with looking like women, the knees will give them away every time. Well, anyway, "Eating Smarties in the Truck."

> City hoves in, rank fields soak
> diesel & manure, nothing grows,
> what shall we eat, corn from Illinois,
> sambas from Japan, diamond bracelet
> in the bank vault, three yellow Smarties,
> the happiness of the world when
> that man asks that woman to dance
> & she puts her cigarette out firmly
> and right away. Gets up taller. Him too.
> She's a little drunk, which is scandalous,
> but just a little drunk, a little scandalous.
> So is he, or he wouldn't have asked her.
> I was alive and watching. I had eaten
> nachos. My scarf was decorated with
> the leaning tower of Pisa. Women were
> getting up and singing & one clutched the mike
> with a silk gardenia in her hair. The emcee
> was manic and the trumpet player

blew at the floor, sadly and thinly,
no matter the song. It was snowing outside
and the orange plough came by shaking the earth, pushing
snow out of the way with a great blade.
How everything forms
& you never know until later what was just
ahead. Deas Island tunnel, traffic converging
on the Oak Street Bridge, coming up from
the States. Couldn't stand
what was on the radio & felt around inside
the nearly empty Smarties box with a free hand.
I miss the sign of his man's knees beside me,
each breath of them under the dashboard
so bony and good natured.

MICHAEL   So cinematic.

DENNIS   Wonderful.

PETER   That is a novel.

SHARON   I'll never be a novelist. But I was thinking about Julie's precise calibrations of gesture when she said, "Strange behaviours of these places." This is novel material for her, too.

MICHAEL   In your poem you can see this woman standing up and making the decision, yes, I will dance with you, and putting the cigarette out firmly. It's wonderful stuff.

SHARON   Thanks.

PETER   Stands taller than he does.

JULIE   And I'll never see a snow-plough in quite the same way, either, because it pushes the snow out of the way with "a great blade."

PETER   Julie?

JULIE   I'll read the last poem in *The Woman Downstairs*. I don't think this needs a lot of explanation. There is a speaker.

PETER   This is the one that got into *The New Yorker*.

JULIE   Yes.

PETER   You got a poem in *The New Yorker*.

ALL   Wow.

DENNIS   We're breaking through.

PETER   Are you rich?

JULIE   Oh, yeah, I'm rolling in it.

KAREN   Real fame.

JULIE   No explanation, I'll just read. It's called "Who We Are Now."

The man who runs the parking lot at St. Hubert & Duluth
holds our keys in one closed hand, curses this country
with the other. *In Soviet Union, I am doctor, like Chekhov* — his
fifth identity in the last six months. *Here I clean hospital
after midnight. You must pick up keys by eleven.*

My friends plan their lives in a nearby Greek restaurant:
plans subject to jobs, lovers, children, or lack of same —
most of all, this constant gnawing at who we are,
exactly what we're supposed to be doing here.
After the meal, the wine, strong Greek coffee,
a ballpoint meanders on the paper table-cloth, variations
on the same story — each year, less embellishment.

I have seen him wave off customers he didn't like the look of:
In Greece, I am anthropologist — he barks, shaking his fist
at a blue Chevette that has backed out in search of a meter.

Quebec people are racist — Canadians are worse. I do not think,
he says, squinting at us, *that you are pure Canadian.*

When we finally head home in our reclaimed vehicles,
it is always early April, always snowing, always unseasonal.
We huddle in the glow of the car's dials and gauges, stare
into the red light at Cherrier like some kind of second sun,
longing for sleep, for dreams to redeem us.

I am Armenian, he states proudly, *and this place is dead.*
In Moscow, my cousin has fourteen fruit stores.
He thrust the wrong keys at us, I point to the correct hook.
East Europe is living. Next year, I sell antibiotics in Bucharest.
Good business, he says, releasing our keys. *Good night.*

KAREN   I bet he really was Greek.

JULIE   Yeah, I think he was, and he continued to outdo himself for months after the poem was written. Then they came along and paved over the parking lot and put up a condominium, just like the Joni Mitchell song. So he's disappeared.

KAREN   Well, he's out there somewhere.

JULIE   He is out there, and guys like him, and he's going to resurface. He has that tendency.

MICHAEL   Oh, there'll be a sequel.

JULIE   He'll pop back up, yes.

PETER   Do you think we could do this again?

MICHAEL   Sure, I'll be here tomorrow morning.

JULIE   We'll all be here tomorrow.

KAREN   Let's go to Lake Nora Arms.

MICHAEL   Listen, the breakfasts there are fantastic. I'll have you all up, you're all welcome.

SHARON   I'll take you up on that, Michael.

JULIE   I'll be waiting outside when you step out in the morning, looking up with doggy eyes.

MICHAEL   Oh, my goodness. I never thought poetry would be so wonderful.

PETER   I never thought it would be so funny.

MICHAEL   Well, being let out of our homes gives us access of joy.

JULIE   Exactly.

PETER   Back you all go to your homes. Julie, how do you like being on the radio instead of delivering other authors?

JULIE   I think it's swell, Peter. I've had a lot of fun this fall, it's been great, but I've always wanted to sit behind the consoles and push the buttons and now I'm going to do it. They're sitting before me, multi-coloured. Any minute . . .

KAREN   Uh-oh.

DENNIS   Julie goes out of control.

JULIE   Yeah, I'll just try to keep my hands down.

PETER   Let me thank all of you. Karen Connelly read from *This Brighter Prison*, Julie Bruck from *The Woman Downstairs* and Dennis Lee from *Riffs*, all published by Brick Books. *Lake Nora Arms*, by Michael Redhill, is published by Coach House Press, and Sharon Thesen's *The Pangs of Sundays* is published by McClelland & Stewart.

ON BUTTER TARTS AND
DOUGH BOYS AND
RICE KRISPIE SQUARES

The sweetest chapter ever told.

✉ I grew up in England and well remember me mum's treacle (or syrup) tart — and remember that it had bread-crumbs mixed with golden syrup filling. Golden syrup is slightly thicker than corn syrup. We had a special "syrup spoon," with a hole in the bowl of the spoon and a hook in the handle, with which to hook the spoon over the edge of the syrup tin, so that the excess syrup could drip back into the tin.

There is no recipe for treacle or syrup tart in my copy of *Mrs. Beaton's Book of Household Management*, but my copy of *Good Housekeeping's Cookery Book* (Revised Edition 1960) includes the following:

Syrup Tart
6 oz. shortcrust pastry
2 oz. bread-crumbs
3–4 tbsps. syrup
Juice of ½ a lemon

Line a plate with pastry as directed for a Flat Tart. Mix the syrup, bread-crumbs and lemon juice together, and pour this mixture into the pastry. Bake in a moderately hot oven (425°F, mark 7) for 20–30 minutes, until the pastry is cooked and the filling golden-brown. Cool and serve. Top with whipped cream if liked.

Yum! I can taste it. Come to think of it, me mum sometimes used desiccated coconut instead of the bread-crumbs. We would have syrup tart, hot or cold, for dessert — or, as we called it, "pud" or "arfters" — as in "What's for arfters, Mum?" And if that seems strange, another "pud" at our house was Yorkshire Pudding, served hot with jam. It was delicious, too!

Patricia Black
London, Ontario

✉ My mother, who is French-Canadian, always rolled out her left-over pastry into a rectangle, sprinkled it with brown sugar and cinnamon, rolled it up and cut it into pieces. She then baked it in the oven.

She never called the results "dough boys." She never called them anything. One day a few years ago, the subject came up with a French-Canadian girlfriend of mine named Micheline. She told me that she, too, was familiar with the tasty tidbits, and that they are called "petes des soeurs." Translation: nun's farts.

We laughed and after some deliberation, decided they were so named because nuns are such holy, sweet women, even their farts would be sweet.

Sandra Bilenkey
Brampton, Ontario

✉ Searching for something to take to a class pot-luck (I teach adult immigrants in Surrey, British Columbia), something quick and easy, but likely to please students from a variety of dietary backgrounds, I chanced upon good old Rice Krispie Squares. I slid them onto the table with the wonderful assortment of samosas, pakoras, spring rolls, empanadas and Polish pastries, and waited to see the reaction of my students, many of whom hesitate to try new foods.

To my amazement and delight, the *Canadian* gourmet treat was a big hit (except with the Muslims, who suspected the pork content of the gelatin in the marshmallows). In fact, the only other food that has crossed cultural borders so easily is pizza — which my Punjabi students have spiced up and claimed as their own!

Capitalizing on this enthusiasm, I based a lesson on the dictation of the recipe, complete with lots of discussion of variations and nutritional value, and a homework assignment: go home and make Rice Krispie Squares!

Margarine, not butter; chocolate chips, peanuts, raisins, too. . . . And to go with it, try serving it as my husband did on my last birthday — with a bottle of good French Cognac, by candle-light, of course!

Carol Thibault
White Rock, British Columbia

✉ My mother and father are immigrants from Northern Ireland. They came to Canada in 1957 and immediately settled in Calgary. A few years later I came along and my parents raised me as best they could using their own background combined with the ways of the new world. In all their experience, they never ran across the phenomenon of Rice Krispie Squares.

I was a bored four-year-old, stuck inside for the duration of winter. My mother considered our snowy environment to be like Jupiter — not to go out in unless absolutely necessary. So to keep me occupied, she bought me a water-colour paint set. Eventually the paper I was painting lost its novelty and I turned to painting my own face. With my mother's back turned, I made the finishing touches on my personal make-over and headed for the door.

The day before, I had seen a little girl about my age go inside the house across the street from us. I decided to investigate. Once outside, I made a bee-line for her house to show off my colourful personality.

She wasn't home. But her mother welcomed me inside, wondering all the while if she would have to call Child Welfare, since in my hasty advance I'd forgotten my coat. Without even commenting on my multi-hued face, she brought me into the kitchen and offered me a very strange-looking substance. It looked similar to the fishing maggots my father used. There was a sticky white resin holding it all together. Forgetting everything my mother had ever taught me, I screwed up my face and said, "Eeww! What's that?"

Without batting an eye, this strange adult, who may have been hiding another little girl in her house, said, "Why, this is spider-web cake." That sounded reasonable to me. So I took the slab she offered, made my excuses and backed towards the door. As I dashed through the drifts across her front lawn, she shouted out, "Chrissy will be home at three-thirty."

When I burst into the safety of my mother's kitchen, full of the recognizable Irish baking smells I knew so well, my mum was flabbergasted. I was out of breath, covered in paint and clutching something sticky and beige. "It's . . . it's spider-web cake, Mum!" Unable to put the gluey concoction down, I timidly took a bite. It was the sweetest, gooiest, yummiest thing I'd ever eaten. My mother confirmed the maggots to be Rice Krispies and rooted through the cupboards until she found a box with the recipe on the back. Then my Irish mum, years after she'd become a citizen here, became a real Canadian — she made me Rice Krispie Squares.

Julie Pithers
Winnipeg

✉ When my husband, Jim, and I decided to get married five years ago, we set the date for three weeks hence — not a particularly long time to "do" a wedding. We *meant* to make a wedding cake, but things busied up in both our jobs and we decided the wedding could go ahead without one.

We lived in Calgary then, and my mom — Iris Black, who lives in Edmonton — kept calling — as mothers are wont to do — to see what she could bring. I kept saying — as daughters are wont to say — that she didn't need to bring a thing — "just yourself" — but I did, during one of her calls, mention she could bring some Rice Krispie Squares! (She makes *great* squares, and we had always looked forward to her making some when we visited her.)

You guessed it. Just before the ceremony, Mom presented us with a beautiful three-tiered Rice Krispie cake! And what a hit it was! Just the thing for an informal, at-home wedding: three round tiers — each one ringed with tiny pink flowers, and on the top a pair of crystal love birds. In good wedding tradition, there were even pieces of "cake" wrapped in plastic wrap and tied with bows, as "take homes" for each of our guests. (I'll bet that none of *those* pieces of wedding cake were thrown in the garbage once they reached home!)

The bottom layers of the cake were eaten that day, but the top tier, complete with love birds, moved with us to Saltspring Island a year ago. While it is unlikely we will ever *eat* the cake on some future anniversary, it *is* allotted a spot, front and centre, in our china cabinet. Hey! Tradition is tradition!

Thanks again, Mom. It was fun — and good!

Carol Helset
Ganges, British Columbia

✉ The greatest improvement in the making of Rice Krispie Squares came with the introduction of the microwave. Never again must one soak the pot overnight, then labour at scraping away those burnt bits that adhere to the bottom like Krazy Glue. In the microwave, the marshmallows puff up and soften in one minute, and the butter melts in thirty seconds. If you then add the vanilla and stir like mad while adding the four cups of cereal, you can dump the resulting glob into the pan and press it down with a damp spoon before it cools enough to think of sticking to the bowl.

Four minutes from start to finish, max!

You might add stuff to Rice Krispie Squares.

You might shape the mixture into animals, trees, snowmen and decorate with cherries, chips, currants, whatever.

You might roll it out and fill it with cream, making a log with appropriate seasonal decorations on top.

You might even let your imagination soar and make a whole village, a space station, dinosaurs — there is an infinity of variations.

But the pristine, unadorned Rice Krispie Square is still the basic, comforting, good-for-the-soul munch it has always been.

I think my husband's breakfast this morning consisted of a piece scooped raggedly out of the pan.

Excuse me, I must go and even off the edge.

Margaret Steel
Calgary

✉ Just this past weekend I made Rice Krispie cake for the first time. The idea struck me as I was cleaning out my camping supplies and came across three-quarters of a bag of marshmallows, still moist and fresh, from this summer's camp-fires. I became obsessed. I improvised with other cereal and with rice, wheat, and corn crispies, giving a varied speckled pattern to the cake. (Yes, *cake*.) I also tossed in half a bag of slivered almonds that had been in my cupboard for some time. It was simple and delicious, and with only a little help, the whole pan was gone in less than twelve hours!

Now please understand, I am a thirty-year-old single male with little or no baking skills or desires. Three of my male friends around my age accepted pieces eagerly over coffee Sunday afternoon. We rationalized about the light and relatively healthy aspects of the cake as we reached for seconds or thirds.

The subtle variations seemed endless to the creative mind — varying cereal types, adding nuts, chocolate chips, peanut butter and so on. When I do my grocery shopping later this week, I will be planning this weekend's Rice Krispie cake, too.

Brad Lindeburgh
Winnipeg

✉ The last time I made Rice Krispie Squares I attempted a little modification, something I have now discovered one should *never* do! I used the latest and greatest in mini marshmallows — multi-flavoured, multi-coloured ones. My five-year-old daughter was completely disgusted with the resultant nondescript greyish tinge — whatever happened to that rainbow of colours? — and closely correlated taste, while my three-year-old son was bitterly disappointed that he couldn't select a "been" (his word for green, his favourite colour) one, since of course some of the original marshmallows had been green. So much for that little experiment, I think, as I continue to munch through a seemingly endless supply of dull grey squares, my husband being of the same opinion as my kids.

Actually, my particular favourite is a modification taught me by my teenage Scottish nieces on their last visit to Canada. They melt down two or three of their favourite chocolate bars, Mars and Bounty being their particular choices, and coat the Rice Krispies as per usual. I am somewhat partial to Skor bars done this way, and I am tempted to try out Smarties, obviously undaunted by past experiences. I am also quite keen on using Kraft caramels as a coating, if I can allow myself the ten or more hours it takes to individually unwrap the little suckers! In the days immediately following Hallowe'en, I'll admit to having been caught, on more than one occasion, trying to sneak some of the aforementioned goodies out of my kids' stash of treats, so that I can dilute some of that sugar-rich and fat-rich stuff with a few cupfuls of at least semi-healthy Rice Krispies. This usually leads to the cold shoulder on the part of my family, who consider this nothing less than sacrilege. Oh, well, back to the plain old marshmallows!

Maggie Laidlaw
Guelph, Ontario

✉ The *Five Roses Cookbook*, published in Montreal 1915, has the following recipe:

> 1 egg
> 1 cup brown sugar
> 1 cup currants
> butter size of a walnut
> flavour to taste

Beat all until full of bubbles. Drop from a teaspoon into lined patty tin and bake in quick oven. One cup dates may be added if desired.

I rather suspect that raisins took the place of currants at a later date, as we got our currants from Australia, and I certainly remember shortages from time to time. My own 1945 Purity Flour cookbook has the following recipe for two dozen tarts baked in muffin tins, and this is the one I chiefly remember.

> 2 eggs
> 2 cups brown sugar
> 2 tbsp vinegar
> 1 tsp vanilla
> half cup butter, melted
> ⅓ cup currants, chopped raisin, dates, figs or nutmeats

Beat eggs only until well blended. Beat in sugar and add vinegar and vanilla. Stir in the melted butter and fruit. Line patty tins with pastry and fill half to two thirds full with butter mixture. Bake in hot oven for first 10 mins and then reduce temperature to moderate and bake for 20–25 mins. or until filling is firm.

No doubt there are other recipes about. It was the vinegar that always shook me — but without it the taste was not the same.

Constance E. Dwyer
Coquitlam, British Columbia

✉ Years ago when I first started dating my soon-to-be-husband, he told me he often made pies and tarts. I, who had never made either, expressed my disbelief. On his next visit he presented me with six butter tarts.

We enjoyed five of these slightly runny, raisin-filled wonders right then and there. The taste? They were made by my one true love, so how could they be anything but perfect?

And what of the fate of the sixth Perfect Butter Tart? I wrapped it in cellophane and have saved it ever since. It's too sweet to mould and only very slightly crumbled. It has travelled with me through more than a dozen moves in my college years and is now safely tucked away in our matrimonial home.

I'm always glad to be reminded of my husband's culinary skills, because on our wedding day he retired his recipe file and all that's left now are crumbs.

Susan Patterson-O'Neil
Cobden, Ontario

✉ It's about those left-over scraps of pastry. Me same Mum, the one who made the treacle or syrup tarts, used to knead all the scraps of pastry together and then roll them out to about the size of a saucer. Then she would plop a couple of big spoonfuls of jam or marmalade into the centre of the pastry, wet the edges and fold the pastry over, sealing the edges and then pressing them together with a knife handle or a thumb. She would cut two or three slashes in the top of the pastry (to let the steam out) and brush the little "turnover" with milk or beaten egg. This would be baked right on an old saucer or a baking sheet. Absolutely delicious! Now, do you want to hear about her steak and kidney pie, or her flaky pastry cream horns, or custard tarts, or Bakewell tarts, or milles-feuilles, or her vol-au-vents — or her Caraway Seed Cake, or her éclairs or her meringues or her macaroons? Typically English, she was a plain meat and two veg main course cook, but, oh, what a pastry cook; what a cake maker! I hadn't given a thought to any of these goodies until the mention of syrup tart the other day — and I now I can't stop. . . .

Patricia Black
London, Ontario

✉ I think the best butter tarts are still Mrs. MacDonald's. In the 1930s Mrs. MacDonald had a bakery in North Toronto on the west side of Yonge Street between Bedford Park and Woburn. Her tarts were filled with raisins and a runny syrup all contained in a shortbread crust about two inches high forming a little cone-shaped cup. In the ten-year-old set there were two ways of eating a tart without dribbling. You could start from the top by biting around the edge and enjoy the raisin top first. Then you could drink the inch or so of syrup on the bottom. An expert could nibble a hole through the bottom edge, suck out the syrup and then turn the tart upside down to eat it from the bottom to the top. Of course, there were those who took a big bite and coped with the cascade of syrup as best they could.

Ed McKenna
Nepean, Ontario

✉ Gram Proctor from Marsden, Saskatchewan, *did* make the best pastry in the world; she always said it was because of her "cool hands" (due to her Icelandic blood?) and the fact that she didn't handle it too much. Her pastry was always nice and thin and flaky; it definitely would *not* withstand the fall-on-the-floor test. Now her *tart* filling *was not* runny and she always used currants.

Here's the recipe:

    1 c. brown sugar
    3 tbsp butter (size of one large egg)
    1 egg
    1 c. currants (soaked in hot water, then drained well)
    Vanilla

Cream sugar and butter together, then add remaining ingredients.

Don't overfill the tart shells, writes my mum in her copy of the recipe to me when I got married. Mum (Carrie) and her sister Verla have continued to make Gram's tarts and apple pies (usually for birthdays and holiday dinners) and have come a close second; but my mum is hot-blooded and somehow her pastry is never *quite* as good.

The memories of Gram in her wonderful bog farm kitchen, at the hutch with the pull-out enamel pastry tray, are very dear to me. She was all the things you want a grandmother to be — cheery, kind and warm, and she loved a good joke, even the slightest bit naughty was okay with her.

These memories do sustain and nourish us; we're so fortunate to have them. My "out west" summers in the fifties and sixties were truly golden — just like Gram's pastry.

Laurie McGaw
Shelburne, Ontario

✉ One of my earliest memories of growing up in Scotland is of watching and helping my mother make some very delicious tarts. These were always a family favourite. Nobody else's mother made these tarts, but all my friends loved them, too.

Lots of people asked my mother for her recipe for "Canadian tarts." We never knew why they were called Canadian tarts — we just ate them up as soon as they came out the oven with the centres warm and gooey.

When I came to Canada twenty years ago, I found people eating Canadian tarts all over the place. They were called butter tarts in Canada, but it was my mother's recipe all right.

They will always be Canadian tarts to me, and yes, my mother's recipe has raisins in it.

Kay Sutherland
North Vancouver

✉ Butter tarts are at their best frozen! It's what makes them a truly Canadian delicacy. I first discovered the truth while hiding in the pantry out of Ma's sight. I couldn't afford the luxury of letting my purloined pretty defrost, so I gobbled 'er down quick before I could be caught with the goods. I soon had the entire family converted, and to this day it is only in a semi-solid state that we sample its sweetness.

Jack Vander Hoek
Ottawa

A Life on the Land

I first met Michael Kusugak electronically, as they say. He read from his wonderful children's book *Baseball Bats for Christmas* for us, and afterwards, by satellite link, I talked with him from his home community of Rankin Inlet, on the western shore of Hudson Bay.

Since then, we've become friends. I've read from his work before a Toronto Symphony Christmas concert (I talk about it whenever I can); he's introduced me to many northern ways. He's visited with me in Toronto — he came down to perform some string games at a huge gala we staged for literacy at the historic Winter Garden Theatre — and I've visited with him in Rankin Inlet (we held our annual golf tournament on the ice there in 1994).

He really does straddle two worlds. His house, and the studio next door, where he works in Rankin Inlet, are jammed with CD players, faxes and modems — all the gadgetry of modern life. But outside, on the shore of the bay, his Ski-Doo awaits, ready to take him at any time to a way of life that has scarcely changed in a thousand years, and which still resonates through the letters he writes, now, to *Morningside*.

April 2, 1993

✉ We slept at our cabin last night. Spring has definitely sprung. Soon we will be chiselling our way through eight feet of ice at Isluuqtuuq (lake of big trout), Diana Lake, and others. It is our most favourite time of year here. This community empties at the end of the working day as people hop on their snowmobiles and sleds and head out to the fishing lakes. We all head back to catch some of the play-off games of the NHL in the evening.

It is truly a most wonderful time of year. The temperature will rise and the snow will soften so that you cannot walk on it without sinking up to your knees. The ptarmigan will fly around in flocks. We will shoot at them with our .22s as they walk around on the bare patches of dark ground. The best recipe for ptarmigan breasts is the shake-and-bake recipe in the old *Northern Cookbook*. Delicious.

My son Benjy will drive us out to the lake. My favourite is the one called Qingaugalik. He is getting pretty good at finding his way out there. We will bring our ice chisel and scoop with ten-foot handles. We will find a spot on the lake that is most likely to have fish, shovel through about three feet of snow and chisel a hole about a foot in diameter. As the hole fills with chips of ice, we will scoop it out and chisel some more. We continue this until we hit water. Sometimes, though, when you pick a spot too close to land, you hit bottom before you hit water. I don't know which is more annoying, messing up the blade on your chisel or the thought that you have just chiselled through eight feet of ice for naught.

You should come fishing with us sometime. Just being out there is worth the trip. We drink a gallon of tea and eat piles of caribou, bannock and pilot biscuits. Being out in the open air does something for the appetite. Like I said, we just go for the fun of it. I don't remember the last time I actually caught a fish.

But I remember the fish that Makiggaq caught at Qingaugalik. It was some years ago. We had gone out on a Saturday, and I had chiselled a hole about two feet in diameter. Sandy caught five nice trout in the hole and we came home. Sunday was a gloriously beautiful day so we were headed back out when we came upon Makiggaq along the way. He waved his arm up and down, which is a "Come!" gesture in Inuktitut, and we went over to the bit of bare ground where he had pitched his tent. When I arrived, he told me to look in the big box he had on his sled. And there was the biggest lake trout I have ever seen. It was almost as long as I am tall. And, even though it was already gutted, I could barely hold it up with both hands. Makiggaq said, "One guess where I caught the fish."

I said, "No!"

He said, "Yes! I caught it in your hole at four this morning."

Needless to say I try my luck at Qingaugalik every spring. Maybe Makiggaq's fish has a cousin lurking in the deep somewhere. You should come and help me catch it sometime.

Taimakalauq,
Michael

April 13, 1993

✉ This is the season of hockey tournaments. Our government's policy to install indoor arenas in every community has done wonders for the sporting community. Nathaniel, my son number three, went to Yellowknife with a Tykes team and had a good time. Benjy, number two, went to Churchill. His team came in third. It must be difficult playing against teams that have artificial ice. Our rink has already been closed once this season because of melting snow.

We had a Keewatin Tykes tournament here not too long ago. Rankin Inlet fielded two teams. Nathaniel was in Rankin Inlet team number two, so we took in a lot of the games, cheering his team on and just generally being good parents. They played against teams from the communities of Arviat, Coral Harbour, Baker Lake and Repulse Bay. And with all those teams came mothers and fathers from their respective communities to escort them and to lend moral support to their teams. Needless to say, it was a hard-fought tournament, both on the ice and in the stands.

There was screaming from the stands and there was more officiating from the stands than there was on the ice. Fortunately, all this hoopla was completely ignored by the players and officials on the ice.

Once, as we were heading for the confectionery for hot chocolate between periods, we came upon a scuffle between two women. Mary, who had a child in our team, asked, "Is this serious?" One of the women said, "Yes!" as she struggled to protect herself. We, actually Mary and her husband, separated the two protagonists and, making sure there was plenty of distance and people between the two, we left the rink for the lobby. With a final "Bitch!" from one of the women, the fight was over.

Rankin Inlet Team Two was a make-up team that included my son, a pair of twins, Bobby, the littlest guy in his league, and a little thin girl call MacKenzie, who cried so hard when she was hit against the boards that their coach had to carry her off the ice the way I carry my son to his bed when he falls asleep on ours. They, miraculously, came to the final game undefeated and, in a nail-biter of a finish, defeated Rankin One 5 to 4.

I would like to pay tribute to one of the greatest artists I have ever had the pleasure of knowing. John Kavik died in Yellowknife early last week and was buried on Saturday here, in Rankin Inlet. I remember seeing his birth date on one of our many government lists when I was a budding youngish bureaucrat. I think it just said 1897.

When we first moved to Rankin Inlet in the early sixties I used to go to the Anglican church occasionally, and I remember this old man sitting in a pew when everybody else was standing and singing a hymn. It was Kavik.

A Frenchman by the name of Claude Grenier came here and set up an arts-and-crafts shop in those old days, and I would interpret for him even though his English was terrible and I did not understand a word of French. Kavik did some crude pottery, building vases with figures of people smoking pipes and standing with their arms akimbo. They seemed to me a wonderful comment on my people's new extravagance: endless amounts of tobacco for our pipes coupled with a care-free life. I am proud to have some of them in my house. But it was for his work in soapstone that he gained national recognition.

The local soapstone here is a very dark grey in colour and will not take a shine. It is extremely hard to work with, but Kavik took advantage of this quality and produced carvings that can only be called avant-garde. He produced masterpieces that were executed with such finesse they evoked a sense of primeval tenderness, a harsh reality coupled with care and tenderness. And art collectors took notice. His carvings were in demand the world over.

In a light-hearted spirit with which he overcame many of life's difficulties — he had led a very difficult life — Kavik played with another great artist, Tiktak. They caricatured each other in stone and laughed. Their caricatures are now prized collectors' items.

He had a little tent out at the Meliadine River once and, in his seventies, thought nothing of walking into town for supplies and, with a load on his back, he would walk back again. It is a distance of some six or seven kilometres, one way.

I saw him driving a Ski-Doo once. I think it was in 1980. He was going down the main street in front of my office very slowly, but just to make sure his machine did not get away on him, he was holding back on the handlebars as hard as he could. His heels were digging into the ground on either side of his machine. I don't think he ever reconciled himself with modern machinery.

Sandy said he was one of the very first people she tried her newly acquired Inuktitut on. After trying to tell him something she had learned and getting quite annoyed that he was having so much trouble understanding what she was trying to say, she finally discovered he was stone deaf.

But once having met you, Kavik never forgot who you were. He talked, joked and laughed. He truly enjoyed himself when joy was in hand. In his own way he instilled in us a true respect for our elders. When I look at his carvings and at the northern lights, I will remember Kavik. He was truly a great man.

Taimakalauq,
Michael

December 5, 1992

✉ As I write this letter I am winging my way westward once more, towards Winnipeg. This afternoon I will head home to Rankin Inlet.

It is simply amazing how the land changes below the surface. I guess my people are still too young in the modern age to realize the value of land ownership. We have given away at least eighty-two per cent of our land and almost all of the subsurface rights. We have also thrown in all aboriginal rights. All this for a mere $580 million. Our Territorial government spent more than twice that last year. And we get the money over fourteen years.

But it was not a fair fight. Our negotiators (if you can call them negotiators) told us every time they insisted on something the Feds would walk out and they would have to relent to get them back to the table. And we had no lawyers. Our people did not understand the terms of the agreement. Every time they asked a legal question, the answer was "Ask the federal negotiators." And to top it all off, Inukti- tut is not one of the legal texts in the agreement. How can that be when almost all of the so-called beneficiaries of the agreement are Inuit? I do not understand it, but the people have spoken; almost seventy per cent said yes. I guess you can see I was not one of the people who said yes.

Anyway, on to more pleasant things. Many little dramas are played out in this vast country of ours. And none have a happier ending than a catastrophe that has been averted.

There was a Peterhead boat that was taking on water in the high seas. The bilge pump had failed and, when the engine got wet, it too quit. Another Peterhead, which had answered the distress signal, arrived in the nick of time but it could not come alongside the sunken boat to take on the four people (two adults, a mentally retarded boy and a little boy of three or four). They floated an aluminum boat towards these people, and they all managed to get into it, but the alu- minum boat swamped and they all ended up in the frigid waters of the Hudson Bay. I guess some of the people were in the water for close to a half hour before they managed to fish them out. David Talugak, one of the adults, told me he might have given up if his little boy had not told him, "Daddy, I'm scared." They are all okay, thank God.

This is a wonderful business we are in. I did some readings and story-telling in a school called Blossom Park in Ottawa this week. On my way out the door for a bit of fresh air, a little boy called out to me, "Wait a minute. Wait a minute."

I asked him, "What would you like?"

He said, "I want to hug you."

With a lump in my throat, I gave him a big hug and it just made my day. There is hope in this world.

Taimakalauq,
Michael

September 6, 1993

✉ We had a frost the other evening. The veggies in our cold frames have flowered and I have to start a fire in my shed where I work every morning. How do I do that, you ask, in this country with no trees? Well, there is so much scrap wood around: old crates, pallets, building scraps, two-by-four ends, old canoes, plywood, old sleds and all kinds of other left-over wood. We harvest it all in the summer, cut it and burn it in our wood stoves. And it has been wet for the last while. It rains every day now; not all the time but on and off; showers, I guess they call it. The sun peeks through the clouds in between the showers. It will be like this until it gets cold enough to freeze.

The birds are flocking now, getting ready to make their long trip south. We have been throwing all kinds of grains and crushed, dry dog food in front of our house. The snow buntings and other little birds just love it. I can see them out there now, running around and pecking. They also like left-over pancakes. And just down toward the sea a bit, you can see a flock of Canada geese, feeding among the wispy, yellowish-brown grasses of autumn. Up in the sky you see big flocks of geese, Canadas and Snows, flying by, practicing their letter V. There are also a lot of immature gulls flying around, screaming, forever hungry. I never know what season I like best.

Boats have been arriving every other day. There are barges carrying cargo from Churchill, Manitoba. Construction of every conceivable thing is in full swing. Houses, office buildings and apartments are going up all around us. What was wilderness two years ago, on the northern edge of Rankin Inlet, is now a major moonscape with buildings springing up on it. They bulldoze everything, rebuild it with great masses of gravel, bury pipes in it, put up power poles and build things on it. Yvo — remember Yvo? He is still the smartest of us all — got into the gravel hauling and land development business and is laughing all the way to the bank. His giant trucks are on the move twenty-four hours a day. I don't think the guy ever sleeps.

There was a yawl that came through here the other day. Someone was ferrying it from Churchill, Manitoba, to Cape Dorset on Baffin Island. He was planning to sail through Coral Harbour and right on through to Baffin Island if the weather held up. Have you looked at the Hudson Bay lately? It is a huge body of water. I don't know that I would want to be driving a tiny yawl around in the middle of it.

A tour ship anchored off the coast here a couple of days ago. There were a lot of people. They especially seemed to like the women wearing their amautis, parkas with the big pouches on the backs of them, carrying their babies. Anyway, they appeared on the horizon, completely unannounced. They disembarked in inflatable boats in the afternoon, walked around and sailed that same afternoon. I sometimes wonder what people get out of an outing like that. Sandy and I once visited England. I did not have time to read all the plaques that give you historical information about the dungeons, towers and crows and various other stuff so I took pictures of them all thinking I would read them later, at my leisure. Well, here it is twenty years later and I still have not read all those things I took pictures of.

My baby turned five this spring and started school this fall. Already, he seems to be talking a lot more Inuktitut than he usually does. Our own Arctic College graduated a hoard of teachers from its Teacher Education Program last spring, and now we have qualified Inuktitut-speaking teachers in all our communities. Isn't that wonderful?

On to other things: Some years ago, the American military decided to abandon their DEW (Distant Early Warning) line which was a network of radar stations stretched right across the North to detect anything coming over the North Pole from the enemy beyond. They decided to replace it with FOLs (Forward Operating Locations). Don't you just love those acronyms? Anyway one of those FOLs is here in Rankin Inlet. They extended our airstrip to six thousand feet and paved it. Now landing and taking off on a 737 is a wonderful experience, definitely not like the old days when the planes used to blow half the runway away every time they landed because it was all sand and gravel. But there is also a wonderful aside to this story.

They had a big pile of pavement left over. The hamlet bought the pavement and got the company to lay it on the road that comes down from the airport, around The Bay, in front of the Co-op and back up to the airport. They also put a tiny bit of it on one of our playgrounds. Pavement is a whole new experience for us. We have never had any here before now. We bike on it, we roller skate on it and we roller blade on it. And Terence broke his arm on it. He was our first roller-blading casualty. I saw him at the Co-op yesterday. His arm is in a cast but he is okay.

Taimakalauq,
Michael

December 22, 1993

✉ *Qaajurnaq* is a word I have not encountered in the English language. It means "I know it is going to be cold when I go out there." You say it with a shudder down your spine. And it is a word that is apt this morning; the weather people say it is −38°C. The stove here in my office is labouring to heat this space; I can still see my breath.

Outside, the scene has taken on a different feel. The snow that was softish and creamy yesterday is now hard and has an angular feel to it, like a Lawren Harris painting. The multi-coloured fuel tanks, up the hill, all have frost up to the level of the fuel in them. The creamy yellow one is almost full, the red one is half empty and the one on the right is full; it has frost right up to the top. I cannot tell what colour it is.

The front end of my snowmobile is buried under hard snow and so is the front end of my sled.

Down towards the sea ice, I can see my ten-year-old son, Nathaniel, and his cousin, Wayne, skiing. Kids do not know the word *qaajurnaq*.

Up the hill, around the fuel tanks, two ravens are doing aerobatics. They are in a dogfight. One of them has a morsel of food in its mouth and the other is trying to take it away. They do rolls, spins and loops up in the sky. Up, over, to the right, down and around and up again, one right behind the other. Billy Bishop would have been envious of their flying ability.

We have not much more than five hours of daylight now. The sun comes up at around ten o'clock and sets before three. But that does not dampen our Christmas spirit. And, soon, the days will get longer and longer. It is amazing how fast you notice the change.

Tattys, our neighbours across the street, have their house wired up with lights of all colours; Susan Aglukark's new Christmas CD is played on the radio practically non-stop. All the kids sing along to it, "Little toy train, little toy truck (*sic*) . . ." Kusugak, my five-year-old, keeps closing the curtains and turning all the lights off so that our tree and the Christmas lights in our house will shine brighter. Qilak, my oldest son, is back from Lakehead University; we are almost ready for Christmas.

A few years ago, I started going to the Anglican church here in Rankin Inlet. Armand Tagoona, our minister, was the nicest man I have ever met. Two years ago, though, tragedy struck our little parish: Tagoona died suddenly and the church that he had built during the days of the North Rankin Nickel Mine was destroyed by fire. We have, since, been holding services in various places around town. The latest home of The Church of the Holy Comforter (can you believe it, a church that is named after a blanket? Heh, heh!) is the gymnasium of our elementary school. We have been planning to acquire a more permanent house of worship but the insurance on the old building was not enough and raising funds is a slow process. In the meantime, we make do, setting up chairs in the gym and returning them to the classrooms when the services are over. At midnight Mass, we will sing hymns by candle-light and take turns reading from the Bible; I am reading from Isaiah this year. Christmas is always wonderful.

Taimakalauq,
Michael

February 16, 1994

✉ The Churchill weather office just said the temperature is –34° and there is a weather warning in effect. But the weather is just gorgeous.

The sun was shining through the mist over the floe edge at eight o'clock this morning. It is not at all cold, the sky is blue and the sun is bright. I do not understand weather people. But the weather has not been kind to us this winter.

Actually, it began with our hot-water tank.

We built this house in 1984. It has served us well, but last spring, I removed and threw away the metal stick that is supposed to keep our hot-water tank from rusting inside. The thing was rusted into a solid glob. I decided I would just replace the hot-water tank sometime soon with a more energy-efficient one. Well, the sometime soon was not soon enough, apparently, and our hot-water tank developed a major leak. I had to turn the thing off and drain all the water out of it.

In the meantime, the circulating pump on our main water-line also quit. It, too, was rusted into a solid block. But we still had the heat-trace. I should explain that the circulating pump circulates the water from our house to the main water-line so that it will keep moving and not freeze in winter, and the heat-trace is an electrical water-line heater, which we use as a back-up for the circulating pump. As luck would have it, our water-line froze anyway.

As a matter of fact, the whole town was frozen up. There was a sign on the door of the snack bar at the Northern store that said, "SNACK BAR IS CLOSE TIL WATER-LINE IS REPAIR. MGMT." The Leo Ussak School shut down, the RCMP had water-line problems, and numerous other homes were without water. I don't think Dan, our plumber, slept for weeks trying to keep up with all the freeze-ups. But that is not what I wanted to write to you about. I wanted to write about poverty.

When our hot-water tank quit, we were taking showers in other people's houses. My ten-year-old son, Nathaniel, called from a friend's house and said he would like to sleep over. My wife told the friend's mother to make sure he took a bath before he came home. Well, our bigger boys snatched the phone away from Sandy and said to the mother, "Please don't tell your daughters." I asked them why and they said the girls were going to think we were poor because our hot-water tank was not working.

Are all kids like this? My bank account goes a little too deeply into the red sometimes, we sometimes run out of oil, we sometimes get threatening letters from the phone company and the power corporation. We do not drive a fancy snowmobile; we do not have a car or truck; and we only have our cable connected during the hockey play-off season and the baseball season. But we are not poor; we are never hungry, we are never cold. I do not feel very poor.

My father told me a story once. He said when he was newly married, he was not a successful provider. One day, a man and his son came to visit him in his igloo in Repulse Bay and asked why his baby would not stop crying. My father explained to him that hunting was difficult and he had come home without any meat. As a result, the baby was hungry and his mother did not have any milk in her breasts for him.

The man asked my father why he had not told him of his baby's hunger. He said the man dispatched his son immediately for food and they ate for the first time in many days.

Our fortune had changed for the better by the time we moved to Rankin Inlet in 1960. But the man who showed my father compassion has long since gone, leaving no surviving relatives. Till his death in 1973, my father had dreamed of some day finding a long-lost relative of this man so he could repay him for his kindness, but it was never to be. We just have to be content to consider ourselves lucky he was there when we needed him. And, of course, to follow his example when we find others in need.

Some day, my kids will know why I never feel very poor. I was the baby crying at my mother's breast.

Taimakalauq,
Michael

"I'm Writing of a Dream Christmas . . ."

Well, maybe not. But letters at and about Christmastime have become such a *Morningside* tradition that we now plan on doing at least one full hour of them just before we break. They're sometimes sentimental, sometimes funny and sometimes (I should warn you) sad. But always, as you'll see, they evoke the spirit of Christmas of the past, of the present, and, we can all hope, of the future.

✉ This is not a memorable Christmas story in the usual meaning of the word. Rather, it is simply an incident from a Christmas of a long time ago. So long ago that I hate to count the years that have intervened.

It happened in Saskatchewan, where I was born and grew up. I suppose I was about ten years old at the time and lived in a small village. Now, it was the custom to hold a Christmas concert in the one-room school. At this concert the children became shepherds, wise men, or Joseph or Mary or sang in a chorus or perhaps recited a poem, haltingly or otherwise. And all became angels . . . at least for one night. The audience, made up of doting parents, loved it. "Did you see our Johnny, didn't he do well?"

For the children, of course, the best part of the evening was the Christmas tree and the presents piled beneath it. You ask, "How did they get there?" Well, as usual, call on the women. The Ladies' Aid of the only church in town would undertake to enumerate all the children in the village and surrounding farms and coal mines, oversee the collection of the necessary money and buy the presents. It is an interesting historical note that at that time Eaton's Mail Order Department in Winnipeg had a service for just such an occasion. An organization such as the Ladies Aid could send in a list of the number of children they were catering for, how many girls, how many boys in each age grouping and what the value of the gifts should be. And of course, the money to cover the cost. Ten days or so later a big parcel would arrive in time (hopefully) for the big night with all the presents wrapped and marked.

The incident that sticks in my mind happened this way. The concert had been a huge success, as usual. Santa arrived in the nick of time (is that why he is called St. Nick?) and gave out all the wonderful goodies. Everyone was happy. Everyone, that is, except one boy, Tom, of about my age, whose name for some inexplicable reason had been left off the list. No extra presents to cover such an emergency. What to do? Well, as my mother was the president of the Ladies' Aid that year, I was asked to "volunteer" to give up my gift so that Tom wouldn't be left out. I was assured, of course, that I would get something later to take its place.

Sure enough, a few days later I received my package. The present I had been given was, if memory serves, a book. The replacement turned out to be, wonder of wonders, a hockey stick.

Now I ask you, what ten-year-old boy in the middle of a Saskatchewan winter wouldn't give up a book for a brand new hockey stick?

And I ask you also, how can I remember such a minuscule incident as that from over half a century ago when I can't for the life of me remember where I put the screwdriver I was using the day before yesterday?

Lachlan Salmond
Victoria

✉ We were a poor family living in what was then the quiet city of St. Catharines, Ontario. It was 1959 and everybody knew everybody.

Most of the land on the north end of town was either orchard or vineyard. There was a thriving amusement park in Port Dalhousie.

Kitchen knives were still sharpened by a man who roamed the streets pulling a portable grinder, ringing a bell and smelling of garlic. Milk, eggs and bread were all delivered by panel truck or horse-drawn carriage, and stores had a delivery service. But that is another story.

While many kids my age — I had just passed my fifth birthday — were probably dreaming of bicycles or hockey sticks, I was just happy to be up and walking. I'd only been doing so for about a year.

I'd been born with clubbed feet. Only the previous year had the heavy metal braces that held my feet in place been removed. I'd not been given permission to wear anything other than orthopaedic shoes, and my activities were limited to walking. I wasn't supposed to run and I definitely wasn't allowed to cycle or skate.

Anyway, each Christmas the firemen banded together and held a Christmas party for the underprivileged. Over the year they collected old, damaged, or discarded toys and rebuilt them to give to kids such as me.

This particular Christmas there must have been about forty kids and their families at the party. It was a gala affair complete with turkey dinner, ice-cream, apple pie, Santa Claus, and the whole shebang.

After dinner it came time for the Santa Claus procession. The jolly old fellow wandered onto the stage where the curtains had been drawn to reveal a mountain of toys.

The very first thing I noticed was a white wagon parked beside the pile of toys. It was a big wagon, much larger than the little red metal ones that would become so popular a few years later. It was well-built, with a good foot and a half or more between the floor and the floorboards. The handle was jet black and the wheels bright red. From the moment I saw it, I wanted that wagon.

The children were called up to Santa Claus in alphabetical order. Having a last name that started with a W meant that I would have a long wait.

When my name was finally called, I made my way to the stage and on to Santa Claus's knee. He asked me if I'd been a good boy and I told him I didn't know. He then wished me a Merry Christmas and handed me a stocking.

I watched as the helper went over to the mountain of toys and pulled down a teddy bear. My heart sank as I realized that my wish probably wasn't going to come true.

Sadly, I began to make my way towards the helper and the toys. If I could not have the wagon, at least I would get one last close look at it. The helper handed me the bear and I began to toddle off the stage, tearfully looking around for my mom, who I knew was somewhere close by. As I was about to step down from the stage, I heard a voice behind me.

"Wait a minute, little boy, I have something else for you. Perhaps your teddy bear would like a ride in this."

I turned around just in time to see the helper reach for the handle of the white wagon and begin pulling it towards me. My heart leapt as I realized that my wish was coming true.

The remainder of the evening, which couldn't have been more than an hour, I was the terror of the party. With one leg buckled on the floorboards of the wagon, and the other poised over the side, I raced around the room making sharp corners and nearly running over dozens of toddlers. At home I did the same, racing around the house on my four wheeled perambulator and many times winning the dis-favour of both parents as I crashed recklessly into walls, furniture and younger siblings.

When spring came and the snow cleared, I was out on the sidewalk practising. I learned to take quick turns off our private walk and onto the public one in front of our house. I became an expert garbage hauler and eventually took on passengers.

In fact the wagon was with me and my family for years. When we moved to Niagara Falls in the mid-sixties, I would use it to haul pop bottles my friends and I collected on Clifton Hill. Much later my mom would use it in place of a stroller for my kid brother.

At various junctures it would be used on paper routes, during Cub Scout paper drives, as a ride at penny carnivals, a stage coach for a bunch of back-yard cowboys, and yes, even to pull around my sisters' dolls from time to time.

The white wagon would survive almost every toy in our house. And when there are seven kids in a house, of which I was the oldest, it says something for a toy that was already second-hand when I got it.

The last time I saw the white wagon it had just received a new paint job and was looking as good as the day I got it. It was the late seventies, and my youngest brother had long since graduated to a ten-speed.

I don't know where the wagon is today. I haven't seen one like it in years. But that white wagon still carries some of the dreams and memories from long ago.

William Webster
Whitehorse

✉ The winter I was eight came early. For two years, we had been the only family living at Falls River, the plant where my father was an operator for Northern B.C. Hydro, which supplied electricity for Prince Rupert. About every six weeks, we travelled the nearly forty miles to Rupert to get the groceries and other necessities in a small converted wooden gill-net boat. This time, though, we were frozen in solid by Remembrance Day.

Christmas was coming closer, but my younger brother and I were not aware of the mounting concern of our parents that resulted from the cancelled trip to town. Not only had Christmas shopping not been done, but food was going to be rather scarce before the long freeze-up was over.

The ice in the bay grew daily thicker. Daddy took the big saw and carefully cut around the boats so they would not get crushed, as the tides went up and down even this far up the river. Weather worsened. Six feet of snow, and the thermometer plummeted, along with our parents' hopes for a "good" Christmas. Nevertheless, my brother and I were confident Santa knew where we were.

Three days before Christmas, the sky finally cleared and the ice and snow sparkled. About eleven o'clock in the morning, Mum suggested we walk down to the wharf and watch my dad cut the ice. Always ready to put aside the morning correspondence lessons, we quickly bundled into warm clothes and fairly danced down for this unexpected treat.

Daddy had nearly finished cutting by the time we got there. Then he did a rather unexpected thing. He walked into the middle of the bay and shovelled a large patch of ice clean. Next he took a forty-five-gallon drum and rolled it into the middle of the clean patch. Imagine our puzzlement when Daddy then stuffed it with rags and lit the whole thing on fire. Thick smoke billowed into the sky.

Within minutes an unusual sound began to drone in our ears. Louder and louder, until it swept over the tree-tops, a small airplane roared over our heads and began to circle. On the third pass, a box fell out of the plane, headed directly for the cleared ice. Another and another and another! It was the most exciting thing we had ever seen — boxes bouncing everywhere. Mom, grinning, explained it was our groceries, and Christmas dinner was inside. When the pilot waggled his wings, we waved madly and he disappeared into the blue.

Christmas morning, there under the tree was my coveted walking doll. We revelled in the toys and goodies "Santa" had flown in. Christmas dinner was resplendent with turkey and all the trimmings. And yes, even the bottle of Lamb's finest for my father survived its long drop.

It was many years before I knew just how the feat was accomplished. My father had talked to the hydro company by radiophone, our only link with the rest of the world. A wonderful, still unknown employee took time to do all our shopping, plus added a few extra treats, carefully packed, taped, and tied each box, and took them to the seaplane base. Frozen food was kept in a freezer until the weather finally cleared and the pilot was able to make his Santa flight. It's a Christmas I shall always remember.

Shirley Cochrane
Prince Rupert, British Columbia

✉ It was Christmastime again, and I was fed up with the hype and commercialism and having to cope with all the gift buying, wrapping, dinner preparations, entertaining and the thousand other things that intruded into my life at that time of year. I swear I had baked at least seven pounds of butter into shortbread and made three batches of marmalade to give to all the old souls I knew who lived alone. I had made God knows how many things for the Christmas bazaar, sung with both the church choir and chorale innumerable songs of good cheer at churches, concerts and seniors' residences. Let's face it, my Christmas spirit had hit a new low.

I left the office the day after a snowstorm had covered the black ice on the streets and slid down Peel Street on my way to Gare Central to take the commuter train home from the office. As I inched my way along the icy street, I thought it might be a good idea to pick up a box of chocolates for the secretaries in the Dean of Students' Office. They often came to my rescue when I was short-staffed, and since my office consisted of just me and my secretary, they did get the sos from time to time. I hurried into the Laura Secord store on the corner of Ste. Catherine Street. If I didn't pick up something for them today it would be too late, and damn, there was an old lady at the counter taking her time picking out single items with much thought and deliberation and inquiries about prices to the only clerk in the store.

I'm going to miss my train, was the thought that was running through my head, and that night was yet another performance — this one at a seniors' residence in Côte St. Luc. I needed every minute to make it to the church where I was being picked up at 6:45. I looked at the woman, stooped, shapeless in a worn, ill-fitting coat, scarf over her head, old-fashioned overshoes. She carefully picked a chocolate Santa, two candy canes, two chocolate bells and another Santa, while fingering the change in a well-worn purse. The clerk took the money as it was carefully counted out, put the purchases in a bag and said, "Merry Christmas" as she handed her the little sack. I was getting more impatient as the minutes fled by.

"Oh, dear!" exclaimed the elderly lady. "I did hope you would wrap them. You see, these are Christmas gifts for my young friends, and I don't have any Christmas paper."

Suddenly my exasperation turned to shame. Here I was going through the motions of Christmas giving and she, with her limited means, was giving her all. How could I have been so disenchanted?

"Excuse me," I said, in my cheeriest voice, "I just happen to have a spare piece of Christmas paper in my briefcase. I'd be pleased if you would take it. It really is extra, I don't need it." I have no idea why I had a sheet of wrapping paper in my briefcase — it was just there.

"Oh!" she exclaimed. "How kind of you, thank you, thank you." I gave her the paper and wished her happy holidays. She tucked the paper inside her coat and off she went with a smile to wherever her humble home was, to wrap the gifts for her little friends.

The clerk, who probably was just as jaded as I was, thanked me warmly for noticing the situation. I could hear the quiver in her voice, and I must admit I had a lump in my own throat.

I missed my train and had to wait for the next one, but as I passed the time waiting, a verse, I think it is from Matthew, came to mind. "If you have done it unto the least of these, my brethren, you have done it unto me." Merry Christmas in the true sense of the word.

Meribah Aikens
Town of Mount Royal, Quebec

✉ I know "Rudolph, the Red-nosed Reindeer" came out in September 1949. I had graduated from the University of Toronto in the spring of that year and by the fall was attending the Ontario College of Education. Many of us were still on our DVA allowances, but to supplement these a friend and I took Saturday jobs at Simpson's. (This was the store at Yonge and Queen, of course. There were no malls then with their Eatons and Simpson's "anchors," and as far as Toronto was concerned, The Bay did not exist.) We really wanted to work in the book department or perhaps men's wear, but we were sent to radios and record players. (Television sets were still a thing of the future.) I hated it. Customers had so many technical questions that I couldn't answer, and because commissions were involved besides salary, the regular, full-time employees resented us and did everything they could to keep the paying customers to themselves. But what I came to dislike most was "Rudolph, the Red-nosed Reindeer." Our department was right next to records, and "Rudolph" was the latest hit. That demo was played constantly, from store opening to store closing. I remember thinking, "Why are you doing this to me, Gene Autry? I've never done anything to you." By Christmas Eve that rinky-dink tune and those asinine words were more firmly set in my mind than anything else I have ever heard in my life. And every time I hear them, I am back trying to beat a salesman to a customer who will ask me questions that I cannot answer.

"White Christmas" also strikes a chord in my memory. The time of its release, 1942, was, I think, one of the reasons initially for its popularity. Canada had been at war for three years, and the United States for almost one. Thousands of young men who had grown up with white Christmases were serving away from home, and the song had just the right degree of sentimentality to tug both at their heartstrings and at those of their wives and sweethearts back in Toronto or Saskatoon or Moncton. I'm sure I'm not the only one to have received at least one tear-stained letter and the explanation, "I can't help it. They're playing 'White Christmas'."

Oh — and why do I remember, after all these years, one of Bob Hope's wartime jokes? "My Aunt Martha gave her girdle to the scrap rubber drive, and now she's dreaming of a wide Christmas."

Fred Farr
Thornhill, Ontario

✉ In 1945, Jim, my husband, had just returned from naval duty, we had just been married and we were celebrating our first Christmas in our first apartment. We bought a Christmas decoration that cost us more than we could afford at the time, but it represented for us a return to civilian life away from the restrictions and austerities that had been an integral part of World War Two. It was a church covered with a white waxy substance to represent snow with a Santa and reindeer attachment that went around the steeple playing "Jingle Bells" when a knob was turned.

A tradition grew up around the ornament. When all the decorations had been put in place and the tree was trimmed, only then was the box containing the church unpacked. The church was placed as the centre-piece on the dining-room table and the youngest child turned the knob that started Santa around the steeple to the tune of "Jingle Bells." As the years went by, as the family grew, each of the four children and then their children learned to appreciate the tradition that had built up around the church, as the symbol of the beginning of Christmas festivities.

In 1989, the tradition was broken. All the preliminary steps were taken, but when the knob was turned nothing happened. All the children (some now forty years old) were disappointed, but Jim and I recognized that a mechanism cannot go on forever; after all, it had been bought forty-four years before. However, Jim very gently removed the top of the church to see if he could identify the problem. Lo and behold, there was a little field mouse with her babies cowering in a nest that she had made with the cotton batting that had been protecting the big fragile Christmas balls.

The mental picture of the little pregnant mouse looking for a safe haven in which she could safely give birth to her offspring and finding it in a church, whose entrance was so small that none of her normal predators could enter, stimulated our imagination. It reminded us of the true meaning of Christmas — the celebration of the birth of Christ, whose mother Mary also had to find a safe haven where she could lie while waiting for the birth of her child. Living on a farm, we had been accustomed to accepting that all creatures were creations of God. My husband very carefully replaced the top of the church and returned it to the attic. It seemed like the Christian thing to do.

Shortly after Christmas, the top was once more removed. The baby mice were all gone. The cotton-batten that had been around the mechanism was removed. The knob was turned and once more Santa's sleigh and his reindeer turned around the steeple to the tune of "Jingle Bells." We were ready for the next Christmas, but somehow the tradition of letting the youngest child turn the knob of the church as a symbolic gesture will never be as dramatic as it had been on the Christmas of 1989.

Jean Morrison
Vankleek Hill, Ontario

✉ We came to Canada from England in 1969 as newly-weds with not much money, few possessions and no relatives in this country. It was our second Christmas, in 1970, that this incident occurred. I was an occupational therapist at the Manitoba Rehabilitation Hospital in Winnipeg, and often at Christmas we, as staff, were given presents as thanks by patients; these were usually chocolates or cookies, but this time I was given a plant. If my memory serves me well, my patient was a woman who was probably in her late thirties and had something wrong with her knee.

The plant was a cutting of hers from a Christmas cactus. It had two or three leaves and one beautiful pink bloom. I had never seen a Christmas cactus before so was very pleased with this magnificent flower. I took the plant home. The bloom died but I kept the plant. It was many years before I was to see the plant bloom again.

I watered and fed the plant and it did not die. It grew lots of leaves. But its various locations in our homes obviously did not suit it. It took the move to British Columbia well, but again, when we lived in Squamish, all we got were leaves. In 1977 we moved to North Vancouver and the Christmas cactus was relegated to the bathroom as the green leaves were very nice but it was quite big by now and becoming rather a dust collector.

Finally in about 1980 when the plant was ten years old, I was wondering what to do with it as it was looking woody and bedraggled. I thought I would feed it well and put it in a south-facing window of our living-room to give it a last chance before throwing it out. Towards the end of November, to my surprise, I noticed little nubs growing out of the ends of a few of the leaves. These turned out to be buds and we had half a dozen of the most beautiful blooms that Christmas.

Since then I have kept the plant in the same place and we have been rewarded with a wonderful display of more and more blooms every Christmas. The blooms last for about a month during the whole festive season. People often remark about the plant, how lovely it is, how do I get it to bloom at Christmas, and where did I get it, so I tell them the story.

Whenever I see the plant, in all its glory, I think of the lady who gave it to me. I thank her for all the pleasure I, my family and my friends have had each Christmas and, although I am sure she will never know, I wish her the same beauty in her life.

Liz Parslow
North Vancouver

✉ The year 1958 found me teaching at the Department of National Defence School in Radcliffe-on-Trent, England. As Christmas approached, a Canadian chum, his wife and I decided we'd spend the Christmas holiday in Italy and, if possible, the three or four days over Christmas in Milan. I was an opera fan and the idea of perhaps seeing two or three operas at La Scala was very attractive.

My chum had a small English car and would drive through France, cross the border into Italy and proceed on to Milan. Since his car was a Morris Minor, we decided that we would keep our luggage to a minimum and take only one gift for ourselves. Each of us would open his gift Christmas Eve at a little celebration we had planned.

Several gifts from home had arrived for me but these would probably contain Christmas fare, so I decided to leave them behind. One day a parcel arrived for me posted in England but with no name or address of the sender on the outside. This was the one I would take to open on the eve of Christmas. It was small, of negligible weight and would be a surprise. I had been in the United Kingdom for four years during the war; a friend from my war years no doubt was sending me a gift.

Our travel plans proceeded according to schedule. We were in Milan on Christmas Eve, saw our first opera, and returned to our hotel for our Christmas celebration. The candles were lit, the Asti Spumante was chilling in the ice bucket, the panettone was waiting to be cut, and we were all just a little homesick thinking of family and friends in Canada. We popped the cork of the champagne, the tray of coffee arrived at our door, we cut the cake, poured the coffee, toasted the season and now it was time to open the gifts. I snipped the string from my parcel, unwrapped the paper and there was a dirty shirt I had left in a London hotel room a couple of weeks before. Christmas, Milan, 1958.

James C. Potter
Brampton, Ontario

✉ Memory can cheat: at times it can betray, but often enough it is the balm of our years, giving comfort to the wounds of time. Mind you, there are occasions when I look back to my youth and wonder if my recall is more selective than absolute. I suppose it must be a trait I share with my mother. Her success as a poet in her later years stemmed directly from a luminous memory of her eventful life.

My aunt Vera was almost the antithesis of her sister. Solid and down to earth, she accepted fact without undue coloration of memory — an easy enough accomplishment given the comfort of her wealthy life.

It was Christmas in England. I was at Vera's for a short stay before going home. Her house was an oasis, well removed from the vicissitudes of a business trip to London.

Late in the afternoon of the second day, we were enjoying a drink by the fireside. "I want to see the Garth," I said. "Think I'll go there tomorrow. Is it far from here?"

"Oh, dear," she said. Her distress was unexpected. Recovering, she said, "Not too far; about an hour on the Newport train. I think I should go with you. Your mother . . ." She paused, and then thought better of it. "Yes. We'll take the 9:40. Right after breakfast."

The Garth was the ancestral home. "It was the grandest house on Eden Road," my mother loved to recall. "All brick and stone it was, with white marble cornices. A garden in the front, a full orchard in the back." Her eyes usually became misty at this point. "I had such a lovely room, upstairs, at the back, overlooking the orchard. The maids' room was on the third floor, but they had no view."

Time and again, when things bore down on us in the midst of trying times, my mother would escape to happier days when my grandfather owned a printing business in Wales. Taking me with her in her mind's journey, I enjoyed garden parties, sunlight and music. "When your grandfather entertained his managers and their wives at Christmas, it was usually in the larger parlour. I would be sent off to play in the garden. I remember a winter sun glistening on a deep snow, and the carols . . . It was all so lovely."

My mother would often sing lyrics from light opera. I learned of the oak-panelled music room where my mother and Vera sang duets for their voice teacher, "Mr. Simon, such a kind man he was."

On days when the Vancouver rain was pelting down, the wind pressing hard against the windows of our boarding-house rooms, my mother sought light and warmth from the Garth's sunnier times. She told me how she loved to sit on the hallway bench, watching the soft gules of ruby light coming through the window set in the front door. Some rays, playing through the bevelled edge of the cut glass, split into rainbow colours that shimmered on the tile floor. The little girl who became my mother would fold up her white-stockinged legs and hug her knees as she gazed at the light rippling before her child-wide eyes. . . .

And now, after all the years, I was to see it for myself. Vera stopped at the third house, just down from the top of the hill. She turned and looked at me.

It was a long, narrow, dark brick building, crammed into a thirty-foot front lot. Set back about twenty feet from the road, it displayed a patch of grass and a rhododendron bush. The brick at the corners of the house was brightened here and there with desultory blocks of squared marble. A pane of crimson glass was inset near the top of the front door.

A woman came out to the porch of the next house. She had been watching us through the holly decorating her side window. "Well, Vera," she said. "It's been a while since we've seen you." Then, "You must be Mary's son. I would know that chin anywhere. Season's greetings to you. How is your mother?" Her words tumbled out in a rapid Welsh lilt. "My, it must be years since I last saw Mary playing out there in the snow when her father and his foreman enjoyed a mulled ale in the kitchen."

I said that my mother was fine, and after a few more words to Vera she went in, returning to her vigil at the window.

Vera looked down and said, "Mary had a vivid imagination."

"Still has," I said. "The maids?"

She looked puzzled. "Sarah came on weekends," she said.

"The orchard?"

She knew now. "A plum tree in the back." She laughed gently.

"And the singing lessons?"

"Oh, yes." She smiled in memory. "A Mr. Simon. He used to teach us in the parlour. A kind man."

And I knew that the ruby window light shone true.

We slowly walked back down the hill. "What will you say to her?" she asked.

"I'll tell her it has remained unchanged since the day she left it," I replied. "Lovely as ever."

Derek Scrivener
Surrey, British Columbia

✉ Mike and I spent our days tracking lynx and coyotes near Kluane National Park as part of an ongoing ecology study of the northern boreal forest. Late afternoon of Christmas Eve found us transcribing our day's data from tape to notebook. Four o'clock and pitch black — Christmas is truly a celebration of light, and during the solstice season in the south-west Yukon, this was becoming remarkably clear.

Winter life in Kluane is not lavish, but it *is* better than that which I have found elsewhere. This was to be my first Christmas away from home and I wasn't sure what was going to happen. How would I react? I need not have worried: a combination of friendship with the others in camp and the spectacular natural beauty made my traditional family Christmas in Toronto seem very far off indeed. To say I did not miss my family is wrong; to say I did not miss Toronto is not.

Stopping by first was Sabina, giving out home-made cards — a lino-block print of a snow-shoe hare darting through the bush, entitled "100% White." Next in was Susan with a plate of home-made candies and sweets from her and Mark, and finally came Manon. Visiting from Whitehorse for the holidays, she had also made home-made cards containing personalized notes and these she gave out with a hug and a smile as wide as the Alsek River. I had met Manon only once before, about two weeks ago in town, and now I was the recipient of not just a card but a generosity of spirit that would show itself again and again in the year to come.

Mike and I looked at each other in embarrassment with the sudden realization that we were both left empty-handed in this spontaneous outflowing of generosity. Over our shared Christmas Eve dinner (no different from any other night), we discussed how to best express our gratitude, but with so little time it seemed impossible. We taxed ourselves to the limit (being typical Canadians) and still drew a blank, so we decided to consult the near-empty case of beer in the refrigerator (otherwise known as the floor). As I took up my guitar, we started to rhyme off "The Night Before Christmas" as best we could, but got stuck on "They meet with an obstacle, mount to the sky." That was when the idea struck.

Change the words around, set it to music and go carolling to all the cabins. Perfect! Not only would we be able to give our own home-made gift (though one could argue that Mike's and my voices are anything but a gift), but our lack of Christmas cheer would be rectified, as well.

An hour or so later we took our brand-new song out into the wintry Yukon Christmas Eve and headed to the first cabin while muttering apologies to Clement C. Moore.

> 'Twas the night before Christmas
> And all through Kluane
> Not a creature was stirring
> Not even a bunny.
>
> The trackers were nestled
> All snug in their beds
> While visions of lynx tracks
> Danced in their heads.

It went over wonderfully, thank you very much. We found warmth and fellowship in abundance.

Our final stop was at Sabina's small dinner party, and here we stayed late into the evening. Sometime after midnight, Christoph, a Swiss Ph.D. student, excused himself but was gone far too long for a routine trip to the outhouse. (At thirty below one does not dawdle.) When he did return, he asked us to bundle up and follow him.

Outside, the sky was clear and a myriad of stars danced their way across the heavens. The snow creaked underfoot in the Yukon cold and a waxing half moon hung in the west. In my excitement, I again felt like a child in awe of the magic of Christmas. It was a feeling that had been lost for years. Emanating from the sparse bush in the distance was a glow that seemed to flicker as if mimicking the stars overhead. We approached it in silence.

When I stepped into the clearing and saw the lighted tree, I was breathless. Recent snow still clung to its boughs and sparkled in the light from the candles Christoph had just lit. We circled around it and stood in awe of a beauty that will never be matched. Christoph spoke words of reflection — what the true implications of Christmas are in this secular society; the rising threat in the Persian Gulf that would eventually erupt into war in under a month; and our own remarkable life in the Yukon bush. Again there was silence, broken this time only by Mike's husky, T.C., who had found an old hare cache nearby and started crunching away on a femur. The solemnity now broken, the candles were extinguished, and we headed home having spent enough time idle at thirty below.

Christmas morning found everyone together for a pot-luck waffle breakfast — bring your own topping. There was everything from chocolate sauce and somebody's mom's home-canned peaches to Worcestershire sauce. (Try it, it's good!) A long ski through the eskers north of camp followed by a cleansing sauna and a marvellous, full Christmas dinner rounded out the day.

As I made my way through the woods to my lakeshore cabin, I thought back over the last twenty-four hours, my first Christmas away from home: the darkness, the lights, the new friends and simplicity and unpretentiousness of life.

This fall, after a series of bizarre occurrences, I find myself again in Ontario. On Christmas Day I will again be with my family in Toronto and I look forward to it, but my heart will be somewhere far to the north and the west in a home to which I hope to return soon.

Ian Adams
Dorset, Ontario

✉ In December 1963, I was in my last year as a student nurse at the Montreal General Hospital. The scheduling that year had made it impossible for me to leave for home before December 24, so there I was, deciding whether I should spend much of Christmas in a little room in residence or whether I should spend it on the train. I decided in favour of the train.

I was very familiar with Montreal's Central Station and always looked forward to the atmosphere there in the few days leading up to Christmas. There was always a big raucous crowd at the far end of the station. Mostly everyone would be carrying shopping bags filled with wrapped gifts; there would usually be a couple of people with guitars and there'd be lots of excited children. When that big white-on-black sign was rolled into place listing the destinations — Trois Rivières, Quebec City, Montmagny, Rivière du Loup, Rimouski, Mont Joli, Campbellton, Bathurst, Newcastle, Moncton, Amherst, Truro, Halifax and Sydney — there was a cheer and a good-natured crush as we all prepared to go down the stairs and board the Ocean Limited. These were eastern Quebecers and Maritimers going home for Christmas.

It wasn't like that on Christmas Eve, 1963. The station was dim and quiet, the way airports are late at night. There was a straggling handful of us waiting to board; we were subdued and cheerless.

It was late evening when we got on the train, but even still, most of us gravitated towards the club car and soon began to talk. We exchanged stories of who we were, where we were going, why we were travelling on Christmas Eve. Some people were in my situation — they had worked up until that afternoon. One young couple had planned to stay in Montreal for Christmas and had decided at the last minute that they couldn't bear not being home.

We talked about who would be meeting us at our various station stops and about little family traditions we were missing by not being home tonight. By the time we went off to our berths and roomettes, we were feeling quite warm and cheerful, the way you do when you've made new friends.

When we congregated in the morning — a sunny Christmas morning — in CN's dining car, we were already rolling through the impossibly white snowy Quebec countryside along the St. Lawrence River.

It was then that we began to lose some of our crowd and we established an instant tradition: at each station, as someone was leaving the train, all the rest of us would gather around the door to wave to the family on the platform and to sing a rousing chorus or two of "We Wish You a Merry Christmas." We just kept waving and singing until the train pulled out.

By the time we were crossing the Gaspé peninsula, heading towards northern New Brunswick, we were having a real Christmas dinner, drinking toasts to each other and to our crew and acknowledging that so far, believe it or not, we were having a pretty good Christmas.

By mid-afternoon, our numbers had dwindled, and as we approached the broad sweep of the Miramichi River valley, I began gathering my stuff together to be the next one to go. At the Newcastle station, I was waved and sung off the train by fewer people than there'd been earlier but with no less enthusiasm. My mother and father and I stood on the platform watching the train out of sight as it continued on towards Moncton.

The five-mile drive to Chatham was a merry one as I reported all the details of the trip. Everyone — including me — was surprised at the exuberance of my mood, everything considered.

There was one more surprise. Although both towns had the quiet empty streets and the unmistakable atmosphere of Christmas Day, in our house, the calendar had been set back. They hadn't wanted me to miss the special feeling of Christmas Eve, so the presents remained wrapped under the tree, the mince pies were on the counter ready to be baked, and the turkey was still in the bottom of the fridge, ready to be roasted with all its trimmings on Boxing Day.

When I'd left Montreal the night before, I had resigned myself to having no Christmas at all. I ended up having two.

Sharon Fraser
Halifax

✉ I met my husband while I was working out west in Saskatchewan, cooking for a big wheat-farming operation. My husband was just one of about eighteen young men who drove the teams to harvest the grain, working from before sun-up till long after sundown. He had been born on a reserve but had travelled all around North and Central America. He was an excellent horseman and so always was able to find work.

We married after the harvest and decided to return to Prince

Edward Island to live on my mother's family farm. My mother had left the Island when she was quite young, travelling first to the Boston States and eventually winding up in Saskatchewan, where I was born. She named me after my father, Guido, who died of influenza before I was two years old. My mother died soon after, and I was raised by an aunt.

Anyway, to make a long story short, my husband decided to go to Prince Edward Island ahead of me to find work. I was to follow. I'd taken on some extra work as a seamstress and had several fancy dresses to finish.

Grandmother and Grandfather wrote that we were welcome to live with them, that, in fact, they would be happy to have some lively youngsters on the old farm.

Three weeks after my husband left Saskatchewan, I received a letter from him. He sent enough money for train fare to the Island and said he would meet me at the station in Charlottetown. I would arrive two days before Christmas.

Oh, my, I looked forward to seeing my husband and beginning a whole new life. I remembered my mother's description of the farm and hoped my grandparents would let us have the big room over the kitchen, the one with rose-bud wallpaper my mother had chosen as a girl. I had planned a garden and was thinking about preserving crab-apples as the train pulled into the station.

My husband was not there. The station master said no one had come and gone. There was no message for me. I waited for an hour, thinking, "He's delayed on the road. Perhaps the horse threw a shoe. He'll be along any minute now." There was no telephone and I had no idea, really, how to get in touch with my grandparents except by going to their place.

The station master wanted to close up, since there were no more trains until morning, so I sat for another hour, my feet on the trunk of our belongings, outside the station.

I'll admit it now, though for years I never would: I began to cry in disappointment and frustration. How could he not meet me after I'd come so far! I was hungry, too, having eaten every scrap of the food I'd packed for the long train ride.

Though I was dressed in my winter coat, I was chilled and bone-

148

weary from the long journey. I'd envisioned sinking into a soft feather bed after a welcoming meal and a hot bath, but here I was growing colder by the minute, a stiff, damp breeze from the Hillsborough Bay not helping matters one whit.

I didn't realize until I saw the person coming towards me that I'd noticed someone in a house across from the station looking out a window at me periodically. It had registered, perhaps, on a subconscious level. A woman wearing a thick shawl hurried across the street.

"My dear," she said to me. "You must be near frozen. Come have a cup of tea and a bite with us. You'll be able to see your man coming from our window."

I'll never forget the comfort in those words. I stood up stiffly, wiping my eyes so as not to appear foolish, and off I went with the kindly woman. She and her husband were just having their evening lunch. The kitchen was warm and friendly; a plate of fresh biscuits sat on the open oven door and the tea kettle whistled happily on the stove. The woman helped me off with my wraps and sat me by the window where I did, indeed, have a fine view of the station.

As it turned out, my husband did not arrive until the next morning. The man — Clive — went across to the station sometime after we'd had those hot biscuits with butter and jam and cheese. He brought my trunk and suitcase to the house. The woman — her name was Marion — made up the guest bed for me and I spent the night.

As it turns out, my husband was delayed because a neighbour's barn had caught fire and everyone went to help. The animals were all got out in good time and some of the barn was saved, but it was dawn before my husband left the site. He figured I'd have gone off to a rooming-house for the night and would know to look for him in the morning.

I know it seems a small incident in a large and long life, but my desperation was soothed by that woman and her husband — strangers — in a way I never forgot; an Island way, perhaps you'd call it. What happened way back then set the tone for my life here, and any time I have considered moving to another place, I recall that dark December evening, two days before Christmas, when I first stepped off the train. Though I've lived through many troubled times (and fine, joyous ones, too, of course), I think that lonely wait at the end of the railroad line was somehow my darkest hour. And then came a smiling woman from across the way to invite me in for tea.

Guida Sparehawk
Charlottetown

✉ My mother died when I was eight and I need a new one.

She would be seventy now. I can only imagine what she'd look like. Her thick wavy hair would be pewter-coloured, the part in probably the same place. She'd still be stylish, still wear great clothes, expensive shoes and accessories, and there would be laughter, warm and social and big like her jewellery.

My new mother would have old Elvis records and pictures of Pierre Trudeau with his roses and she'd be able to recall exactly where she was when she heard about JFK. She'd throw marvellous dinner parties, and my father would kiss her neck while she put the finishing touches on the hors d'oeuvres.

The whole family would fly in each Christmas. The house would be full of people and poinsettias and candles shaped like choirboys and there would be little reindeer all around the punch-bowl while the good dishes gleamed on the extended dining-room table.

My mother would have a new outfit for the holidays, something with sequins that would shimmer and dance in the blinking tree lights. The living-room would be full of love and Bing Crosby while a million snowflakes fell outside the bay windows in the white, silent night.

While her granddaughter helped ice the shortbread cookies, she'd recall the Christmases when we were kids and how it seemed like yesterday. And just as we were putting the cookies away, her grandson would stroll into the kitchen and snitch a few on a cool teen-age wave of Walkman rap. My mother would laugh, licking icing from her fingers, and joke about how kids can never have enough cookies or love.

That is what I've always wanted from my mother: to be surrounded by love and belief. I want this from my new mother.

I want her to appear in my heart and let her love make me more capable of loving others.

I want to show her this and never let her die again.

Bev Robson
Vancouver

✉ There are fleeting, seemingly insignificant moments in life that forever change us. Mine came on a mercilessly cold Winnipeg winter day when I was nine years old.

It was Christmas, 1923. Our family lived in a simple wooden house, not far from the meat-packing plant where my father worked. Money was scarce. Times were hard. We children knew, without asking, that we should not expect much for Christmas. Mother and Father would do the best they could.

Because the winter was so severe, Father splurged most of his Christmas cheque on the "women" of the family. Christmas morning brought squeals of delight as we each opened our present: a pair of warm woollen stockings. We were lucky, and we knew it. Though the thick stockings sagged about our knees and ankles, scratched our legs, and stretched with each wearing, they would protect us from the winter winds as nothing else could.

"Take good care of these stockings," Father cautioned us. "They must last you all winter. There isn't money for more."

Not many days later — when the trappings of the season were gone and the warm magic of Christmas was all but forgotten — I went into the back yard with Mother before school to hang the washing on the line. It was a bitter day: too cold to snow, almost too windy to stand. The clothes froze in our hands.

As we worked, we watched the neighbourhood children, laughing their way to school. But that morning we saw one child who was not laughing. With her head down, she hung back, her body braced into the wind as she clutched her thin coat tightly around her.

Without a word, Mother lowered her hands from the clothes-line and crossed the street. She spoke briefly with the child, then gently took her hand and disappeared behind the old shed that stood there.

Moments later, Mother and the little girl emerged again. And then I saw . . . I saw what Mother had done. She had taken off her stockings and put them on the child. Mother had given her precious Christmas stockings to a little girl she didn't even know.

We never spoke of it. The child went on her way to school and Mother returned to the clothes-line as though nothing had happened.

Many experiences have coloured my life, but none more profoundly than witnessing that single, unheralded act of goodness rendered by my mother on that wintery day in Winnipeg, when I was nine years old.

Carol Laycock
Lethbridge

✉ I did something last Christmas that I won't do again. It was close to midnight on Christmas Eve, and I had been busy all day, busy as a mother could be that last day, rushing to have everything ready. I iced the Christmas cake and made mince pies and a jelly salad and the children wrapped their gifts, a bit clumsily, and they yelled at each other, "Stay out." They were a long time getting to bed and to sleep. It was almost midnight. Robin, my husband, had fallen asleep in his chair. I'd finished wrapping the last present and made the stuffing ready to go in the turkey. So I put on my parka and went outside.

It was a typical Manitoba night. The moon rode high and I looked at the stars. They scattered star-dust so deep I wanted to gather it in my hands. I wondered which star had led the wise men. Any would have been worthy. I walked quietly, careful not to disturb anything. I was going to see if the cows *really do kneel* on Christmas Eve. Legend tells us they do. After all, they were there at the beginning, at the first Christmas. They know all about it. There is wisdom in their eyes, a wisdom of the ages. They are patient and giving and ask only for food and water and a warm barn. They repay us by giving us their milk, their calves, and finally their meat and their hide. They stand peaceful, calm, and look at us as if to say, "Don't fuss, take it easy. Just do the best you can. There are warm days ahead. Shady trees and green grass at the end of it all, a quiet rest and the nicest journey of all." They are wise creatures.

I thought back to the sick heifer, a little Jersey with mealy muzzle and the kind of eyelashes a film star could envy. Then she was suddenly ill. The vet came and punctured her with needles and the latest cure and left us with pills and said to keep her warm and hope for the best, but her eyes had been dull and glazed and she lay still and she was dying.

Was it the medication, the care, the faithfulness, the spirit that made her want to live, to kick her heels to the sunshine and race to the meadow? I had crept down to her stall and in the doorway I saw her. She was kneeling. I stepped back, feeling I was intruding at a sacred moment. Then slowly she stood up and I had entered and she took the soft hay and the warm gruel I offered her. She was going to live and she had been kneeling to give thanks.

So knowing this, and that the cows are said to kneel on Christmas Eve, kneeling to worship Jesus and to honour their ancestors who were at the birth, I went to the barn door and lifted the latch. Suddenly my hand was stopped and I stood as if a voice had spoken. "If you go into the barn you will wake the dogs! Tippy is in there with her pups, and Deena. You will disturb the cows. You will be an intruder and cows don't kneel if you stare. Do you *have* to have proof? What if the cows *don't* kneel. You will always be in doubt. You will even wonder if they ever *did* kneel!"

I dropped my hand and turned back. I was a silly woman and I was prying. Did I have so little faith that I had to steal down to watch? I pulled up my collar and pushed my hands into my parka pockets. What a bright cold night it was, and how thankful I should be. Our cows were deep in straw and our children snug in bed. Then I stopped. The cow chains were rattling, one after the other; a little late came the last. That would be Betty. She is old and stiff. It must be midnight. *They were kneeling.* How could I have ever doubted them?

Molly Douglas
Courtenay, British Columbia

153

✉ Christmas is a time when we expect our children to be on their best behaviour, so it is surprising how the season brings out the worst behaviour in parents. This is best illustrated in the annual ritual of the children's Christmas pageant.

My first encounter with this phenomenon was during my daughter's first year at nursery school. I realized something was amiss when I went to pick up Adrianna after school not long before Christmas. The mums and the occasional dad would normally congregate in the front hall to wait for the children to come streaming out of the large oak door, proudly waving their latest drawing. This rainy day, however, the parents were huddled around the notice board, running their fingers down a piece of yellow foolscap and muttering loudly.

Phrases like "Not fair" and "My daughter would have been more suitable" drifted up from the huddled group of damp raincoats and dripping umbrellas. Pushing my way to the front, I found the source of contention. The yellow paper pinned to the board contained a class list with the pageant characters neatly printed beside each name. Beside my Adrianna's name was written MARY in large blue letters.

It's funny how unrealistic parents can be about their children, claiming they have attributes of beauty and intelligence far greater than those of any other child. So when it came time for selecting who would play the leading roles in the pageant, parents naturally felt that *their* offspring would be the best choice. I personally did not succumb to this immature behaviour. I knew that Adrianna, being the prettiest and the one with the most stage presence, was the obvious choice for the part of Mary. And I said so.

The nursery school teacher appeared at the door and fluttered about among the discontented parents. She tried to placate them with phrases like "But playing the part of a camel can be so beneficial for their social development."

One dad, whose child had been relegated to playing a sheep, was incensed that his curly-haired prodigy had such a lowly part in the play. He bleated on while a mother, the kind that allows her son to bring only carrot sticks for snack, complained that all the angels were girls. "Angels are androgynous," she whined. "There should be an equal number of boy and girl angels."

By the time the evening of the pageant arrived, very few parents were speaking to each other. Each believed his or her child was going to outshine the others, so busied himself adjusting costumes so the child could see out of the misplaced eyeholes, or practising lines one last time. You would have thought it was opening night on Broadway.

Not to be outdone, I pushed and shoved my way to the front row and deftly slipped into the last good seat, seconds before the mother of a wise man. Despite her remonstrations I refused to budge, hoping that my position as the mother of Mary would, at least in her eyes, justify my actions.

Although the parents intended to focus their attention on the unfolding drama on stage, there were numerous distractions. The primary one was Olivier, my two-year-old son. He had been as determined to attend the pageant as I had been to leave him with a sitter. He won. With the promises to sit still and be quiet completely forgotten, he pranced up and down the aisles. Twice I had to stop him from eating the macaroni glued to the top of the "frankincense" box, left on the stage steps by an un-wise man. I sensed, rather than saw, the daggers emanating from the eyes of the parents behind me as I tried to get my overactive son to sit down.

"Sit," I whispered to Olivier as I patted the chair beside me. "Sit," I said more urgently as the nursery school teacher walked out to address the audience. "Shit," he repeated as best he could, in a loud voice, and flopped down into his seat.

The secondary distraction that evening is a curse of the nineties — the video camera. Gone are the days when parents would pop up momentarily, take a picture with their flash camera and sit down while casting apologetic glances to those around them. Now the dads with their video cameras (it is usually the fathers who are entrusted to this task) stand up for minutes at a time and ignore the coughs and sighs of the parent behind them whose view is completely blocked. Even with my front-row seat, I had to struggle to see over the heads of fathers who had crawled up front for a better vantage point.

The confusion in the audience was mirrored in the pageant itself. The first problem was one of enunciation during the annunciation. The angel Gabriel became struck with stage fright! The mother who had convinced the teacher that her son should be part of the heavenly host stood up at the back of the room and gesticulated wildly.

"Behold," she mouthed at him.

"Beware," he cried, and then on a roll, continued, "I bring you some news."

"Quack," went Olivier as he caught sight of the angels' feathery wings, "quack, quack."

Joseph started to giggle, clutched himself and rushed off stage. The three wise men arrived to visit the single-parent family, but only two gifts were presented to the baby Jesus. One left the stage in tears to look for his lost frankincense. From the crunching coming from the seat beside me, I hoped that there was something left of the gift to offer to the baby.

Mary sat patiently waiting for her presents to arrive. Despite my best sewing efforts, her blue robe kept slipping off one shoulder, making her look rakish rather than saintly. As the pause in the proceedings lengthened, two little angels started to argue devilishly over who had the biggest halo. Then a bored shepherd began to poke his sheep with the tin-foil-covered staff.

The pageant over, the audience clapped enthusiastically and let out long sighs of relief. It represented the culmination of hours of costume making, learning of lines, rehearsals and more rehearsals. The squabbles and jealousies were forgotten and the proud parents exchanged kind words about the children's achievements.

Adrianna put the whole evening into perspective for me. Sucking on a candy cane in the back seat of the car, she said, "Next year I'll let Sarah be Mary." When I asked her why, she replied, "Because her *mother* really wanted it."

Wendy de Feydeau
Hudson, Quebec

✉ This was going to be the best Christmas ever. Everything was planned. All the gifts were bought and wrapped. The tree looked just as a Christmas tree should. The house glistened from all the cleaning and polishing it had received over the past week. Oh, yes, this was going to be the best Christmas ever.

Such were the thoughts that raced around in my head as I looked at my world that Christmas Eve. Some of the children, the still single ones, had come home and were tucked in bed. Somehow the simple, homely acts, like tearing the bread for the stuffing, peeling the potatoes and turnip in readiness for Christmas Day, were part of the observance of that day. There was the still lingering smell of mincemeat pies in the air, although they had been taken from the oven hours ago, before we went to the Christmas Eve service at the church.

The children laugh at me. I seemed to have surrounded Christmas with so many traditions. Like setting the little statues of the wise men on the window farthest from the crèche, so that each Sunday of Advent, they could be moved a little nearer, a window at a time, until on "Old Christmas," January sixth, they were at last at the manger. Serving turnip was another tradition. Christmas dinner didn't seem like Christmas dinner without turnip. And as the children would all tell you, each Christmas was going to be the best Christmas ever.

At last, all the preparations finished, I agreed with my husband that it was time to go to bed, fully aware that in four hours' time I had to put the turkey into the oven. Our old farmhouse settled itself for the night, with a creak of roof timbers, and a rattle of the bathroom window, to the accompaniment of a final wheeze from the furnace.

Morning came all too early. Only half awake, I crept quietly downstairs. Yawning and squinting at the bright light of the kitchen, I headed for the coffee maker, from which the odour of fresh coffee teased my senses. I noticed that the tea-towel I had put over the big stainless steel bowl of shredded bread for stuffing had slipped during the night, but that only half registered. Still groggy, I sloshed milk into my coffee. The tea towel moved as I looked at it.

Must be a bit of a breeze coming in that window, I thought, as one does in old farmhouses.

I reached over to secure the towel in its place.

What happened next is hard to explain. One really had to be there to appreciate it. Imagine as you read the next few sentences that they are all happening at the same time, not separated as they must be in writing.

My hand touched the cloth. A moving object touched my hand. My hand, clutching the cloth, flew in the air. A large grey mouse leapt from the bowl. I screamed (something I never dreamt I could do).

The mouse ran towards me. I dashed to the back door calling, "Kitty, kitty," as I opened the door. Six cats raced in in answer to my distress call. One spied the mouse and made a leap for the kitchen cupboard. The others, not to be outdone, leapt after him.

The mouse scrambled back into the bowl and tried to bury himself in the bread. Six cats gave chase. Bowl, cats, bread, mouse, like the fall-out from some weird explosion, seemed suspended in the air. There were yowls as cats bit and swatted each other in mistake for the mouse, then a crash as the bowl landed upside down on the floor.

From within the overturned bowl could be heard the muffled sounds of a cat. We stood there, five cats and myself, in a ring around the bowl, each looking intently at it. Something brushed my ankle. Thinking it to be the tail of a cat, I paid no attention. Suddenly the supposed tail began to make its way with pointy little footsteps up my leg under my housecoat.

That's how the family found me. Leaping up and down, flapping my housecoat, screaming at the top of my lungs. The mouse had exited my housecoat and run up my neck to cling like Velcro to the top of my head.

Husband, wise man that he is, grabbed me by the hand and dragged me into the sun porch, opened the door and pushed me outside. With a swat, he sent the mouse flying off the top of my head, out into the new-fallen snow, where the creature scampered off, leaving a tiny trail of footprints. Back in the kitchen, we lifted the bowl to find a thoroughly annoyed cat still hissing underneath.

And that's how a new Christmas tradition started in our house. I tell the story now as if it only just happened, but it is kept fresh in the mind each year as we all sit around a large bowl in the kitchen, shredding bread for stuffing and telling about my best Christmas ever. Tell how the cats spent Christmas Day looking suspiciously at one another. Describe the screams that awakened the sleepers. Roar with laughter at the sight of me doing a wild dance, screeching at the top of my lungs, on a floor covered in cats and bread-crumbs, with a mouse hanging onto my head like grim death.

But it's the laughter and family that make these the best Christmases ever.

Bev Walker
Picton, Ontario

158

✉ Recently I was thumbing through cookbooks and loose recipes trying to decide what I'd bake for Christmas.

Recipe ingredient requirements included four squares of chocolate, six eggs — on and on, all very rich and yummy.

While perusing these expensive and caloric recipes, my mind flashed back to the early fifties when I was living in Atikokan and packing a lunch box for my husband, who worked shifts at the mine.

One easily made cookie recipe was the old favourite hermits. You know the spicy ones where if you don't hit a nut in the first bite, you hit a date. Moist yet chewy and easy to make, these cookies could be whomped up in half an hour, start to finish.

One day my husband had just left on afternoon shift when our elderly Scottish neighbour came over to visit. Mrs. Munro dearly loved a cup of tea and I enjoyed having my teacup "read," which made for a mutually enjoyable visit.

On this particular day I served hermits with the tea and Mrs. Munro thought them delicious and asked for the recipe. We had our usual comfortable exchange of stories — mine recalling episodes from the days as a city girl fresh to Manitoba farm life and hers from a similar urban background, only taking place as a bride on an isolated bush farm in north-west Ontario. After a while Mrs. Munro took herself off home.

Weeks passed before I had occasion to drop in next door. Of course, Mrs. Munro insisted that I stay for tea. As we sat down at the table, I was passed a plate of what looked to be ginger snaps. I took one. Mrs. Munro said, "I made your cookie receipt but they're nay as good as your'n." With great difficulty I broke off a piece of the hard, dark brown, lumpy-looking cookie while denying having any such recipe. Rather crustily Mrs. Munro remarked, "Aye, it's your'n receipt."

While trying to chew, and completely mystified, I repeated that I couldn't remember ever having made a similar cookie so I asked Mrs. Munro to name some of the ingredients.

My hostess obliged, complacently recalling, "Well, I didn't have the shortening so I used the lard. And I didn't have the brown sugar so I used the white. And my friend Molly Van Drunen up at Dance always said that a cup of snow is as good as an egg any day."

My recipe?

Please don't try these substitutions in your Christmas recipes. Take it from me, you won't like the results. Happy baking!

Kathleen Harrison
Thunder Bay

✉ I had a bit of good luck last Christmas. On the first of December, I had emergency surgery, which left me and my abdomen out of condition for most of the pre-holiday season. Now that in itself was not a whole lot of fun, but it did lead me to discover something that will affect all my future festivities.

Hark then to Moffatt's Law, discovered after fifty-eight years of research: stress, of the seasonal kind, expands to fill the guilt allotted to it. There you go. All we know and all we need to know about holiday madness.

This all came to me in a flash of Christmas lights last year. Before that, I should point out, I yearly felt that it was too bad my Christmas days were spent doing exactly what I would like least to be doing — cooking. And I invariably felt guilty about feeling that way.

So for years I planned and prepared the mighty Christmas menu dictated by my grandmother and yours for my brood of eight. Every holiday they, with significant others of the day, would join my husband and an exhausted me to sip, gorge and groan over a laden table. Afterwards, their compliments would seep through my semiconscious haze, but I was not deceived.

I am not a chef. I can feed fifty people faster than anyone I know, but I am not a cook. With eight kids one tends to shovel not sculpt food. Fuel the hordes, was my rule, and let McDonald's do the rest. Except, of course, at Christmas. Then even I would try to shine. It was, after all, the dinner of the year.

But last year, just home from hospital, I knew that I was not going to be able to do Christmas dinner, and the guilt started rising. Now I usually do guilt very well — else what's a mother for? — but this time it didn't work. I guess it couldn't get past my poor middle, which was feeling exactly as if I'd been stabbed in the stomach. Which, of course, I had.

Not to worry, said my husband. The entire holiday feast is being done by the kids.

Our kids? Our kids are Boomers. That is to say, they think the basic kitchen utensils are coffee grinder, garlic press and corkscrew — roughly in that order of importance. To the best of my knowledge, none had ever cooked anything free of peanut sauce or pasta. And this was the dinner of the year!

Well, it was out of my hands. Almost. The youngest daughter arrived, nude turkey in her arms, early Christmas morning. "I figured I'd cook it here, Mom," she said. "The house has to smell like turkey cooking or it won't be Christmas." She is the poet in the family.

"So," she added. "Just how do I go about this turkey thing?"

"Sop half a loaf of bread in milk, add a chopped-up onion, two stalks of chopped celery, some salt, pepper, and sage, stuff all its stuffable parts and put the bird in the oven at 325," said I.

"Yuk!" she said. "And actually, I got this recipe for chestnut stuffing with pine mushrooms . . ."

Nevertheless, the house soon smelled of Christmas.

A few hours later, the rest of the crew appeared with everything from cranberries (steamed fresh with chopped oranges, honey and ginger) to brandied mince pie with cheese-cake topping and red and green Jell-O for the grandkids. The table was set, a great meal served and eaten, and — have mercy! — the dishes done and away. Magic!

Well. I may be a slow learner but this year let the carols ring forth. I am prepared to meet the day. My holiday house will be a guilt-free zone! Yea though I walk through the busiest kitchen, I will feel no nasties. My family's talents have at last been revealed, and it serves them right. Henceforth, I leave the creativity to them. I will play with the grandkids, I will answer all phone calls. I will co-ordinate the chaos. I will lift my voice in praise of the dinner of the year. But I will not cook.

Free at last! Free at last! Amazing what a little major surgery can do.

Donna Moffatt
Errington, British Columbia

✉ As last year, I fly non-stop to Montreal and arrive in mid-afternoon. My December visit. Better to call it my December mission, for I am certainly no bearer of good tidings. If anything, it is I who need visitation.

Every Christmas, even before Mother died, I made the eastern pilgrimage to visit Father as his darkening world lapsed from year to year. The taxi waits in the K-Mart parking lot while I run in for his favourite candy and nuts. Christmas lights blare, "Winter Wonderland" blares and "We Three Kings" blare. It's the same racket every year, but I shouldn't be surprised: I, the parachuting December visitor, buy the same gifts for the same reasons, blithely assuming Dad's taste in treats hasn't varied. Even if they did, he couldn't tell me.

Open fields, long winding driveway, snow-drifts, locked door, buzzer, reception desk, echoey corridors: my personal touch with the Hall of the Forgotten, niched by the world to run out their string of years, shielded from the outside world by the outside world, some abandoned by relatives — infants on an alien doorstep. I know my way and hurry down the hall. Turn left and turn left again. Slippers and nightgowns whisper and shuffle, and I recognize the black-haired man still swaying at his doorway. While waiting for the elevator, I remember the thin man chanting, "Come on. Come on. You come?" in his reedy voice. He could be inviting me into his room

On Ward 3 I move past more rooms until I find Dad in his sunroom, dressed for contracting: open plaid shirt, baggy green pants, runners without laces. I think he smiles because he recognizes me but I am not sure. As usual, he continues standing, head bowed, shoulders hunched. I manoeuvre him to the window and a couch to talk but this is his only world and he its only citizen. I have no passport, no currency and do not know the language. His world cannot be mine; it is the only part of his life I cannot manipulate.

My wrist-watch itches and burns and I force myself not to peek. It's been less than an hour and I have yet to look him in the eye. Already I am thinking of the weather back home, the Walker contract, the committee I chair every third Wednesday. Already I am outside, escaping down the long, winding driveway, but Dad's dry cough drags me back and my fixed look through the window tries to reach beyond our silences to Montreal's lights reflecting dully on an overcast sky.

The silence wraps both of us. Dad is comfortable in its arms, I am not. A tourist with no hope of securing a tour guide, I wish I hadn't come, and at the same time am glad I did. Having done my December mission for years, I realize it's as much for myself as for Dad. But that does not make it any easier. What do I say to this stranger, even if he does understand? Hallway noises — staff, wandering patients and distant calls for help — crinkle the sun-room silence but they are too fragile, too brittle to build on. I remain quiet.

Finally, I sense I can leave, knowing the trip was not in vain, that the money and time were not wasted. After more wrestling with my conscience, I will again come to the conclusion I need not return until next year. My words of leaving are as those I used when arriving — awkward and strained. I escape to the hall, the elevator, the snowdrifts and my waiting cab. I am a Christmas Pharisee. I can't stop me. I am the somebody nobody knows.

David Nadeau
Three Hills, Alberta

✉ In December 1944, our Canadian General Hospital, with twelve hundred beds, was in Ghent, Belgium. We had been living under canvas since our arrival in Normandy in August; our diet since then had been a nutritional but monotonous variation on the theme of Spam, dried peas, dehydrated potatoes, powdered milk, powdered eggs and prunes *ad nauseam*. Its only virtue was in comparison to the meagre rations available to the civilian population. When the army announced that Christmas dinner would be traditional turkey, real potatoes, fresh vegetables and plum pudding, you can imagine our delight.

On Christmas Day we had more than two hundred patients on our ward who were able to come to the table, so tables were set up in the long corridors. With Christmas decorations made from whatever we could buy in the city, plus our donations of candy and cigarettes that family and friends had sent from home, we were able to set up an attractive table for the patients' Christmas dinner.

Just as the patients finished their dinner, we had a frantic phone call from Nursing Sister Jeanie, who worked in the out-patients' clinic across the canal. She had just discovered that the orderlies were to be served their Christmas dinner on bare tables. The orderlies were our great source of help and a tower of strength in running our wards. Could we come over and bring our table-cloths, decorations and any candy we had? One sister was sent scrounging to the sisters and medical officers for cigarettes or candy. By hard work, we managed to create a festive-looking table. Then it was time to go back on duty, no time for lunch or a rest, but a cup of tea on the ward would see us through until we had our own turkey dinner.

The night staff ate at six o'clock, and we had our dinner at seven-thirty. To accommodate all the sisters in our mess, the tables were set up in an E with the food being served from large pots on a table at the end of the middle bar of the E. We four who missed lunch got the last four seats just beside the serving table, which meant we passed all the plates from hand to hand. Finally as those on the middle bar of the E were being served, one of the sisters said she thought the pots sounded empty; would there be enough? Supreme optimists, we said, There is always enough dinner at Christmas. Well, you guessed it — the pots were empty. If only we had stuck a thumb in each plate as it passed by.

We had our Christmas dinner — Spam, dried peas, dehydrated potatoes and prunes. Don't know if there was any plum pudding left or not, we were laughing so hard that we did not know the difference.

Jean MacAulay
Sackville, New Brunswick

✉ Rain drummed on the roof and spattered against the window panes of the old farmhouse. Such a deluge! It couldn't be Christmas Eve! Anyway, this year, 1941, I didn't want Christmas to come. My little sister had gone to bed, but my mother, my brother and I were definitely stalling. None of us wanted Christmas to come. Dad had died, and how could we have Christmas without him?

My brother made another trip to the barn to check the animals. Mother kept putting finishing touches on the Christmas preparations. I stood in front of the window at the ironing board, pressing and re-pressing our best clothes, getting them in perfect condition for the special day. We were all putting off going to bed, for when we awakened it would be Christmas, Christmas without Dad.

There was nothing left to press. I stood by the window, staring out into the blackness of the night. Faintly through the darkness appeared a light. A car was coming down the lane — on Christmas Eve, at this time of night! It seemed impossible. It turned in the drive, paused and circled, and was gone.

We heard footsteps, voices and a sharp rap. The door burst open and in stepped two airmen. They were chattering, greeting us in English. Was it English? Yes, different though — London Cockney, I'd say, hard to understand. They were putting down their kitbags, throwing off their greatcoats, kicking off their rubbers.

"Where did you come from? How did you happen to get here?"

Listening intently, trying to catch the accent, we learned they were Alf Keen from Surrey, England, and Tom Leach from London. They were stationed at Trenton Air Base in the Commonwealth Training Plan. They had seen a letter, from my mother, posted on the barracks wall, asking for two lonely airmen for Christmas. Mother had never heard back from the invitation and had forgotten about it.

Now there was something to do. Soon there was hot coffee, Christmas cake, shortbread and conversation. Alf had a wife, a son and a little red-headed girl. Tom, younger than Alf, about my age, said he had no family and offered no explanation.

Now we were looking forward to Christmas. The airmen tucked some gifts under the tree, and my brother and I scurried about looking for something suitable to be wrapped for them.

Things were going to be different. I could go to bed and sleep now. Just before I dropped off, I was sure I heard someone walking through the house, but that would be Santa, of course. I laughed softly.

It was rather early when we gathered around the hemlock tree. Mother lit the candles and soon something wonderful began to happen. My little sister and Alf were forming a beautiful relationship. She saw in him the father figure she was missing, and Alf saw, in the little red-headed Canadian girl, his daughter in England. She showed him her gifts and he took her on his knee and they played the Christmas games over and over again.

Tom went down to the barn with my brother. Mother and I prepared the Christmas dinner, and I heard her humming carols as she worked.

When it was dinner time we spread out the feast. The goose was golden brown, bursting with dressing. To go with it were mashed potatoes and gravy, turnips and cranberries. The carrot pudding was plump and delicious. Everyone agreed it was the best Christmas dinner ever. Mother smiled.

When we had finished, Alf became quiet with a far away look in his eyes. "I wonder what they will be eating at home," he said. "The rationing is so bad now."

"We'll make them some food parcels," my mother replied.

That night we all went to my aunt and uncle's farmhouse. It was exciting seeing our cousins and introducing "our airmen." Alf talked, laughed and teased. The girls tried to flirt with Tom, but he was quiet. We ended the evening singing carols around the piano.

More snow fell. The next day we showed the airmen what winter in Canada was like. We made snowmen, had a snowball fight, got out the sled and skis.

When evening came the airmen had to go back to base. It was hard saying goodbye. "We'll write, we'll see you again."

"We'll send your wife and children food parcels," Mom said.

The look on Tom's face had changed in some way.

"Lucky thing," he said, "on Christmas Eve I looked around your house for a gun. Lucky thing you didn't have one or you would have found a dead man down in your barn. I lost all my family in the London bombings. I didn't want to go on, I was going to end it all, but now that I've found this loving family, I've decided to go on. Perhaps I can make it."

I knew then what had been bothering Tom. I put my arms around him, kissed him and whispered, "You will, Tom, you will."

That was fifty years ago. We never heard from Tom again. I hope he made it.

Letters and parcels went back and forth to Alf and family. The other day on impulse, I phoned him and was excited when he answered. I knew the accent.

"Hey, Alf, do you remember December 1941?"

After a thoughtful pause, he answered, "Pearl Harbor. Is this a contest?"

"No, no, do you remember Christmas at the farm in Ontario?"

"Now, I wouldn't be forgetting that, would I!"

"How are you, Alf?"

The answer came clearly and firmly. "We're still doddering along."

Marion Sherwin
Baltimore, Ontario

✉ Grandma is ninety-eight this Christmas. In spite of declining health, she forges on with characteristic determination, hope and wit. We thought we might lose her last October — how many more heart attacks can her frail body take? — but, true to form, Grandma rallied again. "I couldn't miss a Christmas party, now could I!" she quipped on the way home from the hospital.

"No, Grandma." I laughed. "It wouldn't be a party without you."

I remember my first Christmas party with Grandma. I was just a kid. I remember tearing across town on my bike to visit her on the day my big sister dropped the bomb: "There is no Santa Claus," she jeered, "even dummies know that!"

My grandma is not the gushy kind, never was. I fled to her that day because I knew she would be straight with me. I knew Grandma always told the truth, and I knew that the truth always went down a whole lot easier when swallowed with one of her world-famous cinnamon buns.

Grandma was home, and the buns were still warm. Between bites, I told her everything. She was ready for me.

"No Santa Claus?" she snorted. "Ridiculous! Don't believe it. That rumour has been going around for years, and it makes me mad, plain mad. Now, put on your coat, and let's go."

"Go? Go where, Grandma?" I asked. I hadn't even finished my second cinnamon bun.

"Where" turned out to be Kerby's General Store, the one store in town that had a little bit of just about everything. As we walked through its doors, Grandma handed me ten dollars. That was a bundle in those days. "Take this money," she said, "and buy something for somebody who needs it. I'll wait for you in the car." Then she turned and walked out of Kerby's.

I was only eight years old. I'd often gone shopping with my mother, but never had I shopped for anything all by myself.

The store seemed big and crowded, full of people scrambling to finish their Christmas shopping. For a few moments I just stood there, confused, clutching that ten-dollar bill, wondering what to buy, and who on earth to buy it for.

I thought of everybody I knew: my family, my friends, my neighbours, the kids at school, the people who went to my church. I was just about thought out, when I suddenly thought of Bobbie Decker. He was a kid with bad breath and messy hair, and he sat right behind me in Mrs. Pollock's grade-two class.

Bobbie Decker didn't have a coat. I knew that because he never went out for recess during the winter. His mother always wrote a note, telling the teacher that he had a cough, but all we kids knew that Bobbie Decker didn't have a cough, and he didn't have a coat. I fingered the ten-dollar bill with growing excitement. I would buy Bobbie Decker a coat.

I settled on a red corduroy one that had a hood to it. It looked real warm, and he would like that.

"Is this a Christmas present for someone?" the lady behind the counter asked kindly, as I laid my ten dollars down.

"Yes," I replied shyly. "It's . . . for Bobbie."

The nice lady smiled at me. I didn't get any change, but she put the coat in a bag and wished me a Merry Christmas.

That evening, Grandma helped me wrap the coat in Christmas paper and ribbons, and write, "To Bobbie, From Santa Claus" on it — Grandma said that Santa always insisted on secrecy. Then she drove me over to Bobbie Decker's house, explaining as we went that I was now and forever officially one of Santa's helpers.

Grandma parked down the street from Bobbie's house, and she and I crept noiselessly and hid in the bushes by his front walk. Then Grandma gave me a nudge. "All right, Santa Claus," she whispered, "get going."

I took a deep breath, dashed for his front door, threw the present down on his step, pounded his doorbell and flew back to the safety of the bushes and Grandma. Together we waited breathlessly in the darkness for the front door to open. Finally it did, and there stood Bobbie.

Forty years haven't dimmed the thrill of those moments spent shivering, beside my grandma, in Bobbie Decker's bushes. That night, I realized that those awful rumours about Santa Claus were just what Grandma said they were: ridiculous. Santa was alive and well, and we were on his team.

Carol Laycock
Lethbridge, Alberta

✉ My kids don't write much. I gather it is culturally inappropriate to write in the east. But every so often — or every so seldom, as I see it — they call. Recently, Drew, the youngest, phoned from Quebec City. He had called to tell me about an incident on a bus. He had struck up a conversation with an elderly man (quite possibly someone over fifty-five) who had lived right next door to Drew's less-than-posh address in the late forties. It was still a family neighbourhood then, and directly across the street, where there is now an abandoned store-front, he had worked for years in a bicycle sales and repair shop.

Reminiscing, he told Drew that those had been very tough times in Quebec. Unemployment was high, there were few social services, and many families in the area were struggling with poverty. Even so, he said, people were somehow kinder, more gentle then. For instance, he remembered when a skinny, ragged little boy, maybe four or five, used to wander into the shop almost every afternoon.

The first time he appeared, he just walked around the shop staring wide-eyed at the shiny new bikes on display. Then he looked up at the guy at the counter and lisped, "You got bikes!"

"Right," he was told, "and you can look, but don't touch." And he never did. All through the summer and fall, right into a fierce winter, he would quietly come in, scout the new bikes and then stand silently watching customers at the counter.

There were few calls for new bikes that hard winter. People would more usually come in to ask for a new bolt to be put here or there on their old bikes. And the little guy always listened and watched with solemn interest.

One day, close to Christmas, the boy came in, poorly bundled — shivering — and stood watching until there were no customers at the counter. Then he came right up to the front: his eyes barely topped the counter. Reaching up a badly mittened hand, he showed the sales clerk a rusty old bolt and whispered, "Will you put a bike on my bolt, please?"

He was still too young to know that causal sequences don't often reverse — like you grow big, but you don't grow small. I remember my kids thinking that way.

The man told Drew that the boys in the shop had a great laugh at that, and they told the little guy that that just wasn't the way things worked. They felt pretty badly after he was gone, though. He had looked surprised and even a little frightened by their laughter. Then he had put his head down and walked quickly out of the shop leaving the rusty bolt behind on the counter.

It was some time before the boy returned, but two days before Christmas, he slipped in and began his routine inspection of the bikes. He kept his eyes down this time, and he didn't come anywhere near the counter. He just stopped at each bike, gave it his usual serious attention and moved on. After he had looked at the entire display, he turned and quietly started to leave. But, just as he reached the door, one of the men shouted from the back room, "Hey kid, you forgot your bolt!"

And out of the back of the shop, they rolled a shiny kid's bike. They had built it from spare parts on their own time and painted it a bright, sparkling Christmas red.

Donna Moffatt,
Errington, British Columbia

THE 49-SECOND ESSAYIST: PART TWO, 1992–93

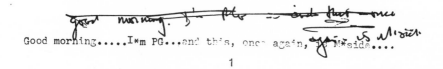

Good morning.....I*m PG...and this, once again, is M*side....

1

From ~~all~~ the montage of memories ~~that linger from~~ the summer that ends for me this morning, one stands out.

I was playing golf near Watson Lake in the Yukon. The course there, which is called Greenways Greens, is the work of one man, an ex-superintendent on the Alaska Highway, who took his own bulldozer to the Yukon bush a few years ago, and carved out nine holes for himself and his friends to enjoy.

Just as I was putting out my own round on this particular August morning, a helicopter appeared from the azure sky, and fluttered noisily down behind the ninth green--somewhat distracting, if you're trying to make a three-footer, but intriguing all the same. The pilot was a man named Ken Birss, who, when he is not flying choppers, sculpts powerful life-size figures out of hardwood. Ken invited a few of us for a ride. We took off from Greenway's Greens and headed a bit north of the B.C. border--which is marked on the landscape by a cleared line through the spruce and jackpine--and up the Liard River. In a canyon on the Liard we hovered for a while over the concrete memorial to the scientist and explorer George Mercer Dawson, the man

171

who first surveyed the border we had seen from the
air, and whose name marks so many Yukon sites.
Though we were ~~hovering~~ _sitting_ high enough for a raven to _in the air_

2

~~the soaring under~~ _soar beneath_ us, we were close enough to
Dawson's monument to read the inscription.   Born
1849, it said. Died 1901.

1901. My own grandfather was a teenager when
George Dawson died, and my father was born only ten
years later. To put it another way, 1901 is to me what,
say, nineteen _fifty_ - one is to my granddaughters, one
of whom starts school tomorrow--not really history,
but part of our own time.

Ken Birss waggled a lever, and the helicopter rose
again, a noisy magic carpet. We left the ravens and
joined the eagles. Below us, the tops of the poplars
were turning yellow against the scrubby bush. It had
snowed in Edmonton the day before, but here in the
north the air was golden with sunshine and sweet as
chardonnay. There never was a time this summer, I
am convinced, when any two places had the same
weather.

_As_ We swung east, I was still thinking about how
recently ~~it had all opened up.~~ _this country had been_ _to what we now call civilization._ _said now_

"You know," ~~said~~ _said_ Ken ~~Birss,~~ "if I overflew the golf
course we could go five hundred miles before we'd see
the mark of another human. People in the south
think we're running out of land. I guess they're right.
But up here, the wilderness goes on forever."

The sculpture Ken Birss is working on now, in fact, shows an American native in the forest, discovering the first foot-print of a European. Even that, when you think of it, doesn't seem so long ago.

172

September 15, 1992

It wouldn't have bothered Bruce Hutchison, the great journalist, that on the day he died — yesterday in Victoria, and peacefully in his sleep — Paul Martin, the great politician, died, too, and that's what made most of the news, including the tributes on *Morningside* yesterday, and *As It Happens* last night. Bruce Hutchison didn't make news; he wrote it. He wasn't a celebrity, though he was a confidant of every prime minister from Mackenzie King to the present; he was a reporter, a journalist, a writer. The fact that he knew — and understood, and loved, and wrote about — this country as well as anyone ever has was of no more concern to him (and probably less) than the joy his garden gave others or the house he built with his own hands gave him. He wrote *The Unknown Country* in 1942, after, I read this morning, a liquid lunch with some editors in New York (liquid lunches were not a part of his routine), but its rolling phrases and passionate insights stand up today, as do many of his other books and articles and columns. He was very wise. Bruce was ninety-one when he died, two years older than Paul Martin, and like Paul Martin, he leaves a rich legacy.

Bruce Hutchison, 1901–1992.

October 9,1992

If Robertson Davies wins the Nobel Prize, a friend of mine said yesterday morning, while the rumours were still flying and before the announcement came that it had gone instead to the West Indian poet and playwright Derek Walcott . . . if Davies wins the Nobel *and* Michael Ondaatje wins the Booker . . . *and* the Blue Jays win the World Series, the referendum will go about 80–20. Yes. A fanciful idea, of course — and that particular friend happens to be firmly in the Yes column — but I know exactly what lay behind it. You should have been here yesterday afternoon, when we spent an hour taking calls about what we had hoped to be the media's coverage of the constitutional debate, but which turned out instead to be mostly about the deal itself. People — the people who called us, anyway — are just upset. They don't understand the details. They want more time, more explanation. Whatever they make of what's in the accord, they sure don't like the politicians who forged it. Don't trust 'em. They're troubled, and they just want some good news. That's where the literary awards and the baseball fit in, I think. Robertson Davies — who Mordecai Richler says is the only Canadian who actually looks like a writer — got edged but Ondaatje's still alive, and he's the favourite. And how about those Blue Jays? Overpaid, over-hyped — but, wow, they're ours, aren't they — even without a single Canadian in their line-up? And when the immensely likeable Dave Winfield waves that toothpick in the air, or when the wonderfully skilled Robbie Alomar steals a base when everyone's looking at an intentional walk, or even when the latest rent-a-hero David Cone bears down and . . . well, you know what I mean. Wouldn't it be nice if life were that simple? Meantime, isn't it fun trying to root them home?

October 21, 1992

GOOD MORNING . . . I'M PG . . . THIS IS M'SIDE . . .

The only thing that could have made it better, surely . . . well, except for having the umps call that third guy out and make the first triple play I've ever seen a reality (and how about Devon White making that catch as he went up the padded wall like Spiderman . . . or how about the mighty slugger Dave Winfield laying down a *bunt* in the nail-biting ninth?) . . . the only thing that could have made it better would have been if Anne Murray had sung maybe just a line or two in French. I know, I know, it's a problem. But there was such a wonderful feeling in the SkyDome last night — or appeared to be from the vantage point of my living-room — that I don't think anyone would have been upset. Look, they cheered the Marine Corps' gracious gesture, didn't they? (Is there anyone left to apologize for that gaffe in Atlanta, do you think?) They practically cheered the *hot dog vendors*. And . . . well, it's just a thought.

November 16,1992
Sorry as I am to return to this usually happy job on a note of sadness, I can't, for the moment, shake the double whammy in the news this morning of the deaths, yesterday, of the man called Dr. Peter in Vancouver and, earlier on the weekend, the artist Greg Curnoe in London, Ontario. You'll remember Dr. Peter, I'm sure. He was on *Morningside* just two weeks ago, talking about the process by which he'd kept a television diary of his disease, and even if you hadn't seen those programs, you could hear in his voice the rare mixture of humour and courage and wisdom that kept him going. I thought of something a friend of mine said about AIDS — that it's like the First World War, when the best and brightest young men of a generation went up out of the trenches, and the rifles and the artillery shells picked off a future novelist here, a future prime minister there. Dr. Peter was thirty-five.

There was a random and senseless aspect to Greg Curnoe's death, too. Greg was bicycling — he was a passionate cyclist and the image you may know him best by is his multi-coloured profile of a bike — when a pick-up truck mowed down several members of his club, killing him and leaving others injured. He would have been fifty-six on Thursday. *He,* I learned to my regret this morning, hadn't been on *Morningside* for several years — I say regret because he was always good and unpredictable company. He is the star, in fact, of one of my favourite being-on-the-radio anecdotes, but because it's old history now and features one particularly naughty word, I'll tell you that some other time. For now, I just want to say I mourn his death.

December 4, 1992
We had a silver tea service in here once, you know. It would have been 1974 or so, I think (all our books are packed this morning, and there is no way to look things up), and the guest was Pierre Elliott Trudeau. We sort of dressed up for him — for him and his phalanx of men in suits, all of whom appeared to be wearing hearing aids. That was the time I asked him if he had ever considered that if the War Measures

Act had been imposed when he was a young activist lawyer in Montreal, then he might have gone to jail, and he replied . . . well, it doesn't matter — though he did use the word "bitch." The memories tumble this morning — our last day here, at 354 Jarvis St. On Monday, *Morningside* — and a lot of other programs — will begin originating from the brand new Broadcast Centre in downtown Toronto. But this has been home for longer than most of us can remember, and coming in here for the last time this morning, using the side door that, like so much of this rambling old red brick structure, has been rebuilt more often than a politician's ego, just brings back too many images to ignore.

I honestly don't remember if the silver tea service we rented was used in this studio, R, or next door, in E, where they now do *Stereo Morning*. This is where Judy LaMarsh had her Persian rug, though, when this part of the radio day was called *Judy*. This is where René Lévesque smoked a cigarette and yelled at me, and where Donna Williams turned the lights down. It's where Angela Hewitt played the piano and Moe Koffman did his jazz imitations, and where Stuart McLean and I burst into giggles. This is where Joe Clark, in his shirtsleeves, reminded me during a newsbreak that I had once turned him down for a job at *Maclean's*.

It was down the hall from here, in Studio F, where I talked with Lester Pearson. That was almost the last interview the man everyone called Mike was to give, and I can still remember his warmth and candour, and the twinkle in his eyes when we talked baseball. F is small. It was crowded in there when we had the entire membership of the Canadian Brass bring in their booty from a scavenger hunt we'd sent them on, and even more crowded when they filled the category of "a live furry creature," by bringing in Angelo Mosca of the Hamilton Tiger Cats. F is where Barbara started doing *As It Happens* in '71, and Bill Ronald and Phillip Forsyth Smith before her. Before *that*, Mark Starowicz and Warren Davis and I used to break out a bottle of scotch while the last hours of old *Radio Free Friday* — we used to sit here for six hours a night then, so we could insert some live items for each region — wended their way west.

I used to drink tea in *Radio Free Friday* days, from a Styrofoam container big enough for a milk shake, and one time, just as we were going to air, I spilled a whole, hot, fresh double-cupful into my lap and had no alternative but to excuse myself to Maggie Morris, who was sitting in for Warren that night, and pull my pants down.

I was a rookie then, but the awe I felt about this building's heritage is as real today as it was then. Lorne Greene read the news from here, you know, and, as he recalled one day years later, it was here where he returned for a guest appearance on an Andrew Allan drama and kept asking the control room if Andrew would want this, or if Andrew would mind if he did that line again, until Andrew Allan said over the PA, "Please tell Mr. Greene that Mr. Allan would like him to keep going and that afterward, Andrew will buy Lorne a drink."

This is where Alan McFee and Tommy Tweed set the clocks ahead. This is where Max Ferguson paced the halls, working out the unique genius of his one-man skits. This is where the Air Farce started, where Bruno Gerussi did Captain Canada, where Byng Whittaker said "Sssscooot," and then scooted across the street to the Celebrity Club. (Joe Austin, the actor, always said he was too well known to go to the Celebrity Club.) This is where Dodi Robb produced *Matinee*, where the Happy Gang knocked for admission, where John Drainie did *Jake and the Kid*, where J.B. McGeachy (Hamish to his friends), did *Now I Ask You*, with Morley Callaghan and Ralph Allen and James Bannerman, where Lister Sinclair wrote his plays, where Lucio Agostini composed his music, where Don Harron started as a child actor (so did Michele Landsberg, by the way), where Vicki Gabereau made her debut, where . . .

Enough, I guess. This was an old building even when I got here. I auditioned upstairs for a program to be called *In Dispute*, a kind of poor man's *Fighting Words* — Nathan Cohen used to work here, too — and later sat in for Bruno and, just down the hall, began my own first daily gig.

It was *This Country in the Morning* that Pierre Trudeau appeared on, and Danny Finkleman, and Helen Hutchison, and Bruno and Vicki and Andrew Allan and Elizabeth Webster and Yvon Deschamps and Maureen Forrester and Sylvia Tyson and Max and Allan and Lister and a lot of other people who have become part of my life — even after, as in some cases, they've left it. We did it here, and after it Michael Enright took over, and then Harry Brown and Maxine

Crook, and then Judy with her Persian rug and then the incomparable Don Harron and, eventually, me again. And now we'll take it all downtown. The move, as I say, is all but complete. Most of our books, which we packed this week, have already gone ahead of us — and the posters from our walls — I still have the original of "As Canadian as Possible Under The Circumstances" — and our files, our shelves and even the monitors by which we listen to ourselves each day. The trick now, I think as I prepare to do the last *Morningside* from here, is to wrap up the memories, and take them with us, too.

December 21, 1992
GOOD MORNING . . . I'M PG . . . THIS IS M'SIDE . . .
Weekend diary of a not-quite (this year) last-minute shopper. Saturday morning. Up and at 'em. Early bird gets the parking space. Hit the toy store. *Love* the toy store. Want to stay, want to play. Ah, well, spend, spend. Is there a recession? Owner says sold only one copy of $2,500 rocking horse. Not to me, I can tell you. Buy instead . . . can't tell you. Too many radios on. Hit cookbook store. Having good Christmas. No wonder. Cheap, practical, fun. Curse *Morningside* anyway. *Surreal Gourmet* sold out. Should learn to shop first, interview later — or keep big trap shut. Move on. Mystery store. Curse *Morningside* again. But — look, over there. Good. Dangerous in here. See too many things *I'd* like. Give to *close* relatives, I guess.

Noon now. Been making trips to car. New meaning to fill 'er up. Other drivers look enviously at parking spot. Look *angrily* when I deposit parcels and go back for more. Into the spirit now. Burning plastic. Buying for kids like sawing legs off table. Have to keep evening up. Tough. Home.

Next day. Normally, have mixed feelings on Sunday shopping. Not at Christmas. Whoopee. Fill in blanks. Even up table legs. One store — there *is* a recession — offers thirty per cent off sweaters, but fifty per cent if you draw red ball from closed bag. Get lucky. Too smart to try again. Go, go. Shop, shop. Three P.M. Drop, drop. Four days left. Phew.

January 5, 1993

GOOD MORNING . . . I'M PG . . . THIS IS M'SIDE . . .

I remember a couple of summers ago, not quite a year after the government had changed in Ontario, when both Bob Rae, who'd won the election, and David Peterson, the man he'd beaten, showed up at an event where I happened to be. You couldn't help noticing the difference. Premier Rae, who'd been whisked up by helicopter, looked tired and drawn. Pale. David Peterson, by contrast — who was wearing cowboy boots and an open-necked shirt — was tanned and fit. Smiling. Relaxed. Who, you couldn't help wondering, had won — and who had lost?

I was thinking about that this morning. Grant Devine is in our Regina studio, awaiting a kind of exit interview about his days as premier, and, though I can't see him, my guess is he's feeling pretty chipper.

January 15, 1993

GOOD MORNING . . . I'M PG . . . THIS IS M'SIDE . . .

They were orange, Nick Harris says, burnt orange, and not the pale green that somehow sticks in my memory. Nick's probably right, too. He worked there, after all, and I just used to visit. "There" is CKGB, the radio station that used to be upstairs from the *Timmins Daily Press*, the newspaper where both Roy Thomson (he owned it) and I (I was a callow reporter) got our start. "They" were the leather couches in the lounge at CKGB. I used to go up there after work and listen to, for instance, *Stage 54* — CKGB was a CBC affiliate. *That* memory's clear, and so, I learned yesterday, when I returned to Timmins, are a thousand others. They came rolling back as I drove past the Esquire restaurant, where we used to go for coffee after we'd put the *Press* to press (that's where, on the day I got my first byline, I blurted out my name instead of my order when the waitress asked me what I'd like) or when, later on, I squeaked across the snow in the crystal northern air, and remembered walking Norma Andreghetti home after the Jeunesses Musicales concert I was supposed to review. (I faked that review, as it happens, and, when I learned the next day that the concert had been cancelled, absorbed a lesson about newspapering I've never forgotten), or when I . . . well, enough. The couches were orange, and they're not upstairs any more.

January 27, 1993

GOOD MORNING . . . I'M PG . . . THIS IS M'SIDE . . .

The day will come, I suppose, when we'll no longer notice that Madame Quelqu'une was the first woman to do that, or Ms. Someone Else the first woman to become whatever. By then, women will have broken all the barriers — my own guess, for what it's worth, is that the last of the firsts will be the presidency of a major bank — and we'll just honour people who do things for what they've achieved as *people*. But that day is certainly not here yet, and, quite properly, the tributes to Mme. Jeanne Sauvé, who died yesterday in Montreal, remind us of her impressive "firsts." Does this diminish her memory? On the contrary, I'd say. It's hard not to think that just as Jackie Robinson, the man chosen to break the colour barrier in professional baseball, had to be not only a good player but a great one, as well as a remarkable human being off the field, so too have many of the women "firsts" had to be not *equal* to their male counterparts, but *better than* them. Surely that discriminatory principle is doomed too. So — let's recognize all the women who, like her, have helped to pave the way for a future that ought to be.

February 15, 1993

GOOD MORNING . . . I'M PG . . . THIS IS M'SIDE . . .

Short sentences. No asides. Don't say, for example, "Dare I say." There. That's got it. *Double Exposure* did me on Saturday. Very funny, unfortunately. Had me here. Reading billboards. Had me doing *looongg* . . . sentences. Lots of asides. I'll fool 'em, I said. How's this? Too bad, though. Lots to say today. Stuart first. Then Quebec. Then Russia. Hour two? Willy Russell. He's the playwright. Wrote *Educating Rita*. Wrote *Shirley Valentine*, too. After that native justice. On the one hand, more "traditional" sentencing. On the other: native women, who want, in particular, harsher terms for abusers. Then, in hour three, two people who collect coupons. And I mean *collect*. One of them has won a scholarship for her daughter, two bikes, a computer, a VCR and . . . oops, there I go again running on. Next thing you know I'll say — dare I say? — dare I say.

March 18, 1993

GOOD MORNING . . . I'M PG . . . THIS IS M'SIDE . . .

True to his word, Robertson Cochrane, the *Globe and Mail*'s word columnist, has boned up on scurryfunging for us. "I found it in the OED2," he faxes, "described as a 'jocular formation . . . with little or no discoverable connexion'" — (there's an x in that connexion by the way).

Is this making any sense to you? If you missed yesterday's class, Robertson Cochrane was here with his new book. I offered him, as a little gift, a new (to him) word, scurryfunging, which in turn had come to us from Rhonda Porter, of Richmond, British Columbia, as part of our recent scholarly foray into toothbrushes, which scurryfungers once were — except that Robertson Cochrane, who dashed from *Morningside* to his library, found another use, from *Punch* in 1894, which used it to mean wriggling or squirming, as in "So he scurryfunged around with his stomach on the ground" (there's a song in there somewhere, I think). Anyway, that's that, except Bob Cochrane also discovered the verb to "fungify," meaning to fulfil or perform a certain function in office, and if I don't fungify what I'm paid to do here quickly, we'll never get to spring, will we?

April 19, 1993

GOOD MORNING . . . I'M PG . . . THIS IS M'SIDE FROM YELLOWKNIFE

One of the people on the plane that brought us here from Edmonton on Saturday was a kind of commuter. He lives in Nanaimo, but his job is tending a power plant on a dam a little north of here. His weekends — one of which had just ended — are fourteen days long, and when he gets to Yellowknife he stops only to pick up groceries for twenty-seven days, then boards a chopper to go to his lonely work. Says the fishing's good, though; in summer (which is not far off), the whitefish come right up to the dam, and he's taken as many as seven in an hour on his barbless hook. Someone else was barely setting down in Yellowknife, before boarding another flight to Gjoa Haven, east of Coppermine, where he'd set up a team of local women to help him conduct a survey on diet and nutrition in the north: how many helpings of Cheez Whiz did you have yesterday, how many caribou eyes? It's important; his wife's working Baffin Island this week and they'll be feeding the results into a computer this summer in Campbell's Bay, Quebec. At breakfast in the hotel there was a guy who'd been conducting written scholarship exams for Trinity College School in Port Hope, Ontario, but he also told me the new second nine at Twin Rivers, Newfoundland, is just as tough as the first, where people fishing the salmon stream have to wear hard hats to protect themselves from flying golf balls. The three women at the table next to me were speaking French, and the five men behind me German, but when I fell into conversation with Abraham Reuben, a sculptor who grew up in Paulatuk, but now lives in Saltspring Island, where his wife is expecting her first llama to stock their mountainside farm, he told me he was just back from Siberia where he'd needed simultaneous translation in — I think I have this right — Saha, Evenk, Even, Nolgan and Yukagir — to hold discussions on a circumpolar art exhibition he's working on.

And so on and so on. I sometimes think, on my all-too-infrequent sojourns into the north, that everyone here has a story. Northerners certainly travel more than the rest of us — even the people who grew up here on the land when they travelled all the time. And those who are drawn north by the same magnetic pull that brings me back year after year seem to keep moving. A guy could write a book, I sometimes think, just setting up shop over a coffee-pot somewhere, and writing down the tales of everyone who happened by.

April 20, 1993
GOOD MORNING . . . I'M PG . . . FROM YELLOWKNIFE, NWT, THIS IS M'SIDE . . .
Excerpts from a northern diary, day — what? — anyway, yesterday.

Hotel phone rings alarmingly early. High tech reached here long ago. This week, in fact, is the twentieth anniversary of the satellite *Anik II*. There are pineapple slices next to your flapjacks if you hang around for breakfast, and to leave a wake-up call you just punch a code into your touchtone. Works, too, though I'm old enough to remember human voices. Flick on TV. Very southern. Very American. Not *quite* Bruce Springsteen's fifty-seven channels and nothin' on, but not much Inuktitut either. Good to see Maple Leafs will open quest for Stanley Cup on one of our local stations tonight. Detroit. Thanks, *Anik*.

Still another glorious day in the offing. In spite of these difficult hours — it may be nine thirty-five in Newfoundland when we hit the air in a few hours but it's just after six here in Yellowknife — the sun is up (and I mean *up*) long before we roll the theme.

Three forty-five. Quick shower. Another ten minutes saved not shaving. Feel like part of the majority here. Even when there's no carnival going on — they were worried about having enough snow for the ski races a couple of weeks ago — I'm sure more guys have beards in the north than elsewhere. La, de dah, off to the salt mines. CBC Yellowknife feels like a good place to work. The Atrium's a bit smaller than at the Broadcast Centre in Toronto, but the pictures are nicer. People get on with each other here — in a lot of languages. After *Morningside* finishes this morning — nine o'clock and we're through for the day — there'll be a home-made breakfast brought in by the staff. Smoked char, caribou ribs, muk-tuk, quiche. Traditional Métis quiche, says George Tuckaroo, of the Dene language unit, pouring some home-made maple syrup onto his bannock.

Program goes well — or so I think; I get buoyed up here. Still can't figure out why more Canadians don't come north for holidays. Not cheap, of course — but neither is Amsterdam. Ah, well, their loss.

After breakfast, a bit more work. Tape this, tape that. To union headquarters to hear their side of the most bitter strike I've ever dealt with. Can't get away from it. Even interview with pleasant reporter from local paper turns, eventually, to the strike. On the day of the explosion, she says, last September, she didn't know what her role should be. Bought doughnuts for her colleagues. Dropped into pub on way to office. Dead silence. Two guys squaring off. Fists raised. One backed into her, crushing doughnuts. "Can't you see you're shoving that woman?" someone yelled. "Sorry, lady," said one combatant and threw a fist past her ear at his opponent. Not funny. *Everybody* here has been touched by this strike. Still, it's Yellowknife — and the north. After lunch off to Yellowknife River, patches of open water showing now, to look for birds for Tuesday's program. Guide says we're in luck. Year's first ducks just sighted. Four of them. Clamber awkwardly to top of rock. City shoes slip. No ducks. Sunshine, though, and the freshest spring air in God's universe.

Busy, busy. Quick nap. Dinner with old friends. More caribou, more char, more muk-tuk. Pass on muk-tuk — which is whale blubber, when you get right down to it — though someone says try soy sauce on it. Try Caesar salad instead. Kids eat with us. Why not? Kids part of *everything* here. Swap grandparent yarns with woman I've known since first trip here. Think Arctic air preserves youth.

Nine o'clock. Off to bed. Leafs lose. TV depressing. Night, night. Sun still shining.

May 6, 1993

GOOD MORNING . . . I'M PG . . . THIS IS M'SIDE . . .

One time in another life, when I was writing a column for the *Toronto Star*, I decided to investigate — honestly, this was in the name of journalism — the then current local phenomenon of luncheon establishments where the waitresses worked with their bosoms, shall we say, alfresco. On a hunch, and a tad too self-conscious to venture into such waters by myself, I invited to accompany me a colleague I both liked and admired — and occasionally feared, if you want to know the truth. The colleague was the cartoonist Duncan Macpherson. I picked him up in the spacious office from which he viewed the world through his peculiar, piercing lens. He tucked his sketch pad under his arm, and we ambled off into the noonday sun. When we reached our destination, Macpherson — even now, the day after his death, it's hard to think of him as Duncan — drew not the shirtless subjects of my intrepid reportage, but me, seated at a table, though there is, in the background, a detached and solitary figure, with a tray, one bra-less breast jutting over my shoulder as I pretend to scribble a note. I look

— what? — perplexed. It's very funny, and I treasure the drawing, which I pocketed instantly, as I treasured Macpherson's genius.

That sketch, in a way, was typical of him. He drew what he saw, and what amused or offended him, and he drew always with unerring brilliance. There may have been — there may still be — other cartoonists in our history whose comments equal his for wit or insight, but none could or can — or, perhaps, ever will — draw as well as he. He drew politicians and statesmen — remember John Diefenbaker as Marie Antoinette, or LBJ as an eagle — and a kind of everyman who looked, for all the world, like Robert Thomas Allen, whose articles he used to illustrate for *Maclean's*. But he never drew, as someone said, hairy monsters called war.

He was as much an artist as a cartoonist and his death, at sixty-eight, from cancer, leaves a void.

A Little Chapter on
Being Big

Some weighty opinions from a large minority.

✉ The notion that I am simply an extension of the person who gains twenty extra pounds by eating a bit too much is *wrong!* I have never been a so-called "normal" weight — not even for one day. My mother was dying of a chronic infection before I was born, yet I weighed almost eleven pounds (and was very short). I had a grandmother who was very large (and who died in her late seventies of cancer, not heart failure). I shared this grandmother with four half-sisters who grew up in a different home than I did. One of these girls was downright scrawny, two were of a shape considered perfect, and one looked like me. The mother of these girls, knowing me, put this child on an extremely restricted diet before she was six months old; the result was an adult of about two hundred pounds who gained weight once she left her mother's starvation regime. One of my "perfect" semi-sibs had one child with the family curse; remembering her sister crying herself to sleep from hunger, she decided to go the exercise route. My half-niece became a swimmer and swam a few local lakes; she grew up to become two hundred fifty pounds of solid muscle. As for me, I have tried everything, and this included complete fasting for thirty days in hospital. And, no, I did not lie in bed for thirty days! I was up and dressed; I helped the nurses make beds, I looked after the flowers, I ran errands around the building, I kept water flasks full, all on medical orders. My weight swung wildly for the first three or four days and then it settled down to a steady loss of just over a pound a week. After thirty days of zero caloric intake, I had a weight loss of six pounds; at that rate, I would have to go completely without food for well over two years.

My earliest memory, probably from age three or so, was of a woman looking down at me and saying, "Such a shame . . . her mother was so pretty." I almost was sent to an institution for the severely retarded at age five because I had a low thyroid test (I have had seven of those over my lifetime, with two low, two high and three in the middle grey area), and the doctor believed this proved that I was abnormal; as luck would have it, I taught myself how to read while an institution was being arranged, so I was not sent away. Incidentally, I have taken thyroid pills many times with absolutely no change. A very kind teacher in about grade four thought she was giving me good advice when she suggested a circus as a place where I could earn a good living when I grew up. The people who raised me did allow me to stay in school past my sixteenth birthday, thank goodness! As they said, no man was ever going to marry me, so I needed to finish school. I went off to university on my own. I got a job and then I got another job and I discovered that not all men wanted to stay away from me. And then I married a wonderful person who is still around after almost forty years. However, to get a diaphragm before I got married, I had to go to the only Protestant doctor around, and he didn't want to give me one because he didn't support "unnecessary" medical devices. He said, "No man in his right mind will have sex with you." Medical types are really something! One kept me waiting in his office for two hours and was astonished that I went that long without eating; he had calculated, using "foolproof equations," that going two hours without food would lead to a drop of over five pounds, and he couldn't understand how come there wasn't a difference in the two weights his nurse had got that afternoon; he finally decided I had nibbled on chocolate when her back was turned. Then there was the one who I made the mistake of convincing that I didn't eat more than my thin husband did; he concluded that since I really believed that I didn't eat all the time, I was out of touch with reality and therefore mentally ill. It took years to shake that diagnosis from my files. And nurses! They think nothing of making jokes standing beside my bed. One seriously told me that there was something in skim milk that would make me lose weight; curious, I asked her if this magic ingredient was in unskimmed milk, and she assured me that it wasn't. I now avoid the medical profession as much as possible.

And then there are others. They are the religious types who come to me on the street and give me a Bible, urging me to forsake the sin of gluttony. There was the little grey-haired lady who had the seat beside me at a public event and who spent the first hour telling me to commit suicide. There are the hundreds of people who assume that I am mentally retarded. Almost everyone I meet is astonished to find out that I have a grandchild — they can't believe I have children, because they can't believe I have a husband, let alone the one I do have, who is somebody any woman with any sense would be glad to have.

Anonymous
The Maritimes

✉ I weigh one hundred ninety-one pounds.

This comes as the most incredible and awful shock to me, a person who has dieted, watched weight, been careful, managed to keep the sugar and butter out of my cooking, since being told I was overweight by a doctor in 1954.

I have struggled to maintain my weight for almost forty years.

I did an excellent job, too, vacillating between one hundred fifty and one hundred sixty-five. What I didn't know was that I looked really very acceptable. I am five feet eight and a half inches tall, and looking back to the photographs I have around the house, I see that I looked just fine, thank you.

For forty years, I looked fine, but never believed it.

I was always wanting to lose that extra ten pounds.

But now I am an older woman. I believe I am becoming wiser. I have allowed myself to find my levelling-off point. I am eating what I want and feel better about myself because I am not depriving myself of daily marmalade on my toast, dessert when I want it, or buttered popcorn with TV.

I can't believe how freeing it is.

I feel like a wise old woman of the tribe who looks like a woman is allowed to look, fat belly (and why not after birthing and nursing four babies), heavy thighs and pendulous breasts.

I look about me and see that I am definitely not alone.

Mufty Mathewson
Edmonton

✉ Over two hundred pounds — two hundred twenty-two and a half pounds and five foot three inches, to be exact.

They say I was born hungry. Almost nine pounds at birth. "Big for a girl." Family photographs show a serious three-year-old with huge eyes and skinny legs. Perhaps the camera lied. I was "too big." "Too big" to be cuddled, "too big" to be carried, "too big" to sit on somebody's lap, "too big" to be loved. Paradoxically, my curious questions went unanswered as I was told I would only be let in on adult secrets when I was "bigger." So I grew. I become "chubby." In desperation, my mother canvassed relatives for their neighbours' children's cast-off clothes, in an attempt to clothe this big little girl, too big for her skinny sisters' hand-me-downs. At age nine, it was decided I was no longer "pleasantly" plump; the family doctor put me on my first diet. It felt like severe punishment in the absence of an offence. I cried in the doctor's office. I subsequently lost the requisite ten pounds and earned the two-piece bathing suit I did not really want. I still shudder at skim milk and celery sticks.

They say fat people do not have will-power. I dieted. I lost twenty-five pounds and regained thirty-five. Lost twenty and regained thirty. Lost another twenty and regained thirty-five, lost thirty and regained fifty. I even lost fifty and regained eighty. I still thought I was lazy and undisciplined. I dieted for eighteen years and put my life on hold, waiting till I was thin. I could not go out and dance or play tennis or run or go to exercise class or swim or talk to men because I had to wait till I was thin because fat girls were not allowed. I dieted for eighteen years. Eighteen years in which seldom an hour of wakefulness went by during which I did not think of my twin enemies: food and my fat.

I have quit. Quit wasting so much energy on one small detail in my life. Therapy helped: I began to feel good about myself in other ways, and began, despite all logic, to "think thin." I began to give permission to myself to live, even though I was still fat. I started to taste food and enjoy it, and even to eat in public without feeling self-consciously embarrassed at every mouthful. And I started to go out and do those things I had always wanted to do.

I ski and go country dancing. I work out, play volleyball, make pottery. I am learning to play the congas and the saxophone and have gained a reputation as an amateur singer. I built my own six-teen-foot cedar epoxy canoe and take it wilderness tripping; I have carried it on my shoulders a kilometre over a rocky portage. I earned my Master's degree and am an ESL teacher and I own my own home. *And I'm still fat!*

I still have huge brown eyes. My hair is thick and extraordinarily shiny and soft. I have a pretty face and a friendly manner and nice clothes that fit. My goals have become health and fitness, not thin. But I would like to feel attractive to men. I have felt attractive for short bursts of time, once even feeling attractive for an entire evening. Occasionally it is a non-issue. Usually, I feel men consider me a pleasant, interesting-to-talk-to woman whom they would never imagine holding in a tender embrace. I spent the first thirty-five years of my life believing I was physically repulsive, so that those men who were not loath to touch me did not count, as if they were perverts or just too blinded by their temporary lust to see me as I was. Too big.

If I were monarch for a day, I would decree that clothing sizes be changed. In the past, I always knew I had really lost a lot of weight when I could finally fit into a size large. (My best friend of twenty-six years is willowy slim and she wears "large" underwear!) Now I must shop in specialty stores that have euphemistic sizes that start at size one. (I am a four.) As monarch for a day, I would decree equal-opportunity body sizes in advertising and magazine illustrations, television and movies. Plump people selling toothpaste, big people in sitcoms not about big people. Tall, short, fat, thin, pear-shaped, round, robust, big, none would be too big, too anything, just different. Like flowers in a garden, fruit from an orchard, same yet different, appreciated for their uniqueness, all loved for who they are, not judged for what they are not.

I now have many ways of describing myself. I am a Baha'i, a teacher, a singer, musician, dancer, potter, canoe builder and wilderness explorer, a friend, lover, and a sane, independent woman. I am still fat, but I am strong and healthy.

Bonnie Cook
Dundas, Ontario

How to Sail, Play Golf, Ride Your Bike and a Whole Lot of Other Things All Winter without Actually Leaving the House

Or, for that matter, moving to Vancouver — though George Bowering, who writes about baseball, is already there. (One of the most commented upon billboards I wrote during one of the long cold winters covered by this book began, "That settles it. I'm moving to Vancouver.")

These are, mostly, commissioned essays. We just asked writers we knew who were passionate about *summer* pastimes to share some of the reveries they use to get through the darkest days.

✉ The Bloodvein. The Thelon. Missinaibi. Fond du Lac. The names echo in midwinter, and they recall places you have been; places that have stayed with you all of your life.

I think of them. Every time I get in my car I play "The Grand River Song" from Labrador, just so I can hear the line "poling up Gull Island Rapids in canoes." I meet friends at Quinn's to talk about July, I write away for maps and I write Alex Hall in Fort Smith, Northwest Territories. I think of Samuel Hearne and David Thompson, and I reread them: I make plans.

But the greatest gift canoeing can give in February is, ironically, an immediate response to the season you inhabit. In a canoe you can't help but feel the body of the country, notice the shapes of islands or hills, hear the cries of birds and wind, respond fervently to the hundreds of small things that make up the world about you. Having been taught, or given, this way of looking at the world, February becomes, not a dream of change, not a longing for the cry of a white-throated sparrow that, somehow, will obviate all in its song; no, February becomes itself.

There are the obvious things, like emerging from work and finding the afternoon brilliant, sun on the contours of snow; or driving your son to hockey practice in the evening and noticing how much longer the day is, the sore-looking winter sunset later every week. There is still cloud that will last and last, long into March; low sky and raw cold, gloom and salt-mist and ice. People fall and break their wrists; black slush drops off cars in underground parking garages, and all the world can seem coloured by the filthy light.

But there is also, if you look, a touch of lavender in the lengthening days; even in a snow squall there is an internal brightening, a luminosity, an opening up; things *are* alive.

If you really move in the cold it will make you feel wonderful. Sure, you can sweat and get a chill that won't seem to go away; you can also go inside and feel yourself get warm, light a fire, sleep under many blankets, and imagine the blue Arctic outside — that's where the wind you hear came from — and realize just how safe you are.

Hundreds of years ago, when Jacques Cartier saw Labrador and the north shore of the St. Lawrence, he called it "the land God gave to Cain." No sane human being would deny our place here is formidable country in a long winter. The rocks and ice share a similar hardness; there isn't a lot to eat. But when I look at February, and open water seems an idea, an abstraction, I recall the attitude that was communicated to Father Paul Le Jeune in the earliest of our literature, an attitude that helped save his life.

In 1633 Father Le Jeune spent a winter with the Montagnais, now called the Innu. He wrote about it in *The Jesuit Relations*. Le Jeune was ill, and he was what we would call depressed, what an earlier time would call a black night of the soul. If, according to his theology, the moral world was in depravity, then how much more absent God must have seemed when the physical universe had turned to monochrome iron and famine. But God, or hope, the spirit of place, whatever you want to call it, showed itself to Le Jeune in the words of his companions, the native people who made him appreciate where he really was:

"Do not be sad; if thou are sad, thou wilt become still worse; if thy sickness increases thou wilt die. See what a beautiful country this is; *love it*; if thou lovest it, thou wilt take pleasure in it, and if thou takest pleasure in it thou wilt become cheerful, and if thou art cheerful thou wilt truly live."

M.T. Kelly
Toronto

✉ As I gaze out my studio window overlooking the snow-covered garden, the radio drones on about yet another snowstorm, yet another day of subzero weather. It seems endless. One freezing, dreary day after another. Who wants to go out in such weather? It's a penguin's paradise out there, a polar bear's utopia. But for us thin-skinned urban humanoids, hell *has* frozen over.

But, still, I distinctly sense a lurking presence down two flights of stairs, at the far end of the wine, potato, and herb cellar, wedged in behind a jumble of cross-country skis, skates, and hockey sticks, gleaming faintly in the dark and shivering slightly with well-concealed impatience: my bicycle! My springtime, summertime inspiration! Panacea for any writer's block! A sleek extension of my No. 4 Finest Sable Winsor & Newton paintbrush. Most days, every day, I write and illustrate for six or seven hours in a row, without moving, wrapped in the haze of the world I am creating: a paper world, a two-dimensional world. My fingers cramp, my legs are numb and my back aches. But on bright spring days, when I run out of creative energy, I throw on my shorts, T-shirt and baseball cap, run downstairs, jump onto my bicycle and wheel off into the wind and sunlight and speed and sounds and smells of the day. A solitary artist re-enters the world. . . .

I head for Mont-Royal, Montreal's beloved mountain, rolling under the bright green arcs of the newly leafed trees, past grey churches and secret synagogues. People are out! Everywhere! Heads thrown back, smiling faces pale in the white sunlight, walking slowly, slowly, for the first time in months. Shoulders dehunched, coats open, chatting on street corners or sipping an espresso at a sidewalk café in the early afternoon. Everyone calls in sick at work on those first warm days — those who still work, that is. I buy a warm bagel at La Boulangerie Cachère and ride up Avenue du Parc, swerving between buses and cars, their windows rolled down, Greek music blaring, hefty arms hanging out to catch the rays. Past Jeanne-Mance Park: the first baseball game of the season is in progress, the players lunging awkwardly for the ball, slipping on the damp grass. Then I turn sharply onto the winding mountain road that ends at the foot of the towering multi-bulbed cross.

All of a sudden the air is silent and green. It smells of last autumn's wet leaves and this spring's new grass. My legs aren't cramped anymore. I change gears with a satisfying click! My heart beats in rhythm with my pumping legs. I change gears again and I feel lighter than air. Going from chilly purple shadows to blinding warm sunlight, up past the giant stairs, past the stone watering trough, above Lac aux Castors, where dozens of people are stretched out on blankets: the first suntan! Past the 1960s' sculpture garden, then up, up the steepest ascent and finally circling around the belvedere overlooking this beautiful, glowing city basking by the St. Lawrence River, the many silver bridges, the tree-lined cemetery that always reminds me of Italy. I am breathing hard, my face flushed red with the sun and exertion, beads of sweat rolling down my back.

Just in time, I begin the long, cool descent, swooping and gliding between dogs and joggers, seagulls, squirrels and even fat old raccoons sauntering along the way. Mustn't brake too fast on the rutted gravel road. . . .

Leaving the mountain, I head towards Parc Lafontaine, taking a bicycle lane. This is easier going, except at the intersections, where cars and cyclists alike ignore all signs, signals, or lights. A cacophony of horns, squealing brakes, and *"Nom de dieu!"* Then I ride once around the park on the designated path under a long sinuous green leafy tunnel, then around the lake with an eye out for the park police:

cycling is not allowed here, but the view is beautiful. Green and black ducks glistening in the sun as they paddle around in circles. Teen-agers smoking and strumming guitars. The first ice-cream vendor of the season!

Ice-cream cone in hand, I pedal precariously through the Plateau, up busy Boulevard Saint-Joseph, skirt the mountain and glide home. My bicycle does not go back into the basement. No, it will await impatiently by the door until the next escapade. I'll go up to my studio and put down on paper the colours of spring.

I glance out the window. It's still snowing. Big fat snowflakes against a pearly-white sky.

Marie-Louise Gay
Montreal

✉ Vancouver people don't like being inside the house. As I sit inside my house on this early February day, wondering whether I can wait another two weeks to get out on the ball field, I cast my mind back three months to the last time I was on the field. Oh, the mind is a wonderful thing. The body, on the other hand, leaves something to be desired.

That's not quite right. I think I have seen a few bodies that bring the idea of desire up. Let's say that *my* body leaves something to be desired. At least for someone who has to live inside it. Living inside this body, which I have done, incidentally, for more than half a cen-tury, keeps me in touch with last summer. Let's be more specific: with last ball season.

For instance, my left hand. Sometimes I bang my left hand against a door jamb, and then I say something in a theological manner. This is because last July I got my left hand broken by a moron who kept run-ning instead of sliding while he was trying to steal second base. A large moron. I got a perfect throw from our catcher and the large moron ran his leg bones right into the tag. I knew my hand was bro-ken, but I figured shock would make everything all right till after the game. Next two times up I bunted and drew a walk. But in the last inning we had the winning run on base, so I bit down hard on my imitation chewing tobacco and hit a liner over the drawn-in left fielder. We won, and I drove to the University hospital. "You again?" asked the admitting nurse.

I also have a dark thing that used to be a bruise and is now a scar on my right knee. That's from the diving stab at a grounder I didn't make in the same game, an inning after I broke the hand that was now pretty snug in my glove.

Over the years on Vancouver ball diamonds, I have broken a toe and a nose and a wrist and a cheek-bone. I've got a concussion during the annual New Year's Day game. I've had a bruise that ran from my knee down to my foot and up to my pain threshold. Baseball's been very good to me.

That's why I long for summer. In summer the sun shines and the puddle disappears from the batter's box, and that familiar phrase rings out across the park: "Did you bring the Ben-Gay?"

I remember the summer and I long for the next one, but even I will admit that I am not really in the summer of my life. For years now people have been telling me I'm too old to play ball. My family tells me that. My own team tells me that. Once a bookstore clerk I had never met before told me that.

But my hero is the Mexican mural painter David Alfaro Siqueiros. The Mexican government jailed and exiled him seven times for being a leftist activist. The last time they let him out he was sixty-five years old. There were four thousand people waiting outside the prison. They had already rented the biggest theatre in Mexico City for the celebration and fiery speeches. The official release time was noon. But this was summer. Siqueiros said he wasn't coming out till the game was over. He was a sixty-five-year-old first baseman, and his team was in the pennant race.

I'm the oldest guy in my league now, and I always did run the bases like a sewing machine. But I make up in savvy what I don't have in acceleration. Here in February, the trunk of my Volvo is already loaded down with bats and balls and gloves and neat's-foot oil and batting gloves and baseball hats and a catcher's mask. For the past two summers I have even added a deck chair.

No, no, I didn't say rocking chair.

And I bought a new Rawlings Spin-Stopper bat. It cost me more than I told my wife, and it's top quality. It'll be good for years.

George "Whip" Bowering
Vancouver

✉ I snip the thread from the grasshopper fly I have finished. Severed from its creator, like a newborn from its mother. Full of hope it sits.

I have plans for you, grasshopper. A voice from the radio informs me that it's 3:00 A.M. and twenty below outside. Frigid February.

I rub my feet together, below my fly-tying bench. The woollen socks feel toasty. It's on nights like these that I wish Vivaldi had only three sources of inspiration, not four. What I'd give for an ultraviolet index reading, instead of another wind-chill warning.

It's a nightmare out there.

I gently remove the fly from the vise and look at it.

A grasshopper.

Summer.

I hear and feel the water against my waders. A full harvest moon hangs in a July night. Bright enough that I didn't need to use a light when I tied the fly to my line.

I stand knee deep in life, the grasshopper secured to the line, nestled in my hand.

My eyes see shadows and greenery — not snow-drifts.

The not-too-distant howling of coyotes replaces the howling blizzard.

I wonder if they swim in packs and mug fly-fisherman. I've been fishing along a half mile of river and it's only 3:00 A.M. I've still got the rest of the night to fish. The fly rod, the line and my arm move as one. The line makes a gentle woosh as it slides through the rod guides. I can just hear it above the gurgle of the river as I wade slowly downstream.

Gone are the tentative find-your-feet-again steps of spring. The pre-kindergarten-kid in the snowsuit waddle is replaced by a firm purposeful shuffle.

The rod bends and breathes with the rhythm of my casting.

The river is no longer the solid, silent, white winter ribbon, it now flows with life.

The snowmobile tracks are gone, replaced by raccoon footprints and my own, in the mud. I miss those little guys in March.

The line pulls the fly across a cloudless sky. It lands near the bank with a plop. There's a swirl. I lift the rod. The line momentarily becomes alive. It is no longer solely mine. The bass is gone. Too slow! My laughter drifts down river and is lost around a bend.

Once again I am alone.

There are pike downstream.

I know this river with the intimacy of a lover. We fished here daily over the last thirteen summers. This is where I go on those can't-sleep sticky summer nights.

The river tolerates me and I sometimes fit in.

There are bottles of fly line cleaner and insect repellent on the front seat of the wagon, not bottles of gas-line antifreeze. There's a growing pile of empty coffee cups on the floor. Sandwiches taste better here. Sitting mid-stream on a rock, watching bats and night-hawks hunting moths.

Listening to the noise of life. The river, the chirp of the crickets, the frogs, and the occasional splash of a beaver-tail.

Gone is the whirr of Howdy Doody's bald car tires, spinning on the black ice outside my fly-tying studio.

I miss the marsh gas.

The smell and the feel of the swamp. Crunching through bull-rushes. Fly-fishing for carp. Thinking about it makes me want to roll in the stuff, waders and all, in some primeval Pavlovian response. God I'm suffering from midwinter quagmire withdrawal.

By the time I fish down to where the pike are, it will almost be light. The grasshopper fly will be replaced with a mud puppy or a Zontcar. Something big and ugly to get their attention.

The sky will have its pre-dawn colours. The fly slips quietly below the surface of a slow pool at the end of a long cast. The fireflies, like the stars, will soon be gone, kingfishers and ospreys taking their place. The second snag is a fish, white and green. Pike looks angry when the fly is removed and I watch it swim away.

I reel in and start the long trek back to the car, dodging the dew-covered webs in the long grass. The ones with the big black and yellow spiders. The webs are as pretty as snowflakes before the dew melts in the sun. I try not to damage them, although I do like to dangle the occasional fake fly in them to see what happens.

I won't have to turn on the heater or scrape the ice from the car windows. I strip off my waders and put them in the car. The door closes with a satisfied click.

Maybe breakfast at a truck stop, perhaps grab a coffee to go. After all, it's just past 7:00 A.M. I know a great spot for crappies and rock bass on my way home.

I've boxes, brimming with small woolly buggers, winkies and mickey finns in just the right size. I could take my wind-surfer out, and go fly-fishing for largemouth bass. Naw! I'm too lazy to lift the board onto my roof racks.

Another empty coffee cup adds to the pile on the passenger-seat floor. Vivaldi is sucked out onto the gravel road behind me, past my elbow, through the open window. Make up words and sing along to the glances of curious dairy cows. I'm sure their tails are keeping time like big four-legged metronomes.

Make a detour.

Sunfish. The very name gives you warm fuzzies in February. *Sunfish.*

Twitching small red-tailed woolly worms, muddler minnows or grasshoppers along the edges of weeds. The sunscreen glistening on my arms. Its taste in my mouth after it's been slapped on below a wide-brimmed hat. Sunfish. Yellow and orange like the summer sun. I love the taste of SPF 15 in the morning.

If someone asks me if I saw the moon last night I'll say no . . . I fished it. And so little grasshopper . . . I have plans for you.

Ian Colin James
Guelph, Ontario

✉ In the long sweep of life, if these things can ever really be measured, one of the happiest moments with all my clothes on was the rainy afternoon I broke ninety on the golf course. Not only did I break it — I smashed it, throttled it, *killed* it.

I shot eighty-eight.

I even had a witness, who walked me back to his cottage beside the first fairway and poured me three fingers of single-malt Scotch. It was a gracious thing to do, for, as I recall, I won sixteen bucks off him that day.

The glow of that triumph lasted for days. And the embers warmed me throughout the whole of the following winter.

As a Canadian who does not live in Victoria, I am happy that golf has an off-season. Winter is a time to enjoy old shots and anticipate new ones. It is a time to browse through golf magazines, all of which have how-to articles on improving your game, all of which are variations on a single theme: reach the green in regulation, take two putts, and you will attain par. Easy.

In winter, you never imagine wounded duck hooks or banana slices, or — horrors — the whiff! In winter my fairways are always soft and green, my skies blue, and my breezes gentle. One of my partners is an Englishman who has a serious disdain for those effete North American courses where the conditions always are ideal. When confronted with golf-course perfection, he snarls, "Where's the weather today?"

My son and I have played winter golf in pubs on those video games. These are the ones where you deposit a fistful of loonies, then drive the ball by sliding your palm over a recessed rolling sphere not unlike a large underarm deodorant container. I regularly drive three or four hundred yards straight down the middle — when you err to one side or the other, the computer creates the sound of branches crackling — but on the green I regularly take ten putts to hole out. Recently I have discovered that the more beer I drink, the better I putt.

As for the real game, this golfer's thoughts in winter are about golf's most attractive element — its accessibility. No matter how hard I try, I cannot imagine duplicating the way Roberto Alomar goes to his right to accept a wicked one hopper, or any slapshot by an NHLer, or any basketball slam-dunk, or the way Joe Carter poled that home run over the left-field fence last October. I can, however, imagine beating Fred Couples, who happens to be one of the best golfers in the world. Not over an entire eighteen-hole match, not even over a single fairway, but on a given shot, for a given moment, yes.

I am realistic enough to admit I could not do this with any of my woods, or long irons, but from a seven-iron to a putter — yes! One dewy morning on the fourth hole at my favourite course, I hit a perfect eight iron from a hundred and thirty yards out. The ball rose off the grass in a perfect arc heading directly for the flag, bounced with a small splash on the green, then rolled into the cup. If Fred Couples had been my partner that morning, he would have awarded me that ultimate golfing compliment. He would have said, *"Shot."*

Many winter nights I have gazed into the fireplace and replayed that eagle shot, and the wind howling outside my windows did not seem nearly so fierce. What other sport, besides low-life events like bowling or horseshoes, allows you to accomplish something like that?

Another thing, in winter I never think of what golf spells backward.

Martin O'Malley
Toronto

✉ History is full of the accounts of famous sieges . . . Syracuse, Troy, Malta. They may all be dismissed by a flick of the wrist. These are nothing compared to the true state of affairs that exists between Canadian gardeners and their winters.

Every year without fail a great bullying force of perishing Arctic chill with seemingly nothing better to do from November to March comes joy-riding down the jet stream, just for the sheer delight of testing our mettle. A cornered citizenry is bombarded again and again by an artillery of bottomless temperatures, maniacal winds, and choking snow.

Classically, in such times, there are two responses. The first is to stay in. To a gardener this is anathema. The second is to cave in, sell out to the enemy, join the ranks of those winter hearties who briskly ski, skate or hike through lung-burningly cold temperatures . . . and put aside their gardening. They tell themselves — and us — they actually like winter.

This is high treason. So also is "try to regard this as a precious time of rest for your plants" and "think of how many pests and diseases it kills. At least we don't have to fight the kudzu vine up here."

Not for me such perfidy. Hear this, oh you Forces of Darkness. Here is one who will not yield. I will garden straight through the winter. Winter does not exist, only days when the weather is less co-operative than others.

Such denial works well for me. So do those other time-tested stratagems: anger, rationalization, indulgence, the use of euphemisms. (See above.) They will work for you. I can state categorically I have never once failed to turn the adversary back from the gate.

Frost makes its first appearance here in Halifax about Armistice Day. This is a teasing blow on the part of our opponents, a period of testing. Insignificant as it may seem at the time, this small incident will establish character, set the stage for the action to follow. We must get it right. I purposely go out and celebrate by planting spring bulbs. Oh, I *could* do this earlier, when the ground was still soft and easy to dig, when the air was still warm and my fingers not benumbed. But don't you see. I *wait* to do this job till then just to thumb my nose at Old Man Winter and his thugs. They don't frighten me. Besides, I didn't start this, my conscience is clear.

Now the gauntlet is well and truly down. The elements know they are not dealing with a sissy here. Real winters are not for sissies. But I'm Canadian!

Like aggression signals employed the natural world over, the sky changes colour, from a gentle blue to a hard steely silver. The goldfish pond freezes over. The advance begins.

Just like the ancients say, I'm getting my garlic in, on December twenty-first. By now the land has been thoroughly intimidated. There I am, pickaxe in hand, scrubbing up the frozen ground all for the sake of a half dozen garlic cloves and maybe a late-delivered lily or two. And when I'm finished I go for a walk in the park, navigating so as to have a leisurely chat with all the many native witch-hazel still cavalierly in bloom.

Such defiance is taken as a challenge. The battle is joined. It is the first of January and we are visited with several heavy storms in succession. A fortnight of minus twenty.

Thank goodness. I thought that thermometer would never drop. Without such a good and proper cold snap, how on earth would the early buds be set! This is precisely the weather I need to bring in some boughs for forcing . . . forsythia, cherry, amelanchier . . . great long stems, all table-tops are covered. I laugh in the face of the Polar

Tyrant. He is screeching at the window, jaw clenched in a terrible grimace of rage and disbelief. The temperature drops another five degrees, the wind-chill howls at minus forty, the days shrink further in terror.

On the other hand *I* find these days particularly useful for carrying out so many long-delayed serious pruning tasks, don't you? For instance, that old apple tree just *must* be revived, it's been looking on its last legs nigh these many years. The line of dirty old Scotch elm must be lopped off in preparation for a hedgerow. And the *Magnolia acuminata* is starting to monopolize the whole back yard again. It must be persuaded to take only its fair share of room and light. I never seem to have the time to do these things when the days are fair.

All the clippings get used for something, stacked and waiting to be used as support canes for early peas, weft for the hedgerow, or thrown into the compost. Always there is the compost to see to. My best friend in the garden, especially in the winter. Compost is never not warm, even if you have to break through a frozen top crust some days. It, too, never gives up. Inside all is damp and yielding and smells not of rot but redolently of all the fresh smells that went into it.

By now the enemy is completely confused. What manner of creature is this ant who won't give up? There is a slight lull in the action. It pauses to regroup. Taking advantage of the break, I ride out toward the horizon to forage for stray harvest. There are Brussels sprouts to be picked. Like all members of the cabbage family they are much improved by freezing. It sets both the texture and flavour. Unlike some members of the brassica, Brussels sprouts are held well off the ground, well above the snow. This keeps them from jelling out. There are the last rose hips to be brought in, they make a delicious syrup for curing the grippe, which of course people mostly get because they spend so much time indoors breathing stale air. There are Jerusalem artichokes to dig, and parsnips, too. These last two have been perfectly, and without our labour, stored underground all the while in conditions of even temperature and humidity. There is a feast still to be scavenged from the landscape — go ask the natives.

With a terrible, punishing renewal of determination the weather returns. We begin to break all records for misery everywhere. It is the coldest, snowiest, windiest, longest. This is psychological warfare.

Winter is trying to break us from within. Precisely the moment to respond by setting out for a spot of planting! Take your packets of calendula, cosmos, marigold seeds, head for those bare spots fortuitously left by the February blasts and go to work. Of course you'll be covering your seeds over with a bag of kitchen leavings run through the blender or food processor. And water them well, no point in having them blown away.

One final thing. While you're out there, casually look around and muse aloud as to what your grafting plans for the next few weeks might be. Now grafting, it must be said, is a truly uncomfortable job. Best done just before the sap begins to flow, you are stock still in the cold, fiddling in fine detail with your gloves off. I have a friend who relinquished a career in landscaping for one in law the evening after the first day she spent grafting. "Anything," she said, "would be easier than this."

Sieges are won first by that side that can outlast the other. And secondly what you want is to lure your opponent into a fatal error. I find the mere mention of the word grafting does the trick every time. The Forces of Darkness panic. In an effort to compound our troubles, to heap suffering upon suffering, they deliver their hastily assembled final blow. Ice. Perilously it is beneath our feet, above our head, sheathing every surface taken for support by hand.

But that's it, that is *precisely* the fatal, mortal slip, if you'll pardon the pun. Only an extra ray of light, of longer, higher sun could convert all that snow to ice.

As though we wouldn't notice. As though we wouldn't press the advantage! Along about the third week in February, the light changes, long before the temperature comes up, long before the northerlies blow themselves out. Tree buds begin to colour up, and the swallows, those minstrels of battle, begin their rondelets heralding victory for the power of light. Look over your shoulder, oh you doomed legions. Winter withdraws. As I knew it must. Not gracefully, with many a Parthian shot. Once again I have won. It is not too soon to move a plant or two.

Jill Cooper Robinson
Halifax

✉ The sails are up, rumbling and snapping in the westerly breeze. The little ship tacks back and forth at her mooring, tossing her head this way and that. When she has the wind on her port side, you call *Sheet in!* and you drop the mooring line. The sails fall quiet and the boat gives a little lurch as she takes the wind, heels over, and moves out into the harbour. You're off — maybe for an afternoon, maybe for a summer cruise to distant ports. Maybe — someday — across an ocean or around the world.

David Stevens, the legendary Lunenburg shipwright, once told me that the greatest thrill of boat-building was that little lurch as a new vessel felt the wind for the first time and moved off under her own sails. That's *it*, he said, the thrill of a lifetime, the birth of a ship.

I know what he means: I feel something of that thrill every single time *Silversark* leaves her mooring. And that's always been my winter reverie — the delicious moment, at once memory and promise, which leads me into sleep on a cold winter night, when the wind is howling and the hard pellets of snow are ticking against the windows.

For me, that's the lure of sailing itself: the promise of new places, new people, new experiences, all set in that sensuous context of whistling wind, salt spray, sea-wrack smells and the companionable gurgle of the water. That lurch away from the mooring is the preface to nights of dazzling phosphorescence in the inky water, adrenaline-fuelled charges into unfamiliar harbours, close encounters with pelagic birds and whales, shrieking squalls and oily calms, streamers of light pouring downward through the clouds and upward from the horizon when the aurora borealis reaches for the zenith of the midnight sky.

In winter I write about sailing, reliving the fears and delights of cruises past. I plan and imagine cruises yet to come, and I read about other people's cruises. For me, sailing and boat-building, reading and writing, all bubble together in a single savoury stew of enjoyment.

I sail most happily with Joshua Slocum and Arthur Ransome. Slocum was the laconic Nova Scotian who set off, ninety-nine years ago this spring, to become the first man ever to sail around the world alone — and to write a classic book about it, a book so fresh and evergreen that it never fails to repay another reading. Both Slocum and Ransome built their own boats, too. Ransome, an Englishman, was a glorious children's novelist, and I sometimes think my notion of a desirable woman first formed itself around the figure of Nancy Blackett, one of his characters. Certainly Lulu, who now shares my life and my cruises, bears a striking resemblance to the spunky, adventurous girl in Ransome's *Swallows and Amazons*.

During World War One, Ransome was a correspondent in Russia; he hung about in Moscow cafés with young revolutionaries and eventually married Trotsky's secretary. He also had a boat built for himself in Riga, Latvia, and what he had to say about boatbuilding is so *right* that I stapled it to the shop wall when I was building my own boat. Here it is:

> The desire to build a house is the tired wish of a man content thenceforward with a single anchorage. The desire to build a boat is the desire of youth, unwilling yet to accept the idea of a final resting-place. It is for that reason, perhaps, that, when it comes, the desire to build a boat is one of those that cannot be resisted. It begins as a little cloud on a serene horizon. It ends by covering the whole sky, so that you can think of nothing else. You must build to regain your freedom.

Yes, exactly. And that's the other thing I like to do in the winter: build boats. It took eight and a half years for us to build *Silversark*, and I confess to a certain sense of loss mixed with the joy I felt when she finally gave that first lurch and sailed away from her mooring.

I wish I had time to build another: to go out to the shop in the frosty mornings in my snowmobile suit, fire up the wood stove, straighten up the work-bench and plan the day ahead with Lulu and our various confederates. To savour again the turpentiney smell of new-sawn pine, the hay-barn aroma of oak, the exotic perfume released when the saw rips through afrormosia. To devote myself, humbly and completely, to shaping and moulding one of the most beautiful of all human artefacts. And then to go home in the evening filled with honest, comfortable weariness, leaving the fire glowing in the cosy shop, the day's work glued up and clamped and left to set overnight.

I've only been able to build one boat since, a gleaming black skiff designed to stow on *Silversark*'s foredeck. I can't even work on *Silversark*; with her stanchions and tabernacle in place, she's too tall to fit inside the shop in which she had her long gestation. So Lulu and I dream of a workshop forty feet long and twenty feet high, tall enough to accommodate *Silversark*, and with plenty of room around her for tools and lumber and glue. A shop big enough to accommodate the fantasy — and it is only a fantasy — of building another boat.

If I could do that — divide the winter days between reading and writing about boats and actually building them — then the winters would be almost as good as the summers.

Winters are made for dreams and warm workshops.

But summers are made for sailing.

Silver Donald Cameron
D'Escousse, Nova Scotia

Living with aids:
A Mother's Story

For some seasons before those reflected in this book, the name Mary Grant was familiar to me. Mary, a wry, wise, Christian woman not far (I would guess) from my own age, wrote to me from her home in Tisdale, Saskatchewan, about various things — chatty letters, often, that were among the dozens and dozens I try to read every day that just keep in touch with things. Then, a few years ago, Mary's letters took a sad — if bravely faced — turn. (There was one, in fact, in *The Fourth Morningside Papers*.) Her son Regan, a promising opera singer, had AIDS. Her letters about Regan's progress — and sometimes setbacks — continued. He returned to Tisdale. I was moved and sometimes inspired by their family's story, and one morning we invited the two of them to come together to our studio in Saskatoon. We played a piece of music from a tape Regan had made not long ago, and then we talked.

PETER GZOWSKI   Thank you for deciding to do this. It cannot be an easy thing to do, even though I think we're all friends in a way. Mary, tell me why you came to think you should appear on *Morningside*.

MARY GRANT   I think primarily it's because I feel that education about this illness is crucial, particularly to our young people. If we don't help them to understand ways of prevention and their own responsibility and their own protection then we're going to lose a whole generation of young people.

REGAN GRANT   I think my feeling is not so much for young people as for older people who just don't understand it at all. I think that mostly younger people are very aware of how it's transmitted and so on but a lot of older people feel that because they don't have to deal with something like this, or have never had to, then maybe it's not so important. But if you think about it, it's important to everybody no matter how old you are because this is a disease that affects human beings and not certain groups of people, and it's something we all really need to be involved with.

PETER   Regan, you're thirty-one now and you were living in Toronto when you found out you had the HI virus. Tell me about your life at that time.

REGAN   Well, I was still in university studying when I got the news. It wasn't really a shock because I had been living a life-style that was certainly open to the infection. My doctor had seen some things in regular blood tests that looked a little bit abnormal to him and so he suggested that I take the test. When the results came back, I was very sad but I really wasn't very angry. I certainly didn't tell my folks about it because I knew they would just worry to death. I did share it with a few close friends, but for the most part I didn't tell people about it and it didn't make itself manifest until the first time I went into hospital with an AIDS-related illness. But it didn't really keep me from being happy or looking forward to things. I didn't think of it as an automatic death sentence. I didn't think of it as something that couldn't be handled or dealt with. I'm afraid that's what a lot of people I know who get the illness — that's sort of the outlook they tend to take, at least they used to. Maybe not so much any more. Even in the past couple of years attitudes have changed. But I decided I was going to continue to live. I wasn't going to roll over and die, and certainly my family has been behind me in that decision.

PETER   How did you break the news?

REGAN   Well, I didn't, really.

MARY   He lied for two or three years.

REGAN   It was when I first got pneumocystis pneumonia. I went into the hospital and Mom had called my place in Toronto to talk to me. My roommate answered the phone and said I wasn't there. Eventually my mom found out I was in the hospital and she phoned, and that was when she realized I had something much more serious than just pneumonia. Once the news was out, I think there was a lot more anger on my family's part than on my own in dealing with it.

PETER   Is that true, Mary?

MARY   My initial reaction, I think, was fear of what might happen to Regan given where he was living. I feared for his safety as much as anything. But one of the most difficult things I had to deal with was that for a few years Regan had been very promiscuous, and I think that's something we have to accept with sexually transmitted AIDS — somewhere along the line of contact, one or more people have been something less than moderate in behaviour. I scarcely believed this of Regan because it was so foreign to his nature. From the time he was a child, he had a keen instinct about what was right and what was wrong, and what would be acceptable and what would be unacceptable, both in our family and in his community. To find that he had been so thoughtless and so careless with himself and with other people was pretty hard to take. He was warm and generous and loving and outgoing and very thoughtful and considerate, and those are probably the things that got him into trouble — because he likes people, and he wanted people to like him. He didn't want anyone to be angry or annoyed with him and he just didn't seem to know how to say no. I had a great deal of anger and guilt to resolve because I hadn't given him the direction and guidance he needed, obviously, in order to survive in situations where he ought to have. As parents, we all fail our children in many ways, and this is one of the ways we failed Regan. Youth is such a terrible time. There's so much feeling and emotion and so little notion of how to handle it. We have to give our children better ways of handling things.

PETER   Most of the parents listening to you make that emotion-laden speech are, if my instincts are right, reacting the way I'm reacting, which is to say, Mary, don't be silly. It's not your fault. It's not anyone's fault. I'm sure, Regan, you must feel the same way.

REGAN   Well, yes, I do. I knew what I was getting into, or at least I should have known. I really have taken the blame for this myself, and that has made it easy to deal with, I think. I think if you can accept the responsibility as yours for getting AIDS, then the whole world opens up in front of you and you don't have to be mad at anybody or have to blame anybody. You just have to realize it's your problem, and you have to learn to deal with it, you have to tackle it, you have to learn to go through it, and you have to learn to accept the support and love and the care that people have for you. Otherwise, you will roll over and die.

PETER   I want to talk about life in Tisdale. Mary, it was your idea that Regan come home, wasn't it?

MARY   Well, there didn't seem to be any other solution because while he has very many loving and caring friends in Toronto, neither of us could see that there would be anyone who could or would be able to care for him while he was convalescing, provided, of course, that he ever did get better, which, for a while, was in doubt. He made the decision himself. He decided that if he was going to die he wanted to die at home, which of course meant Saskatchewan. So I said fine, now we have to concentrate on getting you well enough to travel, because in order to air ambulance him home, we were looking at upwards of ten thousand dollars, and of course we didn't have that kind of money. He had to concentrate some effort into making at least some kind of recovery so we could travel, and I said I would stay until he was ready to travel. I figured if I left he probably wouldn't get out of there. It took us a month, and he was pretty weak when we got on the plane, but we made it.

PETER   What's it like in Tisdale? This is a small town, people talk, people have prejudices. Regan, what's it been like for you to be back in town?

REGAN   It's been pretty great. The people who knew I had AIDS were good friends of Mom and Dad, and as a result we didn't have to worry about bad reactions. Certainly nobody has suggested that this kid should be put in a sanatorium somewhere.

PETER   Nobody has shied away physically or anything?

REGAN   No, but sometimes when I go in the Co-op and we're shopping, there's an area there that people sit, and I think they're looking at me, but who knows? It doesn't really matter, because I don't know who they are anyway.

MARY   That's probably why they're looking at you. *They* don't know who *you* are.

REGAN   Probably. But living in Tisdale has been just great. One of the first things I remember after finally getting out of hospital was listening to cars run over the snow on the street outside, and just the way the snow scrunches . . . I thought, I would never hear this in Toronto. Birds outside the window in the spring. Just the peacefulness really helped me to recover quickly.

PETER   I went through some of your mom's letters. Mary, you wrote last November, after Magic Johnson announced that he's got the HI virus. You said, "Those of us locked in the battle against this dread disease are aware of a double standard. A perception of good AIDS and bad AIDS, acceptable and non-acceptable AIDS. It matters not to me if my son was infected as a health care worker handling contaminated products, through a careless sexual contact, male or female, or had he been an intravenous drug user. The unbearable fact is that he will die before his time of a hideous disease for which there is no cure. What an appalling waste of life." But when I hear Regan talk about his life in Tisdale, what it's been like, it doesn't sound to me like people are judgemental. Maybe that's Tisdale and not the rest of the world?

MARY   Well, I know from the battle we had in our church over sexuality that people are polarized. Just because we haven't had any evidence of it in relation to Regan, it doesn't mean it's not there. I'm sure there are still some people who feel that AIDS is a judgement on homosexuals.

PETER   So there was a little tension in your own church? And your church is really important to you?

MARY   It is very important to me, yes. And there was a lot of tension a few years ago. We lost some people, and I don't know whether any of us came to a consensus on what the answer should be, or whether we just agree to disagree and get on with life as a church. I personally don't feel that sexuality is a choice. It's a condition of being, a given. It's what you do with your given where the element of choice comes in. Promiscuity is a choice. So are moderation and celibacy. To say that AIDS is a judgement on homosexuals is pretty grim. That puts God in a context I just can't deal with. My God doesn't do things like that.

PETER   Can I change tacks for a minute here? Regan, you've been given a great voice. What's happening to your singing?

REGAN   Well, it's going quite well. Saskatoon Opera Association is putting on a production of *Barber of Seville* at the end of February and I'm in that, and I'm getting some music together for a recital I'd like to give at the end of April. Not in Tisdale, but in Melfort, which is the town down the road where I grew up.

From the time I got sick it took about five months to have the energy to produce the voice again, but it seems to be mostly back to normal. I love my music. I don't want to ever have to give it up. And it's going fine.

PETER   Is the AIDS ever out of your mind? It must become such a defining part of your life.

REGAN   To me, no, it's not. Every day, I have to take several different pills and drugs to control the disease. Every time I get up in the morning and pull out my syringes and put them beside the bed, and I know why I'm doing this, I'm reminded that I have a disease that at present is only controllable. It's not curable. I can't go swimming because I have a catheter stuck in my chest for my intravenous treatments. Every time I take off my shirt at night before going to bed, I see this thing dangling there. So no, I'm never away from it, but again it's not something I'm really depressed and upset about. We're learning to manage it and handle it and to deal with it, and so life goes on.

PETER   Mary? Would you answer that differently?

MARY   Well, I guess it's always there, but when he's well, as he is now, it's in the back of my head. I only let it out when he gets one of his infections that he's susceptible to. I think I mentioned his toes in a letter, I was really quite worried about his toes.

PETER   I got that one this morning. You say, "Regan's toes are healing nicely and he continues well. He gave us a scare a week or so ago. Lost his lunch three or four days in a row. We had fears that meningitis was out of control again, but it seems it was just his mother's cooking that didn't agree with him."

MARY   Yeah, well (laughs). He has to take care what he eats because for some reason his stomach is very sensitive, and that was one of the big setbacks during the weeks he was in hospital in Toronto and supposedly recovering. Every once in a while he'd start losing his meals. Physically that was very draining for him. It would mean something was wrong with his medication or the meningitis, what he was taking for the meningitis just wasn't strong enough to sit on it. So of course every time he has an upset stomach or even whenever he goes quickly to the bathroom I'm afraid that he's losing another meal and I get worried again. But most of the time, so long as he's well, I put it away and try not to think about it, except of course at daily prayer time.

PETER   Do you have access to the kind of medical services you need in Tisdale?

REGAN   Well, no. We come into Saskatoon for those. The Royal University Hospital has been at the forefront of the breakthroughs in medical science. Most of my prescriptions have to be picked up here in Saskatoon. Probably if we went through a lot of paperwork we could get them sent out to Tisdale, but this is where my doctor works, so it's just as well that I come here once a month to see him. For lesser things, like my toes, for instance, we have all of those taken care of in Tisdale. There is an excellent medical staff in Tisdale, and they jumped to the call when they found out that there was going to be an AIDS patient in their hospital. Nobody said boo, nobody said I don't want to go near him, nobody said anything like that. They did their job. It was wonderful.

PETER   Mary, during your daily prayer, do you ever say God bless Tommy Douglas? Because I just think of what you would be paying if we didn't have medicare.

MARY   Yes, that's right, the costs are really prohibitive. We've been very fortunate that Regan's doctor has put him on exceptional drug status, so outside of the initial eleven-hundred-dollar outlay, which was returned to us through AIDS Saskatoon, our costs have been minimal, and we're grateful for that.

PETER   I want to read one more passage from a letter you wrote, Mary. This is from quite a while ago, January 2, 1991. You wrote this after Regan beat an infection that was thought to be fatal. "Some miracle of love, prayers, strength of will, and determination, assisted by the necessary medical procedures once they were implemented, combined to effect a quite remarkable recovery from an infection that ought to have proved fatal. This recovery surprised quite a number of people and stunned one gloom-and-doom urologist who solemnly pronounced an imminent demise. The look on his face while watching the patient he had given up for dead, doggedly traversing the corridors in his wheelchair, was almost worth the weeks-long ordeal." Whence cometh your strength, you two? Mary, is it in your church? In your Christianity?

MARY   Well, it's in my faith, I guess, in my belief. I pray a lot, but not formally. Most of the days my prayers aren't necessarily verbalized, but they're there. I think I mentioned a miracle in one letter. It was probably just a turn of phrase. If we had a miracle it was effected by the knowledge of the amount of prayer that was being offered. I have never in my life seen such an outpouring of love and care and concern as there was in that hospital room. The walls of Regan's room were covered with cards and letters and messages, some of them just handed in on little slips of paper, that said, we love you, we're praying for you, we hope you'll get better. The only walls that were empty were the window walls and the wall above his bed where all of the equipment was, and I'm sure that the knowledge of that amount of concern had a very beneficial effect on his recovery. I don't think that prayer is something that ought to be offered with the hope of changing circumstances or changing situations. It changes us so that we can handle the situation and deal with the things that are given to us.

PETER   Are we hearing about an exceptional mother-and-son relationship? Is the whole family like this? There are two daughters and another son, and of course there's your dad. Regan, is the whole family together?

REGAN   Well, I'm not sure. Mom, maybe you should answer this. Mom and I tend to talk about these things more than I do with my siblings or my father. My dad is very reticent about things like this.

PETER   No kidding?

REGAN   He's so staunch, so stoic, so . . .

MARY   . . . Scot.

REGAN   Yeah, there's something behind that strong-man kind of veneer, but we never really talk about it. It's hard for him to verbalize things like this. My older sister, well, she sometimes talks about things like this. My little sister, no, she doesn't, hardly at all. My brother . . . he sort of dismisses it all out of hand, but you know it doesn't affect my relationship with them at all.

MARY   You're still very close.

REGAN   Yes, we are, and I believe in many ways, having HIV has been something that has drawn us even closer together. I went to a different church in Toronto, and indeed that has been a source of strength for me. It's very comforting to know that there are people halfway across Canada who are praying for you. It's the thought of being cared about that really keeps me going. I believe in God very much. I also believe you can't just say that you're Christian and say you love people. You have to really live it, and that's been a part of my life, especially since getting this disease.

MARY   He talks as much as I do.

PETER   I know what's going to happen. You're going to go down the elevator and across the lobby and out into the main street of Saskatoon and you're going to get in the car and you're going to look at each other and you're going to say, gee, we should have told him this or said this or something. So I want you to do that now instead of in the car on the way home. Mary, what have I missed?

MARY   I don't know if you've missed anything. I don't pray for a miracle, but perhaps I should tell you what my prayers are. I pray for strength for our journey, no matter how long or short it may be. Strength to cope with what we know is ahead of us and for our family to hold together and to continue to be a source of comfort and support for us.

PETER   Regan, what did I neglect to ask?

REGAN   I think the only thing I really want to add is that people should know AIDS is something that is definitely preventable. It is something that can be controlled. It does not have to get into epidemic proportions, such as it has, say, in Central Africa, but people have to have the willpower to say, no, I'm not going to get involved with activities that leave me susceptible to getting this virus. I know it sounds like Nancy Reagan, just say no, and I know that it's not always easy, but I think that is really the only way we're going to stop the spread of this disease.

PETER   Don't take those chances.

REGAN   I really believe that's the way to stop it.

Regan Grant died peacefully at the family home on June 28, 1992.

"A Clock with Hands Tells You How Long Till Lunch"

And other reflections on the advance (or otherwise) of technology.

✉ Back in the early seventies, I, like most people, was wearing a spring-driven watch. Every Sunday when my father and I would set our watches to the one o'clock beep on CBC Radio, my cheap but sturdy Timex was usually a minute or two out. My father had an electric Bulova with a tuning fork contraption inside it, which — *mirabile visu* — kept it accurate to within a few seconds each week.

Then the first digital watches appeared. Forget their sleek, modern black faces and those bold red numbers that appeared for a few seconds with the push of a button — the true wonder was their accuracy. The cheapest digital watch was accurate to within seconds *per year*, and our Sunday one o'clock ritual soon became superfluous. I became the proud owner of a series of digital watches, the cheap black plastic type with time, date, stop-watch and alarm. They were dependable, accurate, water-resistant to various degrees, lightweight and, most of all, desperately cheap. During the eighties, it was often more economical to replace the watch than replace the batteries.

But somewhere along the way it dawned on me that *I didn't like reading numbers*. It was harder to digest the information at a glance. Instead of looking at a watch face and thinking, "It's almost six o'clock," I would have to read an exact number and analyze the information it represented.

So after fifteen years, I went back to an analogue watch, an electronic quartz model this time, just as accurate as its digital cousins. I was happy again — most of the time. It turns out I had become addicted to those ubiquitous gadgets, the stop-watch and the alarm. Back to carrying a travel alarm on trips, measuring pizza delivery time by the oven timer — my muttered complaints were endless.

I might still be complaining had my wife not presented me with the perfect watch — an analogue model with a four-function digital display tucked up above the watch face. I cannot help but think that in this case, I might have my cake and eat it, too.

Alan Brown
Scarborough, Ontario

✉ About four weeks ago, I bought a new analogue watch because digital watches (a disposable commodity those days) just don't work for me. In the past three years I've been through about fifteen of them, from the cheapies (three dollars or so) to the mid-price range (twenty-five dollars is the most I've paid), and all of them have stopped working after a few weeks. They might give a little warning signal, such as intermittently flashing a really weird sequence of numbers for a few days, but eventually they all end up showing me a completely blank face, as if we've reached the apocalypse or something.

I live in Australia and was just about to embark on the long-ish trip that brought me here, so when I found an analogue watch that had a peripheral stripe with what I supposed to be numbers indicating the twenty-four-hour clock, I snapped it up. "That'll come in handy," I told the sales clerk, and she smiled indulgently and nodded. A couple of hours later, in the airport, I noticed that the half-red, half-blue stripe trimming my watch face wasn't a twenty-four-hour clock at all. Can you imagine? The numbers running down the right side of the circumference, which was blue, were: 5, 10, ¼, 20, 25. At the bottom, the character ½ was half on the end of the blue, and half on the beginning of the red stripe running up the left side. Continuing to move clock-wise, the numbers on the red were now 25, 20, ½, 10 and 5. Written on the blank part of the face on the right side, in blue, was the word PAST. On the left, in red, was the word TO. I had bought a watch with a key explaining how to read it, like a map. What's worse, I had told the sales clerk that I would appreciate such a feature.

What we surrendered when we let digital watches take over in the seventies and eighties was a little bit of the ability to understand things in proportion to one another. An analogue watch face — as the very name suggests — is a spatial metaphor for time, representing it as a circle. When we used to learn to read a clock, we were also learning a little about relating time to space, which can get pretty philosophical, when you think about it. Digital timepieces have taken a lot of the meaning out of reading the time.

Madeleine Clews
Perth, Australia

✉ Digital clocks are a part of my life. They tell me the time when I drive or turn on my stereo or VCR. They tell the time well enough, but they have no soul, no character. They are just part of the machinery.

I have two favourite timepieces. Both are analogue, and both are mechanical. They are turn-of-the-century pocket-watches. One was made by D.A. Reesor, a Brandon, Manitoba, jeweller, sometime between 1885 and 1900. The other was made by the Elgin Nat'l Watch Co. sometime around 1900. Both watches are silver-coated, stem-wound, and have twenty-four-hour faces. The Elgin uses Roman numerals, the Reesor plain numerals. The Reesor is stem-set and has a screw-on back and screw-on bezel. The Elgin is a lever set watch; it has a screw-on bezel and no back. The workmanship on both watches is beautiful, and I find the movement of springs, gears, wheels and escapements in mechanical watches and clocks absolutely fascinating. Neither of my watches keeps perfect time — but neither do the digitals in my possession. Each loses about a minute or so every third day and has to be reset accordingly. This is not an onerous task. I find that winding a watch or two daily can be a very pleasant ritual.

Holding the smoothly worn, rather weighty silver case in one hand and setting and winding with the other hand is curiously relaxing and comforting. The thirty seconds this operation takes can be easily spared.

I am sorry that I know nothing about the previous owners of either watch. If I were Sherlock Holmes I could, no doubt, open the case, gaze at the workings through a hand lens and state that the watch was owned by a retired military surgeon from Halifax, who was left-handed, smoked cheroots, drank brandy, raised Siamese cats and budgerigars, and kept gumdrops in his watch pocket. Alas, I can do none of that. I can, however, try to imagine who might have possessed these watches before me. Was it a blacksmith, a lawyer, a miller, a butcher, a farmer, a sawyer or an outlaw? Perhaps the Reesor left Brandon in 1898, in the waistcoat pocket of a bank clerk who had left his job, sold all his possessions and headed for Skagway with the thousands who flocked north to the Klondike gold fields. Perhaps the Elgin adorned the pocket of the first motorist to drive his — or her — new-fangled horseless carriage between Toronto and Hamilton, or Fredericton and Saint John. I am now a small part of the ninety-plus-year-old history of these watches. Each time I take one out and check the time, I am not only sharing that precise moment with those around me, I am sharing a moment with all the unknown hands that have held, set, wound and pondered these watches for nearly a century.

Brad Allen
Thamesford, Ontario

✉ I received my first digital watch for Christmas in 1979, when I was ten years old. I opened the small package, labelled "Open Me Last," with eager anticipation. I had never before been so close to this kind of cutting-edge technology: both my parents wore analogue watches, and my own Mickey Mouse watch — Mickey's eyes moved from side to side to count the seconds — also sported a big hand and a little hand. (It was years, literally, before I understood the horological term "second hand"; watches have two hands, and, logically, one is the first and the other is the second.) The new watch was all black and at the push of a button displayed the time in bright red numerals on a little screen. I was fascinated and wandered around for several days afterwards, ostentatiously checking the time every few minutes. When school reopened in the new year, I found out that the watch was less fascinating than inconvenient: it was a two-handed timepiece and defied my checking the time while carrying anything in either hand. Eventually the watch began to guzzle expensive watch batteries at an alarming rate and was duly retired in favour of Mickey.

Several years later I received a new digital watch as a birthday present. More sensible than the black Mark I model, it had a continuous display and would even show the date and count the seconds when I pressed the bar below the screen. It had one major flaw, though: because neither the face nor the numbers lit up, I couldn't see the time in the dark. Alas, a rambunctious softball game smashed the crystal, and the most accurate time the watch gave after that was "blob after splotch." Mickey returned to my wrist.

In 1986, after Expo ended in Vancouver, I bought an official Expo watch for twenty dollars. An analogue watch. Mickey, I felt, was growing old, and I wanted the new technology as represented by the official watch's rotating face and changing patterns. But I threw over the Expo watch for the red airplane watch, which deserves its own explanation.

I saw and fell in love with the red airplane watch in 1987. Instead of having a flat or slightly curved crystal, the red airplane watch's crystal arched up more than a centimetre from the face. The face itself had an aerial view of a resort and affixed to the second hand (so *that's* what a second hand is!) was a tiny silver airplane, which circled the resort as time passed. The watch later died of a broken hairspring, which would have been as expensive to fix as the watch had originally been. . . . I was heartbroken.

Since then, I've had (only) two more watches — both analogues. My oversized everyday watch has a face that's 3½ centimetres across, so that I'm able to see unequivocally when it's time for lunch, or so I tell everybody. It spoils me for my dress watch, a silver Alfred Sung number whose hands are almost impossible to read without a good squint.

So, the score stands at Analogues: 5, Digitals: 2.

How the heck is a clockwork toy supposed to work in the digital age? Long live analogue time!

Adrienne Brown
Vancouver

✉ I prefer digital clocks. I think the reason for my preference lies in my experience — or in my lack of experience — with analogue clocks. When I was a child in the forties in Trenton, Nova Scotia, we had only one clock in our house, and that one was a wind-up alarm clock in my parents' bedroom. We rarely referred to this clock during the day. Instead, we got the time from the radio or a factory whistle that blew on shift changes. The only clock I saw most days was a large clock on the town post office. It had roman numerals for each hour and ornate hour and minute hands. Once a minute, the minute hand jumped forward to the next minute mark. I looked at the clock every day as I walked by on my way to school chiefly because I hoped to see the minute hand jump forward and never, as far as I can recall, to see the time.

Now, when so many appliances come with clocks attached to them, we have many clocks, all digital. We also have in our bedroom a twenty-year-old digital clock, which has a light that shines the time on our ceiling. I've grown really fond of this feature, because when I awake in the middle of the night hours before I have to be up, I merely open my eyes a slit to check the time before rolling over and falling back to sleep — a very user-friendly clock indeed. That light is a sort of technological miracle because it has beamed the time twenty-four hours a day for twenty years without burning out.

Phyllis Chapman
London, Ontario

✉ So much trouble in life happens when we try to put analogue situations into digital formats. Analogue formats sweep through the shading and nuance that make life a continuous process. Digital, on the other hand, describes a series of binary, yes-no choices: On or off. One or two. Right or wrong. Yes or no. Win or lose. In a digital situation you either are or you aren't.

Some things in life are analogue, others are digital: Disease is analogue, death is digital. Sex is analogue, pregnancy is digital. A broken arm is analogue, a lost arm is digital. Separation is analogue, divorce is digital.

Kind of fun, but a lot depends on knowing which is which. Take the recent referendum, in which the federal government took an analogue document, like the Constitution of Canada, and reduced it to a digital, yes-or-no format. Nothing but trouble.

In Canada, especially in the news media that define our public issues, we are always confusing analogue and digital. Abortion: Right or wrong? Will Quebec stay or go? Is this athlete, movie star, economy or country on the way up or down?

Time and life are analogue. Put them in digital formats, whether on your wrist or your news media, and you've got trouble.

John Gray
Vancouver

✉ An analogue clock allows you to be approximately right. With a digital one you can be precisely wrong.

Despite advances in cockpit design, most airplanes still have analogue clocks. They are much easier to use during instrument approaches than digital clocks. In fact, most cockpit gauges remain analogue today. They show at a glance if you're in the ballpark.

One pilot wrote: "A clock with hands tells you how long to lunch."

Also, analogue read-outs make it easy to judge a rate of change. The best altimeters have digital displays, but the designers left in the hands. Taking them out would cause a pilot walk-out.

Sander Schimmelpenninck
Oakville, Ontario

✉ For years it has been my business to take perfectly innocent things of all sorts and inflict computers on them. Little clocks that used to be content marking time now count up, down and sideways. Ovens may now want to know whether you're cooking beef or a cake, and presume to conduct themselves differently. All manner of farm implements unabashedly claim intellectual superiority over the rubber boots standing in front of them: the unholy amalgam of blinking lights and silicon somehow knows that the bovine who just stepped up to the trough is Blossom and not Primrose and should, therefore, get two squirts of this and a dab of that for breakfast. We have lasers and more computers to explain to the water which way to flow through field drainage tiles.

Sometimes I think I'm living in a virtual world: I park myself in front of a computer that could always be counted on to be a Macintosh, if nothing else. Now it periodically and transiently undergoes a metamorphosis and emerges as an IBM: the butterfly re-enters the cocoon and emerges as a worm. The screen is cluttered with everything I've done for the last nine years — as is my very tangible desk — as well as the contents of all the other Macs in the neighbourhood. Look closely: is this letter actually going to end up stored in the brute in front of me, or on the *New Yorker*-sized, battery-operated miracle on the shelf by the back door? This letter could be faxed (who the hell let that become a verb?) to your computer and end up before your eyes without ever having been committed to something as quaint as a piece of paper. Mama wouldn't let me build a pipe organ in the house (taking the narrow view of things again), so beside me is a thing about the size of an ironing board which, with the help of the Mac, puts me in a most richly reverberant great church, at the console of an organ as yet uncommitted to wood, tin and air. When the rigours of the technological rat race get too much to bear, I descend into something solidly, tangibly baroque. Right.

I've fought all of this, long and hard. You may remember an item from some years back about a stinky diaper being changed in the printed-circuit-board processing lab. That diaper would have been hung outside to dry on a clothes-line. Nothing virtual about a clothes-line, especially on a January morning, and before you get to thinking that I'm a MCP or something, the odds are slightly in favour of me having hung them there, especially in January.

227

Technology impedes the enjoyment of technology betimes. Last Sunday we were out for a fly on one of the most glorious afternoons in memory. There are lots of things in our little plane, and the offending item this past Sunday was the satellite navigation system. This sounds pretty smarmy, but they're priced somewhere between a clothes dryer and a gas furnace these days, and for this, you get to know where you are to within something like twenty-five feet. The little thing can tell which *side* of our fifty-by-two-thousand-foot runway through the hay-field we're on, to say nothing of which end. So there we were, floating above that outpost of heaven located in southern Ontario's dairy land — Wingham, Hanover, that area — and it suddenly occurred to me that I didn't want to know where we were to within twenty-five feet, or our speed over the ground to within one knot, or that, if things kept on as they are, we'd be home in thirty-seven minutes and eleven seconds. Know what I did? Turned the little beggar off. Deprived it of electrons. Floated around with the hawks and seagulls for a spell and ended up back home, just like we used to: There's the bog south of Wingham, there's the Exeter sewage lagoon, there's the corner of Lake Huron at Ipperwash, there's the junk yard up from Melbourne, there's old Ginger the Horse at home.

So you've retained a curmudgeon to spit in the eye of Technology, have you? Good.

Ted Spencer
Appin, Ontario

✉ There must be more than a handful of us using manual typewriters in preference to the word-processing jobs that require only a small degree of literacy to operate.

From the *Toronto Star*, March 12, 1988: "When replacing a type-writer ribbon, take the old one and put a few drops of light machine oil around the outside layer of ribbon and put it inside a small plastic bag for a few weeks. It will then be as good as new and will even make a blacker impression."

Anne McCaul
London, Ontario

Nov,15, 1991.
Ottawa, Ont,

Dear Morningside,

Heard your segment on manual typewriters ast week and, knowing it would generate (in the mechanical sense of the word) a lot of finger-tipped blistered responses, I thought I'd add this one,
As you can probably tell by the script, I am writing this on what my wife derisively refers to as "the dinosaur", It is, in fact, a 1922 portable Underwood, an Underwood No, 5, to be exact, I could go on for hours about what it needs to be fully restored, not the least of which is a new ribbon, roller and pinch roller, but I love it nonetheless,
Sure! it takes a kind of determined skill to hammer the keys just hard enough to impress; sure! I'm constantly "X"ing out errors; sure! it takes forever to type a simple letter, but what can I say about things beautiful that has not already been said?

J. P. Onion

Ottawa,

✉ Re fax machines: I love them. I live in Manotick, outside of Ottawa, and my daughter lives on Quadra Island. Send a letter? Why? It takes ten days, and I can write her a letter at work and send it to her after hours (cheaper) and she has it next day. The news is still fresh, and I still phone her twice a month for more personal contact, but a letter by fax between us is great. Often on a noon hour in British Columbia she will fax me a letter — what a great booster for the day!

Janet Downey
Manotick, Ontario

✉ Rest assured: I believe the telephone booth will be here for some time to come. Although cellular phones are fast decreasing in both price and size, there will always be a need for a place to make that emergency call. How do you get in touch with your husband when you've had a long hard day on the road and your cellular batteries wear out? Where do you go to call the insurance company when, in the bustle of a business crowd, someone knocks your elbow as you're about to clinch that multi-million-dollar deal and your cellular goes flying down three flights of stairs and is run over by the janitor's work cart? How do you arrange a job interview if the cellular you stole off Eaton's shelves needs to be assembled before use — and the instructions are all in Japanese? What do you use to pass on the vital information you just obtained in sensitive negotiations if you're a high-level government official in a foreign town, and you never know what reporter with a scanner might be lurking nearby?

Not to mention, if there were no telephone booths, how would mild-mannered Clark Kent rid the world of evil?

Roma Quapp
Ottawa

✉ I was snowed in at Halifax at the end of a business trip to the Maritimes. I had a friend in Hubbards, more or less on the outskirts of Halifax, though a small town — at least then — in its own right.

We had partied well and truly the night before, and rather than doing the usual tourist things, my friend suggested a trip to Chester, another small town, to meet some other friends. I went into the bar alone while my friend parked the car. I was just inside the door when I heard the waitress ask whether Bee was there.

"He's coming," said one fellow. "He's parking the car."

"That's okay," said the waitress. "I really want some guy named Cadham who is apparently with him. There's a phone call for him."

The call was from Air Canada. They'd got a flight together and I could get back to Montreal if I could make the airport in twenty minutes.

The Hubbard operator had been at the previous night's party and knew the plans to make for Chester the following day. Finding me was therefore no problem for her.

Try that with your modern electronic do-everything-but-find-the-guy-in-Chester telephone.

Jack Cadham
Foam Lake, Saskatchewan

✉ Personally, I don't want to see a beautiful summer ever again — not until someone de-invents the leaf-blower. What use is a beautiful summer when all it does is encourage leaf-blower operators to get out there and assault my eardrums and all the flora and fauna in the neighbourhood? What kind of mind invented this horror? Who marketed it? Underemployed ear doctors? People who have problems with intimacy? (I bet one of them is busy at his word processor right now churning out the leaf-blowers' self-help manual, *Actualizing Alienation Through Leaf-Blowing*.) I really would like to know why anyone on this planet needs more than a rake and the wind to deal with the leaves in his life.

Annabelle Cooper
Toronto

✉ My bank has been diligently trying to persuade me to take advantage of the new technology — the automated teller — and I have resisted all their efforts. And, in thinking about it, it's not because I'm uncomfortable with the technology. It's the sociology that's influenced my choice.

Since deciding to try to live the life of an artist, I find that I've become something of an urban hermit. Once I get busy working on one project or the other, it's not inconceivable that I go for six days without having any face-to-face contact with another human being. Thus, my infrequent trips to the bank aren't strictly for business; they also give me the opportunity to have a visit and chat with people I've come to know over the past two decades. The employees of my branch have seen me go from being a scruffy, five-foot-nothing dwarf of a hippy and wanna-be psychologist to a balding, bearded, broke, successfully impoverished artist. And, somehow, I don't think an ABM is going to enquire about my latest project or show or how things have been going, nor am I going to be able to ask it how the latest addition to its family is doing or whether its spouse is still a dedicated bicyclist.

For the time being, I'm going to continue to resist having the machines completely take over my life and try to find some simple pleasures in actually talking with real, live people.

Jerry T. McNeill
Edmonton

✉ There is more than one brand of Swiss Army Knife. We all know about the Victor Inox, but many people don't seem to have heard of another very legitimate brand of SAK, namely the Wenger Inox. The Wenger is usually about half an inch shorter than the Victor, and the Swiss cross logo is slightly different, but the big difference is in the scissors. They have no spring to lose! Instead of the spring there is a lever, which connects the scissor blades with the knife's main spring. Being a (Swiss) precision machinist by trade I appreciate this detail very much. Admittedly this knife has one drawback that outdoors people and others that eat out of cans might consider major: the can opener. The one on the Victor is more refined, on the other hand it can also break easier. Since the Swiss Army is impartial in its dealings with its civilian suppliers of SAK, Wenger and Victor both manufacture the identical SAK for military purposes, and Wenger incorporates the competitors' can opener in its army issue knife. It's like driving a Ford with a GM engine.

Fred Schenkel
Creston, British Columbia

✉ I've only ever had two kinds of knife with which I've been totally happy. One is a Russell belt knife made in the Maritimes, and the other is the red-handled one.

I discovered the Swiss Army Knife a long, long time ago during a holiday trip in Britain when I needed a corkscrew for a picnic on the Scottish moors. The blades of my basic model, the screwdrivers, the bottle and can opener have been invaluable at times, but to this day I haven't had any real use for the pointy tool next to the corkscrew. The fact that I'm almost never without the knife is readily apparent from the faded knife-shape on the hip pocket of all of my Levi's.

A few years back, when my muscles seemed to obey the mind better, a good friend and our mutual collection of three mid-teen boys hiked the West Coast Trail. That's the one on the ocean side of Vancouver Island and runs between Bamfield and Port Renfrew. To the energetic it's about a hundred kilometres of the most spectacular walkable coastline in British Columbia. To those of us past the magic forty, who get all our exercise pulling our chairs closer to the dining table, it seemed a lot farther than that. A third of the trail was steeply uphill, a third just as bad downhill, a third along the pebbly beach, which is like walking on ball bearings and another third through salal and other rain-forest underbrush still soaked from rain weeks before. I know that it doesn't add up, but in retrospect the sum of the parts was much greater than the whole, both in effort and enjoyment.

About half-way along the trail one has to cross the Nitnat River, a fairly good stream that empties Nitnat Lake into the Pacific. As it is too deep to wade and does not have a cable car or Burma bridge, as do some of the other streams along the route, crossing is by boat and in the hands of a member of a local native band. I'm told that back in the early days of the trail these crossings were by canoe, but our transport was a small outboard-powered craft. The fee was two dollars per person.

While ferrying us across, our contemporary Charon offered to sell us live crabs at the same price, two bucks apiece. We agreed to buy one each, as our seafood menu up to that time was limited to goose-neck barnacles because all shellfish harvesting was closed due to recent red tide in the area. While goose-neck barnacles are possibly the most delicate-tasting stuff to come out of the ocean, they're only available at low ebb and are often in inaccessible places, so we were happy to augment our backpacker's freeze-dried food. You know the stuff. Much like an airline meal, it looks like food, feels like food, but doesn't taste like food and probably isn't.

The crabs turned out to be huge, individually too large for our biggest cooking pot. That evening we took turns cooking them, half a crab at a time. My tool of choice in dealing with this feast was my Swiss Army Knife.

During washing up I found that while I had been ever so meticulous in getting out the little bits of crab stuck in the various crevices of the knife, my nose told me otherwise. So into a fresh pot of boiling water went the knife, along with our other utensils, plates and Sierra cups as part of our effort towards backpacking hygiene.

Imagine my shock when, after the required boiling time, at the bottom of the pot I found the sterile but skeletal remains of my knife and a couple of equally clean but curly red plastic bits. No one at the time had thought of the fact that the red part of the knife is plastic, a plastic that turns very soft in hot water.

My immediate angry reaction, mostly at my own stupidity, was to chuck the bits as far as I could into the surf, but ecology prevailed and they were packed out with our other trash. As it turned out, it was difficult to part with old friends, skeletal or not, and I wound up taking the knife home. Eventually I replaced the plastic parts with teak and would be using the knife still had I not taken it with me sailing. On water, as we all know, only things of value ever fall overboard. My original SAK is now probably encrusted with barnacles, but a number of its younger cousins have not been far from my hand since.

By the way, I heard or read somewhere that, aside from dropping them in deep water, SAKs are never lost. Soon after you buy a new one the old one turns up. There must be something to that, as at the moment I have three.

Still, through all these years I've yet to find out the real reason for that pointy tool next to the corkscrew.

Al Vitols
North Vancouver

✉ My father, before his retirement, worked in the sulphuric acid plant division of Cominco, a lead-zinc smelter in Trail, British Columbia.

One of his jobs — I swear I tell the truth — was to don a rubber suit, like a deep-sea diver's suit, and dive into house-sized tanks of one-hundred-per-cent sulphuric acid and use an oxy-acetylene torch to weld patches over holes the acid had eaten in the one-inch-thick steel plate.

After one such repair job, he climbed out of the tank, stripped off the suit and reached, naturally, for a cigarette and his Zippo — the one I'd given him for Christmas.

Oops! Plunk! Damn! The lighter had slipped out of his hand and dropped into the tank of acid.

What to do? Re-suit and dive in to rescue it? Nope — too tired after the last swim. Almost end of shift anyway. I'll get it out tomorrow, or the day after. Unfortunately, life being the way it is, he never did get around to rescuing that lighter. Not, at least, for about a year. When next he was required to weld a patch on the inside of tank No. 5, twelve months had gone by.

Same routine — suit up, dive in, weld a patch over that crack that's developed in the tank. Routine repair except — hey — what's this shiny lump of metal lying on the bottom of the tank?

The shiny lump of metal was the stainless steel case of the Zippo lighter.

Now I'd love to say that after emerging from the tank he used that Zippo to light his cigarette, but that would be stretching credibility too far, wouldn't it?

No, the acid-soaked lighter did not function. My father did, however — purely as a matter of curiosity, and with a roguish sense of humour — write a letter to the Zippo folks, explaining that the lifetime guarantee they offered probably did not cover eventualities like a year-long swim in pure sulphuric acid.

No, indeed, the Zippo people responded — they hadn't had that in mind when they offered their guarantee — but they did have a Zippo museum, where retired lighters and their stories lived on.

In subsequent letters, it was agreed they would swap his acid-etched Zippo remains for a new model. They even had his initials engraved on the new one. His old lighter's remains now lie in a Zippo museum, I believe in Pennsylvania. His story was told in a half-column ad in *Time* magazine, complete with photograph, for which he received twenty-five dollars — they refunded, as well, the cost of postage he spent mailing the corpse to them.

My current Zippo lighter, a solid brass model, has lived a much tamer life. True, the hinge pin broke after two or three years of use, and I considered sending it south of the border to be repaired. Figuring transit, repair and return could take six to eight weeks, I decided not to do this. I replaced the missing hinge pin with a carefully customized length of paper clip which, since it's now about a year old, I should probably replace again.

What a machine this Zippo is! Two or three different breakage points are areas a good backhouse mechanic can fix himself — if not, send it to the manufacturer, for repair at no cost.

Aarne Martin
Vancouver

CLEO IN JAPAN

Cleo Paskal, whose chapter this is, is in Montreal these days — so far as we know. With Cleo you can never be sure. In *The Fourth Morningside Papers*, she appeared from South Africa and Mali, where she had gone, as she said, "to shock myself out of my Euro-centricity." This time, she's been in the Orient, from where she wrote . . .

February 2, 1993

✉ I have a friend, Toshiro, who is a Japanese anthropologist. He wrote his Ph.D. at Cornell on the Jews of St. Lawrence Street at the turn of the century. Now he teaches at a university in Japan. Last fall, he took his seminar students on an ethnic tour of North America. They crossed the continent visiting native reservations, Harlem and synagogues. One day, after attending high holiday services in Mont-real, he mentioned to me that he planned to write a book about Japan and that he needed help with the research. Three weeks later I was in Japan.

I am based at Meiji Gakuin University, just south of Tokyo. I occupy an amorphous position somewhere between student and dean, a situation rather confusing to the hierarchy-conscious Japa-nese. They don't quite know how to treat me. I haven't made things easier by doing stuff like roller-blading around campus. To stay on the safe side, something the Japanese love to do, everyone treats me really well.

This is a very strange institute of higher learning. It is brand-new, impeccably clean, well-lit, with a kind, knowledgeable staff who really want to help you learn. Even the administration people are gentle. It's a sort of Platonic ideal of a university. But the whole thing shuts down by 6:00 P.M. It is 7:13 P.M. now and I am the last person left in the building. The security guard has just been by and has given me a quizzical look. So much for the "hard-working Japanese" myth.

Universities are one of the only areas in Japanese society where people are allowed to be individuals with individual interests. Even given that, my faculty, International Studies, is known as a collection of some of the most eccentric people in Japan. I deal mostly with four professors. The main one is my pal Toshiro, whose current fascination is jazz in Harlem. You can hear his office from down the hall. Another professor specializes in Africa and was one of the founders of Japan's anti-apartheid movement. He keeps his own carton of sake in the faculty fridge and occasionally shows up in full East African dress. A third seems to specialize in places with great beaches. He throws superb parties. The fourth professor is very, very quiet, kind and gentle. He is studying the American military occupation in Japan.

Soon after I arrived, the four of them took me out to dinner. They ordered lots of beer and lots of sake and, as an afterthought, some food. When the glutinous brown mass arrived, I asked, "So, what kind of food is this?" They looked at each other like they had never thought to ask, seeing as how they didn't really intend to eat it anyway. After some poking and prodding and conferring in French (their common second language, as most of them had opted for Parisian graduate schools), they declared it cow intestines and ordered some more beer to congratulate themselves on such fine analytical detective work.

It isn't only the professors who allow themselves to go a bit batty within the safety the university. Most students sacrificed their childhood to pass the insanely rigorous entrance exams. Their three years of university are probably the only time in their lives they will be allowed to indulge in discovering what interests them. As soon as they graduate, most will become corporate cogs.

Actually, the vast majority of students don't wait that long. My friend Mew is a second-year university student in Toshiro's Ethnic North America seminar. She is already worried about job hunting. She takes after-school classes that teach her how to write CVs, how much leg to show at interviews, and how to answer interviewers' questions. During the course of finding a job, Mew will probably send out hundreds of CVs and submit to dozens of interviews. Most university students spend more of their final year attending interviews and courses on how to job hunt than attending class.

It is especially difficult for women. Many companies hire based on looks in order to find potential wives for their male employees. Needless to say, Mew's job-hunting courses have taught her that, when asked if she will continue working after marriage, the answer is no. No point rocking the corporate boat, especially because new statistics show that the unemployment rate in Japan is now a shockingly high 2.7%.

But, in the meantime, Mew is still a university student. A very excited university student. Next week Toshiro will bring American Indian Movement leader Dennis Banks to visit the campus. Turns out Mew loves to dance to native music. Who would have guessed? She'll have to leave early, though, her job-hunting course starts at four.

Yours,
Cleo

March 2, 1994

✉ It's called "surprise fork syndrome." You get it when you've been in Japan long enough to understand the rail system and have ordered at least one meal from a vending machine. It strikes suddenly, usually in a restaurant. You sit down and prepare to order from the picto-menu. The waitress comes over, spots your genetic make-up and disappears. She comes back, bows politely and generously, graciously, offers you a fork. You might have lived in Japan for forty years and be a chopstick virtuoso. It doesn't matter. You are a foreigner and no foreigner could possibly understand things Japanese.

Some Westerners take it well. They understand the waitress is only trying to be helpful. Others get nasty and make a point of ordering really soft food just to show off their chopstick skills. The rest are happy to see a familiar object, if only a fork.

Foreigners in Japan have been known to go to pathetic lengths to remind themselves of home. A guy I know at the Canadian Embassy in Tokyo hosts weekly happy hours featuring specially flown-in Molson's. An old university buddy, who had been living in Japan for three years, insisted on celebrating our reunion by opening up one of his prized possessions, a can of Campbell's beef and barley soup. I once saw a tin of Spam being sold for twelve dollars.

Personally, I am coping pretty well, even though I still can't identify most of the food. Yesterday I bought a package of dried apple slices. Turns out it was dried squid slices. Also, the Japanese aren't big on sweets. Chocolate cake is rare, and as a result, Diet Coke is even rarer.

It's enough to drive you to cultural desperation. Even when you think you're watering your cultural roots, like by paying twenty dollars to go see an American film, it's never quite the same. Movies are invariably a wash-out. No matter how funny the movie is, you and the guy from Wisconsin in the third row will be the only ones laughing. I don't know whether it's because the rest of the audience just doesn't get it or because the person who did the subtitles is criminally incompetent. Whatever the reason, you usually end up laughing six times as loud as you would back home, just to prove to the people sitting next to you that, for once, they're the foreigners and no foreigner could possibly understand the subtle humour of the Three Stooges.

But no attempt to preserve ersatz culture, no matter how pathetic, comes close to those made by the U.S. military. Occasionally, when I really need a fix, I resort to listening to FEN, the Far East Network, U.S. Armed Forces Radio. They deal with cultural isolation by ignoring the existence of any culture that isn't American. In between songs by country singers you wish you hadn't heard of, they run segments like "Swap Shop with Captain Conners," which feature such memorable bits of radio as: "Sergeant Franklin has a six-piece solid wood dining-room set he'd like to sell for $1,200 or best offer. You can reach him through the guard station at the Yokosuka base." There's also "Outdoor Trivia" with questions like, "Which kinds of rock can explode when they get too hot, like in a camp-fire?" Sorry, I didn't hear the answer. I was laughing too hard.

My favourite FEN disk jockey is Harry Newman. He is a complete gloom-monger whose patter consists of nothing but statements like: "Mothers, don't leave your children unattended in the kitchen. Pots falling from the stove could result in burns and scaldings that last a lifetime. In fact, you should always have boiling saucepans on the back burner, just in case. Remember, prevention is safety in the making." Great stuff, especially considering most Japanese think themselves lucky to have two burners in their tiny kitchens.

FEN also runs a TV station, which features long-forgotten American classics. I never miss *Stubs, Best Cowdog in the West* or any of the *Love Bugs*.

But since the vast majority of Western culture that makes it to Japan is brought in by the U.S. Army and Hollywood, is it a surprise that waitresses think foreigners are too dumb to use chopsticks?

Yours,
Cleo

April 2, 1993

✉ It's good to know your value on the open market. In Canada, there are lots of people just like me, so I rate balcony seats at a hockey game. In London, I can pass myself off as an exotic American and can usually bag something in the vicinity of decent seats at *Les Miz*. In Mali, a village chief once offered a male travelling companion one hundred camels for me, but only because he thought I would make a good tourist attraction. Now I'm in Japan, and the question is, what am I worth?

A friend of mine, Takeo, has a grandmother who is an *o-miai* co-ordinator, a *nakodo*, the Japanese version of a matchmaker.

The *miai* from *o-miai* comes from the verb *miau*, which means "to look each other over." The O part just makes it all polite. The *nakodo*, usually an unpaid older woman, arranges formal meetings between prospective couples. To make things even more relaxed, both sets of parents attend, as well. If the couple likes each other or, in the words of one participant, "If I think I could sleep with him," another meeting is arranged. After three or four meetings, wedding invites are sent out.

Statistics are hard to come by, as most Japanese couples would prefer to say they met through AA than through *o-miai*. Most guess around thirty per cent of marriages are arranged. Takeo's grandmother alone has been the mysterious, but beaming, guest of honour at more than two hundred and fifty weddings.

Takeo and his parents live with his grandmother. I asked him if I could come over for dinner. It was such an extremely un-Japanese thing to do that he was shocked into compliance. Foreigners can get away with anything in Japan.

Exactly one week later, I brushed my hair, put on a dress, and went to meet Takeo at Tokyo's Ikebukuro train station. From there it was a twenty-minute ride to his house. As we chugged closer, Takeo progressively straightened up his appearance. First he pulled a bland tie out of his jacket pocket and knotted it tightly. Then he tucked in his button-down shirt, combed his hair and brushed his jacket. I knew we had almost arrived when he took off the ring his girlfriend had given him.

The house was about a ten-minute walk from the station, pretty close by Tokyo terms. It was two storeys, with Takeo and his family living upstairs and Grandma living downstairs. It was her house. The path up the side to the entrance was lined with bonsai trees. The door wasn't locked; in fact, I don't think it even had a lock. We took off our shoes and went in.

It was a stupendous greeting. Mom, Dad, kid brother, and Grandma all rushed out of different corners of the house bowing and yelling welcomes. I felt utterly unworthy.

The inside of the house hadn't changed in probably sixty years. The dinner table was long and low. We sat on the *tatami* floor, the room heated by a stove. The walls and most of the furniture were wood. There was no TV. Nor had they made any concessions to a western palate. It was a purely Japanese feast. *Sashimi*, *tempura*, thinly sliced vegetables, home-made *miso* soup, tofu cubes and, proudly displayed at the end of the table, to be admired and maybe eaten, a melon.

"Do you always eat like this?" I asked Takeo. "No," he replied, "you're the first foreigner ever to visit. They wanted to make a good impression."

During dinner, we smiled at each other a lot but conversation was pretty awkward until Takeo asked me if there was anything I would like to know about o-miai. What a pal. I asked his grandmother what she thought was important in a good marriage. "There are only two things that are important," she answered. "First, education. The man must be equally or better educated than the woman. Second, height. The man must be taller."

It couldn't be that simple, could it? Two hundred and fifty weddings. I tried to apply her rule to a question I had been asking myself for months: why were so many foreign men married to Japanese women and so few foreign women married to Japanese men? Most put it down to Japanese women being desperate to escape an oppressive culture and foreign women being unwilling to be the virtual house slaves many Japanese men expect of their wives. Grandma didn't agree. "It's simply a question of height. Foreign men are tall so Japanese women like them. Foreign women are tall so Japanese men don't like them."

So where did that leave me, a short foreign woman? Grandma answered, "You're an exception. I think I could make you quite a good match, seeing as how you are so short." Finally, a culture that appreciates my special physical qualities. It's good to know your value on the open market.

Yours,
Cleo

May 2, 1993

✉ The Okinawan Islands, dotted along the southern tip of the Japanese archipelago, should be known for their coral beaches and hyacinth groves. They're not. They're known for having been the only bit of Japan actually captured during World War Two. The Americans are still there. The area was directly occupied until 1972, and Okinawa main island still has the highest concentration of U.S. bases outside the continental United States.

It was well after midnight at Birdy's bar, an off-base club for American Green Berets from nearby Kadena base. It was the Friday after pay-day but there were no soldiers in the bar. They were all in Somalia. Rumours were that some of them were among the eighteen who had died in the botched attack on Aideed. The Okinawan barmaid casually wondered who had been among the dead.

The Green Berets might not have been there in person, but their spirit was pervasive. On one side of the cash register was a photo of Nixon and Elvis shaking hands. On the other side was the "Welcome Military Personnel" sign given to favoured businesses during occupation. Tacked above the bar was currency from all the places the American patrons had visited or perhaps invaded, including a Canadian two-dollar bill. Faded, lacquered movie posters papered the walls. Grant, Garbo and Bogart smiled down at the patrons. In a corner was a transcript of Martin Luther King's "I had a dream" speech. In another corner was a karaoke machine. Fish tanks rainbowed with tropical fish and plastic American Indians were on the counter and behind the bar. A Russian officer's hat hung from the wall like a trophy. It had the feeling of a cosy, well-worn officer's club, which, of course, is basically what it was.

I was there to meet one of Japan's most notorious radicals, but I didn't know what he looked like. I sat next to one of the two men at the bar. As I sat, the man turned and smiled. "Hello," he said, "my name is Chibana Shoichi. I own a supermarket, a small supermarket."

It wasn't exactly an understatement, but it wasn't exactly the whole story, either. Everyone in Japan knows Chibana Shoichi, though they might not recognize his name. People usually refer to him as, "You know, that Okinawan guy who burned the Japanese flag." Sometimes they'll add some reference to heroism or treason, depending on their politics. But everyone knows him.

In 1987, at a baseball game on a U.S. Army base in Okinawa, he took off his shoes, scaled a concrete wall, and set fire to the *Hinomaru*, the Japanese flag, with his pocket lighter. He climbed down and waited to be arrested. The police were so shocked they didn't know what to do. So Chibana went to the local McDonald's and had lunch while the prosecutors tried to put together a warrant. Then he turned himself in.

Since then, he has been vilified by right-wingers and beatified by left-wingers. Now he was buying me a beer.

The bartender, looking rather effete in oiled-down curls and Lennon glasses, served us our beers and quietly left.

I asked Chibana the obvious question. "Why?"

"Do you know much about the history of Okinawa?" he asked.

I said I knew the islands had been independent until the Japanese had unilaterally annexed them in the late nineteenth century. The Japanese had done their best to eradicate local languages and culture, replacing them with Japanese and Emperor worship. Then came the destruction of the war and American occupation.

"That's all true," he said, "but empty. It doesn't explain the damage Japanese education did to Okinawa, to Okinawans. During the war, we were taught that the Japanese were divine. That there was no worse shame than to be captured by the barbaric Americans. Because of that, thousands of Okinawans committed suicide rather than surrender. When the Americans landed, mothers slit their daughters' throats then set themselves on fire. They killed the ones they loved best to save them from what they were taught to believe was a fate worse than death. Okinawans who did try to surrender were killed by Japanese soldiers who thought they would betray them. All this was done in the name of the *Hinomaru*, the flag of the Japanese military during the war. Now that flag is the unofficial flag of Japan. Germany changed their flag. So did Italy. But Japan didn't. The war isn't over here. We still have Japanese education and U.S. bases. When they decided to fly the *Hinomaru* in my village, a village where hundreds died in its name, a village that is built around a U.S. base, many old people came to me and asked me to stop it from happening. I was the logical choice because I am self-employed and can't be fired.

"I didn't think it was such a big deal. The response was shocking. East Timorese, Puerto Ricans, American Indians all come to me. I say, Please don't consider me a representative of Okinawan dissent, but they still come.

"I didn't expect the response from right-wingers, either. They tried to burn my store. I couldn't imagine that. But there was also unexpected support. Sixty-five lawyers from as far away as Tokyo have volunteered to defend me. I don't even know most of their names.

"Honestly, the thing that surprised me most was that no one had burned the *Hinomaru* before. People think I am a crazy radical. In the context of Japan, the act looks crazy, but in the context of the community, it was not so strange. A supermarket without customers is impossible. If they thought I was crazy, my customers would go elsewhere. They didn't stop coming.

"Speaking of which, I have to go. If I don't get home soon, I won't be able to get any sleep before the farmers' market opens in the morning. You have to get there by five or else all the good fruit is gone. It's not easy running a supermarket."

Yours,
Cleo

June 2, 1993

✉ A surprising number of people know only two things about modern Japan. First, the Japanese eat raw fish. Second, they're sexist. When word got out that I was going to Japan, a guy I normally consider about as enlightened as an eclipse called to warn me about the evil sexist Japanese. Actually, I think his exact words were, "Hey, babe, watch yourself, 'cause I won't be there to take care of you." I started to wonder how bad it was going to be.

It hasn't taken long to find out. There's a lot of talk about corporate sexism. About women having to quit promising careers once they get married. About sexism being so ingrained in the culture that women actually speak a different, more deferential version of Japanese. That's all true, but pretty remote from the lives of most Japanese women. The mom of the family I am staying with, Yuki, was quite a well-regarded professional before she got married. She put her career on hold when her first child arrived. Now her daily routine is pretty typical and quite punishing.

She gets up around seven, hangs out the wash she did the night before and wakes up and dresses her two girls, aged one and three. Then, if she didn't do it the night before, she'll pack her husband's lunch. By the time her husband wakes up around eight, she is cooking them all a hot breakfast. After her husband leaves, she cleans up and takes the children to a small local park. There, she meets other mothers escaping tiny apartments. Yuki knows most of the women by sight and sits and chats with them while the children play. There are unspoken rules about what they can discuss. Yuki's husband, for example, has a prestigious job so Yuki can't ask the other women what their husbands do. If she does, courtesy dictates that they must ask her her husband's profession, and when she tells them, they might think the whole conversation was set up by Yuki as an excuse to brag. The women in the park have a common bond of motherhood, but they rarely become friends.

After the park, Yuki makes lunch then puts the kids to bed for an afternoon nap. While they sleep, she cleans up and does regular chores like balancing the family books. If she's lucky, she'll have time to read the newspaper. Once the kids are up and dressed, the family usually goes food shopping. There are no large food stores like Loblaws or Safeway, and the fridges are very small. Almost every day, Yuki has to go to a variety of small, spaced-out stores to get food. Not particularly thrilling under normal circumstances, but with a thirty-minute bus and train commute at either end and two small kids in tow, it's my personal definition of hell.

Back at the house, Yuki unpacks and prepares dinner. Her husband usually gets home around 7:30. That is remarkably early by Japanese standards. There is a joke that many Japanese children think their father only knows three words — food, bath and bed — because by the time they get home from the office, they're so wrecked that's all they are capable of.

After dinner, the kids have about an hour to play with Dad, then they are bathed and put to bed. Yuki cleans up, puts in a wash and tends to all the things she didn't have time to do during the day. For example, while I was there, she stayed up until two o'clock for a week in order to get off all the family's New Year's greeting cards.

It's all pretty mundane and probably sounds very familiar to quite a few Canadian parents. The difference is that there is practically no societal support for parents. Women are expected to just disappear for a few years, re-emerging only once the kids are in school to get a low-level job to help pay the bills. Often husbands are rarely around, or, if they are, they sometimes exact as much care as the children. It is very lonely. Yuki is considered one of the lucky few whose husbands actually know the names of their kids.

Another thing that makes life more difficult for mothers is the exorbitant cost of baby-sitting. Leaving your kid in the care of your neighbour's teen-ager can get you branded an uncaring mother. Baby-sitters are almost exclusively older women whose own children have grown up. They are professionals and get paid accordingly. This set-up causes a serious social problem. For many women, especially in the cities, their first direct contact with babies comes in the delivery room. A lot of women have no idea what they are in for. Several have told me that if they had had a chance to baby-sit when they were younger, they would have had second thoughts about rushing in and having one of their own as soon as they got married.

Unsurprisingly, there is starting to be a backlash. Surprisingly, it's coming from older women, not young college students. Increasingly, on the same day her youngest child gets married, the mother considers her family duties over, and she serves her husband with divorce papers. Usually the husbands are completely shocked. These divorced men were so dependent on their wives that they either collapse and shrink into something else or barely survive. Some don't even know where their underwear is. A few of these newly divorced women have squirrelled away money during the marriage. Others are so eager to be free, they don't care what happens next. It is as if suddenly, at the age of fifty or sixty, they are being born again.

So that about sums up sexism in Japan. Now, on to raw fish. That's actually a bit more complicated. You see, it all depends on if you're a man or a woman. If you're a man, you eat a piece of sushi all in one bite. If you're a woman, you eat it in two. It's much more feminine that way.

Yours,
Cleo

MORNINGSIDE'S OWN BIRDS
OF THE AIR

And beasts of the field, for that matter. The animal kingdom in all its variety continues to attract our listeners' attention.

✉ A day to rekindle doubts and superstitions.

This morning, a morning of winter cold and bright sunshine, seeking a last view of the countryside in its eclipse plumage before tomorrow's blizzard arrives, I drove along the Corkstown Road. This is a frequent eddy in my current life. I can see horses. I enjoy horses. I prefer them stoutly fenced. The fences along the Corkstown Road are very reassuring. Some days there is a sparrow hawk on the power line by the long straight. It knows I am harmless in the aspic comfort of the car. The sparrow hawk prefers humans under glass. I stop and wonder what it can find to eat so late in the year. It ignores me. A brown horse, bored with inhaling the rough brown grass, looks up and swings its head on that lovely strong neck, which horses have patented. A horse that has been looked at by television cameras does not need my praise. Beyond the brown horse is a white horse. I call up a memory of a childhood chant: "Good luck to you, good luck to me, good luck to every white horse I see."

And there we were, in this triangle of high wire, high fence and high technology, each taking the morning as something to be enjoyed, something not to be questioned. I wondered about their thoughts. The brown horse, failing an apple or a sugar cube, ambled horsefully away; tomorrow the horses will be turned out in the next field. The hawk, seeing a cricket three fields away, whipped across the meadow and was gone to lunch.

Farther on, a railway line crosses, shuffling out from an underpass and curving slowly away north-west between the fields and an untidy rise of shale and sumac. It's not sumac any more. It was a hill of fire in the early fall, but now it is just skeletons and clinkers. I wonder if the hawk and the horse care.

I roll with gentle dignity across the corduroy sleepers and the rails. The rails live in a world of their own, dreaming of the freight train that rumbles through at 4:00 A.M. The wooden ties turn and groan in their sleep. I set the car at the hill to the west and ignore the thundering sewer of trucks and cars on the expressway to my left. A lonely runner, proud in his agony, comes over the brow of the hill. I flash my lights and wave. We are both pilgrims in search of something yet to be revealed. This is a kinship I do not have with the horse or the hawk. The runner waves. A bond; a modest togetherness of Adidas and Pirelli, sharing the road on a morning that only God can give to man.

On the crest, where, in season, signposts encourage campers to nest for the night and, in a different season, stout padlocks convey a different message, we are introduced to Kanata, a city that, like Gargantua, sprang fully formed into the mortgaged joys of the world. It is what it is.

Before a beetling plunge puts me down on level terms with dog walkers and the hustle of purposeful traffic, I look at the horizon, scalped by pioneers. It must be five miles to the edge of visual experience. I mentally lay that yardstick across the land five hundred times and see Vancouver. I look over my shoulder and see, two hundred horizons away, Newfoundland. Did they feel lonely, the pioneers, adrift in an ocean of land, paddling up nameless rivers, crossing endless lakes? Or were they like the brown horse, intent on immediacy, sparing only a quick glance at tomorrow's field?

And in the overhead of this musing world I see geese. One, two, three . . . ten, eleven, twelve . . . clouds of geese, skeining, streaming, arrowing . . . not just one, two, three individuals but explosions, barrages, mushrooms of Canadas. Geese I thought long gone were only now turning south. Had they heard a private weather forecast?

Should I believe them? Perhaps the sparrow hawk was wrong. Two hundred horizons to the south there would be new grass and sunshine. A thousand crickets, a thousand grasshoppers, five hundred mice away, the sparrow hawk could perch upon a warmer wire.

What would the white horse do? If only I had more horse sense I would know the answer. Geese once warned Rome. Are they warning us this will be a hard winter, a winter of savage winds come to ransack us? Three hundred and six car lengths to the mile, three hundred and sixty thousand car lengths to the south is sunshine. Why on earth do people say, "Silly goose"?

I say, "Gone goose . . . smart goose."

Craig Parry Hughes
Ottawa

✉ I first homesteaded in this country some twenty-five years ago. I remember one drizzly overcast day in the fall. I had most of my harvest in the bin and I was doing my fall cultivating when I stopped for supper. As I got off the tractor and the world was once again silent and sweet without old John puffing and snorting around the field (old John is my John Deere tractor), I heard what must have been a thousand geese from the sound of them. I ran to the house to get my gun and with some luck perhaps get one for supper. But when I came back out, the geese had not yet arrived. I thought that this must surely be a big flock to be heard from so far off. I stood there for what seemed an eternity, but it could not have been more than five minutes. As I stood there, the noise of all these thousands of snow geese rose to such an intensity that it drowned out any other sound. When they finally came into view, it was not like any flock of geese I had ever seen, but a cloud that darkened the sky. As they passed overhead I stood in awe. I could not bring myself to shoot at such a marvellous sight. The flock was over a mile long. I know because my farm is a mile long, and the flock was stretched the full length of the farm. When the last little straggler had finally passed overhead, I wished I had a movie camera to record all this, as surely no one would believe what I had seen, and I didn't shoot even one. But then I would only have to clean it and —

well, beans and wieners didn't taste so bad. I had just started cooking my supper when I heard a second flock fly over, and it was as big as the first. I could not believe there were so many geese in the world. This flock was followed by a third flock that was just as big.

During the night as I lay in bed, I heard geese flying overhead as I drifted off to sleep. In the morning when I went out to greet the day, the sun had not yet crested the tree-tops, and in the pre-dawn light it seemed that I was in some magic world, as during the night it froze quite hard and the mist that hung in the air from the day before was now suspended frosty crystals that sparkled and shimmered like a million tiny jewels. As I stood there drinking in this marvellous sight, I thought perhaps it must have snowed because my fields looked white, but then it really was hard to see through all those sparkling jewels drifting all about me. I took a step closer so I could see, and then, as if thunder had broken this silent sparkling world, ten thousand wings of snow geese thundered to get airborne, and with this came the cries of alarm from ten thousand snow geese. For what seemed like only a moment, the world was vibrating with the cries of snow geese and thundering wings. It shook me to my soul. A few minutes later the world was silent once again. The sun broke over the tree-tops and all the sparkles melted into the sunlight and I stood there wondering if I had really seen this marvellous sight, or was I just dreaming. But as I stood there shivering in my long underwear, I knew that I had seen what perhaps no other man has ever seen.

Vic Daradick
High Level, Alberta

✉ In 1967 I was struggling to learn the finer points of flight test engineering at the United States Navy Test Pilot School in Maryland. I was one of two Canadian (RCAF) students on our course. It was a very tough course. Only the best of the U.S. Navy and Marine Corps aviators were selected. The head of academics was a man called Tom Moore. He was a talented teacher and he slow-talked like the Mississippian that he was. The Navy wanted high standards in their flight test program and was prepared to "bilge" poor performers. A person got "bilged" for any one of a number of things, including failing too many quizzes.

One morning we were presented with a Tom Moore special: a rather tricky quiz on aerodynamics. I was bent over my desk, operating my trusty slide rule at high speed, when I heard a plaintive cry from across the room. One of my American Navy colleagues cried out in a loud and agonized voice: "I did not come to the Test Pilot School to learn how to be a ?£$*??!!* Canada goose!"

When I worked my way towards the bottom of the page, I discovered the source of my colleague's agony. What to my wondering eyes should appear but the following question: "You are a Canada goose leading your squadron to winter quarters. How should you brief your formation to fly so as to achieve optimum fuel efficiency?"

My first reaction was an onset of the same panic demonstrated by my colleague. But, as a Canadian, national pride dictated that I solve the puzzle. But how? Then I realized that all I need do was to apply some aerodynamics called "lifting line theory" that suggested if one knew the gross weight and wing span of the goose, one could predict where the geese following the leader should fly to take advantage of the wing-tip vortices produced by the goose ahead. I got full marks on that one, and I did not "bilge" the course.

Ken Mitchell
Picton, Ontario

✉ Some people react with disbelief when told about turkey vultures. Many folks think they are giant crows or ravens, or some kind of great black hawk. Besides, they argue, don't vultures and buzzards pick at the carcasses of carrion in Africa?

Where we live, in the Ganaraska Forest region, it is not the Canada goose that heralds the coming of spring or fall, but the migration of the turkey vulture. Our home lies directly beneath a migration route. The vultures fly in a graceful, circular dance, a ballet, with the hot-air thermals, round and round, never flapping their wings. When I'm out hanging up the laundry, with only the sound of bees buzzing and the song of birds and the whisper of the forest filling my ears, I spot the vultures flying overhead, and I feel relaxed, at peace. I cannot express how connected I feel to the change of the season, to my sense of place in the forest when I see these magnificent creatures.

Their flocks, which I think of as families, usually number seven to eleven or twelve, sometimes less. We have never seen more in a group. I note that these are ideal numbers when working co-operatively, when striving towards consensus in decision making. I think, does a coven not ever go above thirteen?

Last fall, though, I observed several families converging over the Wilmot Creek at Bowmanville, then following the 401 westward to Niagara. The larger group numbered nearly thirty, and they were flying very low. I could distinguish, with the naked eye, the juveniles, with white heads, from the adults, with the red heads. They all have that silver-white portion on the underside of the wing, which glistens brilliantly when sun-rays reflect off them.

The families pass by our home in the spring, but one pair lingers on through the summer. We see them searching for food over fields and roads. Sometimes we come across one picking at road kill, doing its bit in the circle of life.

I am a vulture-watcher, and somehow feel a spiritual kinship with these dark, mysterious gypsies of the sky. They are my gauge of the seasons. When I don't see them for a while, I miss them, feel as though something important about my being is missing.

Helen MacDonald
Newtonville, Ontario

✉ Some two hundred and twenty kilometres north-west of Vancouver are the Yuculta Rapids. This is a place where at certain tides the water eddies and boils, whirlpools form and sucked-under logs have been seen shooting out of the water like ICBMs launched from a submarine. A spectacular place to see but not to be in, unless one has a fast, flat-bottomed boat and good "local knowledge." A couple of years back I was lucky enough to be in the company of one such knowledgeable skipper and in the right kind of boat travelling through the rapids while searching for a film location.

In the middle of the rapids near the aptly named Whirlpool Point, we could see many hundreds of birds actively diving at the huge vortices, fishing the upwelled herring schools. Although it's a spectacular sight, there's nothing terribly unusual about that, as gulls do that whenever the opportunity presents itself.

However, when we got closer, it was obvious that, while there certainly were a number of gulls, most of the birds were bald eagles. I counted well over a hundred fishing, but a much larger number by far were perched in the fir trees lining the shore. At first glance it looked as if some giant had taken handfuls of white cotton balls and thrown them into the dark branches, as all one could see at a distance were the white necks. At closer range we could see that they were eagles either eating or resting up for the next course or, perhaps, having an afternoon nap, having eaten too much. I have a certain affinity with the latter.

That evening, back at the lodge bar, when an American tourist commented on the great numbers of the U.S.A. "symbols," my skipper confided to him that they were actually plastic, remotely controlled birds, distributed by the B.C. Ministry of Tourism for the benefit of our American tourist friends. Apparently the mechanical killer whales were getting too expensive.

The other eagle experience doesn't involve numbers. It took place while filming a hang-glider pilot for a now almost forgotten late-night live television show on the CBC.

Just south of the 49th is a place called Cherry Point. Along with an oil refinery, it also boasts a long, high bluff at the waters' edge. As this bluff more or less faces the Strait of Juan de Fuca, any kind of good westerly wind provides a healthy and continuing lift above its face.

The glider pilot, the subject of our short film, told of many occasions when he was joined above the bluff by an eagle, flying wing to wing, and executing all of the hang glider's maneuvres in perfect unison. Occasionally it would separate a bit and do some turns on its own, as if to say, "Hey, can you do this?" If the wind was right, they'd spend hours flying together, and only a call by Mother Nature would bring the pilot to earth.

Al Vitols
North Vancouver

✉ Doris Mills first "discovered" birds in 1916 while on her honeymoon at Scarborough Beach, Maine, and there she compiled her first bird list. From then on she recorded all the birds she encountered at home in Toronto or abroad, and every year until her death, in 1989, she completed an annual bird list.

In 1936, Mrs. Mills began to keep a journal about her birding adventures rather than simply compiling lists of birds. By this time she had become part of a loosely organized group of amateur ornithologists who often scoured the ravines and waterfront together to find birds. She was in her early forties, but almost all the rest were young men in their teens or early twenties.

One of the young men she occasionally birded with was Farley Mowat, recently come to Toronto from Saskatoon. Of their first meeting she wrote:

January 8, 1938
Eight Long-eared Owls had been seen in Sunnybrook Park and so Henry Barnett (who knows where they might be found) said that he would try to show them to me on Saturday morning. At 9 o'clock I met Doreen Barnett, Barnie, and Farley Mowat at the corner of Blythwood Road and Mount Pleasant.

Farley is such a character that I must explain about him.

Barnie was at the eastern gap one day birding when he saw on the ground a piece of a broken pipe. A little further on he found another piece. Soon he met a boy who asked him if he had found a pipe. The pipe had been his! He is a bird student from Saskatoon, is sixteen, but very short and "young" looking; wore, on Saturday, a Scotch tam-o'shanter and woollen plaid scarf with his hiking clothes, his father's army boots, etc. He has a round face and blue eyes and seems to belong somehow to the out-of-doors, and he is quite a remarkable ornithologist, according to Barnie, and later, my own observation. Has been banding birds, and has keen eyes and considerable knowledge.

Barnie, the tall and overgrown (Barnie is 15), and Farley, the short and undergrown (smoking a pipe and being quite a man, for some time I judge), these two have become real friends and are two of the keenest bird students in the city.

Farley knows the Long-eared Owl well in the West and once saw thirty nesting pairs, he told me.

We parked the car just within the Sunnybrook Park gates and walked across a snowy field to a large pile of hay on the edge of the ravine. There flew up from the weed seeds a number of Tree Sparrows. Redpolls were flying with undulating flight. A siskin flew over our heads. We heard the call of a Downy Woodpecker and soon saw him at the base of a tree below us. Chickadee notes sounded in the air. We heard the sweet notes of goldfinches.

The Long-eared Owls were known to roost at the top of the pine trees on the north side of the road and at the top of the wooden bank. The boys started upward, examining every tree, while Doreen and I kept to the road and looked at the treetops skirting the roadway.

We had gone but a short distance when Barnie gave a shout, and motioned for us to look quickly to our left. I just saw a large owl disappearing into the dense growth of hemlocks on the south side of the roadway and near the top of the hill. It was the last of eight Long-eared Owls which the boys had disturbed and which had flown from their hiding place on quick and silent wings. I was surprised at the size of the owl in flight. How long his wings looked, and how long his tail. A beautiful bird he looked in a costume of two shades of brown, seen against the dark grey blue green of the hemlocks.

One owl remained on its perch in a pine tree high up the bank, and Doreen and I climbed up to see him with all haste.

"Be quiet!" Barnie shouted. Our ascent was a slippery one up the snowy hill, but we reached the bird ere he had flown. And, indeed, the ninth Long-eared Owl was very still and seemed undisturbed. I had never seen a Long-eared Owl before, so was especially thrilled. I noticed his rufous cheeks and long pointed ears and quickly made a note of him in my notebook. When we drew near and Barnie clapped his hands, the owl drew himself up very straight and his eyes were shining amber, very round and fierce and glowing. Barnie commenced to climb the tree and the owl flew suddenly and silently.

He seemed only about 9 inches on the perch, but when he

flew he seemed twice the size, with long wings and a long tail. Again I was struck with his two-toned appearance in flight, a light buff and dark brown against the green of the trees and blue of the sky.

The owl flew to the opposite bank which is as densely wooded with hemlocks as the bank we were on was wooded with pine. In the dark foliage of the trees he disappeared. And now we heard a Blue Jay screaming and screaming with cries of indignation and could see him across the ravine, or roadway, hopping from limb to limb and tree to tree in agitation and excitement. He had discovered the owls and was warning the whole neighbourhood.

Beneath the pine trees where the owls had been resting were many dark pellets on the ground, the snowy ground. These were about the size of horse chestnuts and were filled with the fur and bones of field mice. One contained the white skull of a little mouse.

The boys gathered a pocketful each of the pellets — and Barnie discovered too late that his lunch was in the same pocket (so part of the lunch went to the gulls at Sunnyside, but the precious pellets were kept to be examined later).

Long-eared Owls feed largely on field mice. A few small birds are taken, but they are mouse-owls and need to be protected. The pellets beneath that particular roost seemed to be composed of the remains of mice and of nothing else.

In 1939, Doris Mills married Murray Speirs, a young student of ornithology at the University of Illinois. Murray completed his Ph.D. in the 1940s, and eventually joined the faculty at the University of Toronto. Doris Speirs became fascinated by the evening grosbeak and made the study of this handsome yellow, black, and white bird a life-long project. She joined professional associations, met all the professional ornithologists, and spent thirty years researching the species both in the field and in the literature before publishing life histories of the species for the Smithsonian Institute.

John W. Sabean
Pickering, Ontario

✉ I have played host to several invasions of carpenter ants. At the time we were living in an old house, home to spiders, sow bugs and occasional ants — no problem in our live-and-let-live house.

But one spring, long before ants in their natural quarters would have been active, the "occasional" stragglers developed into a foraging column running along the back of the kitchen sink, up the wall, and into a crack in the roof panelling. They being large black carpenter ants, and the house being made of logs, I grew nervous. While ants don't actually eat wood, their industrious tunnelling can have similar weakening effects on structural timber. My hospitality could prove ill-advised if it meant I would one day put my foot through the floor.

I am generally less concerned about insect plagues than about the poisons society unleashes against them. But I decided the ants had to go. An aerosol bomb was not an option, for environmental reasons both inside the house and beyond. I also doubted it would do more than kill the scouts, leaving unscathed the main body of troops in battalion HQ somewhere in my walls.

The best lethal agent I could find was a bait, a sugary solution laced with poison, dispensed in a small plastic squeeze bottle. A similar product is sold in little flat tins with ant-sized, punch-in holes around the sides. Both take diabolical advantage of the nurturing habits of the ants: they suck it up and take it back to the nest to feed the non-foraging members of the community, including the larvae and the queen. When the queen dies, and there are no replacements, the once populous, well-organized colony disintegrates.

I put drops of the stuff into short sections of clear plastic tubing where only the ants could reach it, and watched as increasing numbers of them streamed in to collect their new-found, deadly bounty. In time, the hustling work parties diminished to a few uncertain stragglers, and eventually even these failed to show.

Indiscriminate use of such poisons could inflict spin-off damage on animals that prey on ants, particularly woodpeckers. I'm reasonably sure that nothing except my "target" quarry succumbed since they lived inside the house where, to date at least, any kind of ant-eater has yet to set foot.

Bob Waldon
Alert Bay, British Columbia

✉ My sister named her turtle Maggie and mine was Jiggs, after two well-known comic strip characters of the day. If memory serves me, they had been plucked from the putrid water of the local Woolworth's turtle tank in exchange for the comfort and security of a dented old galvanized wash-tub, which was kept under the stoop in the back-yard of our house in Fort William.

From time to time they were allowed out for exercise, and to compete against each other in races over a prescribed course carefully laid out in the mud. As they were about the same size with no distinguishable features, we painted an initial on each shell with nail polish, M for my sister's and J for mine, in order to distinguish ownership.

I don't recall having to deal with their excretions. I can only presume that our long-suffering mother dealt with such details, as indeed she must have done with the rats, guinea pigs and assorted rodents that regularly infested the household.

Disaster struck one afternoon when the neighbour's dog slipped his tether, using the brief moment of freedom to knock over the tub, which lay undiscovered until some time later, leaving no sign of its inhabitants.

The search went on by flashlight into the evening hours, but to no avail. After a suitable period of mourning, we moved on to caring for a couple of freshly hatched Rhode Island Reds.

The Lakehead winter came and went as only it can, with its freezing temperatures and great drifts of snow. It must have been sometime in May or June when one of the turtles was spotted by our mother as it emerged from a hole under the fence around her vegetable garden, apparently none the worse for wear. We couldn't tell whether it was Maggie or Jiggs, as the nail polish hadn't survived the winter's rigours.

It must have been able to burrow (if that's the appropriate terminology) below the frost line.

The voice of the turtle wasn't heard in our part of the land until many years later, when four of the little critters and their tank were left in the care of our young family while their owners went on vacation for ten days. Despite lots of TLC, on or about the fifth day, their shells began to soften; by the ninth day, all had expired. Frantic calls were made to pet shops for miles around, but no luck.

The news was broken by our guilt-ridden children within the first tense moments of the neighbours' return. Cause of death was later determined to be disintegration of some sea shells, which had been inserted into the tank's salt-free water by one of the turtle minders who was concerned about the sparse habitat.

Despite their loss, the neighbour's kids and ours have remained good friends ever since. And now their own kids are into hamsters, which frequently find their final resting place inside some inaccessible hot-air register. Personally, I would much prefer drawing the turtle-tank cleaning duty every time.

Deryck Thomson
Sidney, British Columbia

✉ While on a recent trip to Thailand my friend and I engaged a car and driver for three days to do some un-touristy things. One morning we went to a monstrous covered market, not meant for tourists at all. It was noisy, colourful, exciting, and fabulously interesting. Here and there I noticed large wash-tubs filled with water and containing many smallish turtles, about six inches in diameter. I asked Chusak if people ate them or bought them for pets. "Neither," he replied. "People buy one and then release it in the nearest river or canal. It makes them feel good because they have done a kind deed. The turtle also feels pretty happy." The next day someone catches them — and the cycle begins again — also providing more jobs. What a delightful idea.

Stuart Cranston,
Pakenham, Ontario

✉ My husband and I opened a neighbourhood pub a little over a year and a half ago, which we called Buffalo Bob's. Three months after opening, the two of us took a break and went to Seattle for a weekend.

We spent quite a bit of time shopping for unique items for the pub, and one of the things I purchased was a rubber pig (much like a rubber chicken), which my husband thought was rather stupid.

We returned to Calgary and hung the pig at the bar, over the cash register. A number of things have happened to our pig since.

It disappeared close to Hallowe'en of 1992, only to return on the thirty-first of October dressed as a sheep! After that it disappeared for close to two months, and we decided it had been stolen. On the first anniversary of the pub's opening, we received a picture of the pig (in a nice frame) lying on a gas barbecue with a cherry in its mouth! The pig itself, however, did not reappear. A month later, a customer was showing me his holiday pictures of a trip to Cabo San Lucas. In the batch of photos were shots of our pig sun-tanning on a balcony in Mexico! The pig then reappeared and took its place over the bar. It (we're still not sure of the gender) subsequently kept disappearing and reappearing, with accompanying photos of it fishing in British Columbia, with a cigarette hanging from its mouth, eating pork ribs, drinking tequila, driving a motor boat, drinking in a bar in Chicago, hanging out with some waitresses in a pub called the Sunset in Vietnam — the usual holiday stuff! At the moment, we think our pig is on its way home from San Diego.

Amy Brooks
Calgary

✉ It started simply, with the snakes. No, actually, the snakes were after. The degus (pronounced day-goos) came before them. Well, we had the cat first, and he is strange in his own right, but aren't they all?

The degus are South American ground squirrels — really cute guys, related (distantly) to chinchillas. They lived in a three-storey condominium cage, with an enclosed run on the side so they could go up and down at will. They also, apparently, went in and out at will. Every once in a while we all dropped whatever we were doing — me, husband, and the three boys, then aged two to seven — to engage in the degu races. This entailed all five of us running around like crazy, and one degu running around faster than any of us. The secret to catching an escaped degu is to drop a cloth on it. It will stop long enough for someone to swoop down and grab it. The scene was reminiscent of a demented corrida, with tea-towels, sweaters, jackets, and hand towels being flung madly after an escaping furry brown speedball.

We had crickets escaping for a while. (I have to warn you that almost all of these are escape stories.) We only bothered catching the obvious ones. It was kind of nice to have the walls chirruping on warm evenings. Unfortunately, if you're sensitive about that kind of thing, they didn't survive the winter.

Then we got the snakes. Unlike degus, snakes . . . aren't . . . very . . . fast. They are, however, very difficult to find. Snake hunts usually begin when my husband opens one of the cages and calls out, "The boa's loose!" Or the black rat snake, or . . . well, you get the idea. The first thing to do is close all the doors to the playroom. Or what used to be the playroom until the animal quarters squeezed out the kids. This is just in case the escape was discovered soon after being accomplished. This is often not the case. The discovery of the snake is thus frequently a surprise. Such as opening a desk drawer, and stopping in the midst of reaching in for a pencil, because *that*, by cracky, is no pencil. Or sitting at the kitchen table, drinking a mid-morning cup of coffee, and noticing out of the corner of my eye a long green and brown form advancing silkily along the baseboards of the kitchen cabinets. Or the day my sister and I were sitting in the living-room, and she noticed that the Tardis was gone. This is what I call the six-foot-long display case in which lives the iguana. I was delighted to tell her that I had finally prevailed upon my husband to put it in the playroom, and this was now an animal-free zone. I was soon proved wrong, as a snake emerged from the bookcase.

I know you would like to get off the subject of snakes, and I undoubtedly piqued your curiosity by my previous mention of an iguana. Iggy is rather large, being about three feet long, and half of that is tail. On sunny summer days my husband puts a harness on Iggy, attaches a leash, and ties him to a tree in the front yard. This is necessary, by the way, because iguanas, like humans, do not manufacture their own vitamin D, so must receive it from sources such as sunlight or food supplements.

Iggy usually likes to climb into a tree to bask, but sometimes he will rest on the lawn. A neighbour refers to him as our "guard dragon." It makes a change for the letter carrier. On more than one occasion Iggy has — what else? — escaped. One time we thought he was gone forever, but a neighbour fortunately discovered Iggy on top of his cedar hedge. He would have missed the iguana entirely if not for the red harness he was still wearing.

We only once had a fish escape, and he (or she, but most likely he, since almost all our animals, and all our humans except me, are male) must be a very clever fish, for he chose his acrobatic moment when three of us were in the room.

"Oh, Mum, there's a fish on the floor!"

"Oh, dear! Well . . ." and not knowing just what exactly it was I was supposed to do in this particular circumstance, I just bent down, picked him up gently, and plopped him back in the water. He is still swimming happily, but we've since put a cover on the tank.

It is with some shame I mention the other female in the house. Agnes, the ring-necked parakeet, is foul-tempered and as far as she is concerned is sovereign of all she surveys. She makes pecking gestures at anyone coming within pecking distance (she once separated a rat from a goodly portion of his tail) and squawks mightily whenever it ruddy well pleases her to do so. It plays havoc with telephone conversations.

Her one enemy is the iguana, who once crawled into her cage in pursuit of dinner. At the time, she was fortunate to be on the roof of the cage, and she was absolutely silent. Unlike the afternoon we heard her screeching in real panic and ran to the room to find her attempting to run away from the iguana. In addition to having few redeeming features, Agnes is not very good at flying. I grabbed a sheet of cardboard to put between them and shooed Iggy away. This was what she was waiting for. She waddled quickly after him. He turned, with a gleam in his eye. Luckily, one of the boys was now in position and was able to quiet the iguana and carry him away.

Styx, the twenty-year-old ginger tom with a checkered past, is now making obeisance at his master's feet. My husband, Andrew, is making tomorrow's lunch, and Styx knows the mayonnaise will soon appear. He is so delighted when Andrew offers a tiny bit that he purrs — and purrs so strenuously that he chokes when he puts out his tongue to lick. Mmm — maybe I could do something with that, after all.

Deborah McMullen
Ottawa

ENCOUNTERS WITH THE . . . WELL, MAYBE NOT RICH BUT SOMETIMES PRETTY FAMOUS

The people people meet, and why they have remembered them.

✉ In the early years of World War Two, an English widow with an unforgettable, warm, raspy voice moved into her newly built house on Douglas Avenue, in Oakville, Ontario — right next door to our home. She brought with her two golden cocker spaniels and one vivacious young daughter, Kate.

Babby Reid, as everyone called her, was the soul of kindness and generosity. She became a great support to my mother, who was left alone to care for an awkward little girl and a new baby during those long nail-biting war years. Babby, who was older than Mother, dispensed great dollops of good old Yorkshire wisdom and humour while mixing drinks or pouring tea.

Her daughter, Kate, with a mane of thick strawberry-blond hair, enormous eyes and wide, intoxicating smile, soon attracted every young person in town, or so it seemed to me. They swarmed around her like moths to a candle. The Reid household was always awash with men and women of all ages congregating for food, gossip and lots of laughter. To a young child it was Mecca.

Katie, as we knew her, flitted in and out of our house like some exotic bird and soon was put in charge of my baby sister and me on those rare occasions when Mother was able to escape from her domestic duties for a day or an evening with friends. Katie was a tough baby-sitter. An only child and definitely headstrong herself, she certainly wasn't about to put up with any nonsense from someone else — particularly someone who took great delight in making a baby-sitter's life as tiresome as possible. But she was fascinating — full of interesting stories and sudden, touching bursts of compassion. Being in a room with Kate was an electrically charged adventure, slightly dangerous and always exciting.

One day I was hanging out of our upstairs window when I saw Katie come skipping and pirouetting up our front path, calling out, "Mrs. Lewis, I'm going to be an *actress*!" "Damn," I thought crossly. "That was *my* idea!"

Well, Katie obviously did become an actress, and in a very short time, too. By the early fifties she was earning awards for her work on stage and appearing in role after role on Canada's fledgling television network. By the middle of the decade, Kate Reid had become a household name and a veritable star in a country that acknowledges very few.

Babby Reid was immensely proud of her beautiful, talented daughter and always kept us informed of her progress, after our family moved to Quebec, with special tickets to her plays on our return visits to Toronto.

When I did come back to Toronto to try my hand at the business, it was Katie who introduced me to an agent, but above all, who gave me some wonderful insights into her approach to audition pieces. I wonder if she ever realized how truly helpful they were. Later, when I was doing the struggling actress bit in London, I watched her shining performance in *The Rainmaker* in the West End. Again in New York, it was a thrill to catch her backstage while she was playing Caitlin to Alec Guinness's Dylan Thomas.

Our lives took different routes after that and I don't think we ever really met again — but I watched her avidly whenever she appeared on television. I watched with growing sadness at the dimming of that incandescent flame, as a troubled life etched itself heavily into her features. Perhaps that was the way life was meant to be for Kate. Surely no other Canadian actress of our generation was so adept at portraying the full range of pain and vulnerability of the human condition, alleviated by flashes of warmth and generosity of spirit that leapt out of that wide smile and throaty laugh.

Nancy Erb Kee
Brampton, Ontario

✉ 1898–1992 — the Years of A.J. Casson. From horses and buggies to Bondar in space. What were the images of this man's mind? It seems to me bewildering.

I am sitting here in my home, which is really a cabin at mile 71½ on the Algoma Central Railway Line. I've opened my only fine bottle of wine and am proceeding to drink it in celebration of what A.J. Casson means to me as an artist. As I do so, I'm going to try to write some sort of tribute to him, as I feel compelled to do so.

This morning I starting painting at 8:30 as the sun was then high enough to truly see colour. At 9:00 I turned on the radio, a ritual when I paint in the cabin instead of out of doors. I heard that Casson had died. I was indeed provoked to think about him and how he had so much to do with why I am now where I am. Casson, the Group of Seven and Thomson are an integral part of my history.

I studied art at the Ontario College of Art. My greatest mentor there was Franklin Arbuckle. He had just begun OCA's Landscape Class. Casson and the Group of Seven were the beginning of that study, the ideal of the Canadian landscape in Canadian terms, making our own tools and speaking in a Canadian context. My father, in the 1950s, studied at OCA and although he became a CBC set designer he loved painting. As a child I went on many landscape painting trips. He, too, was inspired by Thomson, Casson and the Group of Seven.

In my fourth year at OCA, Franklin Arbuckle took his landscape class to Algoma. We stayed at Spruce Lake up the Algoma Central Railway line. I remember telling Franklin that I would return here to paint. The day after my graduation, with a pack on my back, I moved here to stay and paint. I've lived and painted here every day, six days a week, eight to ten hours a day, ever since. That was ten years ago.

If it were not for Canadians like A.J. Casson, the Group of Seven, Thomson and Arbuckle I would not be here, eighty miles from civilization, trying to capture something of our Canadian identity which I, and they, believed was inevitably tied to the land. "Our Landscape."

I'm thirty-two years old. I live on what I paint. My life is simple, a small cabin, wood stove, gas lights, outhouse, no electricity, no running water except for my legs and no place close by to spend money. I make anywhere from $8,000 to $12,000 a year. The thing is, if it were not for artists like Casson I would not even have that. Now I can live and paint as a vocation. Thank you, A.J.

Chris Cooper
Algoma, Ontario

✉ Mavis Gallant's trip to Mabou — eleven years ago but the sound of her voice and the care with which she read from her own works revived my recollection of her reading to students in English classes at Mabou School. She listened carefully to students as they explained their difficulties with writing; she willingly read some of their short stories and encouraged them to write and re-write.

Supper was around a kitchen table over chicken and wine. Stories of local life were shared with her — and she laughed and entered into the local mode of story telling. And then she went along to the local museum, where she sat in a very straight antique chair and read from her writings. The community shared with her from its treasure-house of Gaelic songs, fiddle tunes, and step-dancing. Several members of the present Rankin Family Band performed for her. What an evening it was, a sharing of talent and creativity. Mavis Gallant's visit to Mabou was important as it inspired a number of young people, as well as their teachers of writing.

Jim St. Clair
Mabou, Nova Scotia

✉ I listened, delighted, to the reading of Gregory Clark's "Miss L. Bruce: A Love Story" this morning. That story holds special memories for me in two ways.

My first-grade teacher, Mrs. Wright, was one of those increasingly rare individuals who sought out the best in her pupils and encouraged us in our strengths, in my case reading and imagining, while magically creating a space for arithmetic in me or spelling in others. She would keep me after class and give me wonderful books to read and all on the pretence that I was being disciplined, because she knew it would go badly for me if some of the others thought that I was being favoured.

When crossed, she was fearsome and she nurtured that reputation as a way of maintaining discipline, but she had a heart of gold and would tour the elementary schools of our town for years after she had retired, just to make sure we were getting on well.

Years later when I was covering an IODE meeting for the local newspaper, there she was; and she recognized me.

"I know you," she said in her brusque teacher's voice "You're Mac-Murchy. Is this what you're doing now, are you a photographer?"

"No," I said, "this is a sideline and I'm trying to get into music school." I was immediately in awe of her as if I was six years old again.

"What do you mean *trying?*" she inquired, her eyes aflame. "You must have gone stupid on me." Then she smiled and winked, and I carry that moment as a talisman to ward off indifference.

As I said, there are two reasons I hold that Gregory Clark story dear. You see, I have a signed copy of that volume of short stories with a personal dedication. I had the pleasure of meeting Gregory Clark on one occasion. I was about twelve and he was around eighty. My father, a writer, told him that I had read his war memoirs at the age of eight and this impressed him enough that he promised to send me a copy of his latest volume of stories. By this time in his life his heart was giving him grief and, in fact, he had already had at least one operation, and it was through his doctors that I met him.

My father and I had been researching a Petun Indian village near Collingwood, which had once occupied the land where some friends of ours had a farm. Greg's doctors had identified and carbon-dated some bone fragments we had found. They had told him, and he insisted on seeing the site. His heart condition did not dissuade him from clambering around this hilly farm. It didn't seem to hinder his life-style at all, except that he was on a Scotch ration and gleefully showed us a U-shaped glass measure that he carried with him. He also took great delight in our activities on the site, one in particular.

You see, archaeologists get unsolicited help from burrowing animals. They often turn up fragments that indicate a possible excavation site, so we always checked around the mouths of groundhog burrows. He thought this was hilarious, hence the dedication:

"To John Scott MacMurchy with best wishes, provided you don't lend it to your dad, so interfering with his exploration of groundhog holes."

He was a warm, delightful man, full of life even as his was drawing to a close, and his stories read like a comfy chair by the fire.

John MacMurchy
Toronto

✉ Thirty years ago, I was a Canadian Wildlife Service biologist studying how arctic foxes relate to their environment.

In the early fall of 1962, I was returning to the "Outside" from the Arctic, via Churchill and Winnipeg, with a cageful of fierce little fox cubs for captive rearing. When I was reunited with my charges at the Winnipeg airport, the evening was sultry and the animals were suffering in the unaccustomed heat.

I hurriedly took their cage outside, to give them the benefit of what breezes there were while I found water to bring them. When I returned, a stranger was bending over them. Concerned that he might get bitten or, even worse, let the cubs out into the night, I greeted him abruptly and even, to my later regret, with a touch of annoyance.

To my regret, because I saw almost immediately that he was being a "good Samaritan," offering the cubs licks from a couple of ice-cream cones, and, when he introduced himself, he turned out to be a most likeable person. That's my memory of Stephen Juba, Mayor of Winnipeg.

Andrew Macpherson
Edmonton

✉ Last Monday night, I walked into rehearsal for a local production of *Camelot* and discovered, to my shock, that one of my Canadian heroes was dead. I had just sat down to pore over a few days of *Globes* that a fellow actor had brought with her and delightedly pulled up the day's arts section with its cover photo of Greg Curnoe. "Oh, a story on Greg, how terrific!" I exclaimed, and then recoiled as Janet replied, "Oh, yeah, he's the one that died this weekend."

How can Greg Curnoe possibly be dead? This summer, when I saw an exhibit of his work at the London Regional Art Gallery, I was incredibly excited, because the artwork was exciting, and new and fresh, and still had lots to say — and Greg still had lots to say, and now that possibility is gone, lost amid a tangle of metal and rubber and pavement.

This Canadian artist touched my life in a lot of ways. As a teenager, already aware of Curnoe's work, I used to be amazed at how normal he was. (Artists, I think I thought, were supposed to be weird.) He showed up at the same functions my family did, because my brother was in the same class as his daughter at school, and he was just your average parent.

Later, in high school, I realized how not normal he was, in the best of ways, when I dated the bassist for a punk band called Bits of Food. The band's nickname was Sons of Spasm, because several of its members (including my beau) claimed Nihilist Spasm Band members as parents, and I always used to think it was the coolest thing in the world to walk into a gig and see Greg Curnoe working sound for his kids' band. Greg supported his three kids, and friends of theirs, in being the people *they* wanted to be, and that was really different.

When I went away to school in Ottawa, I spent a lot of time trying to forget that I was from close-minded, waspy, preppie London — it wasn't a place I felt especially tied to. But sometimes I got homesick for certain parts of it and ran to the old National Gallery on Elgin Street (which was free), and spent some time with the Curnoe works — particularly one that showed a view along the Thames and the bank of Old Vic Hospital, relatively close to the Curnoe home, and a spot where my family did a lot of cross-country skiing. Greg Curnoe's work helped me acknowledge the place I was from and realize that it had a lot to do with the person I am. I still am not overly fond of the city, but there are places and people there that will always be very much a part of me, and I feel truly blessed that some of those brought me into contact with Greg Curnoe.

Lisa Kowaltschuk
Minden, Ontario

✉ In early 1974 I had the privilege and thrill of joining the auspicious firm of Arthur Erickson Architects (AEA). Those were the heady days — masterpieces such as Simon Fraser University, MacMillan Bloedel Building, Museum of Anthropology, and the three-block Courthouse and Art Gallery project. I was the thirty-ninth employee to join the staff, and two months later another thirty or forty had been given a similar opportunity, swelling the tiny office walls. We expanded onto the roof garden, into the basement. There were drawing-boards crammed in every corner of the office, except the famous coffee pit. It was truly one of the most exciting work experiences in my ten-year secretarial career (primarily in architectural offices). Yes, I was a lowly secretary, subjected to three gruelling interviews before finally being hired. But as a lowly secretary I was paid more than the graduate architects who thought they had died and gone to heaven when they were hired to work for their guru, their mentor. They came from all over the world.

One never knew which famous personality would waltz through the door. Another friend of Arthur's? There were many. And sometimes even his dear sweet mother, who once told me the furniture in a reception area should not be too comfortable, lest visitors get the wrong idea and overstay their welcome! We all worked long hours —

273

often well into the night and entire weekends — to meet those never-ending deadlines. We typed draft scripts for Arthur's book taken from tapes of Arthur and his brother Don sitting in the garden "discussing" all his various masterpieces. Arthur travelled almost constantly, and his ever-faithful accountant, Millie, always made sure his refrigerator was stocked with fresh milk, Brie and pears (his regular lunch fare) for his return.

One week in June 1974, the staff decided we should all go out to dinner. Arthur was actually going to be in town and surprisingly wanted to attend. In trying to keep the costs to a minimum, we decided on Chinese, and the menu was arranged. The morning of the dinner, Arthur reviewed the menu and decided it wasn't enough. Millie insisted it was what the staff could afford. Arthur was emphatic that he wanted Peking Duck for all seventy of us, as well as a nice white wine, and he would pick up the tab. He also decided he wanted to have the whole party back to his house for Spanish coffee after dinner. He asked Millie to phone one of the better hotel bars to find out the best recipe and to organize the glasses, ingredients, etcetera, for delivery to his house. The staff were somewhat stunned by his invitation. Arthur was always quite unpredictable, and he certainly knew how to capture one's attention.

Dinner was great fun. It was a balmy June evening and, as we walked through the gate of the nine-foot fence — the only entry into the property — the evening became enchanted. Yes, the garden was wild, but with lights strategically placed amongst the foliage, as one walked over the "bridges" and stepping stones in and around the reflecting pool, bamboo and rhododendrons, it was breath-taking. I recall some of the group climbing the trees for a different perspective (typical architects!). As I walked into the house, it was in darkness, and there in the tiny but very functional kitchen was Arthur, measuring the booze into seventy-odd glasses, all by the little red light of his espresso coffee machine and an ethereal glow from the garden. He was in his element, exuding the usual charm, and he was sharing a very private part of himself with a by then raucous group of employees, most of whom worshipped him. When I exclaimed to him that he could hardly see, he was quick to point out that any more light would simply spoil the atmosphere — the perfect host! We all got a great buzz from the Spanish coffee, and all managed to show up for work the next day — still buzzing!

Arthur was fifty then, and his young, starving protégés in their late twenties and thirties. Many of them went on to be successful, award-winning architects. There were times when he drove many of them to distraction — his sometimes flamboyant life-style, his total lack of business acumen (he admitted it even then) and his huge ego (how else does one design such monuments?). He really was and is a truly brilliant designer.

Gillian Bird
Peterborough, Ontario

✉ My husband and I, visiting on Saltspring Island in British Columbia, attended the weekly market at Ganges Harbour. We were drawn to an open violin case behind which a pre-teen boy was hopefully playing his violin. There were pitifully few coins in the case. We added to them but my husband commented, "He hasn't got a chance — look to your left."

And there, a few booths away, was an ever-increasing crowd and Valdy, an island resident, giving a free concert.

Suddenly, a wonderful thing happened. Valdy left his spot and moved to the boy's side, consulted with him, and then sang to a violin accompaniment. Now there were showers of quarters landing in the violin case and the boy's face, tucked into his violin, was aglow with pride and pleasure.

I've listened to Valdy ever since, and my appreciation of his music has changed from tolerance to pure pleasure.

Kathleen Ward
Birtle, Manitoba

✉ Last Saturday night we held a Gala Dinner and Dance in Fulford Hall to honour the artists who donated their works for a raffle to raise funds for our new "Artspring" building. Valdy emceed the event — beautifully.

Early Sunday morning Valdy called our house, as my husband and I were heading up the clean-up committee and had the key to the hall. He said he'd left his sound equipment in the hall and had a ferry to catch, so was wondering how long we'd be. As we live on the north end of the island, we told him we'd be a while, but would get there ASAP.

It was a misty morning — and a beautiful drive through the Fulford Valley. When we arrived at the hall, Valdy's truck was there, with that famous guitar case in the back of it — open and empty! And from across the road, from the cemetery behind the church and through the semi-fog on that quiet Sunday morning, we heard singing — Valdy's! "What on earth?"

"Just singin' a song for my daddy!" he said, as he crossed the road to the hall.

Only on Saltspring!

Carol Helset
Saltspring Island

✉ I remember Rita MacNeil from the many nights I spent listening to her at the old LBR tavern in Halifax. The LBR (Ladies' Beverage Room) is located in the basement of the Lord Nelson Hotel in Halifax. In the late seventies and early eighties it was dark, grubby, airless — and one of the friendliest bars in town. Word was that Rita really enjoyed her stints at the LBR and was at her best performing before a crowd that included more than just the usual bar creatures. Old men in their "funeral suits" and old women in flowered dresses sat at the rickety tables with their children and grandchildren, waiting to hear a good Cape Breton girl who was making it on the mainland. Everyone enjoyed Rita's songs — I remember the whole bar on its feet, arms entwined, singing "Working Man" — but she did a good job of covering other people's songs, as well. She did a powerful version of Warren Zevon's "Roland the Headless Thompson Gunner," and her version of "Your Cheatin' Heart" could make you cry into your beer. "Bring It on Home to Me" was one of her encore numbers, and it displayed the power and range of her voice to their full advantage. It made me long to hear her do more blues numbers. Rita never sang the verse about "being your slave." Instead, she always ended with "You know I'll always sing for you, anytime, anytime you want me to."

Keep on singing, Rita.

Mary Ellen Wright
Placentia Bay, Newfoundland

✉ In the early fall of 1970, I was driving from Vancouver to Manitoba. One night on the Trans-Canada at a truck stop near Calgary I got into a casual conversation with two young native men who, I found out, were hitching to Winnipeg. I offered them a lift, and, with their two small packs and a guitar, they settled down in the back seat. It was immediately obvious that these were two unusual young guys. Both were well-educated, intelligent and articulate, and, when we weren't talking, they put on an excellent concert for me.

These were the Vietnam years, a bad time, at least in the west, for young people in general and for young natives in particular; I had been shocked to see at first-hand how they were treated by the police forces from Vancouver to the Cariboo. Even at that, I was surprised by what they told me about the gauntlet they had had to run on their trip west, when they were kept under surveillance the whole time. What struck me was the lack of indignation they displayed. They spoke about the harassment with a dismissive humour that was far more withering than anger could ever be. I couldn't relate their experiences to the Canada I thought I knew.

As it happened, I was soon able to witness just what they had to endure. Late at night we came upon a road-block somewhere in Saskatchewan; a couple of hundred miles to the north a Mountie had been killed by a white trapper, who was now being sought. I didn't expect we'd have any trouble — I was a middle-aged white male with a crew cut, and my passengers were natives. But as soon as the police saw them, they were hustled out and taken away for questioning. Half an hour passed, and I became more and more indignant, which I

277

didn't conceal from the policeman who came to question me about my passengers. He became so furious at my temerity that I thought he was going to take me away, too. Finally, they came back, as relaxed and good-humoured and polite as ever, an attitude I suspected was particularly annoying to the police. They might have been happier with the usual inarticulate impotence.

I had to turn north at Virden, so I pulled in at a service station. They thanked me for the ride, I thanked them for the concert, and they walked off, only to come back when they saw that the car wouldn't start. I pointed out that there was nothing anybody but a mechanic could do, and before long they got another ride. In fact, the car had driven its last — the next day I had it towed to Birtle, where it was given the last rites by the GM dealer there.

I have heard Tom Jackson on the radio two or three times since then and would have known him even without the name, because of his distinctive voice. It is no surprise to me that he is getting national recognition. I expect his friend has also made his mark.

Andrew Gibson
Ganges, British Columbia

✉ *Death of a Lady's Man* had just been released. I was in Vancouver promoting *A Man to Marry, A Man to Bury*, and my publicist invited me to a gathering that evening, in honour of Leonard Cohen.

We arrived early, and my husband cornered Leonard to tell him about one of his colleagues at law school, an Adolf Gerloff, whose mother had given him Cohen's first album for Christmas — not because she loved Cohen's voice but because Cohen was a Jewish name and she wanted Adolf to know she could be open-minded. I left the kitchen and went out on the verandah to look for the moon.

Secretly, of course, I hoped Leonard would follow. My publicist had told me he admired my poetry, and I imagined him caressing a dog-eared copy of my first slim volume and telling me, "I always read your poetry in bed." But it was more than just my syntax I hoped he'd get excited about. Taking from his pocket an old schedule of trains, he would look me in the eyes and say, "Greece would be a good place to look at the moon." I would lower my needy eyes and tell him I wished to feed him tea and oranges that came all the way from China, and the next week Peter Gzowski would be interviewing us about our affair on national radio. Leonard would say how our visions complemented one another and I would give an example of finding lines from one of my poems on a dead friend's bathroom wall: "Is there really this much desolation/ or is it just that I have/ found it all?" paired with a line from one of Leonard's songs, "Then picking up the pieces that he left behind you find he did not leave you very much, not even laughter." Peter would say, "Where do you go now?" and Leonard would say, "I only read her poetry in bed."

I watched him coming towards me from the house, in his quiet way. He slid in close as if he felt the need to warn me, "I told you when I came I was a stranger." I would have given him head on an unmade bed in the Chelsea Hotel or any other hotel in town when he spoke to me in that voice full of broken whiskey bottles and desire. "I *really* like your husband," he said.

Death of a lady's man.

Susan Musgrave
Sidney, British Columbia

✉ Re an item about Leonard Cohen picking up his own socks. He does. I have proof. When he stayed overnight in Kamloops, while on tour, he was photographed doing his own laundry at the McCleaners downtown. Unfortunately I don't have the photo, but it wouldn't be any use on radio anyway, would it? This is just to put the record straight.

Christine Allister
Kamloops, British Columbia

✉ One morning in the late sixties my elderly grandmother set out as usual on her weekly shop, from her apartment in London, Ontario.

Coming off the elevator, she found, as she related it, "a nice young man" sitting in the lobby scratching away on an envelope with a dry ball-point pen. Did she have one that worked? No, but there was one in her apartment, so, that being a different time, she asked him up.

Over her cherry pound cake, it developed that he was a poet from Montreal whose dad owned the building. While he was visiting, a poem had come, and he'd had to record it, even just as gouges ground into the paper with a dead pen. So grateful was he to be able to *really* save the poem, and for the cake, that he'd send her a copy, not of one of his books, but of something new — his first record album, just out.

Together, they left the building with mutual farewells and she figured that was probably the end of it. Back home from shopping, later in the day, though, a knock came at the door. Same guy, but this time he had a copy of *Songs of Leonard Cohen* in hand. After parting with her, he'd come to the conclusion it was going to be too much trouble to arrange it for her through the record company, so he'd gone downtown to a local record store and purchased one. He unwrapped it, wrote "To a dear friend, L. Cohen" in the top left corner with her pen, thanked her again, and left.

Gram had never heard of Leonard Cohen but sure enough, that was his picture on the front. She couldn't relate to the woman in the fire on the back, though, and actually she didn't even have a record player. Maybe one of the grandchildren could get into him. And so I received the record, just at the right time in my adolescence to trigger an addiction. Now everyone seems to be on a Cohen jag, but for me he'll always be just another guy my grandmother helped, and who liked her for it.

Peter Ferguson
Kimberley, Ontario

✉ Yesterday, January twenty-ninth, Rick Neilson's helicopter crashed just outside Houston, a small community not far from Smithers, British Columbia. He and four heli-skiers were killed instantly. I can't imagine the number of people who are grieving today, because Rick's circle of family and friends encompassed hundreds. He had so many who loved him, from Labrador to British Columbia. But the horrible aching I and his other friends feel is nothing compared to the anguish that his wife, lover and friend, Allison, is going through.

Rick was passionate in his beliefs and his loves — there were no grey areas. His contempt for bureaucracy and the plain injustices that many people endure was as strong as his love of life and family. He often said that pilots never lived to see old age, and he planned to cram as much in as he could. He tried — and was almost successful — in turning me into a vegetarian. He never followed a recipe and made it look easy, which made it so frustrating when I failed miserably at duplicating his fabulous meals.

Rick was a confirmed nudist and used it to advantage — without shame — sometimes. There was the time I had been house-sitting for them, just after I met them. Noticing that their car was in the yard, I knocked, and getting the usual come in, opened the door to see this lean, bearded guy buck naked and putting a large bundle of celery into the fridge. I guess it was his way to make or break a new friendship, although he did pull on some jeans.

He and Allison could often be found in the woods by their little log house, picking mushrooms and wild violets to candy. Even though they were often just scraping by, the abandoned or mistreated animals in the neighbourhood knew where a free meal could be found.

Besides flying, riding turned out to be Rick's favourite passion, even though he was *really* bad at it and couldn't walk for days afterwards.

As I'm reading over this, I realize that all I've said is what he does, or did — oh, damn — and not what he *was*, what made him so special. And, although I feel it in my heart, I don't think I can put it on paper. Maybe if I explain our final favour to him, it will explain things better.

Knowing that Rick would complain about a conventional funeral and a thousand-dollar fee for a simple cremation service, Allison's family decided today — between great fits of tears and laughter — to do it up his way. Allison's cousin, George, a doctor, trapper, and master carpenter, has agreed to make Rick a custom pine casket from wood they both sawed on the back-yard mill this summer. Little did we realize then what it was destined for.

He also agreed to take on the heart-wrenching task of moving Rick's remains to the crematorium, thus bypassing the need to pay strangers to do the job that loved ones should do — would do, if we as a society weren't so removed from death.

Included for his final trip will be a bottle of Black Death rum, which Allison's dad is bringing out from Nova Scotia. Rick's ashes will eventually end up on an island back home that's dear to the whole family.

Rick celebrated his fortieth birthday last May. You may hear about him from one of his friends at the theatre — oh, did I forget to mention the part where he acted, directed and produced in his spare time?

I guess the best way to judge our friendship is by the code he and Allison used to grade some recipes in a favourite cookbook they gave me one year:

> one check for *Really yucky*
> two checks for *Okay*
> three checks for *Good* and
> four checks for *Right some Jesus good*

It was a four-check friendship.

Sue Redford
Prince George, British Columbia

Sarah Lives

He was, too, in my view: Paul Hiebert, the prairie munchkin who gave the world — or discovered for it — Sarah Binks, the

Sweet Songstress of Saskatchewan. I was introduced to Sarah in the 1950s, when one of my roommates at the University of Toronto (remember when roommate meant only that?) would read her hilarious verse out loud to me in lieu of studying, but Dr. Hiebert himself — he was, when he wasn't composing poetry, a chemistry professor at the University of Manitoba — didn't come into my life until I signed on at *Morningside*'s predecessor, *This Country in the Morning*, in the early '70s. Though he had retired to what had been his summer home in Carman by then — he was born in 1892 — he became, if not a fixture on *This Country*, then at least a favoured guest. He'd come into our studio in Winnipeg — we flew him to Toronto once, for an end-of-season celebration — read some Sarah, and just generally make everyone feel better for having him around.

I dabble in oil paint,
In cinnebar and ochre,
All night I am dissipated
And play poker.

He was such a part of us. Not us at CBC Radio, us in Canada. He was funny and warm and sprightly and wise. He flirted — with, always, a twinkle in his eye. He teased. He won the first ever Leacock medal for humour in 1947 — just as Sarah herself had won the Wheat Pool Medal, "never before presented for poetry." Tommy Tweed and Don Harron adapted Sarah for radio. Mavis Gallant wrote about her. Eric Donkin made a one-man (woman?) show out of one of Sarah's friends, Rosalind Drool, and various serious composers, including the late Robert Fleming of the National Film Board, set some of her verses to music.

But by the early 1990s (Dr. Hiebert died in 1987), I began to wonder if he — and Sarah — were losing their place in history. At one *Morningside* story meeting, we were discussing the works of other and more recent prairie poets when I presumed to suggest they (the poems) were so bad they might be "Binksian," by which I meant, of course, bad on purpose, as only Paul Hiebert could make them. The look of confusion that crossed at least one young producer's face — she shall be nameless here — convinced me.

It was time to bring back Sarah. So we assembled a panel, rolled out some quotations, and even, on a subsequent occasion, got Peter Tiefenbach to drop over from his usual post at *The Arts Tonight* and accompany his usual co-host Shelagh Rogers in a songfest.

Sarah forgotten? Never.

In my little book, in my little book,
I write verses.
Sometimes they don't rhyme —
Curses!

✉ For me it all began in the 1940s, when I was farming with my husband near Leader, Saskatchewan. I read Paul Hiebert's book and learned that the author had taught school in the Leader district.

Years later, after researching the subject, I wrote an article for *Folklore* magazine, from which I quote:

"Historically speaking Saskatchewan was very young when Hiebert came to Leader (then known as Prussia — the name was changed during the First World War) to teach in a one-room school south of town. The entire experience (the pupils, community, lifestyle) made an indelible mark on his young, impressionable mind, and although greatly exaggerated, became the basis of *Sarah Binks*."

And so it is with pride (and some humility, I admit) that I, a Saskatchewan farmer and sometime poet, with first-hand experience of crickets and a cow "with tail-full," living in Sarah's community, claim a sisterly kinship with the sweet songstress of Saskatchewan.

Jean Reinhardt
Leader, Saskatchewan

✉ Forty odd years ago I was christened, elegantly enough, Sarah Miranda Jane. Thanks to my father's literary turn of mind, however, I became Bink, and as such have lived my life.

I believe that my present job title (Municipal Weed Inspector, County of Lunenberg) is proof positive that names are indeed our destiny.

Strangely enough, I once had a poem published in *The Canadian Jersey* (as in milk cow) *Breeder*, leading a friend to refer to me as the Bovine Bard of West Devlin. How oddly is my life entwined with the Sweet Songstress. Coincidental? I think not.

Sarah M.J. Pelley
Lunenburg County

✉ I was a member of what I suspect was rather a sizeable group who failed Paul Hiebert's course in "Qualitative and Quantitative Analysis and Chemical Equilibrium" at the University of Manitoba in 1946. I was also a member of a very much smaller group (in my mind's eye I see only four or five, including Professor Hiebert) to gather in his office after each incomprehensible lecture to laugh and snort and chuckle over the latest chapter of Sarah Binks as the Sweet Songstress and her inimitable poetry gradually took shape over that winter.

Professor Hiebert's lectures were given in Theatre B, in the Junior or Broadway Division of the University of Manitoba. The buildings that housed the Junior Division had been built as temporary military barracks during World War One, or so we were told, on a long triangle of land across Broadway from the Parliament buildings. They were wooden and ramshackle and jammed with students, since they housed the junior years of every course except Agriculture and Home Ec, and the men coming back from the war and anxious to get on with their lives had almost doubled the student population.

So Theatre B on Tuesday and Thursday mornings was full. Every seat on every bench that sloped up steeply from the demonstration counter at the front was filled, and there were often students standing at the back. At ten o'clock the door opened and in came Professor Hiebert. He would take his place behind the long counter, his head barely clearing the top, shake out a few papers and begin, in his small, squeaky voice: "Now, the properties of sodium bisulfide are such that . . ." His voice did not carry beyond the first two or three rows of that cavernous theatre, but it really didn't matter, because Tuesday and Thursday were the days that the campus newspaper came out, and had Professor Hiebert cared to glance up, which it seemed he rarely did, all he would have seen would have been half an acre of *Manitobans*.

I don't know what the failure rate on that course was, but I for one was completely intimidated by it, never understood in any degree the theory behind it, and failed it, not once but three times. My first mark, that spring, was forty-eight per cent on a reread, which meant that it had been forty-nine per cent, and the reread was to decide whether to put it up or down one mark. (I like to think that, if Professor Hiebert had been doing the marking, he would have put it up.) The following September I rewrote the exam, after studying all summer while waitressing at Minaki Lodge. That mark was forty-two per cent, and the third attempt the following fall, after a summer of waitressing and pseudo-studying at Banff Springs, was a miserable thirty-five per cent. Obviously, "Qualitative and Quantitative Analysis and Chemical Equilibrium" was slipping farther and farther from my grasp, so I gave it up and took Economics instead — no problem.

How did Professor Hiebert decide who amongst these anonymous seventy or eighty students had the wit, the humour, the depth to appreciate Sarah and her lyrical genius? Someone once implied that the worthy professor had an eye for the ladies. We were all female. We were probably the complete contingent of women (or "girls," as we called ourselves then) in that second-year chemistry class.

My father used to talk about attending lectures given by Stephen Leacock at McGill in the early 1900s. Dad was a Leacock fan all his life, but if the subject of Mariposa or the *Sunshine Sketches* ever came up during or after those lectures, Dad never mentioned it. We were lucky — we were in at the birth, as it were, and Sarah will always be a sort of beloved, if slightly ditsy, foster-sister.

Rosemary Butler
Milford, Ontario

✉ I first knew Paul Hiebert in the thirties when I was a school teacher in Carman, Manitoba, where he maintained a summer residence. Then in Winnipeg, along with hundreds of war veterans, I attended university and took advantage of the War Veteran's aid program. Paul was a professor of chemistry and taught us that subject in the old Broadway Building in downtown Winnipeg. Classes were large and filled with many war veterans, like myself, all keen and anxious to get our degrees. At that particular time, Paul was preparing his book on Sarah Binks, the renowned poet from Willow, Saskatchewan. Much of the classroom lecture time was taken up by Paul reading, with keen delight, the latest poem of Sarah Binks and telling us of some facet of her developing poetical skills. This was indeed delightful and entertaining, but of course at the expense of chemistry.

Now, some fifty years later, I often pick up my autographed copy of Sarah Binks to read with delight the poems Paul recited to us during those memorable chemistry lectures. I'm certain I have forgotten most of the chemistry he taught, but I do remember Sarah Binks and her delightful poems.

Andrew D. Baillie
Calgary

✉ During the early sixties when I was producer of a TV public affairs show at CBC Winnipeg, I would occasionally invite Paul Hiebert to abandon his retirement redoubt in Carman and come into the big city for a guest spot on TV to embellish aspects of the Binksian oeuvre hitherto unexplored. On one occasion it was decided it was time to bring to the public's attention that remarkable creature, the snearth; according to Paul, the snearth was nature's most perfect example of camouflage. To prove the point, we found a photo of a ploughed field in Saskatchewan, and Paul went into his mock academic mode to lecture, with pointer as required, on the remarkable way in which the snearth blended into the natural setting. Since the photo contained nothing but a ploughed field,

Paul had free reign to marvel with the viewers on the snearth's amazing talent for invisibility.

Ken Black
Toronto

✉ One of my sisters had chemistry lectures from Paul Hiebert and got to know him even better doing graduate work in that department. After she moved from Winnipeg, we had to go out to the university every time she came back, for a visit and a few more chuckles with him. We were regaled with tidbits from his upcoming book, *Sarah Binks*. He told us he and his brother had decided they would like to write bad poetry well.

After we knew the book was published, Mother kept asking at Eaton's book department if *Sarah Binks* was in yet. Finally she was told, "Sarah is in the receiving room upstairs, but she hasn't come down yet!"

While I was teaching in Portage la Prairie, I heard that Dr. Paul Hiebert was to be the guest speaker at the Children's Aid Society District annual meeting. The large dining-room of the Portage Hotel was to be the locale and I bought a ticket early. The room was packed. After dinner, in his opening remarks, Dr. Hiebert said he didn't know why he had been invited to address the society as he had no children and didn't know much about them, so he had brought along the poems of some of his friends to read to us. This was greeted by the puzzled looks of some and broad smiles from others. Some went to sleep, some just looked confused, and the rest of us loved it. One man in a far corner periodically let out a loud guffaw. I wish I had a copy of a poem by Raytha Dovecote, a Home Economist, as I am one. He had a niece who was one, too, so I suppose she inspired that poem.

Some time later Paul Hiebert sent a copy of the manuscript of *Sarah Binks* down east for a "critique." The "expert" who read it must have skimmed it quickly, missing the introduction. His report came back encouraging the writer, saying his poems showed some flaws but were promising, and suggesting he keep on. After that the writer stopped reading *Sarah* when asked to speak and read the critique instead. He thought it even funnier.

I remember enjoying a CBC television interview with him at the time of the flag controversy. The young man interviewing him didn't seem to know how to take this man with the puckish humour. He said he heard he had an idea for the new Canadian flag. Oh, yes, it was a decahedral flag. Each province would have a wedge with its own symbol, then all would be happy as each one could hang it with its own wedge at the top.

Frances McColl
Winnipeg

✉ During my studies in grade-eleven English, I had a teacher who was a devotee of CanLit and introduced us to many wonderful Canadian authors, including Paul Hiebert. By happy coincidence, my little home town of Morris, Manitoba, was only forty miles east of Carman, where Paul Hiebert lived.

So, one fine winter day in, I think, 1974, a group of five sixteen-year-olds made the trek to Carman, with the assignment of interviewing Paul Hiebert.

I'll never forget his house. It was small and looked to my young eyes like an English country cottage. Mr. Hiebert came to the door himself to greet us. He looked like an elf. He was tiny, twinkling and delightful as he led us to his living-room. His house was filled with more clutter than I'd imagined it possible to live in. Papers and books were *everywhere*, and the little figurines and knick-knacks must have numbered in the thousands.

We sat on those old purple-coloured sofas (just like the one my grandmother had) with doilies on the backs, sipped Kool-aid and ate the cookies previously laid out by Mrs. Hiebert, who we heard, but never did actually see.

Mr. Hiebert very patiently answered our not very sophisticated questions about Sarah. For over an hour he entertained us, reading

Sarah's poetry (complete with his comments) and giving extra smiles and twinkles to the young ladies present.

It was an experience I have treasured ever since.

Deborah Bartlette
Delta, British Columbia

✉ Sarah Binks and the Titulation of Saskatchewan: The contribution of the poet laureate of Saskatchewan, Sarah Binks, to the literature of the west is fully documented. Less well known, but perhaps deserving of greater recognition, has been the Sweet Songstress's influence on the province's place names or, to use her own phrase, on the process of titulation. A prime example is one of her series of bovine masterpieces, "Ode to GUERNSEY and ABERDEEN Angus Cattle," which produced six place names:

O Cow, as you DRINKWATER
And masticate the YELLOW GRASS,
    Does gratitude e'er thy thoughts possess?
As you forage the GOLDEN PRAIRIE,
Spare you thanks for the farmer
    Whose ENDEAVOUR your life will bless?
Thro' months and WEEKES of toil
and the sweat of his brow
    beginning with your birth
He works and spends for you.
O Cow —
    know thee thy CUDWORTH?

Bill Barry
Regina

✉ I earned my university credits the hard way — by taking two courses a year at summer school. It was during these summers at the

U. of M. that I met Professor Hiebert. He had already retired from teaching in the regular session but would come back to teach one chemistry course during the summer session. During the lunch hour the faculty members who ate in the cafeteria would sit around one table that seemed to be reserved for them. But Dr. Hiebert picked up his tray and found a place at one of the student tables. He claimed those guys at the reserved table were too boring. We had no problem listening to him talk about some off-hand subject. And it wasn't chemistry. He was asked once how he could read exams so fast that he had the results posted almost as soon as the last student finished writing. "Oh, that's easy," he said, "I stand at the top of the stairs and throw them down. The grades are in the order in which I pick them up on my way down."

One year when we were planning the Education Week activities for our school, I suggested we invite Paul Hiebert as the guest speaker for the evening program. The board was agreeable and I made the arrangements.

We invited Dr. Hiebert to our place for supper. He gave our older two children an outline on how to write a western. I won't go into details, but he insisted that you could not kill a cowboy unless you shot him through the liver. After supper we went to school. I introduced our guest to the school board, and he immediately started telling off-colour jokes. Some of them were so raunchy that some of our board became concerned and one of them took me aside to suggest that we could not let the guy up on stage. Our prim little community would be scandalized! I reassured him and things went on as planned and we had a most entertaining evening.

Years passed. Our son, Garry, was through university and had a job uptown. One day he heard that Paul Hiebert was coming to give a noon-hour lecture at the University of Winnipeg. Since that was uptown too, he decided to go and listen. Paul Hiebert introduced his topic as "The Cow as Leitmotif in Saskatchewan Literature: A Rumination on Udder Nonsense."

Frank F. Enns
Winnipeg

✉ Paul Hiebert gave a talk on that elusive bird, the snearth, on CBC Winnipeg's *Life and Literature*. I sent for a copy of the script and have it — all seven pages!

Here is a brief excerpt:

"My friend Lorne Wallace of the CBC who is an experienced and ardent bird-watcher claims to have seen a pair of these birds in southern Manitoba near Cartwright. They were sitting on one of the concrete posts which mark the boundary line between the United States and Canada and were looking south across the 49th parallel into North Dakota — they were uttering cries of distress but when disturbed by the appearance of a car bearing American license plates they took off with great vigor and headed north all the while uttering cries of disdain. As a rule the snearth scrupulously observes the three mile limit and seldom ventures closer to the border."

No doubt this pair was an offshoot of the Saskatchewan ones.

Frances McColl
Winnipeg

✉ On a trip to the library, while checking the whereabouts of sundry works through the computer facilities, I noticed that fully half of the Vancouver Public Library's copies of *Sarah Binks* were in circulation. The other copy was still in the stacks. I was inspired to pen the following:

Binksiana

When winter's wondrous whiteness wends its way
Across the stubble to the outhouse door
Like highwaymen full tilt across the moor,
I read the Eaton's catalogue and pray
That, when I'm through, the door will open some
And I will find the rope back to the farm
Is yet unsnapped or otherwise unharmed.
"Amen!" I cry as page nineteen is done.

In summer sixty thousand swarming flies
Symphonically surprise their outhouse guest;
Such sussuration soothes the rustic breast,
But not when those damn pests get in our eyes.

Such samples singled out evoke, methinks,
Saskatchewan's Sweet Songstress, Sarah Binks.

David Walmsley
Vancouver

✉ It would be unchivalrous of me not to share a Paul Hiebert original.

Mary,

Sarah might well have concluded her great work Up from the Magma with Now it is Done, one of her finest but still unpublished poems The Author of this new life of Sarah Binks therefore sends it on to his friend,

Mary Elisabeth Bayer, in the hopes that if the going gets tough she will know, like Sarah, that there are still things;

Now It is Done

Now it is done, let others oil the turning
Of that old wheel of wisdom 'til they die;
For me at least the craftiness of learning
Has turned upon itself – and I am I;
And I am I again / the rut and rubble
Of that wise world where only sages speak
Is gone, – once more the sunlight on the stubble

So poured for me, once more upon my cheek
The rain, the prairie rain will beat and bluster,
And warm, wet earth will breath beneath
   the plow,
And yellow in the sun the fields of mustard
And blue the flax will blossom for me now.

Paul G. Hiebert

I also wrote an ode in appreciation, which Professor Hiebert said made him both laugh and cry. There can be no higher tribute!

Ode to Sarah Binks

All hail still voice that shrieks no more
That taught us music hind the kitchen door
That gambolled with the calf and snearth
And now is fallow neath the earth
   (Oh Sarah speak I must
   To you who loved the dust
   In humble admiration
   On behalf of the whole nation)

All hail and drought and dust and drill
Your fearless fury made us ill
And taught us how to run in rhyme
Against both temperature and time.

Sweet songstress, sleep and chirp and snore
If we should hear your voice no more
We know at least you planted verse

Where others flagged, or failed or worse.
So meekly now your cloak I take
From mantle, tremble, shudder, shake,
Sask. hath no greater sound methinks
Than the one and only Sarah Binks.

Mary Elizabeth Bayer
Victoria

✉ I was born and raised in Saskatoon, so I was introduced early to Miss Binks. In 1971 I joined the faculty of the University of New Brunswick in Saint John and the next year introduced the first course in Canadian literature taught at the campus. Naturally, in the interests of regional understanding, I put *Sarah* on the course and began what has become over the past twenty years a tradition. The assignment was to produce a group of poems Sarah would have written had she been born in New Brunswick. The richness of my collection of maritime "Binksiana" will, I am sure, be immediately conveyed by even a few samples.

In 1973 Jane McNulty Binks produced "The Balmy Breezes of the Bay of Fundy."

The fresh, balmy breezes of Fundy,
Caress and refresh all and sundry
Cooling and soothing the furrowed brow
They trickle and fondle the horse and the cow.

Oh I never feel sorry to climb into my dory
Fundy's billows like pillows do flow,
And gently I'm rocked, never shipwrecked or shocked
As if tucked in a cradle I go.

Of your Baltic and Red I'm disdainful,
The winds of the Arctic are baneful.
And being specific, I loath the Pacific,
I consider its hurricane shameful.

O give me my Fundy, whether Wednesday or Monday
Its salty expanses I savour.
O I'll never endeavor, no matter how clever,
From Fundy my fellow to waver.

In 1974 Vivian Wright Binks caught Sarah in a more elegiac mood
in "Sarah's Visit to Enos Turnip's Grave," which begins:

Here in a nook by the Passamaquoddy
Lie the remains of Great Grampa's body!
Oh Great Grandfather, gramp's daddy,
Here's where you lived when you were a laddie!

Several years later Sister S. Manning Binks illustrated Sarah's
sensitive response to her immediate environment in "Hymn to the
Pollutiontown Mill."

Quaint little mill
Grinding up logs,
Spitting out paper
Clothed only by fogs.

Dear little mill,
Set near the river
Takes a great oak
Makes only small slivers.

Fine little mill
Perfumed so gay
Drinks in clear water
Sends scum away.

Grand little mill,
You always shall be
The symbol, the herald
Of prosperity.

Mill of our forebears,
Mill of our age,
Mill that makes poets
By making the page.

O little mill
We love thee so well
Thy beauty is surpassed
By only thy smell.

Sarah's lack of botany is shown by her wrong choice of tree. However, we prefer to think that she is providing an alternative for when they have used up all the softwood trees.

In 1991 Kevin Bonner Binks illustrated Sarah's rare ability to lift the prosaic to poetic heights in the memorable couplets of his splendid "The Potato Is King":

Baked, dollars or golden hash
The lowly tater is solid cash.

The McCains and the Irvings fight for your favour
Though all are aware of your flare and flavour.

And, in his tender "Ode to a Fiddlehead" about to be ravished by "suitors . . . hungry for love," he coined that unforgettable phrase, "fear not fair fern," a cry for social justice worthy of Sarah in her P.R. period.

Winnifred M. Bogaards
Saint John

✉ I would like to draw your attention to a piece of history that seems to have slipped by your watchful eyes — the Three R Society. This society was founded in the 1930s for the Restoration, Reconstitution and Rehabilitation of Fallen Poets. Long before Hiebert wrote his seminal work on Binks, the society's founder, Edith Babb, researched and partially restored Sarah. Edith Babb was old enough to be Sarah's grandmother and yet she recognized the great genius caught up in Quagmire, and within a mere ten years of Sarah's death, penned the now famous (but forgotten) poem, "Owed to Sarah Binks."

I would like to share this with you. I have included it as it appears in *The Collected Works of Edith Babb* (author unknown). You will note how closely the format resembles that used by Hiebert. Both Paul Heibert and John Lennox (Canada's tallest academic) agreed with me (in 1984) that Edith's poem is a splendid tribute to The Great One, Saskatchewan's own songstress, poet and woman. I hope that you will add it to your annals of acclaim.

Owed to Sarah Binks by Edith Babb

A poem's owed to Sarah Binks,
Our poet laureate, methinks.
Her rhymes were many, thoughts were few.
Sometimes her poems combined the two.[1]

This Sweetest Songstress of The West
Is the poet I love best.
The one on whom the muses smiled.
A poet, yet a prairie child.

She spoke of things so commonplace,
The cow, the pig, the human race.
Weddings, death and spreading time;
Immortal now in verse and rhyme.[2]

---

[1] To which Edith adds the following footnote:
To think her thoughts might well have been
Not thought, not written, never seen.
And so we thank the whole Wheat pool
And the diligent searchings of Rosalind Drool.

[2] The effect these immortal rhymes had on the public is exemplified in the following:

Her poems lead one to suppose
She could have said the same in prose.
She captured Fortune in her lair
And won a prize at the Quagmire Fair.

In glory she'd no time to wallow,
For life was more than she could swallow.
Still young, she tread life's last kilometre
And then succumbed to a horse thermometer.[3]

Naomi Norquay
Toronto

✉ It was the CBC's fourth Literary Competition of 1982 to which I submitted Edith Babb's "Owed . . ." (posthumously, of course for she died in 1948 of natural causes). Robert Weaver and his judges failed to appreciate this fine piece of Canadiana and squandered their chance to introduce Edith to the nation.

I have enclosed another Babb gem, entitled "Them Noble Pigs." This is also in *The Collected Works of Edith Babb*. I think that it is one that would have inspired Sarah Binks in her penning of that famous "Hi Sooky, Ho, Sooky" had she been privy to the works of this other Canadian poet.

The following is an excerpt from *The Collected Works of Edith Babb*:

Her poems, so mystical in text,
Made readers cry, "What next? What next?"
They craved the word of this fairest sage.
They couldn't wait to turn the page.

Beyond a doubt Sarah filled her readers with inspiration. I do not know anyone who, having read her poems, did not go on and read something else.

[3] One wonders what heights Sarah would have reached if she had only lived a full life. But even in so short a life she produced a large number of poems. Sadly, many still remain undiscovered. There is much that Sarah wrote that has never been read. Just as there has been much read that Sarah never wrote.

In most cases it is difficult to precisely date Edith's poems. The one exception is "Them Noble Pigs," which Edith wrote the summer she turned ten. This poem is exemplary of the high quality of poetry the poet was able to produce at a tender age. It also brings to light something close to an international literary scandal.

"Them Noble Pigs" pays tribute to Edith's favourite farm animal. Edith entered it in the 1868 "Poetry Contest of the Empire." It contains a few words and phrases that we have long associated with Lewis Carroll's more famous poem, "Jabberwocky." Carroll was one of the judges of that contest and it was he who penned the rejection letter that Edith received — her poem discarded by the judges, *but never returned to her*. Carroll's letter to Edith was short and to the point: "Topic unsuitable for a young lady."

I request that you read the following poem with care and decide for yourself whether or not this has the makings of the biggest plagiarism scoop in English literary history. I present the facts, only the facts: a fine poem written by a ten year old Canadian girl that was rejected *but never returned* by a man whose great prose and poetry graces many a Canadian girl's bookshelf. Read and be your own judge!

Them Noble Pigs

The pig's a noble animal:
The male's a boar and that's no bull.
His mate, the soft and silky sow,
Doth gyre and gimble in the mow.

They hang about the trough for slops
And when it comes they lick their chops.
Then with a dainty, pigly grin,
They push and shove and dive right in.

The menu's never apt to bore
The pigs who only grunt for more.
Aside from comments on their diet
They tend to live life on the quiet.

They do not crowd their thoughts with talk.
They never jabber when they walk.
And with a silent, stoic grace
They quite surpass the human race.

So calm, so cool, so nonchalant.
Them noble pigs is tres gallant.
The boar so brave, the sow so supple.
Each farmyard ought to have a couple.

Naomi Norquay
Toronto

THE 49-SECOND ESSAYIST: PART THREE, 1993–94

For Kathy

good morning....I'm PG....this is A'side....

The only one I knew had a first name was Miss Durward. Frances
Durward, though HOW I knew it I have no idea. It would please
me if she were listening now, since I liked her--she actually
smiled sometimes in class--and am still grateful for the chances
she gave me. *though I doubt she could be.* Miss Hewlitt must have had a first name too,.of course--
she and her sister, in fact, also Miss Hewlitt, lived *the, downstairs beams. from us* in an first floor of our duplex--but if I knew it then I've lost it
now, and Mrs. Lavitt's, and Mr. McInnis's...no, wait a minute, he
was Stuart, come to think of it *wasn't he? wasn't he*, and as I remember that I remember
him standing in grade seven, and tellin us that he could probably
skate backwards through our whole hokey team if he wanted, carrying *Stickhandle* *front of us* *and*
the puck until someone--was it Bill Parkison?--said, no, sir, you *Scope a goal, un til someone*
couldn't, because you'd put yourself offside--and in drags grade *eight*
eight there was.... *eight*

Oh, sorry. It's not just that's it the first day of school
almost everywhere (bye, Stephanie, have fun), but that I spent some
time last night with a book of reminiscens, perhaps all kinds of
people talking about - remembering all kinds of teachers, and what

303

they meant to them and, as may have happened to you just now, I started
thinking about my own, ^(teachers) nd was astonished how clearly I remember
them, half a century later.

September 22, 1993

GOOD MORNING . . . I'M PG . . . THIS IS M'SIDE . . .

Jane Urquhart will be jealous of me this morning. I'm in St. John's, on
a crisp and sunny September morning. Times are bleak here. I'm still
thinking of my conversation on Friday with Brian Peckford, the for-
mer premier of Newfoundland who lives in British Columbia now,
and who speculated here that the population of the province he used
to lead may have to shrink by half, or of the comment a week or so earlier, by John O'Leary, of Frontier College, that the educational needs
of thirty thousand people who've traditionally lived by the fishery
have now all changed. In the store I stopped in this morning, the
woman ahead of me bought *half a package* of cigarettes. If I'm not mis-
taken, a guy on the plane from Halifax last night was actually bringing
in his own salmon — bringing fish to Newfoundland. And yet and
yet. The sun is bright over what the singer John White calls Sig-a-nal
Hill today. You could almost *feel* what the poet Geraldine Ruba calls
"the beauty of the place." As the cab driver said, it's a good day to be
alive. Jane Urquhart was living here when she researched much of the
novel we'll talk about later on. But she's back in Ontario now. She
will, as I say, be jealous.

October 7, 1993

GOOD MORNING . . . I'M PG . . . THIS IS M'SIDE . . .

To tell you the truth, I might not even have looked closely at a story
I've been reading if Jeannette Matthey, the gutsy and vivacious CBC
radio journalist who died yesterday at thirty-seven, had not been on
my mind. I first heard it, on a radio newscast while I was driving down
to work: another small, technological advance in the fight against

breast cancer, the disease that took Jeannette's life — specifically, as it turned out when I called up the wire story, to provide earlier detection among young women. Could it have saved Jeannette? Who knows? You may have heard last night on *As It Happens* a tape she made about her own history. Her voice was still full of its familiar warmth and gallantry — remember those vivid, personal accounts she filed to *Morningside* as the Soviet Union fell apart, stories, she once said, she could tell her grandchildren. But she was angry, too, and she showed it. Too many doctors, for all their skills, had missed the cancer in her young, fit body. So, maybe, if the breakthrough in the news today had occurred ten years ago . . . well, that's pointless, isn't it.

Still, there was this, too, in the details. The new technology they'll start to work with now — a combination of a U.S. government department and private enterprise — is in fact a spin-off of weapons research: a device that was invented to look for flaws in nuclear warheads and experimental lasers will now be used to look at women's bodies. Sounds good, eh? But what, I couldn't help wondering as I talked about Jeannette with her other friends and colleagues here . . . what if that research, and all those millions of dollars, had gone in the first place not to war but to *health*? When, I wonder, will we learn?

October 12, 1993

GOOD MORNING . . . I'M PG . . . THIS IS M'SIDE . . .

A bit more than a year ago, during the first blush of Blue Jay fever — odd, isn't it, that the Jays seem to be doing just as well this year, but scarcely anyone is jumping up and down? — Tom and Jerry, the two Americans who cover the team on radio, started talking about one of the (also American) celebrities in the stands. She was Karen Babb, or, more properly, Karen Babb-*Sprague*, wife of the Jays' young third baseman, Ed Sprague, and she had, of course, just won the Olympic gold medal for synchronized swimming. They should introduce her, said either Tom or Jerry or maybe both, and let the people give her a cheer. I don't *think* so, I remember saying at home. That medal really belongs to one of ours, Sylvie Frechette, who was robbed by a judge's error. Fortunately, the powers at the SkyDome must have heard me; Karen Babb — it wasn't her fault that the judge messed up — stayed in her seat. Now, though, *everyone's* feeling better. Sylvie — at last — is about to get her own gold.

October 25, 1993

GOOD MORNING . . . I'M PG . . . THIS IS M'SIDE . . .

When the people who organized the first-ever Saskatchewan book awards this year first realized they were up against the sixth game of the World Series, they felt a little flicker of apprehension. Saskatchewan takes its sports seriously, after all, and though 420 people had coughed up thirty-five bucks a head for dinner in the Regency Ballroom of the Hotel Saskatchewan in Regina on Saturday night . . . well, you never know.

No problem, it turned out. Not an empty seat in the house, and though word seemed to spread spontaneously around the room as the Blue Jays waltzed into the lead, there was more talk of literature than baseball — at least where I was sitting — as we made our way through beef sirloin, wild rice and Saskatoon berry pie. By the time Dianne Warren, of Regina, had virtually swept the awards for her collection of short stories called *Bad Luck Dog* (and it's probably worth noting that the only exception to Dianne's monopoly, another collection called *Sun Angel*, by Chris Fisher, was also published by the Saskatchewan collective, Coteau Books), not even the fact that the hated Phillies had now forged ahead could dim the air of celebration. Saskatchewan takes its writers seriously, too, and Dianne, all of whose victories were chosen by separate juries, got a standing ovation.

Still, there was the game. When the literary cheering had stopped, a few of us huddled around the table where David Carpenter was sitting. Carpenter, a poet, novelist, teacher and editor — he'd had a hand in Chris Fisher's winning work — is also a baseball fan (and fly fisherman) and through the dinner, it turned out, he had been the source of all those spontaneous baseball updates. Clutched in his hand was a television set about the size of a cellular phone, with a picture no bigger than a match book. And when I leaned over for a peek, there was a tiny Joe Carter at the plate, with an even tinier Paul Molitor and Ricky Henderson prancing on the base-paths.

And then . . . well, you know the rest. We could *see* that Joe had hit it, but to get the facts right — it could have been foul from where I was looking, and then, as even now, a home run seemed too good to be true — Dave Carpenter covered the receiver with his ear.

Still, I saw it, and somehow, along with millions of other people, somehow felt nearly as good for a moment as Dianne Warren herself.

November 2, 1993

GOOD MORNING . . . I'M PG . . . THIS IS M'SIDE FROM WINNIPEG . . . Evelyn Hart, who is the undoubted star of the Royal Winnipeg Ballet and who carries its laurels all over the world, actually didn't appear on the stage yesterday afternoon until well into the second of the three pieces the company presented at a matinée here in its home city. In the first piece, my own non-expert eye was caught by the young dancers of the corps, twenty-four of them, including one, named Cindy Winsor, whose parents come from Preston, Ontario, and who, because she led the graceful parade that opened the dance, did exactly thirty-nine arabesques before her work was over, and never missed a beat. When Evelyn, as everyone here seems to call her, finally did make her entrance, there were no gasps of recognition or waves of applause. Evelyn Hart *is appreciated* here where she makes her base — there was a splendid gala in her honour just a couple of nights earlier. But she is part of a team, too — a quite magnificent ballet company that graces this prairie city.

November 24, 1993

GOOD MORNING . . . I'M PG . . . THIS IS M'SIDE . . . Notes from a morning the first working hour of which I am to spend with Leonard Cohen. Three forty-five A.M. — or thereabouts, I am not tracking the time too carefully at this hour — the *Globe and Mail*, which clumps conveniently outside my apartment door while the world sleeps, has a note in the department it calls "Short List." Mentions *Morningside*. Says Leonard will be here. This fall we've had, among other people, Kim Campbell, Anne Murray, Conrad Black, Margaret Atwood and the world champion baton twirler, among other people. But only Leonard, so far as I can remember, made the news. Five-fifteen. Head out. On elevator, a guy is taking newspapers around to other apartments, the slugabeds. Sees me. Nods. Says, "I see you have Leonard Cohen on this morning." Oh, read the *Globe*, I say. Na, he says, the *Sun*. Gary Dunford talks about you and your good buddy. Good buddy? Hey, all right. Finally, seven forty-five, Toronto time, twenty minutes or so before air. Last-minute visit to . . . er, washroom. Guy drying his hands. Sees me. Nods, says, "Hey, I see you have Leonard Cohen on this morning." "Read the *Sun*?" I say. Nah, he says. Saw him on the elevator.

December 21, 1993

GOOD MORNING . . . I'M PG . . . THIS IS M'SIDE . . .

It's been trying to snow in these parts, and there are lots of promising little dots on the weather map now, so I should probably leave that subject alone for a while. But my bleatings about the lack of white across the country have brought such a nice letter from Mar Craig in Regina that I thought I might pass at least parts of it along. Winter in Regina, she says, demonstrates the need for fifty words for snow, and Mar goes on to list three kinds they had last week alone.

1) "Separate tiny crystals that fall and stay separate, squeaking under your boots when you walk,"

2) "Hoar-frost. Frozen fluffy fog on every surface. In my neighbourhood," Mar writes, "the mature elms form a white lace canopy high above the streets. At my house we have spectacular frost patterns on the windows of the front porch, and a mountain ash tree with huge clumps of scarlet berries encased in crystals. On hoar-frost days you can expect sun all day — enthusiastic sun, blazing straight out of the clear blue sky, unimpeded. In the afternoon, if a breeze comes up it is so slight that the snow falls off the trees one huge flake at a time and sparkles all the way to the ground. Countless slow motion floating sparkles."

3) "Outside my front door one day last week I found a thin layer of snow that looked like sparkling white Cheddar cheese.

"It's a mystery to me," Mar concludes, "why we get so much

attention for drought, flood and bugs, and so little for an early winter spectacle that challenges the most extravagant imagination. It's so beautiful here it is hard to take in . . ."

Merry Christmas, Mar Craig, Regina . . .

January 17, 1994

GOOD MORNING . . . I'M PG . . . THIS IS M'SIDE . . .

Just as Elvis Stojko was leaping high into one of his incredible triple somethings on Saturday night, the cable to our house froze, I think; the picture died and the music of the *Bruce Lee Story* turned to a white buzz. A pipe froze at our place, too, over the weekend, and my car broke down. How cold was it? That's the question Warren Clements posed in Saturday's *Globe and Mail* contest, which will probably get some hilarious answers (wish I'd thought of it, in fact) but up our way, the cold didn't seem very funny. The CAA, when people called to get *their* cars started, was a day and a half behind; plumbers, I think, will be working till July. The temperature? Who knows? Without cable, I couldn't see the weather channel. How did our ancestors handle it, anyway?

January 18, 1994

GOOD MORNING . . . I'M PG . . . THIS IS M'SIDE . . .

Okay, that settles it. I'm moving to Vancouver. Know what the big problem is in Vancouver? (Yes, of course you do, if that's where you live.) The damn daffodils are starting to come up, that's what. And the rhododendrons. The rhododendrons think it's March in Vancouver. They were playing tennis in Victoria yesterday — the people, not the rhododendrons. And I know my phone will ring this afternoon and a guy I know who moved out west from Montreal and joined a golf club where he says the junior champion is sixty-seven years old will tell me about how he played the back nine this morning. Meantime, I still can't get the plumber to look at my frozen pipes — I'm too low a priority, I guess, we have *some* water — and another guy I know said he drove past the place where my car broke down over the weekend and saw a snow-plough stuck in the ditch. I'm going, I tell you, I'm going.

February 18, 1994

GOOD MORNING . . . I'M PG . . . THIS IS M'SIDE . . .

And I say — however sadly — *hurray* for Kurt Browning. Did you hear him? He said sorry to *us*? Geez, Kurt, which of *us* hasn't blown some crucial moment in our lives? Who hasn't failed some important test? But among those of us at home, who, I wonder, would have had the grace you showed yesterday? So, hurray, I say — and "Go Elvis," who, speaking of grace, took a moment after his own splendid skate to hug his fallen team-mate and say, according to a story this morning, "I'm here for you." These games may be marred by you-know-who and *her* team-mate, but, if it doesn't sound too Canadian, you gotta like *our* kids. All of 'em.

April 12, 1994

GOOD MORNING . . . I'M PG . . . THIS IS M'SIDE . . .

Pooh, as we went to air this morning, was still missing.

Pooh — you may have missed this in all the riot of other information — is the Jack Russell terrier — one of two in the royal possession — that went walking with her master, Prince Charles, in the forests of Balmoral, Scotland, over the weekend and disappeared. This has caused quite a flutter, apparently, not to mention raised the prospect of His Royal Highness wandering the woods crying, "Has anyone seen my dog Pooh?" The *Daily Mail* has offered a substantial reward, the ghillies have been peering down rabbit holes, the press is in hot pursuit, but so far — no Pooh.

Hoping I could be of some help this morning, I consulted once again the chart of canine intelligence in the book you may have heard me mention before the news. Would a Jack Russell, I wondered, just be too dumb to find her way home — or, perhaps, smart enough to want to take the same course as Diana? No clues. Jack Russells, according to the book, are not a recognized breed. Now if Pooh had been a border collie . . .

May 6, 1994
GOOD MORNING . . . I'M PG . . . THIS IS M'SIDE . . .
Okay, I cheated. But it was time to leave for work, and I had just one word unsolved in the cryptic crossword. It should have been easy. The clue was "gave everyone a hand" — five letters — and I already knew it went blank, E, blank, L, blank. In five letters? Cryptics are tricky, of course. "Gave everyone a hand" almost certainly didn't mean helped, or assisted, but if not, what? Applauded. I was stumped. So I cheated. I have this little machine, you see, kind of a calculator, about the size of the jack of diamonds. (There's a clue in there, now that I think of it.) Officially, it's a Scrabble dictionary. You punch in the word you want to play, and if it's in the dictionary, the machine confirms it. But it's cleverer than that, too. You can punch in the letters you're holding and, after a moment's pause, it will make some suggestions. Or you can punch in, say, blank, E, blank, L, blank, and it will give you an alpha-betical list of all the possibilities. So (blush) I did. And there they were: belle, belly, bells, cella (the interior of an ancient temple), celli, cello . . . and so on. Did it solve my problem? Well, yes. But I'm only mentioning it this morning because later on we're looking at the Scrabble dictionary and the current fuss over its *very* politically incorrect vocabulary.

The answer? Oh, "dealt" — gave everyone a hand, as in bridge.

May 9, 1994
GOOD MORNING . . . I'M PG . . . THIS IS M'SIDE FROM MONTREAL
Early morning. Still dark, in Montreal. I'm half awake, half asleep. I was on *Cross Country Check Up*, where we talked about bilingualism yesterday — had fun, too, though I'm afraid I may have let my emo-tions show a bit toward the end — when they were holding that

hockey shoot-out on TV. Ah, well. Probably would have lost my cool there, too. Way to go, Canada. Now, this morning, amid my reverie, the phone rings. It's a machine, playing Muzak as my wake-up call. Then, a sultry voice. Wishes me, in French, *une journée agréeable*. *Merci*, I think — yesterday's phone-in still on my mind. More Muzak. Sultry voice comes back, this time in unaccented English. Wishes me a pleasant and *profitable* day. That's better, I think. In the Broadcast Centre in Toronto, there are TV screens that flicker out information about what we do. "Do you know," they ask in English, "that 3,500 people (I think that's the number) *live* here?" In French, it's different. The verb is *travaillier*. Life, I take it, occurs elsewhere. Two solitudes, do you think? They were playing "O Canada" in the elevator when we rode up to work this morning in the Maison Radio Canada.

May 13, 1994
GOOD MORNING . . . I'M PG . . . THIS IS M'SIDE . . .
I can't always remember the whole list. The telephone, to be sure, though Americans sometimes claim it. Insulin, Pablum, green garbage bags — I'm grateful to Stuart McLean for that one — the variable pitch propeller, Marquis wheat, Trivial Pursuit, the snowmobile, the photo-finish camera . . . and basketball, we can sometimes forget (aren't raptors birds, by the way?) . . . and the co-op movement and the vacuum radio tube . . . and, well, anyway, the list of Canadian inventions is a long one. Once I was trying to give it in a speech and someone yelled from the crowd, "You forgot the zipper" — which is a disturbing thing to say to a man standing on a platform. But I *never* forget the Bloody Caesar. A Canadian invented that exactly twenty-five years ago — in Calgary.

May 27, 1994
GOOD MORNING . . . I'M PG . . . THIS IS M'SIDE . . .
"I could hardly believe my ears," writes Kate Stevens, the story teller (and Scrabble player) from Victoria. "You are reputed to believe in

literacy," writes Dennis Duncan from Saskatoon, "yet your comments reveal a most disturbing attitude."

They are not alone. Today, the last of this season, wraps up twelve long years of service for me at *Morningside*, and though I'm sure I've been in hotter water at some time, I can't, this morning, recall when.

What has caused the fuss — we read a couple of letters last week and lots, like Kate Stevens' and Dennis Duncan's, are still coming in — is my conversation a couple of weeks ago with Mike Weiss, the Scrabble guy, in which, apparently, I over-supported the move by some people to get the racist and sexually explicit words out of the Scrabble dictionary. My goodness. A tempest in a pee-pot. People — including some of my colleagues here, who are, I remind you, the best radio producers in the world — think I've taken leave of my senses.

Am I, as I said I was to Shelagh Rogers last week, sticking to my guns?

Probably not, to tell you the truth. I still cringe when I see a racial epithet appear in my favourite word game, but, as someone said to me, if you don't like it don't play it. And as for the other four-letter words, it does seem a bit hypocritical of me to have in my vocabulary words I'll say (if not on the radio) but won't play. So, to keep the peace, I'll cave in.

But here's why I thought this apparently minor matter worth raising today: there's a lot of talk of political correctness in the air — and a lot of evidence of its excesses. At the same time, as the mail has reminded me once again, there are an awful lot of people of good will who are determined to stand up against it.

The (Sometimes) Bittersweet Tug of Memory

In all the years I've done daily morning radio for the CBC, I've never ceased to have been amazed at its power to stir the ashes of memory. Almost anything, it sometimes seems, can strike a chord, evoke an emotion, call up a moment, or a person, from the past. A song, a reference to someone else's favourite relative, or, in the case of one of our most distinguished poets (she had won the Governor General's Award not long before she wrote this), just a young musician in the midst of her first *Morningside* interview.

✉ The Radio as Time Machine

This morning on the radio
Peter talks with a musician.
Five years in Toronto,
she was born in Nova Scotia
where her father
taught her how to play
when she turned three —
her fiddle a sixteenth
the normal size. "Now,"
she says, "it's sitting
on the mantle."
"What would he say," Peter wonders,
"if I asked him
what kind of pupil you were?"

314

"I don't know."
"Well, put your headphones on,
and let's find out."
"She was a good pupil,"
her father says from Halifax.
"Dad?"
"You should see your daughter,"
Peter says. "She's wearing
a big grin. How come you're
so pleased?"
"It's just so good to hear him."
Three years since
my father's death,
I can't help but wish
next time I'm on the radio
Peter will say, "Lorna,
put your headphones on
and we'll ask your dad."
Dad?
Ask him what?
Maybe what he thought
I'd learned from him,
what he thought of me,
— all this time
between us —
even if he had to say
some bad things
with the good,
how I'd be grinning
just to hear
his voice again,
his smoker's cough,
no matter if
the whole country's
listening in.

Lorna Crozier
Saanichton, British Columbia

✉ I was a regular customer at Woolworth's. I was very shy as a child, and my parents were always trying to devise ways for me to learn to talk to strangers. Once every month or so they would give me change (twenty-seven cents, I believe) and instead of going home at noon I was to go to Woolworth's lunch counter for a hot dog and chocolate milk. I was terrified but hungry so at the age of six or seven, I would walk downtown, find a seat at the counter and bravely order lunch, praying to God that no chatty adult would take the seat beside me. The program must have worked, though, because now, unlike most adults I know, I am not embarrassed to eat alone in a restaurant.

That was my parents' money. I spent *my* money in the toy department. That is to say, I spent most of my money on one specific item. India rubber balls. We lived at the corner of Park and Pine streets, which, if you know Brockville, is three blocks straight uphill from the mighty St. Lawrence River. If your India rubber ball got away from you and headed down Park Street, it was history. I lost about four million of them. After the first few, we didn't even bother chasing them. We just considered them a gift for the archaeologists and set about saving up pennies for the next one.

For a while, the father of one of my friends was the manager of that Woolworth's store — not the owner, just the floor manager. They lived in their own home. All six kids were well-clothed and had bicycles. They had their own set of encyclopaedias. The mom didn't work outside the home for wages. If you went there after school, you got home-made cookies and milk. If I feel nostalgic about anything, it would be this: that I grew up in a time when a person could support a family of eight on the salary he earned as the manager of a five-and-dime store.

Deb Chatreau
Tweed, Ontario

✉ We lived on the Alberta side of Lloydminster but went to school in Saskatchewan. The route home took me past the local Woolworth's.

When I was in grade six or seven, some friends and I fell into a bad habit of dropping in on the store, sometimes a couple of times a day, to relieve the candy counter of a chocolate bar or two.

I can only imagine the life of crime that would have resulted had it not been for the sudden appearance of a wise store manager.

Loot in pocket, we were heading for the exit when he materialized, a large man in an important-looking suit.

Confessions were quickly extracted, the candy confiscated and our phone numbers written down. He let us go, promising to call our parents very soon.

So far as I know, he never did. Maybe it slipped his mind, or maybe he knew the best way to strike terror in young hearts.

Had he reported us there would have been big trouble, punishment and then it would have all been over. Instead, my friends and I spent weeks, maybe months, dreading every ring of the phone.

I don't know about the rest of the candy gang, but I have never again lifted anything from anywhere.

Mark O'Neill
Vancouver

✉ I used to spend my lunch breaks in the five and dime drooling over all the little things we could not afford. I was particularly enchanted by all the little bits and pieces in the stationery department. I would squeeze the art gum erasers and smell the chalk and the pencils. I particularly loved to fondle long, new, unsharpened, yellow HB pencils with intact erasers and no teeth marks.

At that particular time we were just graduating from pencils to pens and while reluctant to date myself, I will say that these were straight pens with removable nibs that we dipped into little inkwells. The urge was too strong. I had to have new pen nibs. I picked up a little packet with three nibs and was immediately overwhelmed with hot guilt and furtively stole out of the store with the prize in my pocket.

Back at school I opened my package and put the nibs in my mouth, as one had to suck the oil off before using them in the pen holder. My mind was miles away, dreaming of all the wonderful things I would write with my new pens. My reverie was broken by my teacher calling on me to answer a question. I was startled and unable to speak with a mouthful of pen nibs, so I started coughing and spit out two pen nibs. Where was the third?

For years afterwards, any time I felt the least twinge in my chest, I knew the stolen nib had at last ended its floating journey round my body and come home to stab me fatally in the heart for my crime.

Needless to say, I was forever cured of shop-lifting. However, I still do love stationery counters and new yellow pencils.

Patricia Post
Vancouver

✉ I'm blind as a bat and therefore have little way of telling what new eyeglass frames look like on my face. No problem, I thought, I'll just run across the street to the Woolworth's and pop into one of those automatic photo booths and get my picture taken wearing the new frames. I was about a month too late. Woolworth's in uptown Saint John closed December thirty-first.

I telephoned the other discount and department stores in the city, only to discover there is just one automatic photo booth left in all of Saint John. It's in the Loch Lomond Mall — a good fifteen minutes drive from uptown. I suddenly felt very sorry for the teen-agers in Saint John who don't have access to a car.

Growing up, I didn't know anybody who didn't have at least one strip of black and white instant photos in their wallet or taped to the mirror in their bedroom. Hell, we lived in those photo booths in junior high. We used them when we needed photographs for bus passes and other forms of ID. We'd pile into them on rainy Saturday afternoons when there was nothing else to do. The photo booths were a lot of fun for twenty-five cents.

There was the stool. Who can forget spinning the top to adjust the height? And what about the background curtain in the booth? Do we draw it closed, for a more sophisticated look . . . or have our picture taken against the blank back wall? Then again, we could be really clever and pull the curtain half-way.

The automatic photo booth was the only reason I went to Woolworth's, and I am sorry for that. Maybe, had I and everyone else who only went there for the photo booth bought a few items from the store, it would have lasted a little longer.

Christiane Vaillancourt
Saint John

✉ I remember one of my childhood favourites — the Mello-roll! Two sizes, three flavours — chocolate, strawberry and my choice, vanilla. The Mello-roll, or "ice-cream wrapped in cardboard," was a special treat for my best friend Christine and me.

Most Friday nights and Sunday afternoons during the winter months, we put on our ski jackets (mine a robin's-egg blue colour from the Sears catalogue), our Beatle caps (just like the ones John, Paul, George and Ringo wore) and our stretchiest stretch pants. Dressed just so, we would head to the local arena to skate round and round the rink. During intermission, when the rink was being shovelled clean, we made our way to the corner store where, allowance permitting, we could enjoy our chosen flavour of Mello-roll.

My own children have not experienced such a simple pleasure. Gone is the Mello-roll, now replaced by something much more exotic like a peanut buster parfait, a product more suited to our "consumptive" society. Gone, too, is our neighbourhood rink, replaced by a sports complex complete with multiple ice surfaces, a pool, meeting facilities, offices and debt.

I want to believe my two kids have just as much enjoyment and peace as we did in the days of the Mello-roll. I'm just not sure!

Alice Paige
Pakenham, Ontario

✉ I grew up in central northern Saskatchewan, when horses brought the farm kids to school. In the coldest weather, those kids would arrive at school in tiny cutters painted in bright colours, with short wooden "wings" sweeping back at an angle like the wings of a fighter plane, their sole purpose to keep the little vehicle from overturning in deep snow. I lived in the village and was always amused at the sight of the cutters all lined up at the little red barn the school provided, their smoke stacks trailing smoke from the tiny stoves inside for hours after the frost-covered horses had been stabled. I still thrill to the memory of running after a horse-drawn open sleigh, to stand on the protruding runners at the back, smoothly hitch-hiking to school or around the village, jerking to the motion of the horses' steps. The runners squeaked in the cold snow.

A farmer's field became a winter playground for those of us who lived in that village. Our playground was known locally as "Verge's Hill" — Verge being the owner of the wheat field that included a slope steep enough for toboggans. Our toboggans were huge. It wasn't uncommon for eight or ten of us to line up on a single toboggan, one kid perched backwards on the curl to deflect the huge spray of snow that would be kicked up on our trip into the stand of poplars at the foot of the hill.

Saturday nights were public skating nights on the outdoor skating rink. A dime would be tucked into our mitts to pay for admission to the rink. Then we raced towards the bright light illuminating that magic place. For one winter my father helped as custodian of the rink. To clear the snow he had to push a large wooden scraper with a metal edge on its blade across the surface of the ice.

Flooding the ice meant filling a forty-five-gallon barrel with water, then placing it on a crude wooden sleigh. A pipe with holes along its length lay crosswise at the base of the barrel, and the water sprinkled from these holes in smooth wet lines as my father pushed it back and forth. I loved everything about that rink, even the smell of rolled tobacco on the clear cold air.

Larry Wotherspoon
Nanaimo, British Columbia

✉ Yes, it *is* strange what triggers memories.

Vacuum message tubes . . . Back in the early sixties I did a brief stint in the Nursing School at the Royal Victoria Hospital in Montreal. Visions of tubes colliding in mid flight used to feed *my* imagination. But the great sport of *interns* was to capture a mouse in the building's bowels, put the poor creature into a tube and load it into the system, then make a mad dash to its destination, casually walk up to the nursing station and wait for the unsuspecting nurse to open the tube and discover its contents. It was not uncommon for the reaction to echo through the ward some time between midnight and 3:00 A.M. . . .

Willi Evans Wolfe
Jemseg, New Brunswick

✉ My first brush with romance came when I was six years old. In those days Batman was everywhere. I was carried along in the excitement by the enthusiasm of my brother and the boy across the street. For hours we would leap and careen around the yard inventing bat-adventures. Being the youngest and the only girl, I most often felt the injustice of being cast as the villain. (Well, Catwoman *was* the only girl's part.) Every day we would rush home from school to watch Batman on the television, calling out the fighting words as they sprang off the screen: "Biff . . . Kapow . . . Zonk!"

One day Batman and Robin, in pursuit of a villain, jumped from a great height and Robin fell and sprained his ankle. Batman paused.

"Quick, Batman, follow him! He's getting away!" pleaded the crumpled Robin from behind a brave grimace.

Batman instantly altered his course and swooped over to Robin's side. He wrapped his strong arm around the Boy Wonder and tenderly eased him to his feet.

"Never mind that, Robin," said Batman, choked with loving concern, "we have to get you home and get you fixed up."

Robin tried to take a step but the pain was overpowering and he fell into Batman's arms. Batman drew Robin to him, wrapping his arm around his waist. Robin, leaning into the Caped Crusader, hanging off his shoulder, half hobbled and was half carried to the Batmobile.

My little six-year-old heart melted right then and there into a sugary pink puddle on the floor. Never before had I seen such a moving display of human emotion. I was smitten. From that day forth I never took my eyes off the screen from the opening shot of Gotham City to the last disappearance of the Batmobile over the road barrier and into the Batcave. I strained to recover that moment, watching every movement between them, listening to every word they exchanged.

I still called out the fight words with my brother and jumped off the back porch in a terry cloth cape, but I knew the real magic of the Dynamic Duo had less to do with the Joker and the Riddler than with life back at the Batcave.

Naturally, I had no inkling as to what my young mind was implying, but well over a decade later I heard a radio commentator, going on about some nostalgia thing, mention homosexual undertones in Batman and Robin. A light flashed on in my head. Right! I knew that! Ever since I was six . . .

It's been about thirty years since I've seen Batman and Robin, and I don't think I'd see them again even if I had the chance. I want to keep my first brush with romance as perfect and uncomplicated as I remember it. Needless to say, I will have no truck with the thesis that Batman and Robin were simply "business partners."

Linda Little
River John, Nova Scotia

✉ Lately I've been thinking on my mixed-up feelings when I was issued my helmet from Army Stores at the Little Mountain Depot in Vancouver in the summer of '42.

Every army recruit was issued with two suits of battle dress, woollen underwear, heavy, warm socks, mitts, black army boots and a great coat. From stores he also drew an issue of webbing, pouches, battle gear, fatigues, mess tins, a field dressing, duffle bag and the helmet. The rifle, bayonet and gas mask came later.

The helmet was a bit of a shock. I was appalled by the thinness of the metal carapace that was to enclose my skull. And what about the sloppy strap that held the helmet in place? Worst of all was the discovery that unless I kept my head and chin up and shoulders back, the helmet would slip sideways, thus exposing more of my fragile skull than I chose to an eager sharpshooter somewhere out there in no man's land.

Today I can't recall whether there were large, medium, or small helmets, or if they went by sizes such as 6 or 6½ or 7 like they do for a fedora or a bowler hat. I think all the helmets were stamped from the same mould, a standard, utility issue, and adjustments to the skull size were achieved by fiddling with the inner webbing or tightening or loosening the chin strap.

I can still hear our sergeant at Basic Training Camp at Vernon telling us the capabilities of the helmet and its multiple uses under fire and up in the front lines:

"Now, this is the helmet," the sergeant shouted, holding one up for all to see. "She's a good shield and protector against shell fragments and ricochets. But don't expect too much from a direct hit. She's also useful against falling rocks and debris coming down from a nearby Moaning Minnie or an 88. Or blows from a rifle butt or heavy kicks from an army boot.

"Now, pay close attention. If you're stuck you can use her for a water pail or a wash basin, or even a chamber pot, to use the polite word. But for God's sake, pull back the webbing inside. Some chaps have used their helmet to scrape out the muck in a silt trench. But remember, when all hell breaks out, keep your heads down and hold tight to your helmet."

Most soldiers hated their helmet. It sat on the head like the cap of an earthy, gigantic mushroom. It was an ominous and foreboding piece of gear reinforcing the sense of anonymity, inadequacy, lost identity. Even the weight seem designed to push down on the forehead and give a primordial cast to the visage and lower jaw. But worse, the helmet suggested the soldier's mortality, his tenuous hold on life, the unseen dangers that lay ahead. In poetic vein, it was poor and

323

miserable comfort for the imagination, art, music, language, the seat of the affections.

Thousands of soldiers went through the war without even a nick or a dent to their helmet. We were the lucky ones. But forty-six years later I still see clusters of rusty, soiled helmets, dangling by chin straps from rifles planted as grave markers. And the helmets turn and twist in the wind above freshly tossed earth behind a hedgerow, an outhouse, a barn or a haystack, or on the crest of a hill in driving black rain.

Sam Roddan
Surrey, British Columbia

✉ In 1944, I was in the Canadian Women's Army Corp, stationed in Kitchener. I was on leave travelling by the Northern Ontario Rail to Val d'Or. I had to change trains in North Bay. My train arrived at around midnight and connected to Swastika about five in the morning. There was an all-night canteen across the street from the station, where service people could get a meal, coffee and even a nap. I had my lunch and settled down to wait and read. The canteen person came over to ask me to help a couple of armoured men. Without asking any questions, I said, "Glad to." The woman said, pointing to the men, "They have no arms, I would appreciate it if you would cut the boys' meat and feed them." I went into shock. And then all kinds of thoughts went through my head. I'll never be able to do this without blubbering or crying. And if ever I needed to keep my cool, it's now. I made an excuse that I had to go to the bathroom first. I needed a few minutes to put myself together. The two men were young and handsome. A thought went through my head — I should be flirting with them and not feeding them. I hate to think what thoughts were in their head. While I fed them we chatted as if nothing were happening here. They invited me to take a taxi to visit a friend in Ferris. I spent four hours with these two men. I don't remember what we talked about or even the trip back to the canteen.

Every year when I hear the last post or see the poppy, the memory comes back. I have a good cry, like now, and a rant — "What good did the war or any war do?" Another time at Union Station, Toronto, I saw a long Prisoner of War train full of teen-age boys. They looked so scared. Today I think they were lucky.

Josie Hjorleifson
Duncan, British Columbia

✉ In 1939 Tom and I were living out in the bush in a shack that we built on the property of the Delnite mine about six miles outside Timmins. When war came, Tom and many of the male population of Timmins joined the Sappers and were soon on their way to England.

The scene changes. It is two years later, somewhere in England, and a detachment of the Royal Canadian Engineers has been seconded to a British regiment. It is in the officers' mess and the Canadian mail has just arrived and is being devoured; first the letters and then the newspapers from home. Suddenly an officer from Timmins gives a shout of laughter and the others gather around.

It seems that the Ontario division of the Red Cross has held a competition among its branches to see which, per capita, could knit the most socks, sew the most shirts, write the most pen pal letters and, in general, carry on the good work. "Cedar Corners Branch" just outside Timmins had won hands down; and the Red Cross was loud in its praise. There was great mirth among the men from Timmins and complete mystification among the Brits.

You see, "Cedar Corners" was just that: a cross-roads with a gas station, a liquor "outlet," a restaurant-cum-general store, and a big frame house where "the Ladies" lived. When the Timmins men all pulled out of town, business was suddenly very slow for "the Ladies." But since they were as patriotic as anyone else, they formed their own branch of the Red Cross, with spectacular results.

It remained a source of joy to the homesick Canadians and a source of incomprehension to the Brits — but what could you expect of uncouth colonials who would push aside the *Times* and the *Guardian* and cluster around a rag that called itself the *Porcupine Advance*?

Joyce Tyrrell
Toronto

✉ For forty-seven years, my father owned and operated a corner grocery store and meat market in my small home town of Canton, Ohio. It was located in an old, converted, grey frame house that looked the same as all the houses on the street, except for a painted sign and two large front windows that held displays of produce and toiletries.

The meat department was to the right of the entrance in what had probably been the living-room. Straight ahead was the store's only aisle, which ran the entire length of the building. In the very back there was a teeny kitchen with a table where three people could sit—if the one near the sink sat sideways.

The wooden floor in the kitchen sloped at such a terrifying angle that I always stepped gently for fear of ending up in the stock-room below. Lunch was eaten in that cosy little room. There were no set hours and no restrictions on the type or amount of food.

According to the flow of customers, Daddy would send the clerks to eat in turn, each carrying his choice of fixings. On the busiest day of the week they could always look forward to the hot lunch my mother cooked at home and brought to the store. And at one time Daddy had ten employees.

The store ran mainly on credit. All purchases were handwritten on a small pad. The original was given to the customer and the carbon copy put in the big open-topped file next to the cash register. All the names were visible at a glance. In front of each was a metal divider that flipped to the side on a spring, so the bill could be slipped under the name.

Most of the customers were labourers or factory workers, and during the all-too-often lay-offs and strikes, they could run up huge debts. A six- or seven-hundred-dollar grocery bill forty years ago was astronomical, considering that almost all items cost less than a dollar. And food isn't like furniture that you can put in lay-away until it's paid off.

All the families still had to eat, so more credit was extended, and Daddy might have to carry them for months. There was never a hint of interest or carrying charges. And in all those years he said that very few people disappeared without straightening out their accounts.

I learned my most valued lessons in human relations as a teen-ager working at the Garfield Grocery.

My mother gave recipes and wiped runny noses.

She had infinite patience with a grubby child who had to decide how to spend his three pennies when there were three shelves full of candy in the showcase.

You could often see my father putting a comforting arm around the shoulders of troubled customers who came to him for advice.

They both laughingly, and with ironic pride, spoke of the gumption and ingenuity of the two little boys who took empty pop bottles from the store's garage out back and brought them in to collect the refunds.

Orders were taken over the phone and delivery was free. When old Mrs. Sweeny wanted a quarter pound of lunch meat we were out of, Daddy would get the delivery boy to stop and buy it retail. Time and money spent for no profit.

Do you even know the name of the manager of your local supermarket? And if you do, would you name your child after him or her? More than one of Daddy's customers named a new-born son David after the corner grocer. Living testimonies of love and respect. The same love and respect that they received.

One very hot, humid, summer day, an old man limped slowly into the store and bought a Popsicle. My father went to the kitchen and brought out a chair. He led the customer by his arm and sat him down in the middle of the only aisle.

Then Daddy took the Popsicle from the man's palsied hand and removed the wrapper.

"Here," he said, as he gave it back. "Rest up and enjoy."

The Popsicle cost a nickel.

The memory is worth a million.

Adele "Vicki" Charness
Montreal

X-ER-SIGHS

Slackers, busters, post-Yuppies, thirteeners (for the thirteenth non-Aboriginal generation born in America) . . . The air and the media were full of labels for the people most frequently called Generation X — after the novel by the Canadian writer Doug Coupland. One morning we gathered four of them to talk about their lives and their expectations, and to respond to some of the criticism. That panel drew a lot of thoughtful mail, as you'll see. First, though, here are our panelists. In Fredericton, Linda McNutt, twenty-six, a writer, researcher and theatre director. In Toronto, Dave Eddy, thirty-two, also a writer, and Candace Gregoris, twenty-two, working on a political science degree. And in Halifax, Chris Trowbridge, a history student and sometime campus radio DJ. A lively bunch. We started with Doug Coupland's novel.

CHRIS   I didn't think it defined my existence or anything, but I thought it was a good read.

LINDA   Yes, a good book, great characters.

PETER   You liked it, Linda?

LINDA   Yes, I liked it.

PETER   Were you in it?

LINDA   No. I think the desire to be a story-teller they all have, maybe that's there. The existence of dropping out and living in the desert — not really.

PETER   Dave, were you in it?

DAVE   I felt it pretty much pegged my experience of our generation.

PETER   Really?

CHRIS   This book came out and labelled us Generation X and now people expect all these generalizations about us to be true. I thought the people in that book were really passive and kind of boring in a way. They didn't really do anything interesting with their lives. I don't think that is true of my generation. I think people I know are really creative and interesting and they're not just sitting around waiting for the end of the world.

LINDA   That's the way I felt about it, too. I thought there was very little hope in it, and I think we have a kind of freedom because there is no opportunity out there so we make our own. I think that is something really exciting about us as a generation that wasn't in the book.

DAVE   If there was to be a motto for our generation, if our generation had a motto, it would be "We made a virtue of necessity."

PETER   Meaning...

DAVE   Meaning we have been given less. I think that with each generation — from probably yours to our older brothers' and sisters', the sort of Baby Boom to us — each generation has had less and less. For your generation, perhaps you could say that home ownership was looked upon as a right. And the next generation, it wasn't that they really bought condos, but they were able to spend a lot of money on BMWs and home appliances. And now, a lot of us can't even afford cars, but I think we make a virtue of it. We bike, we rent. You know, our parents had all these ideals about peace and love and ecology, and yet they left a huge pile of garbage. And we're very conscious of that.

LINDA   The expectations are pretty deadly, as well as the garbage. The expectation is that we're supposed to have everything together by the time we're thirty. I remember being lectured by endless tenured professors in their thirties with Volvos about how I should be more socially active.

CANDACE   What a fallacy, though, that people of our age are not socially active.

LINDA   There are more campus activists now than there ever were in the 1960s. And I think we have another backlash we're dealing with. If we're being socially active or we take a social stand, people say, "Oh, you're just doing that because you want to be politically correct, you're just jumping on a bandwagon." We do things, but people think *why* we do them doesn't originate from us.

PETER   People say you only want jobs.

CHRIS   I don't really care if I have the capability to make enough money to consume as much as my parents did, because they consume an unreal amount on a global scale. I don't need a condo and I don't need a wife and kids right away. I'm quite happy to live on a smaller scale and get involved with my community directly.

PETER   I want to talk about jobs and reduced expectations. Linda, you're doing combinations of part-time jobs.

LINDA   Oh, yes. I work for a couple of different theatre companies, both of which are made up of people who work part-time. They might work behind a pharmacy counter or they work for other writers or they do research part-time. They do what they love because they can survive. They make the rent and then they make their lives happy. If they live in cold places, they put on a sweater and grow geraniums. We do the best we can with what we have.

330

CANDACE   Don't you think there are two sides to that, though? I know I'm going to finish my BA and then probably go back and do an MA because when I'm finished there won't be anything out there for me to really commit to. I think sometimes we're accused of lacking commitment — we don't want to commit to anything, we want to be able to move around, float around, do whatever we want to do. But we're in the middle of a recession, and it's extremely hard to find a job.

CHRIS   I agree. A friend of mine graduated with a history BA, Honours, from McGill, supposedly the best university in Canada, and he ended up walking around all summer with a sandwich-board sign to make money.

PETER   Dave, have you had times like that?

DAVE   I've had McJobs, if that's what you're wondering. I think there is an evolution, where we pin less of our identity on our jobs. I think we decide, Well, I'm not going to get rich, I'm not going to sell my soul and wear a suit, because it's just not going to happen, so I might as well do something I'm going to enjoy. I think for our generation there will be fewer traditional jobs. A lot of people will be working out of their homes. There will be smaller businesses. It won't be that you'll walk into a big organization and get a job just like that.

PETER   Do you feel frustrated by that? Does it seem unfair to you? Linda?

LINDA   I'm definitely frustrated by it. I was probably more frustrated before I decided to stop worrying about it and be a writer. It really bothered me before I decided, Well, there's nothing out there, so I might as well do what I love. I went through a Master's program, and most of the people I went through with are waiting tables in Fredericton waiting for somebody to die in the civil service. That's probably why we get labelled as frustrated and alienated and apathetic. But my response to that has been, Well, let's redefine what being grown-up

331

means. It doesn't mean having a house and two kids by the time you're thirty.

DAVE   A good thing that could happen for our generation is that the emphasis on our identities will shift from consuming to producing. For an entire generation of people it's been, "What do you own, what do you wear, what do you drive?" But maybe for us we'll produce more.

CHRIS   I think it's easy for us to sit and complain about not being able to become professionals as easily as our parents did. But what about the diminished expectations of income? There are a lot of people who are more deserving of attention and changes in the social structure than Generation X kids.

LINDA   I think that's why we get accused of being apathetic, too, because we can see that there are people who are worse off than us. The people next door to me collect bottles for a living, and I look at them and feel pretty lucky about what I have, and it is very difficult for me to feel all that bitter about not being a company vice president.

CANDACE   We're defining ourselves a lot more socially. If I'm asked, "What do you care about?" well, I don't care about having three VCRs and twelve colour television sets in my house. I define myself socially, not by what I have. I define myself by the relations I have with other people in terms of racism, sexism, homophobia, things of this nature.

DAVE   We were bombarded by television from the age where you believe everything adults tell you. And then there's an evolution, where you say, "Wait a second. TV exists simply to sell me products." Also we watched a generation, the generation we live in the shadow of, the Baby Boomers, embrace a whole set of values. It was easy in the sixties when you wanted a straight job, so to speak, and you needed some money, if you had dropped out, it was like falling off a log to get a job. Then when the money market tightened, we watched an entire generation . . .

CHRIS   Sell out.

DAVE   Sell all their ideals. We want to wait and develop a set of values we can embrace for a lifetime. And not do this embarrassing public flip-flop the generation before us did.

CHRIS   And they're so self-righteous about it now.

LINDA   Yes, the self-righteousness is probably the most confusing part.

PETER   What do you mean self-righteous?

CHRIS   Well, you know, they were on the barricades in the sixties and blah, blah, blah, and now they're comfortable and they don't really care. I don't see how they've made any real changes in their life-style from their parents. They acted as if there's this big social change going on, but it was all lip service.

CANDACE   Yeah, I once saw an interview with George Harrison, Mr. Beatle there, and he was talking about, Oh, my God I was in L.A. and isn't it horrible and disgusting watching all the cars go by and just think of all the pollution they're spewing into the air. And I'm thinking, Sure, I bet you got a limo ride to this interview.

LINDA   Those horrible car commercials telling us to buy the politically correct car because they really care about the environment. They use it as a marketing tool.

DAVE   "We believed the last thing the world needs is another car . . ."

ALL   "So we built one."

LINDA   We're in the weird position of understanding the parents of Baby Boomers, all of us looking at them from both sides of the generation, asking, "What are they going on about now?"

CANDACE   Some guy in his three-piece suit sitting behind a personal computer writing about how we're apathetic.

LINDA   Yes, and probably has Saran Wrap in his cupboard.

DAVE   We do define ourselves in relation to them. We always grew up in their shadow. They were the first generation to be both a media event and a target market. Let's face it, they were just a generation, like any other. In their teens they were obsessed with hair, drugs and music and they were called hippies. In their twenties, they were obsessed with themselves and called the Me generation, and in their thirties they became obsessed with their careers and household products and they were called yuppies. Until now, we haven't been labelled at all, no one's paid any attention to us. They control the media at the moment, and that's why I think we get such a bad rap.

PETER   I don't want to make too big a deal out of this but one thing I notice about my own children is how television-literate they are. People who grew up with television have all of television's history at their fingertips. You guys probably know more about *Leave It To Beaver* than I do.

CHRIS   We're great viewers.

DAVE   I part ways with my generation on that one . . .

LINDA   Yes, me, too.

CHRIS   But it's like a cultural vocabulary. I think people are pretty critical about it. It is something shared we have. Everybody knows *The Brady Bunch* and *Scooby-Doo* and *Welcome Back, Kotter*.

LINDA   Or you're downtown at the market in Fredericton and everybody's talking like they're on *Seinfeld* saying, "What is that, carrots, carrots? What is that, carrots?"

CANDACE   But I watch shows that give me a literary rush, those television shows that make you feel like you've read something.

PETER   At this very moment at least four people are writing letters saying, "If she wants to feel like she's read someone, she should read something."

CANDACE   But I do, I read every day. But what I'm saying is that the television I watch is not the TV they accuse us of watching. I don't think I'm part of the *Bay Watch* generation. *Bay Watch* is that show where we're going to run around on the beach in our bikinis and save people from the undertow or whatever. I know the interesting people around me watch shows like *Northern Exposure* or they watch *Roseanne*, they get characters you would never expect, who would never walk onto the set of *Leave It To Beaver*.

CHRIS   But don't you guys view some really bad TV sometimes just for fun? I mean, you can watch *Entertainment Tonight*. It's great.

CANDACE   Oh, right, *Entertainment Tonight*.

CHRIS   It's great, you can just see western civilization falling in on itself.

LINDA   *Hard Copy* is the worst.

CHRIS   There's half an hour a night of this . . .

LINDA   . . . Of drudge.

CHRIS   Yeah, it's amazing. I love it.

DAVE   I don't accept this idea of watching TV ironically because it's so bad it's good.

CHRIS   Oh, I do.

DAVE   TV invites you to do that, TV makes fun of itself and asks you to watch it for that reason.

CANDACE   No, I think there is some TV that takes itself too seriously. That's why *Hard Copy* is funny. But I have my own little personal rule. I have personally sworn off *Geraldo* in the belief that I will lose IQ points watching the show. But I don't feel that way when I'm watching *Northern Exposure*.

PETER   Can I get a response to what I think of as the David Letterman phenomenon of television, the trivialization of everything that is important and the inflation of everything trivial?

DAVE   I agree with that. I can't remember who said if Einstein was on Letterman, Letterman would chide him about his jacket or trousers or something. He'd have five minutes and then he'd be off. I do think TV is slowly but surely trivializing everything. You cannot be sincere on television. That's why I don't accept the idea of watching it ironically. People who are sincere on television look like fools. Especially on talk shows. You have to make fun, you have to hang back. That's why it's a cool medium. And I don't think we should buy into it. I think it's Canada's role not to buy into it. It's no accident that Marshall McLuhan came from this country. TV is all created in the States. The States is the circus, and we are the spectators, the critic.

PETER   Dave, what should I have asked you about? What doesn't come up in all these magazine pieces?

DAVE   The magazine articles emphasize what we lack, which boils down to marriages, morals and mortgages. If you were to ask me a question like what do we want, what are we aiming for, what are our goals and ideals — that's something that is rarely asked of us, which is why it is simply assumed that we have none. I think we do have very fervent and passionately held beliefs.

LINDA   We are excited about the future and excited about our relationships with each other.

336

DAVE   It's much more personal, the way we relate to people. It is not going to the barricades, not having sit-ins and love-ins. You could say we're just trying to set an example for the yuppies. Maybe one day they will wind up following our example. Hard to imagine, but . . .

LINDA   It also seems like a valuable thing to look at who is doing the labelling and why. It seems to be a Baby Boomer phenomenon to label us and try to get to the bottom of why we're not doing what they did. And that seems like a very strange way of asking a generation to talk about themselves. "Well, you're apathetic. Respond."

CHRIS   I think we should be viewed on our own terms and given some space and respect, because I think we have a lot of potential.

LINDA   It does a great credit to our spirit that we continue to do anything at all, considering we're being told constantly that we're academically apathetic. When you go to school now, it is for yourself, not to get a job, because realistically, a Master's degree doesn't mean a job. So you go for yourself, which is a hopeful thing. If you choose to get into a relationship, despite statistics about divorce, you're choosing to hope. That's a part of us that maybe the Boomers have missed.

DAVE   I think we're slightly late bloomers, too.

LINDA   We're taking our time and thinking things through.

DAVE   We've all spent our twenties agonizing over what we ought to be. I think you'll be hearing more about us.

LINDA   Yeah, we've thought a lot, and that's not a bad thing for the species . . . to think.

CANDACE   So maybe television didn't destroy us after all.

✉ I am Generation X.

I don't have a real job (how I disappoint my parents).

I have causes: sometimes I march, sometimes I don't.

I don't watch TV.

I shun consumerism and refuse to hoard.

I don't have babies; I won't get married (how I disappoint my parents).

By 2000 I'll have a Ph.D, but I still won't have a real job.

You mistake silent struggle, stubbornness, for apathy. Sometimes we get depressed, those of us in Generation X. We don't fit into the structure we inherited. Call us self-righteous, but we don't want it. We'll do what we like instead.

Paula Price
Vancouver

✉ I am thirty-two years old.

The real Generation X are those that are always forgotten and overlooked, now even by the media's analysis of us. We came into the world in between the baby waves. We are neither Baby Boomers nor are we twenty-something. Following in the footsteps of the hippy group is something we have all become accustomed to, but I don't think many of us can tolerate being lost in the shadow of the next generation of idealists.

There are a lot of disadvantages in being caught between the dominant cycles. We were always subjected to declining services in the education system. Work is less available. When I graduated from high school, the eighties' recession was starting. There was no work. I went to university, but became disillusioned with the make-it-or-break-it attitude and left to try something else. There were no other opportunities, so I went back to school. When I left a few years later, the "jobless recovery" had started. There was some work, but no real opportunities. Many of my peers went back for post-graduate work. I, on the other hand, went on some travel adventures, as did many of my other friends. When we tried to re-enter the work force, the nineties' recession was in full swing. Some of my peers went travelling, some went back to school, a lot of my other peers who were employed were laid off, and possibly a few more accepted low-paying, no-opportunity work. So here we stand. We all have skills to offer and extensive résumés of meaningless work experience and travel adventures.

John D. Macklin
Elliot Lake, Ontario

✉ I guess part of the problem of being in your early thirties right now is that our lack of generational identity is a vacuum the media is seeking to fill. Granted, we of (I'll say it) Generation X have been obscured by the giant shadow of the Baby Boomers who went before us, got all the good jobs, and used up all the safe sex. And when we have nothing better to do, we can usually be eloquently bitter about that.

For example, and this isn't talked about enough, when we were in high school we had to listen to the Boomers' disco music. They wouldn't let go of the pop charts and fade respectably into adulthood the way their parents did. And that the young persons of today are listening to the same damn disco music should give you a good clue as to exactly why we sometimes sound bitter and demographically doomed.

Many of us were complaining about our identity void for years before Douglas Coupland's *Generation X* came out, but we never did anything, like, say, write a best-seller about it. That's just the sort of lack of initiative typical of our generation. I guess if there's one thing most people of my generation have a clearer grasp of than the Boomers, or the younger people coming up (you know the ones; they wear toques even when it's hot and they can't spell worth a damn), it's that there isn't an "enemy." We are *all* the enemy and we are *all* the friend.

Did our parents lie to us? My parents weren't very comfortable with, say, homosexuality, when I was young, but I can't blame them for not being on the cutting edge of social change. They didn't understand quantum physics, either. But they never *lied* to me about anything more serious than Santa Claus.

We *are* a sceptical generation, but by and large most of us have

339

learned (not because we're morally superior, but because we had a chance to watch the Boomers at close hand) that just because you hate your parents doesn't mean there's something wrong with society. It just means you hate your parents.

Here our lack of generational identity has been a blessing. It's kept many of us from facile polarization. Us (good young people) vs. Them (oppressive older people). We don't *have* big solutions *or* big enemies; we're just trying our best in a world that can be complicated and hard because it's full of other people who aren't any better than we are. Anyone who feels anger over that needs to grow up.

Duncan Thornton
Winnipeg

✉ Pity poor me. At thirty-three, I am a year too old for your Generation X panel; living the marginal existence of a Canadian theatre actor, I have never been able to call myself a yuppie. Yet I'm married with a recently acquired house and child (consumption-happy materialist that I am); but my husband is a twenty-nine-year-old — *definitely* a Generation Xer. At least, he knows about all the topics your panel discussed. So where does that leave him? An Xer with a wife and house and child?

As you can see, I have some trouble with all these labels and generalizations. My brother, the consummate yuppie by most definitions, was unemployed for a long period a year ago, and only his brilliance in his particularly hard-hit field (and a lot of luck) have kept him happily employed through most of this recession. So *is* he a yuppie? What about the forty-year-old professional we know who is now living with his wife and kids in her parents' home having lost their house, his business, her job? What label do we stick on them? And incidentally, when will you do the panel on that terrible consuming materialistic generation of parents who, in the case of every yuppie or Generation Xer I know, is keeping us all going through these terrible times? Both "labelled" generations are turning to parents who, in their retirement years, are finding their funds depleted by their yuppie children who are losing their jobs or their Generation X kids who say they can't

afford to leave home. They're the ones I feel for, as I lean on my particular parental units once again for financial and emotional support.

I suppose all I'm saying is that labels don't fit. Particularly in this
recession. And anyway, *every* generation is labelled at some point as
apathetic. *Every* generation goes to parties and discusses social ills
passionately when they're young. And every generation resents the
one before.

Generation X better watch out. There's another one right behind
them.

Alison Lawrence
Toronto

✉ As an avid follower of David Letterman, I was struck by your asser-
tion that he has contributed to the "trivialization of everything
important" and the subsequent elevation of all things trivial. I must
disagree with your analysis.

One of the subjects raised in your discussion was the level of ironic
detachment with which many Generation Xers watch television.
David Letterman has taken this phenomenon a crucial step further by
employing that same ironic detachment as a participant in the
medium itself. What is actually being deflated is the pretentiousness
and sugar-coated moralizing of the popular culture that is the Baby
Boomers' legacy. Although the show smacks heavily of glibness and
cynicism, for many Generation Xers it is easily preferable to the
feigned show business intimacy of Arsenio Hall leaning forward,
unctuously, in his chair, engulfed in waves of "spontaneous" applause
every time he or his guest makes an obvious or politically
correct statement regarding social injustice right before cutting to
commercial.

The problem with this letter is, of course, that, even as I write, a
maelstrom of counter-arguments is raging through my brain, making
me doubt my own convictions even as I utter them. This is the hall-
mark of Generation X: a paralysis of conviction brought on by information bombardment and hyper-education. Machiavelli crushed my
faith in politics, the revisionists my faith in history, de Tocqueville

my faith in democracy, the Gulf War my faith in the media, and post-modernity crushed my faith in myself. The result: a defensive stance of detached irony.

So here we are. A generation of Hamlets. Asked to make choices, but terrified of the fallacies in everything. Capable of greatness, but paralysed by our own self-consciousness. A generation too smart for its own good.

Tom Scholte
Toronto

✉ I was also born in the defined Generation X zone, but as a result of being a child of immigrants, I'll always have more than my parents have. I tire of listening to people of my generation complain that they'll never have what their parents have.

My parents have always lived a simple life-style. When I was growing up we had a large garden and a compost pile, drove the car only when necessary, kept the heat in the house at sixty degrees (this is north-western Ontario, where the temperature dips to the minus thirties or lower) and lived in a mine rental house.

My father, now in his late sixties, doesn't own a car. Instead he cycles everywhere.

These are principles I inherited *before* the current environmental bandwagon ride.

As for work and career, I would never have dreamt of going to university to take a general arts degree and then expect to get a job. Where do people get these expectations? I did go to university, but I studied nursing.

With lower expectations I have achieved more. I'm no longer a nurse, since my work as a nurse gave me the luxury to make a more desired career choice. I'm now a writer doing a patch-work of odd jobs and loving it. As my parents did and still do, I live simply, in a tiny house with the temperature kept low. I have my parents to thank for teaching me the skills to live as I choose, skills that the Generation X offspring of "privileged" households frequently lack. Skills such as signing out a book from the library versus lamenting about not being able to afford a movie, baking your own bread, learning to save scarce pennies towards the piggy-bank of larger and, most importantly, *realistic* dreams.

And as for the cultural vocabulary of TV, I've watched so little television in my life that I feel when my Generation X peers talk TV talk, they're talking a foreign language. But I've read my way to a better life, a life of ideas and realistic *choice*. Choice initiated by my mother reading to me at night while she was learning English. Most of us, after all, do have the ability to *choose*, and this may be the ultimate luxury of being a Canadian.

Eleonore Schönmaier
Ketch Harbour, Nova Scotia

✉ My husband and I married in 1961 when we were very young — twenty-one and eighteen. We preceded the Baby Boomers and although we lived through the sixties we weren't *of* the sixties. We were too busy raising our kids, and so on. We questioned the society we had inherited, too, wrote to communes to decide whether we could contribute to an alternate life-style in that way, and so on. We ultimately bought an old farmstead on five acres and bought books like *Five Acres and Independence*, and made plans for riding out what we saw as the inevitable crash of our economic situation.

Our children now range in age from thirty to twenty-one and we have pretty well accepted that they will never live as well as their parents. Our thirty-year-old, on the advice of a guidance counsellor, opted for community college over university and graduated quite successfully from a business program in 1983. But 1983 was another of those cyclical recessions and she has been either unemployed or underemployed ever since. Admittedly she has complicated her life with a husband and two children, but all the bright promise she showed through her school years has dulled. Indeed, she explained to us one day that she no longer expects a break. She and her family just moved north, where the housing is more reasonable and they can live more simply, and they hope to exist on under- or unemployment. Their old house is heated with a single wood stove and the large greenhouse out back promises some self-sufficiency. Sound sixtyish? She has completed an historical novel, well-researched, better written than many in the genre, but as yet unpublished.

My twenty-seven-year-old son and his new bride, age twenty-four, graduated from the University of Guelph with high hopes of entering a faculty of education. They faithfully have reapplied while he works part-time in a bookstore, and his energetic dynamic wife now cooks for a day-care. She was hired as a pre-school teacher but their budget restraints have changed their priorities, and she can't afford to walk away from a job. They rent one room in a house and have an old car that no longer runs and that they can't afford to fix. They both have student loans, which the banks are pressing to collect. They are mercifully much in love and happy to be together, but the exuberance and confidence they used to exhibit is becoming muted.

My twenty-four-year old daughter is probably the most financially secure, but her job as registered nurse is termed "casual," which means she gets no benefits and can have shifts cancelled arbitrarily. Her expenses in Toronto are high but for a single person she lives quite comfortably. But unfortunately the Xers she meets of the opposite sex are self-centred. They frequently live at home, pay no board, and intend to party for at least five or ten more years. They don't need marriage or family. Of course they don't, because they are caught in a childhood time-warp, where responsibilities can be managed by the previous generation. After all, they're the ones that screwed everything up!

Our youngest daughter just turned twenty-one. She is a student at Ryerson in a business management program. We're glad she has another year and a half to go — it will delay the inevitable. Then she, too, will probably be underemployed, if at all.

Education is something we have always advocated, and we firmly believe that no education is truly lost. However, the energies and potential that we are losing because of the present economic conditions are formidable.

As a parent of four Xers, I am saddened and depressed. We probably lived through the era of the most promise. We assumed, erroneously, that our children's lives would only be better, have more promise. We tried to give them the tools to construct and mould the future, but the medium of the future has been altered and the funding cut off!

Each generation, from the war babies (or Depression babies) on up, have thoughts of disdain for those who went before. We all feel we could have done better, been more sincere, treated the environment better. I only hope the Xers get *their* chance to put their stamp on our society. Who knows what form it will take. To all the Xers, and especially my own few, enjoy the journey and keep on travelling. In the end, that's all any of us have — the journey.

Joyce Ward
Belwood, Ontario

A Rutabaga by Any Other Name Would . . .

Well? A cornucopia of vegetables.

✉ When my wife and I arrived as immigrants to this land from a small group of Third World islands in the northeast Atlantic, we diligently started to explore our new home, particularly by camping and walking the Bruce Trail. On our drives to Tobermory from Toronto, somewhere around Shelburne or Flesherton, I think, we passed — to our total befuddlement — a *rutabaga waxing plant*. Needless to say, we neither knew what rutabagas were, or why it was so essential that they were waxed. Was this to stop them rusting-out, or to remove superfluous hair?

Eventually we discovered that the rutabaga was nothing more than what we knew as the familiar swede, even more ironic given that my wife comes from south Devon, in England, where this vegetable is grown in quantities quite disproportionate to its edibility. We have spent many a Sunday returning from her parents' house, stuck behind trucks laden with rutabagas, spewing clouds of red Devonian soil behind them, not to mention the odd yellow-purple cannonball. Quite a hazard when you are in a small, drop-top sports car — top up or down!

346

My computerized PC Globe lists the rutabaga as a major agricultural commodity of the United Kingdom. Now that is going to be a big surprise to those south Devon farmers.

Edibility? The classic English way is to find the biggest, toughest and woodiest, peel it by taking only the minimum of skin off to ensure that the woody layer beneath the skin remains; boil the bejeezus out of it; give it a brief straining; and dump it straight onto the plate with no seasoning. The point about not being too diligent in straining is to ensure that during the course of the meal, water leaks out of the rutabaga and both dilutes and cools the gravy. You can of course mash the rutabaga with about an equal weight of butter, and put in tons of black pepper — but that is tantamount to treason, even if it does render the beast edible.

Finally, I have to say that the British do not wax their rutabagas at all: a further indication of how technologically retarded they really are. Typical of a people that knit little ski toques to put over their teapots, drive on the left, regard dogs as equals to themselves and think that microchips are something you serve with fried fish when dieting.

Andrew Forester
Toronto

✉ Turnips have a long history. Their properties are listed in the Health Handbooks (*Tacuina Sanitatis*) of the Middle Ages, and they are included in three important cookery books in France; the *Viandier* of Taillevent — 1315–1395 (*nom de plume* of Guillaume Tirel), chief cook of the King of France, and the *Menagier de Paris* (Householder of Paris), written at the end of the 1300s by an elderly bourgeois gentleman, recently married to a fifteen-year-old girl. Following the advice in the book would not only enable her to run a good household, but make her a better "catch" after his demise. She could then "do him proud," as it were. The third book is the *Du Fait de Cuisine*, written about 1420 by Chiquart, chief cook of the Duke of Savoy, Amadeus VIII, who in 1439 was to become Pope Felix V (actually the last antipope in the Schism).

The *Viandier* uses turnips in a potage or thick soup. He then adds that women are mistresses of all this and know how to cook them. The *Menagier* gives more specific information. Turnips should be picked after a frost, washed two or three times in hot water, then, because they can absorb large amounts of fat, cooked in a warm broth of meat — pork, beef or mutton. In the Beauce region (around Chartres) the people liked their turnips fried then sprinkled with "powder," usually a combination of ground ginger, cinnamon, grains of paradise, cloves and a bit of sugar. The menus show that they were often served with venison or stag. He gives another recipe for cooking young, small turnips first in water without wine, then parboiling in water and wine, adding either chestnuts or sage. The other entry in the *Menagier* adds turnip to a very long recipe for making a compote. Chiquart lists turnips in his descriptions for dinners, those for both fast and feast days, but doesn't give a specific recipe.

It seems clear that turnips were used often, and probably not without cause, for, consulting the Health Handbooks, one reads that according to humoral theory, the Nature of turnips is warm in the second degree, humid in the first. Their usefulness might have been the reason for their popularity, as they were believed to increase the production of sperm and make the body less subject to swellings. Could their popularity be attributed to a desire to carry on the lineage?

The entry in *The Four Seasons of the House of Cerruti* advises that though the white ones look better, the yellow ones taste better, and again suggests cooking in fat broth. On the down side, they may bloat the stomach but can activate the bladder, and if they are eaten with herbs and lots of pepper they "arouse young men to heights of sexual adventurousness."

Vive le turnip!

D. Eleanor Scully
Waterloo, Ontario

✉ As one born in England, I had never heard the name rutabaga until I started shopping for vegetables in Canada, where I discovered that the lowly *swede* was here dignified with this exotic-sounding title.

I remember fields of swedes growing in England during the war; formerly used mainly as cattle fodder, the swede became a staple "second vegetable" in the frugal years of rationing. I remember school dinners comprising a slice of the inevitable Spam and watery mashed potatoes studded with the chewy yellow dice. But my grandmother, an excellent Black-country cook, maintained no stew was flavourful enough without the swede. I was allowed to prepare the globe by peeling it and cutting it into chunks because — unlike the accompanying carrots, which she prepared herself — it was not appealing or tender enough to be eaten raw by an ever-hungry child. Once safely in the big black pot, the bright vegetables were accompanied by chopped onions and herbs, potatoes, seasonings and scrag end of mutton (a half a pound of meat per person per week) to make what was called "a fillbelly stew."

So you see, a rutabaga by any other name would smell as sweet in the stock-pot, as far as this cook is concerned.

Hetty Clews
Fulford Harbour, British Columbia

✉ I was born in Yorkshire and there was a strong Scots border influence in the family. We enjoyed "bashed neeps," which is the equivalent of "mashed turnips," so glorious mashed with cream, butter, salt and pepper. And no Scotch broth was complete without cubed neeps in the rich mutton broth thickened with barley. The smell of neeps always takes me home to my Nanna's kitchen, while my husband despises the smell of turnip, as it takes him back to his days as a captive slave labourer in Germany during the war, where turnip soup was a staple.

There is another name used for turnip in parts of England, and that is mangold. In the Yorkshire dales they grow fields of the stuff. It's put through a machine and comes out like raw French fries and is fed to cattle.

Jean Feliksiak
Winnipeg

349

✉ *Rutabagas At Oxford*: The rutabaga is certainly in the *Oxford English Dictionary*. Perhaps it is not in the *Concise Oxford Dictionary* or the *Shorter*... or the *Pocket*... editions, but if you go to the OED itself, you will find it on page 932 of the Q–R volume.

Its use is illustrated with three quotations. The earliest is from a work on agriculture dated 1800. The second is from Shelley's *Œdipus Tyrannus*, 1820:

"Hog-wash or grains, or ruta-baga has none
Of them been ours since your reign begun."

The article starts with "now rare," but if you go on to the third (supplementary) volume of the *Compact Edition of the Oxford English Dictionary*, you will find "Delete 'now rare' and add "'U.S.'" And there are five quotations, two from Britain, one from Canada and two from the United States.

I grew up in England and never heard the word "rutabaga" until my return to Canada. At the same time, I met the strange North American tradition of the college yell, and it seemed to me that an agricultural college might well adopt one beginning "Rutabaga, rutabaga, rah rah rah..."

I have always found the rutabaga quite revolting.

Philip Chaplin
Ottawa

✉ A rutabaga is not a mangold.

A mangold-wurzel (German, mangold = beet and wurzel = root) is a coarse beetroot. How coarse can a beetroot be, one would ask.

When I was a child in Scotland, they were called mangel-wurzels and sliced for cattle-feed.

There was also a radio program for children on the BBC wherein the hero was Wurzel Gummidge and his wife was Earthy Mangold.

We called rutabay-gas swedes in Scotland. What they were called in Sweden I can't say. (Scotch-wurzels, perhaps?)

Jean Cameron
Gloucester, Ontario

✉ Those learned in the works of the late Damon Runyon will recall that his male characters, whether the hard guys with their equalizers or the weasels with their policy slips, were wont to use the term "rutabaga" as an expression of disopprobrium if not as a downright expletive. If a crap-shoot turned out sour, it turned out rutabagas. If an enterprise came up worthless or worse, it came up rutabagas. If the action on a prize-fight backfired, that too was rutabagas. Also, it must be admitted that the occasional doll was so described. For Big Julie, Nathan Detroit and all the others, the rutabaga was synonymous with very bad news indeed.

Whether this usage is just or unjust I shall most carefully leave to some other forum. I was interested to learn that the vegetable is not grown in the United States. In spite of that, it made its mark in Manhattan at a time when Manhattan was a somewhat more agreeable place than it is now. Today, it's strictly rutabagas.

John A. Livingston
Sunderland, Ontario

✉ I have been a Rutabaga for many years, starting out as a Turner, and being called "turnip" in my youth. This moniker has served me well and over the years has attracted a number of fine specimens of bric-a-brac that are wonderful representations of the noble veggie. My unintentional collection of rutabagery includes a lovely custommade neon sign of the word "Rutabagas," many T-shirts, works of art, and (china) dishes featuring Our Pal The Neep, and umpteen recipe booklets. My Rutabaga Cheesecake once won a prize in a bake-off (recipe courtesy of the now-defunct? Ontario Rutabaga Producers marketing board — the same folks who sent me a Rudy Rutabaga T-shirt).

Are you aware that literature and songs have been devoted to our national vegetable? Included amongst other vegoid volumes in my library is a 1923 Harcourt & Co. copy of Carl Sandburg's *Rootabaga Stories* — a popular bedtime read in our home. One of several rutabaga tunes in my repertoire is Frank Zappa's classic from one of the Mothers of Invention albums in the 1960s titled "Call Any Vegetable." The lyric is simply:

Call any vegetable, and the chances are good
that the vegetable will respond to you
(*chorus, in a yodel:*)
ruuu taaa baaa aa aa ga
rut a baa aa aa ga
rut a baa aa aa ga
rut a baa aa aa ga
rut a ba gaaaaaa.

Monny Rutabagas
Victoria

✉ Of course, for better or worse, like it or not, the obvious candidate for Canada's national vegetable is the Jerusalem or root artichoke, or more correctly *Helianthus tuberosus*. The vegetable is native to North America. It was there before Champlain or even Eric the Red. It can be found growing in every part of Canada, and if we let it it would grow absolutely *all over* Canada. It grows in the States, too, but not everywhere there. It likes nippy winters, so I am pretty sure it isn't growing in Jerusalem.

If we serve it properly and don't overdo it, we can learn to love the Jerusalem artichoke in spite of the fact it is so easy to grow. Have you tried it chopped raw in salad? It is crispy like water chestnut.

To be worth eating, root artichokes must be touched by the frost — they can take a lot of such touching. They must also be fresh. Artichokes that have sat sulking for a few days in a supermarket must be cast out to utter darkness (where they will probably sprout).

The usual way to serve artichokes is smothered in white sauce, and it is by no means the worst thing I remember about boarding school. The cookbook will tell you to peel the artichoke and lightly boil it. That is okay as far as taste and texture are concerned, but then comes wind, and the eater explodes methane gas into the atmosphere, and that, as we all know, contributes to the greenhouse effect and global warming. I was not surprised, therefore, to learn that artichokes are a crop of choice for those who are promoting methane or methanol as the fuel of the future. So for human consumption, and in spite of what the average cookbook says, root artichokes need long cooking in order to be nutritious, digestible and politically correct. But if you do cook them a long time, they turn to syrupy jelly. The Indians used a complicated method of steaming them whole in a pit for at least twenty-four hours, after which they sort of drank them out of their skin. I personally don't see this custom fitting in with our modern life-style — but all is not lost. The great Canadian vegetable can play a leading role in the great Canadian soups.

Soup is very Canadian. It is what you need after shovelling snow for hours or after watching an ice hockey game. A bowl of artichoke soup served with hot crusty garlic bread makes a perfect lunch.

Some may argue that the great Canadian soup is split pea. Properly, split pea soup is a French-Canadian dish. If Quebec leaves Confederation, she will likely take her pea soup with her. Now in that event we better see to it that the rest of Canada doesn't fall apart. One way to keep us together is a great Canadian soup that can be enjoyed from sea to sea (omitting Quebec) and one made from our only indigenous vegetable.

Of course there are variations of artichoke soup, just as there are variations of pea soup, and in spite of what the cookbooks say, you really don't have to peel them — I find life is too short for such a fiddly exercise. Just chop them alone or with carrots and onion and cook them in stock until they are very soft, whirr them in the blender until smooth like velvet; after that you can add cream, wine or sherry or just sprinkle with garlic and devour.

Maybe someday, somebody or something can be described as being "as Canadian as *Helianthus tuberosus* soup."

Monica Oldham
Victoria

A Festival of Idiosyncracy

Or, as someone said, there's no accounting for taste.

✉ I hate shopping! The only things I enjoy shopping for are shoes and stationery. But grocery shopping I hate most of all. I avoid it until there is absolutely nothing in the house, when there is a choice between the local G & H (more expensive) or pizza to go. Then my husband says, in his most pleasing and diplomatic tone, "Are you going to do a big shop soon? Because we need . . ." and he adds whatever it is he most wants.

So. Having dined on whatever scraps I could rustle up, I venture off to the nearest Extra Foods market. I make sure I arrive at around 8:00 P.M. because they close at 9:00 P.M. That way I have to hurry and don't have time to spend too much money. (I also think one hour is plenty of time to waste on shopping for food.)

Sometimes I catch people looking at me sideways as I open egg carton after egg carton and jiggle each egg. I do this because sometimes they are broken and stuck to the bottom of the carton. Then I head straight to the opposite end of the store, away from the fresh produce (am I subconsciously avoiding getting lured into buying more by the succulent tomatoes and shiny apples?). When I do end up at the produce section I look around to see whether the person who spotted me jiggling the eggs is anywhere about, because if I'm buying bell peppers (red, green or yellow), cantaloupes or tomatoes, I smell them. Yes, I smell them to check for mould. I have a keen sense of smell and this way I avoid buying any that may spoil in a day or two.

At 8:50 the manager announces that the store will be closing in ten minutes.

Whether I have all the things on my list or not, I rush to beat the other three shoppers to one of the two check-out stands. Exhausted, I pack up my stuff and drive home, grateful that I do not have to repeat this exercise for another two weeks, or three, if I can drag it out that long!

Philippa L. Joy
Pitt Meadows, British Columbia

✉ In our household it seems to be my father who is the little kid in the shopping cart. It is not any specific aisle or section of the grocery store that must be avoided — it's the whole store! There are many weird and wonderful products in even the most ordinary grocery store, and it appears to be my father's duty to seek out every one and bring it home to experiment with. This often results in cashiers yelling across to each other asking what the product *is* before they can even look up its price. My father, never being one to discriminate, finds wonders from all sections of the store: produce, meats and fish (fresh, frozen or dehydrated), cheese products, not to mention the endless variety of spices, grains, beans and lentils to entertain him. Since he enjoys helping my mother with the shopping, her constant comment is, "It wasn't on the list."

His experiments involve every pot, pan, utensil and kitchen gizmo we own, but I must admit the results are usually very tasty and we often can't even identify the original ingredient we perhaps turned our noses up at.

While some mothers have success rolling their children down the centre of the aisles out of arm's reach, we have yet to find a shopping cart designed for a sixty-seven-year-old gentleman with long arms!

Elizabeth J. George
Winnipeg

355

✉ I am a mother of five, grannie of eleven and great grannie of three, so you can see I am in quite an advanced place in life, and really have learned a thing or two.

We have a fiftieth wedding anniversary coming soon, and having been through war, pestilence, flood and all the things that make life difficult at times, I feel that apart from the obvious things like a lot of love, a great deal of humour, much music, libraries, home-made bread and a good pot of soup, which help us cope with stress, there are two very important things that have seen me through. I guess number one would have to be a hot bath — I have always been so grateful for that — and second would have to be an onion sandwich! Maybe, if the day has been really tough, *both*.

I remember once when the bread-winner got ill, the kids were all little, we had no money, and of course I didn't work. For the first time in my life I worried much, not for myself, but for the kids. I got to the point where I was actually casting around for someone to take us on, and settled on a bachelor friend of ours who was kind, seemed to love the kids and I was sure I could get him. Then I found out he *didn't like onion sandwiches!* I tenderly nursed my husband back to health, and he is still going strong. (The bachelor friend is long gone.)

We have found the perfect sandwich recipe after all these years and I would like to share it with you. Brown bread, lightly spread on one side with butter, the other with mayonnaise, then a layer of thinly sliced onion (we have used all types), crumbled blue cheese and thin slices of apple. Serve whole, with a glass of cold milk. *Heaven!*

I am sure for our fiftieth anniversary the main question will be, "Will you make them or will I?"

Jean Clarke
Granthams Landing, British Columbia

✉ I believe it must have started in my childhood, when we used to make weekend trips to the cottage near Coboconk, Ontario. Some-where along the way we would stop at the now extinct Bluetop

Restaurant. This, to date, was the only place I have found where they would garnish your hamburger with a large *slice* of Spanish onion, and nothing else. Best damn hamburger I ever ate. The pungent oils of that thick slice stayed with us for the rest of the trip. Our breath was unbearable, and we did not care.

In June 1990 I was involved in a serious motorcycle accident and spent the summer in hospital. It was there I was re-introduced to my father's long-time passion for the raw onion sandwich. He would sneak one into my room whenever he came to visit, all sealed in a Zip-loc bag which did absolutely nothing to conceal what he had secreted in his pocket. Compared to hospital food it was manna from heaven. It was soon quite apparent to the nursing staff what I had been up to, and I didn't care. I'll bet that sandwich did as much for my recovery as any medicine.

And, to this day, my house is never without a large, yellow Spanish onion, a loaf of white bread and a pound of butter. I eat onion sandwiches regularly, stink like hell, and still don't care.

My father's simple recipe — not to be altered:

Toast two pieces of white bread and butter (not margarine) well.
Slice Spanish onion as thinly as possible with a good sharp knife, by hand (no cursed kitchen machines), the more the better.
Pile slices on toast, sprinkle with salt and fresh ground pepper to taste. *That's all!*

Do not cut the sandwich. Eat it whole, in one piece. And if your eyes water, your nose tickles, your temperature rises and your breath clouds the windows — fine! You won't care.

Alan Woodward
Mississauga, Ontario

✉ I was catapulted back in time to wintry Sunday mornings of my youth, into a huge kitchen where two cast-iron frying pans sizzled, and my five brothers and sisters and I sat around the great maple table waiting for Sunday breakfast. The windows displayed thick quilt-like floral patterns painted by Jack Frost, but our family was cocooned in warmth and laughter, and the room was filled with the aroma of the morning meal.

I remember eating lard sandwiches. They were apparently an import of my mother, who immigrated from Yorkshire in the late 1950s. She met my Polish father here, and when they married, she brought into the marriage her own cuisine, including lard sandwiches. We covered our lard sandwiches not with onions, but with a generous sprinkling of Bovril beef cubes. What made the open-faced sandwich taste so great was the bread, bought at the Oshawa Bakery just half a block away. Made in traditional style by Russian immigrants, the rye bread, French bread, rolls or Babka would still be warm — it literally melted in your mouth. No other bread graced the kitchen table — Dad said all other bread tasted like soap. The smell of baking bread still evokes memories of a childhood rich with the sights, sounds and smells of the community in which I was raised, among Polish, Ukrainian, Hungarian, Italian, German and Russian immigrants.

Lard sandwiches were eaten at lunch. But thinking of them reminded me of our amazing breakfasts. Usually, breakfast was a generous helping of oatmeal; but on Sunday, we were fed like royalty. There would be tea for all of us, and on the cutting board a couple of loaves of bread fresh from the bakery and handily sliced by my father. The frying pans would hold a pound of back bacon and chunks of blood pudding. Then quartered chunks of green tomatoes would be added, followed by the eggs. After everything was cooked, slices of bread would be dropped into the hot drippings and fried until crisp. Oh, such a delight!

Now my two children eat sensibly — hot or cold cereal, juice (never tea), toast, yoghurt and fruit. The bread is already sliced. It comes from the bakery in the village and costs more than thirty-five cents a loaf. Shoppers there do not wear floral scarves or carry their purchases in baskets. They are usually in a hurry. Our windows never display frosty floral designs — it's not as cold or snowy as it used to be. It's quiet. My children know few words in their grandfather's language.

Lard sandwiches, fried blood pudding, bacon, green tomatoes, eggs and bread — not the food for today's cholesterol-conscious individual. But food fit for royalty in the memories of my childhood.

Helen MacDonald
Newtonville, Ontario

✉ Ah, the meal in the hand.

It took millennia for evolution to come up with the opposing thumb for our species. While it is generally believed that it happened to enable us to better grasp branches and tools, the truth is that it took place just so we could hold a sandwich properly. Allegedly invented by the Earl of Sandwich, and later promoted by Dagwood of the funnies, the sandwich now appears to have slipped in the culinary hierarchy. That seems a shame, as it is one of the few foods that's limited only by one's imagination and intestinal fortitude (I beg your pardon).

A sandwich is created, not made, and, unlike Gaul, is divided into two parts — outside and inside.

Although the primary function of the outside, the bread, is to keep your mitts off the gooey stuff inside, it does make a big difference to the final taste. Bread should be fresh and crusty and come from the local bakery. Choose the most appropriate kind and slice it thinly. Pure white is fine, so is the darkest rye, but don't forget the shades in between.

Save the sliced commercial facsimile for those borderline-criminal luncheon meats. They deserve each other. They also deserve "prepared" mustard, the white gorp that comes in jars and tries to pass for mayonnaise, and alfalfa sprouts. A proper sandwich, like the wild Pacific salmon, should be healthy, vigorous and ultimately tasty.

The only thing to be said about the inside, the filling, is don't be afraid to try different combinations, and don't knock 'em till you've tried 'em.

The right lard, on very dark rye or pumpernickel, with a sprinkling of crunchy bacon bits and the lightest dusting of cayenne and salt, is memorable. So is peanut butter and very thinly sliced rings of sweet, mild onion, like the Wala-Wala or Hawaiian or Texas. Try cream cheese and sliced radish with a pinch of caraway seeds and chopped chives on medium rye. Instead of butter, paint a couple of slices of Italian white bread with maple syrup. Pile on thinly sliced cooked ham, a slice or two of tart apple and be careful with the allspice — you'll never be happy with an ordinary ham sandwich again. Or try it with crushed pineapple instead of apple. How about feta cheese, sliced ripe olives and anchovy bits? Try olive oil instead of butter. Try other substances. Forget margarine. Margarine is to butter as coffee whiteners are to cream. And the fat content is identical.

On the other hand, sometimes simplicity is best. Forget egg salad, the stuff that tastes of something undefinable with onion and celery. Enjoy the real taste of eggs and have an open sandwich (an oxymoron, I guess) of thick-sliced free-range eggs on buttered white bread. Make sure all slices have some yolk, use coarse salt and be liberal with black pepper. It's worth the cholesterol.

Malt beverages notwithstanding, the best drink with a sandwich is coffee. Real coffee. God permitted instant coffee to be invented for one purpose only, and that is to lightly sprinkle the powder, mixed with a few grains of cinnamon, over vanilla ice-cream. Certainly not to drink.

Al Vitols
North Vancouver

✉ Standing hip-high in a clear, cold stream, a fisherman only needs his rod, a few favourite flies, a small net, anti-mosquito oil (if fishing before the fall's killing frost), a tin cup attached by elastic to the belt for occasional, refreshing slurps of stream water . . . and maybe one or two wine-soaked cigarillos (the *only* time they can be smoked).

Lunch is a different matter.

Resting on the shore as the noonday sun warms your pinkish hands, the following would be pulled out of your day-pack if you are a "real" fisherman:

– a loaf of fresh French bread
– a chunk of Royal Blue cheese
– a chunk of Edam (or something milder than the above)
– a few Polski Orgorskis (sans garlic)
– 1 lb. seedless green grapes
– a couple of Nanaimo bars (yes, home-made)
– and, most important, a half litre of *vin de table* (red, of course).
This can be of French or Okanagan origin, depending on your present level of nationalism.

Carrots! You gotta be kidding.

Robb Lucy
Vancouver

✉ How could anyone throw away half a red cabbage? Don't they have a freezer? Here is what you do — melt 3 tablespoons butter in a pot, add ½ cup brown sugar and ½ cup wine vinegar, add 6 cups shredded red cabbage, let this come to cooking stage and simmer 2 hours. You can double this recipe or triple it or whatever, just don't throw away red cabbage! It's good to eat right away, but better still if it's left in the fridge overnight and warmed up next day, then freeze the leftover cabbage in portions you would need for a meal, and all you do is warm it up — it's delicious.

Lillian Pedersen
Redvers, Saskatchewan

✉ I hate garlic with a passion. I dislike the taste, I detest the aftertaste and I am revolted by the after-after odour. I can detect garlic from a long way off. The smallest amount will dry out my mouth and cause my lips to swell. Sometimes when a meal is especially well-cooked I won't notice the taste immediately. Give it half an hour, however, and the old after-taste and all its problems will be there to spoil the memory of even the best prepared dish.

Whenever I go into a restaurant I have to conduct an inquisition to ensure my order is garlic-free. This is very often to the embarrassment of friends and family who may be with me. My kids are totally mortified with the ritual I have been forced to adopt. I have to maintain a constant vigil — don't ask, and sure as heck the garlic will be there in the most unlikely of dishes. I have not yet found garlic in desserts, but the time will surely come.

I find it amazing that society condones such an evil-smelling and -tasting food. We are living in an age of personal cleanliness. Before going out for the evening we will shower, plaster ourselves with lotions and deodorants. We will use aftershave or perfume depending on our needs. We will scrub our teeth and suck our breath fresheners. We would be mortified at the thought of any B.O. or bad breath our best friends could not tell us about. Yet the same people are quite happy to consume vast quantities of Caesar salad in the name of gourmet dining. We are totally oblivious to the stench that surrounds us and that will linger for hours if not days.

In the days before we were married, my wife-to-be took me home to meet her parents. Her father prepared the Sunday lunch. It was an especially tender joint of beef with all the trimmings. Unfortunately, his idea of good food was to roast the joint with a sprig of garlic running right through the centre. Every slice had its own imbedded piece of garlic. I ate it all without complaint or comment. I even expressed my appreciation for a delightful meal. It was then I decided it must be love.

For a little while I used to live and work in San Francisco. I worked in one of the large engineering offices in a downtown high-rise. My office was on the thirty-fourth floor. Every Monday morning I would ride a packed elevator along with a bunch of guys who had made the best of the weekend. The stench of garlic was overpowering. Sometimes I would grin and bear it, and by the time we reached my floor my eyes would be streaming, my nostrils twitching and my stomach churning. At other times I would try to hold my breath for all thirty-four floors and would arrive purple and gasping for air. Either way it took an hour and six cups of coffee to recover.

I don't know the answer to this dilemma for garlic-phobes. Perhaps restaurants should have garlic-free areas in the same way we have no-smoking areas. Certainly the perils of second-hand garlic fumes are every bit as dangerous as any second-hand smoke.

My dictionary tells me that garlic is a member of the lily family. This is definitely one case where "a rose by any other name . . ." does not apply.

David Elson
Calgary

✉ My mother-in-law was fully aware of sherry's medicinal qualities for the last twenty or thirty years of her life. She knew that a small glass of sherry taken at bedtime induced a good night's sleep, and furthermore, if one was awakened by any circumstance then another small glass or two could be relied on. She always insisted that she didn't like the taste of her medicine. I certainly understood that it was purely for the purpose that she claimed. When I noticed that she seemed to really enjoy whatever dinner wine we offered with Sunday dinner, I suggested to her many grandchildren that those might make suitable gifts. You know how difficult it is to buy anything suitable for eighty-nine-year-olds. It turned out that she drank all her gifts but never got the soporific effect that she was looking for, so the bedtime prescription continued. Can I mention brand name? Can I mention brown paper bags and derelict winos in the same breath as Bright's 74? Need I mention how increasingly difficult it became for my husband and me to return on a regular basis to the government liquor store, with her carefully inscribed shopping list of two bottles of "74" and one twenty-six of Dubonnet brandy? (Of course you already knew that the brandy was good for the heart.) Indeed, we gradually developed a pattern of alternating visits to the various outlets lest we be recognized, although I'm not sure that our little ruse was that effective, as Victoria, where we lived in the seventies and eighties, had only a half dozen government stores. Once I tried to circumvent the weekly trip to the sherry shop by buying a gallon of the stuff. However, we had to revert to the usual quarts as she was too old and frail to handle the weight of the big jug.

Then there is the importance of the glass. My mother-in-law used a small juice glass, the kind that come in sets of six with painted oranges apparently growing on some sort of English ivy. When one dropped in for the obligatory familial social visit one invariably was poured about four ounces of this vile-tasting sherry in a dusty orange-encrusted tumbler. The only other drink was the aforementioned brandy diluted with flat canned generic ginger ale (and dust). You see, my mother-in-law was not a drinking person.

I do know beyond any doubting that I will never enjoy a glass of sherry. Who can blame me?

Helen O'Connor
Surrey, British Columbia

✉ For the past eight years, a friend and I, both seniors, have been taking bicycle tours around the Maritimes, down the Gaspé Coast, into Maine, and as far away as the Magdalen Islands. We are always accompanied by our two-litre plastic Coke bottle full of sherry. The thought of it keeps us going after fifty or sixty miles with no motel in sight. I have often lain in the ditch to rest with visions of sherry-happy-hour urging me to get up and go.

Once at a border crossing a stern-faced customs woman asked, "Are you people carrying liquor or cigarettes?" I did not lie. I gave her a steadfast look and said, "Do you think that old ladies like us would have such stuff?" I trust she felt ashamed for asking. (All our luggage is in two panniers at the back of our bikes.)

And then the utter satisfaction of happy hour in one's own room after a long day on the road! — with our own sherry, from our own plastic bottle, in a comfortable motel. Could a scotch or a beer compare? No way. We cyclists in our seventies *know* the joys sherry can bring — that floating feeling that wafts us into the dining-room after a hard day's journey.

Frances Gammon
Fredericton

✉ My experiences with sipping sherry both involve aunts. Not the picnic variety, but those who sport silk dresses, camel coats and immaculately coiffed grey hair.

As a child I remember Christmas eves and social evenings at my great auntie Adrienne's scrupulously tidy apartment. A lifelong spinster (and librarian by trade), she ran her home much as she ran her life. It was well-organized, pleasant and filled with things that gave her happiness. Fortunately my large and exuberant family fell into that category.

Along with home-made candies, tea in feather-light china cups (that belonged to *her* mother!), I remember that sherry was always offered. In delicate long-stemmed liqueur glasses served from an exquisite tray. "A nice glass of sherry?" my aunt would enquire coquettishly and always the grown-ups would smilingly nod in the affirmative.

The other aunt whose sherry-sipping is nearly legendary (in our family at least) is my auntie Joan. She lives in a small village in the south of England, a vibrant and attractive widow who is also an accomplished painter.

We're a great family for letter writing and Joan (and my other English relations) regularly correspond with their extended family over here. Joan, like many "arty" people (myself included), is notoriously disorganized, and the majority of her letters begin with the words "I seem to have misplaced your last letter but shall carry on regardless." Her letters, too, tend to stretch on over a period of days, sometimes weeks depending on whether they too get "misplaced." She generally winds them up, though, by sitting down in the evening after dinner with a "small" glass of sherry and finishing them all at once. As the evening wears on and the stack of unfinished letters recedes, presumably the sherry flows slightly more freely. The last few paragraphs are generally a bit hard to follow (the sherry presumably aiding in freeing up the creative juices) but always entertaining.

As yet (being only in my mid-thirties), I'm still at the white wine stage. But I look forward to the day when I too will acquire a taste for "a wee drop of sherry," that most civilized of libations.

Diana Andrew
Lake Cowichan, British Columbia

✉ Late last summer, my sweetheart and I were getting ready to take a much needed holiday. It was going to be a fairly bare-bones event money-wise, but once we got to our hideaway, we really didn't need much. Ah, but just a few little extras . . . wouldn't that be nice? Then we started noticing all that spare change!

We cleared a dresser-top full of pennies into mason jars, took some already full mason jars from yet another dresser, and laid them all out on newspaper on the back porch. I plunked myself down in a sunbeam and started to roll. (That's not entirely true. I used those new, nifty, plastic gadgets that accept the right amount of coin, and then snap shut. Oh, what a great invention!)

There were a few loons, some quarters, lots of nickels and dimes, and the rest — pennies! I rolled, and rolled, and the money just seemed to keep stacking up. I rolled some more, quietly delighting in the prospect of a holiday with some plusses, because of those wonderful pennies. Pennies, pennies, pennies!

Then a little rhyme popped into my head, and I jotted it down on the newspaper, in honour of said coin.

Oh hail the shiny copper, lowly copper much maligned
For weighing down and tearing up our pockets, most unkind.
And yet I choose to praise it, nay, exalt it for I find
It's given us a holiday, a getaway, a place to stay
It's given us a tidy sum, a vodka run, five days of fun,
And really, when all's said and done, a dresser top, defined.

When all the coin collectors had been snapped shut, I think we had close to two hundred dollars. *Wow!* That's a lot of little extras!

Nora Galloway
London, Ontario

✉ On Mother's Day of 1988, some friends and I left Michigan to go canoeing at Point Pelee in southern Ontario. One of the men in our party had grown up in the area, and along the way we stopped at a farm to pick up an old friend of his.

366

The friend turned out to be an impoverished graduate student who professed that the ankles were the most beautiful part of a woman's body. I laughed, of course, sure that he was joking. Later, by chance (or was it?) I wound up sharing a canoe with him all afternoon.

I'm almost ashamed to admit it, but it took me at least a year to figure out that the reason we couldn't keep up with the rest of our floating party that day was because this young man, seated in the back of our canoe, paddled only when I happened to turn around. We did, though, have several hours alone to talk, and I found his kindness, his respect for and his generosity towards other people both endearing and somewhat mystifying. It was a completely new kind of gender encounter for this American girl, especially one who came from the rather jaded world of commercial television.

Well, the "ankles" routine continued throughout our courtship. Whenever anyone wondered at the attraction between us, a seemingly completely mismatched couple, he would emphatically state that he was in love with my ankles. At one point, I remember sitting with my foot in my then-boyfriend's lap as he tried to explain to another male friend — at length — the beauty and symmetry of my ankle.

The moral to this Valentine's tale is that the ankle-man got the girl, and we have now been married nearly four years. It would be impolite of me to share my husband's true beliefs behind his appreciation of ankles, but I will say that it was a gesture of kindness and respect. Personally, I also think that it was an inspiring statement about love: it doesn't matter what you love about another person, as long as you love openly and completely.

Kim Hutchinson
Harrow, Ontario

✉ In North America, not all unmarried girls have been called old maids or spinsters.

During World War Two when many girls were left to fend for themselves, the term bachelor girl became popular. According to Webster's dictionary, a bachelor girl is an unmarried young woman who works and leads an independent life. As the years passed, many of my generation became bachelor women. Between me and thee, an old Ottawa Valley joke: a bachelor girl is a girl who has never married. An old maid is a girl who has never married or anything.

(Miss) Elva Skuce
Ottawa

✉ When the Phone Rings, I Know It's For Me

The last time a man
Succumbed to my charms,
Venus de Milo
Still had arms.
The Coliseum
Wasn't crumbling down,
And no one suspected
The World was round.
But I'm quite contented,
Not "left on the shelf";
I don't live *alone*:
I live by myself. (And love it!)

Corinne Martin
Kelowna, British Columbia

✉ I am the proud owner of a Dandie Dinmont terrier, and almost every time I take her for a walk someone stops to tell her what a sweet dog she is. When they ask what kind of dog she is I automatically start my answer with, "You've probably never heard of the breed, but . . ." Almost without exception their eyes glaze over and they continue on their way.

She is ten months old and the second Dandie I have owned. I was happy to learn that she is in the second half of the intelligence rating — I would never want a dog smarter than I am! I would far rather be able to say that I have forgotten more than she will ever know.

I never tell anyone that she is stupid, just that she is a free spirit. She will sit (occasionally) when I give the command, but I think it's only because she's tired of standing. And she will walk nicely beside me — as long as there is nothing interesting to sniff on the ground.

I live in a condominium and Dulcie (that's her name — I hope you picked up on the alliteration with Dandie Dinmont) is the love of most of the other owners. She thinks everyone gets on the elevator just to see her! The older I get the more I believe that a wonderful, outgoing personality is every bit as important as a big brain, in dogs as well as people.

M.J. Walker
Halifax

✉ I live in the St. Jamestown community in Toronto, in the vicinity of Parliament Street and Wellesley Street East.

These fifteen high-rise buildings have a population that once rivalled, and perhaps still does, the density of Hong Kong.

My apartment overlooks the downtown core of the city of Toronto, a magnificent view of one of Canada's most dynamic urban centres.

At the height of my apartment, I can, on a clear day, see a binocular view of the Niagara Falls tower and the vapour rising from the great Falls.

If the winds are right, I can clearly hear the roar of huge airliners taking off from Pearson International Airport.

I look over the rows of Victorian houses of Old Cabbagetown and feast on the sights of old trees that line the streets below, a sight for which Toronto is famous in the eyes of visitors.

I am also privileged to have, as neighbours, individuals and families from *many* other countries who have come to Canada to discover and enjoy the freedoms and tolerance of our Canadian democracy.

The St. Jamestown community as a whole is a living, practising United Nations.

I don't need to travel to Europe, or to Africa, or to Asia, or to the Pacific, or to South America, or to the United States, or to other parts of Canada, to meet and converse with peoples from those other lands and regimes.

I am now retired and have witnessed the changes in the complexion of Canada for twenty-two years, right in my apartment building.

The St. Jamestown community is a microcosm of the new Canadian identity, politically, racially, religiously, spiritually and culturally.

I live within easy distance of the old historical Toronto *and* the new ultramodern Toronto.

Metro Toronto's marvellous transit system can take me rapidly to any neighbourhood within about a fifteen-mile radius. And I can always withdraw to my flowering balcony boxes or my library of books and recordings — and I can quickly arrive at the best and finest theatres, cinemas and concert halls, gardens and sports arenas in all of North America.

How fortunate can an urban dweller be?

Arthur Reid
Toronto

✉ Red plaid, eh? In style at last! I wear almost nothing else out to the barn from the morning that ice first skins the animals' water in autumn to the morning that I find the goose sitting tight on her clutch in the spring. My red plaid shirts, whether wool or cotton flannel, are all cosy and comfortable. They co-ordinate effortlessly with a wide range of turtle-necks, jeans, coveralls, windbreakers and parkas and can be worn with sneakers, wellies or felt-lined boots as the weather and job demand. Their bright patterns hide the daily accumulation of hay, manure, soil and grease, and they are essential in maintaining what personal neatness is possible on the day that the buff Orpingtons meet the freezer. Best of all, they match stunningly with my bright red 1956 Ferguson 35, making me a cheery picture, suitable for a

Christmas card, when I blow the snow off the drive. Who says *haute couture* isn't for the practical life of the common man?

Jerry Bloom
Campbellville, Ontario

✉ My grandfather kept his old military tunic in a plastic bag in the back of his clothes closet, and once every blue moon he would drag it out to see if it still fit — which it never did, but as he explained, those old tunics tend to shrink when they are put into storage for too long. His tunic had badges of rank and stripes and sashes all over it, and you could tell from the way he looked at it that every emblem and decoration held some special meaning for him. The tunic was a reminder of his youth — of a time in his life when he was young and strong and confident.

My own tunic — my link with my youth — hangs in the back of my closet, too, except that this tunic is blue instead of scarlet, and is made of denim and not serge. My badges are not of rank, exactly, but each one is as meaningful in its own way as my grandfather's were to him. The jean jacket was a uniform in its own right to my generation, with its own special insignia, and the older and more frayed and patched it was, the more authority it carried. My jacket sports the St. John's First Aid Instructor's badge I earned in 1972, and the Department of Lands and Forests crest I kept from when I was a Junior Forest Ranger in 1968. The project DARE crest from my days as summer staff at that facility is still attached to the right shoulder, and over the right breast pocket there is the dark circle of material where a patch with a peace sign was attached. But most meaningful to me is the large embroidered rose on the back of the tattered and faded jacket, painstakingly worked by my girlfriend as a surprise for me for my eighteenth birthday. Obviously the badges and the embroidery on my jacket were not earned in the way my grandfather earned his medals and promotions, but each one nevertheless holds a poignant memory and reminds me of special friends and moments from my younger days.

So there it hangs, worn and moth-eaten, with leather patches on the elbows and along the frayed collar and cuffs. There is tobacco dust in the pockets from the days when smoking was still okay, and smoking roll-your-owns was not just totally cool, but a statement of both frugality and independence. I hitch-hiked across the country in that jacket, wearing it against the weather during the day, and rolling it up to use as a pillow at night, and I remember how I used to keep a rolled-up ten-dollar bill tucked into the waistband for emergencies.

I don't take it out very often now — once every blue moon or so. The last time I did, I let my seven-year-old son try it on, and it was strange to watch him be amazed that his dad owned something that old. I try it on myself, of course, and you know something? My grandfather was right, those darn things *do* shrink when they are kept in storage.

Otte Rosenkrantz
London, Ontario

✉ My desk frequently looks like the entry point for a paper-recycling depot, and some of my parishioners make veiled comments about the general disorder, and how can I ever work like that?

I am convinced the messy-desk people and neat-desk people are a twain that shall never meet. We simply don't understand each other, and likely never shall.

The debate brought to mind a poster above the desk of someone I worked with in my years before ordination. This person had a boss whose desk was not just neat, but completely empty. No piece of paper lasted more than a minute on its polished mahogany surface, but was referred immediately to an underling, such as my friend. Needless to say, the underlings' desks overflowed with paperwork.

Oh, yes, the poster. It read: "If a cluttered desk is the sign of a cluttered mind, what does an empty desk mean?"

The Reverend Robin Walker
Spruce Grove, Alberta

✉ I once read an article written by Katherine Whitehorn years ago, when she had a regular column in the *Guardian*; at least I think it was the *Guardian*. Her solution to the impossibility of cleaning up an untidy desk piled high with unsorted items was simply to put that day's newspaper over the pile and start anew. That way she would have the layers stratified so that whenever she did get around to tidying up there would be some chronological order to the mess.

Jean Smith
Toronto

✉ I was listening to a debate this morning: is a clean desk better than a messy desk? Which turned into a discussion on messy desk syndrome (MDS).

As I was listening, I was staring at the mounds of material on my desk. I had the ubiquitous manila folders, the in/out baskets, the memo pads, the file holders, all full to overflowing. I had a number of must-do's sitting on top, which would work their way to the bottom by the end of the day.

When I do get my desk straightened out, I can't find stuff. Months later, when cleaning out files, I will come across it, and considering it to still be important, I will file it again. You can guess what happens. I immediately forget where it is filed.

In my time here, I have filled, and emptied, two filing cabinets with miscellaneous material, and in so doing, I have come to the conclusion that I spend almost as much time cleaning and sorting as I would searching and finding, so I don't think a clean desk is that much of a time saver.

This situation brings me into a fair amount of conflict with my boss. He feels that a clean and tidy desk is the sign of an ordered mind, and that clutter is a sign of laziness. In my way of thinking, his desk looks like no one works there, whereas with my desk, there is no doubt that someone works there, the evidence is all over the place.

Paul McCaughtrie
Waterloo, Ontario

✉ On a rare day off (I was refinishing the basement) I heard your item on karaoke singing. I was astounded by the rare opportunity to hear *you* sing. I am not sure if it was tenor or bass or somewhere in between but it was unmistakably singing.

I am taking the liberty of sending you an application for the Toronto Mendelssohn Choir, Canada's premier large vocal ensemble. Since its founding, one hundred years ago (making it Canada's oldest performing arts organization), entrance to the Choir has been by *audition*. In fact, the whole choir re-auditions every year. Getting in once is no guarantee that you will stay in.

You are a busy man so I suggest that we come to your office for your audition. It is not particularly onerous. Applicants sing a set piece from *Messiah* (Every Valley . . . for tenors and Why Do the Nations . . . for basses), do some sight-singing and there is also an ear test. We even provide the accompanist.

Don't be put off, Peter. Who knows, you could find yourself with the rest of the Choir singing five performances of *Messiah* next December along with all the other concerts we give in Roy Thomson Hall. If you had been in this year you might have ended up in the sound track of an Academy Award film. That's right, the Choir sang in the sound-track of *Schindler's List*.

Michael Ridout
Manager, Toronto Mendelssohn Choir

THAT SUMMER IN KEMANO

One morning in January of 1994, my mail, with no warning, contained one of the loveliest messages I've ever received. I reproduce it here in its entirety.

```
grandson from vancouver said he will mail this for us


MR. PETER GZOWSKI,
HOST OF MORNINGSIDE
C.B.C. RADIO PROGRAM                          RETIREMENT LODGE
TORONTO  ONT.                                 VICTORIA   B.C.
                                              FEB.1994

    SIR:

    REASON FOR THIS NOTE:     WE WERE ALL FIVE IN THE CONSTRUCTION OF
    KEMANO 1950    1954

    WE CAME   ALL  FIVE FROM FINLAND   AND ALL ABOUT THE SAME AGE.
    THREE OF US REMEMBER A YOUNG CLEAN CUT AND FRIENDLY FELLER WITHTHE SAME NAME
    AS YOURS

    WE ARE ALL OF US AROUND 90 YEARS OF AGE NOW    AND YOU  (IF IT WAS YOU SIR)
    WAS A VERY YOUNG MAN   LOOKING AT YOUR PICTURES IN THE NEWS PAPERS NOW   THE
    AGE IS ABOUT RIGHT.

    PARDON OUR ONE FINGER TYPING AND MANY SPELLING AND PHRASE ERRORS   WE DID OUR
    BEST

      WE THINK THAT YOU WERE THERE ONLY FOR ONE SUMMER OR SO   AND WERE A STUDENT

    AND SIR   (IF IT WAS YOU)   YOU WERE ALWAYS VERY FRIENDLY AND POLITE WITH US
    EMIGRANTS.

    YOU WERE    WE THINK  MOSTLY AROUND THE CONSTRUCTION CAMP   LOCATED JUST ABOVE
    THE  MAIN CAMP  IN KEMANO
```

NO NEED TO TELL THAT WE ENORMOUSLY ENJOY THE PROGRAM   MORNINGSIDE   AND WE MISS
YOU WHEN YOU GO WITH VACATIONS

WE ARE MOSTLY TOGETHER BETWEEN 9 and 10   BEFORE SOME OF US ARE TAKING AWAY BY
THE NURSE TO A BATH AND MASAGE ETC..

NONE OF US WANT YOU TO GO THROUGH THE LABOUR OF WRITING US BACK ETC.   BUT COULD
YOU MENTION SOME DAY ON THE RADIO WHETHER YOU WERE THE YOUNG MAN ? ? ? ?

WE WILL SET A DAY WHEN WE ALL CAN BE TOGETHER LISTING TO THE RADIO ON   FEB. 7
1994   AND HOPE YOU WILL HAVE THE TIME TO SAY SOMETHING ..... BETWEEN 9 & 10.

YOU HAVE KICKED IT FAR IN YOUR LIFE SIR   AND YOU GIVE MANY PEOPLE A LOT
OF PLEASURE   GO ON YOUNG FELLER   MANY AND MANY GOOD YEARS TO YOU SIR.

FROM OLD OLD MEN   WHO ADMIRE YOU.   I AM SWEDE AND
                                 BY : Karl Johansen , FRIEN

I very much wanted to talk to Karl Johansen and his friends, but in spite of the best efforts of *Morningside*'s diligent investigative producers, we could find no trace of them in Victoria's retirement homes. Undaunted, I wrote — and on the appointed day in the appointed hour — broadcast:

By my arithmetic, they would not have been much younger then than I am now, even though, as I remember it, it was a young man's place.

Kitimat. To most people, it was the great hydro-electric site of its time, a mega-project as we'd call it now, maybe the biggest in the world. But to those of us who went there, it was mostly just a giant construction job. Men (if there were women I didn't see them) flocked from everywhere to work there: men who knew heavy equipment or earned their livings with their backs. Engineers and artisans, bush pilots and cat-skinners, labourers and just men looking for a stake. They came from Newfoundland and Portugal, from Italy and Germany and Sweden and Texas and Saudi Arabia and Quebec and the prairies and . . .

I came from the University of Toronto. The five men who wrote to me last week came from Finland.

Only three of them, according to the letter, remember me, or think they do. But their letter, signed by Karl Johansen, and mailed, as he notes, by a grandson in Vancouver (there are no other clues), takes me back, and, I think, deserves an answer.

Yes, Mr. Johansen, the young clean-cut feller you recall (those were the days, eh?) was me. And if the five of you, in your nineties now and still friends, are, indeed, sitting around the radio in Victoria this morning, waiting to hear from me before it's time for your baths and massage, please nod to each other for me, and confirm your speculations. I was eighteen. It was the summer of 1952. After writing my first-year exams, I had taken a bus to Vancouver and signed on for the float plane north.

Yes, as you remember, I did spend almost all that summer in one camp, just above the main base at Kemano. Like everyone else, I lived in a tent, with a wooden floor and wooden siding. At night, coming back from mug-up, we would feed the black bears, until word got out in the surrounding bush, and there were, one evening, fourteen of them waiting for cookies and sweet cakes. One guy, a beached sailor as I remember, coaxed a bear into our tent one night with an orange and the bear peeled it before our eyes. He — the sailor, not the bear — must have been nuts. That bear could have torn us all apart. Another guy, on another night, hooked a metal pie plate full of chocolate milk to the camp generator and sent 110 volts through a bear's tongue. *That* bear went squealing over the creek. But he came back. We never did get rid of them.

The food was good in our camp — I remember taking a can of lobster out to a tower site one day — but the work was grim. There was at least some rain for forty-two straight days, and black flies and no-see-ums all the time. I was a labourer. I operated what we called a Mexican drag line — a shovel with a nine-foot handle — mucking out the footings of the power line. In my blue university windbreaker, class of 5T6, I was the only person in the labour gang with English as a first language. One man, from Portugal, was studying in a bilingual dictionary that must have been written by an academic. "Pray lend me your shovel," he said to me one morning.

Someone in that labour gang told me if I peed on my hands it would prevent blisters. I still don't know if that works. They — were you among them, Mr. Johansen? — elected me shop steward anyway. I wish I'd been better equipped.

That fall, I took my stake and headed down the inland passage to go back to school.

Karl Johansen and his friends, his letter says, stayed four years, from 1950 to '54. A summer job for me was a new life for them. The black flies and the rain turned to snow and howling winds and back again. Four years in the bush, a long way from home, building, in their fifties, a new life for themselves, and building a country, too.

I learned a lot from the men I met at Kitimat. One who lived in my tent had been a chess champion in the Yugoslav army, and when he heard me say I knew at least the rules of chess, he spent weeks carving a set out of two different kinds of wood, only to learn that even if he spotted me a queen and a knight I couldn't give him a game. But he taught me a few lessons anyway.

And so, as I say, did they all.

Karl Johansen says some nice things in his letter. If I can read between the lines, I think it will kind of please him to have confirmed that the picture he saw in a newspaper the other day of the guy they listen to on the radio is indeed the kid on the Mexican drag line they remember from more than forty years ago.

It pleases me, too, Mr. Johansen. When the nurse finishes your massage today, I hope the five of you will raise a little toast to the days we all worked together, and to everything that's happened to us since. Yes, this is me, on the radio. I'm fine, thanks, how are you?

No word. But my reminiscences had struck other chords:

✉ I couldn't believe the nostalgia your letter to the "Veterans of the Alcan Project" evoked in me. Vivid images poured forth as you reminisced about your days as an eighteen-year-old greenhorn at the Kemano section of that huge project. While you ran your "Mexican drag line" at Kemano, I was doing the same summer job as a seventeen-year-old at the gravel pit at Anderson Creek at the Kitimat site. Later that summer I was shifted to a survey job at the shore line site of the soon-to-be-built smelter. There, the trees, stumps, and vegetable matter had to be removed and replaced with an approximately twenty-foot-thick layer of quality gravel. Thousands of huge truck loads were hauled in by "Eucs," "belly dumps" and White trucks. It was a magical place for a seventeen-year-old between grade eleven and twelve. There were three of us on Alcan's survey team — Bill Moser, the engineer; Bill Jenkinson, a commerce student; and me — the three Bills.

My six summers on the project put me in close memorable contact with the cross-section of Canada's workmen and new immigrants and gave me a deep respect for the talents this country receives from new Canadians. In those six summers that I surveyed, I worked with many carpenters. The best was a Haisla Indian from Kitimat village, three miles across Kitimat Arm. The most accurate instrument man was an Estonian named Leon, who fled Estonia by bike ten minutes ahead of the Red Army. I worked with German labourers, one of whom had bullet holes that pierced his stomach and both arms. Imagine my reaction the first time Hans removed his shirt on a hot summer day. I gave "levels" to Italian crews who worked magic with concrete and lived in a bunk house with Portuguese labourers who weren't sure what our toilets were all about.

And during those six summers I came in close contact with the special kind of Canadian who went from project to project across this vast land, living in bunk houses, eating "Crawley McCracken" food, saving or gambling away his relatively good wages. He worked six days a week and often nine-hour days. There were many memorable characters — the cigar-chomping, blunt and feared project superintendent, John Whittaker (the brother of Charlotte), who put in fourteen-hour days seven days a week and couldn't stand for anyone not going one hundred per cent, the neophyte cartoonist Alan Beaton and his character "Joey" perennially clearing the clogged sewer line, the hard-as-nails, effective workaholic instrument man Ken Dagg, the twenty-year-old Arvida-born Bertrand Belanger, who taught our three-man crew French three days a week while we taught him English the other three. There were pilots, pastry cooks, postal clerks, flunkies, radio operators, photographers, draftsmen . . . I could go on and on. Those were very memorable summers for a young B.C.-raised teenager.

Bill Sparks
Oliver, British Columbia

379

✉ I was just nineteen and arrived at Kitimat as a bride in May 1953. Most of the women were wives of the top construction workers. They were older . . . say in their forties and fifties. (Funny, I think of that as young now!)

Arnie, my new husband, said that no wife of his was going to work. I was a secretary and could have easily found work in the offices, but I did as he wished and stayed home. Our home was with my father as he was able to get one of the hastily constructed houses as he was general foreman of the carpenter shop in Kitimat.

To get to our house one had to climb 117 steps. Each Friday all the ladies would line up to get into the only store — the Hudson's Bay Company. This was the day that the boat brought in fresh meat, milk and vegetables. The store was located in the bottom area of a big complex that housed a large mess hall for the construction men. The men who weren't on shift would sit outside on the steps. I would have to wend my way between these groups. There I was, the youngest woman in Kitimat among all these love-starved, lusty men, trying to look straight ahead to get to that store. I never dared to look up at a wolf whistle or any of the sighs when I passed.

There was a big recreation hall where free movies were shown a couple of days a week. If the men didn't like a particular clip they would start to stamp their feet. The projectionist would take that part off — and I mean, *right now*. When I arrived, all the nearest men would call out, "Coming through," and I would go to the head of the line. If any man had not seen my approach and was using profane language, he was nearly done in on the spot!

Behind the rec hall they had an "official" gambling tent. One day one of the electricians was gambling and he won a trailer. His family was staying in nearby Terrace and he brought them in to live in his new trailer. You guessed it — a week later he got to gambling again and lost the trailer!

The men usually worked sixteen hours a day seven days a week. There was no TV or even radio. It was very lonely for me. One day my dad came home and found me listening to short-wave radio to someone speaking in Chinese — just to hear another human voice. My father said, "You poor kid!"

On fine summer evenings when Arnie had time off, we would walk down to where the new potlines were being built. Arnie would explain to me what was being done. The ground for the potlines had to be brought in by a huge dredge that ran twenty-four hours a day. At first it was hard to sleep as you would hear the large rocks hitting the sides of the pipes.

The only way people could get into Kitimat or Kemano was by boat or airplane. One day a lady was seeing her husband off at the boat dock. As she went to drive off she put the truck into the wrong gear and ran into the boat! She was charged with "undue care and attention" and it made a great story for the camp.

As the road was being built to Terrace, we would drive out to see how far they had gone. One Sunday we drove through all the creeks and got to Terrace! We decided that we may as well drive to Prince Rupert since we had got that far. The whole town came down to greet the first train when the track was completed. What a happy day that was.

There was no beauty parlour for a long time, so my hair grew a long way down my back before I took a trip into Prince Rupert and had it cut. Arnie was sorry because he had liked my long, wavy hair. After that I just went to the local barber like everyone else.

When I had my first baby in July 1954, Arnie was outside doing work on the hospital. All his friends bet twenty-five dollars on whether it would be a boy or a girl. When my son Ray arrived, all the men came to visit and would say, "Here's a few bucks for the kid." His bank account was a large amount overnight.

The meals at the hospital were delivered from the construction mess hall. Only breakfast was made in the hospital — by the patients! One never knew what would be on the menu when the lid was lifted. One morning I had just fried bacon, the next day just eggs.

In 1954 the Alcan families started to move into the new houses at the newly built Kitimat. More order came to town. All the crazy, zany construction days were over.

Clare Mosher
Nanaimo, British Columbia

✉ Kitimat, 1952! This is like a mantra to me.

I arrived in Canada in May of that very year with my mother and four sisters. Dad, a civil engineer, had gone on ahead to build the dock at Kitimat. Single-handedly, I was led to believe. So it was left to Mum to get us from Bromborough, Cheshire, Great Britain, to Dad by whatever means possible and by herself. Having ascertained that there were no direct flights, we sailed: by boat from Liverpool; train from Montreal; and boat again from Vancouver. Mum must have thought that voyage would never end. Then arriving in that smelter town she probably wished it hadn't! Mind you, she has never complained about it. Not to me, at least. All I remember of the getting there was tomato soup after a storm at sea. There was hardly anyone down for lunch that day. I dined with the captain. I have, in truth, only a handful of memories before Kitimat. Kitimat is where my childhood truly began.

I celebrated my fourth birthday in a house sent up by barge from Vancouver. The town site, as it was then called, was underway — oh, those glorious "yuke" trucks — no lorry was ever half so grand. But the town site was still just a name when I celebrated my eighth birthday in that same ticky-tacky wooden box on a scruffy hillside. I didn't see the town site again until 1987 when I read at a school there. *It* now presumed to call itself Kitimat.

What a horror it all must have been to my mum, who grew up in a house with its own name, Ravensheugh, and whose parents were well-to-do shop owners back in that civilized little corner of England called the Wirral Peninsula. Her father got in exotic food-stuffs for the local gentry. Now Mum shopped at the Hudson's Bay.

What a horror for my three older sisters. The only boys around were those smelter workers among whom you found yourself. They treated me all right, scruffled my hair if I got too close. But when it came to the girls, my father didn't trust them. He kept a gun by the door in case any of them came sniffing around. And for the bears, of course. I remember watching through the window as a black bear rubbed his matted back against the house. The house hardly moved at all, but the earth did.

Talk about halcyon days! For me Kitimat was a non-stop adventure. I couldn't possibly have slept the entire time we lived there. We built twig huts up in the woods, thousands of them, a complete civilization: the twig hut people. I hunted with my father and the local Kitaamat Indians. The people of the snow. I remember sitting out a rain storm in a rotted-out log cabin eating egg and onion sandwiches on my mother's home-made bread and playing soldiers with shotgun shells while Dad smoked his pipe and chatted with his fellow hunter. I could pluck a duck and gut a rainbow trout as if I'd been born to the wild life, and yet the flannel shorts and red tie under my Cowichan sweater belied the fact. We made fishing flies at the dining-room table. My father kept them in a brushed silver metal box with little compartments inside, each of which had its own transparent lid. My flies were fat. You'd think a fish would have liked a fat fly.

I went out on a tugboat, the *Mackenzie*, every morning with the tugboat man and his wife, who made high apple pies and gave me coffee with cream in it to keep the chill out. It was *every* morning. It must have been or how could the memory take up so much space in my mind? We boarded a battleship once and I sat in a gunner's seat and it never occurred to me to ask what a battleship was doing there. I guess it was over from Korea, but at the time it seemed just the kind of thing a boy might expect to find parked in his back yard.

I painted the rocks around the RCMP station white and was paid enough to buy something at the Hudson's Bay store: a toy truck, a pop gun? I can't remember toys from those days. Life was a toy. The woods were my playroom. Woods! These were forests. We came to Canada expecting nothing less: forests, Indians and bears.

I was uncommonly rich. I'm the only kid I know who had his own paddle wheeler, a real one, the *Delta Queen*. We played on her all the time, running up the gangway and around the decks and up and down her staircases. I suppose we were allowed to: I don't remember any rules. I do remember the sign that said we could no longer swim in the Douglas Channel. I don't think the word pollution was used in those days, but that was the cause. How quickly Alcan managed to bung the place up.

Mostly I remember a lot of benign neglect. A lot of arriving home late for dinner and playing hookey from kindergarten when they actually got the school built. Once, when I didn't quite make it to school, I found a dead shark on the beach.

But I must have made it to school some time. I remember Ritz crackers and apple juice. I remember my first dramatic role. I was a stalk of celery.

I don't remember specific friends, not their names. There was a tribe of us roaming the forest and the dump and the beach and knocking on the RCMP door to see if there were any chores they needed done. All this while my sisters sat at home in crinolines, listening to records from the Columbia record club, and waited for the school to be built so that they could actually meet someone. Anyone. That's probably not the way it was, but their life in Kitimat seemed extraordinarily dull to me. No twig huts, no sharks.

My parents partied. There seemed to be parties all the time. There was no television, no videos. So they put on funny hats and danced the cold away.

In some essential way Kitimat made me. We moved to Vancouver in 1956 and the rest of my growing up was done in cities. Gout forced my father to sell his guns and rifles and I became, willy-nilly, the compleat urbanite. But I knew when we had kids that it would never be enough to let them grow up without knowing something of the wilderness — Heaven knows, there's a lot more of it than city in this blessed country. So here we are these last five years living on seventy-six acres of rock and pine and swamp in the relatively tame wilderness of eastern Ontario. Few skills gleaned in those far-off outdoor days have really stayed with me. Except the feeling of being at home in the woods. And, perhaps, a certain competence at childhood, a deftness with twig houses, a proclivity to play hookey knowing with an unshakable certainty that wonderful things wash up on the beach.

Tim Wynne-Jones
Perth, Ontario

But, finally, paydirt. Late in February, in the morning mail, this:

```
SIR:

DOnt  KNOW WHAT TO SAY    ON FEBRUARY THE 7-th  AT ABOUT 9.10 IN
THE MORNING WE WERE ALL GROUPED AROUND THE RADIO.
YOU SIR  CAME THROUGH LOUD AND CLEAR      WE WERE ALL A BIT OVERAWED TO HEAR YOU
SPENT  MANY MINUTES ON ONE OF THE MOST POPULAR RADIO PROGRAMS IN CANADA
ON US   AND THE STORY OF KEMANO   AND THE CONFIRMATION THAT THE FAMOUS HOST
OF  MORNING SIDE  AND THE YOUNG CHAP FROM THE 50-ies  IN KEMANO   ARE ONE AND
THE SAME PERSON.                        FROM ALL IN OUR GROUP;
THANK YOU SIR    THANK YOU PETER  FOR DOING THIS    YOU GAVE US A GREAT DAY.
FARE THE WELL    NOW  AND IN YOUR FUTURE.
```
K. J.

```
P S  this note was written some time
after the exciting day
grandson will mail this ..
we all had a (what our
scottish nusrse say;
A WEE DRAM) and drank
to YOUR HEALTH SIR.      k.j.
```

385

INDEX

Anne McCaul, London, Ontario 228
Frances McColl, Winnipeg 289–290, 293
Laurie McGaw, Shelburne, Ontario 114–115
Fred McGuinness, Brandon, Manitoba 43
Ed McKenna, Nepean, Ontario 114
Deborah McMullen, Ottawa 262–265
Jerry T. McNeill, Edmonton 231–232
Ken Mitchell, Picton, Ontario 252–253
Donna Moffatt, Errington, British Columbia 160–161, 169–170
Rose Morley, Owen Sound, Ontario 52–53
Jean Morrison, Vankleek Hill, Ontario 137–138
Clare Mosher, Nanaimo, British Columbia 380–381
Susan Musgrave, Sidney, British Columbia 278–279
David Nadeau, Three Hills, Alberta 162–163
Ian Nicholson, Kanata, Ontario 35
Lyle Nicol, Kenora, Ontario 53
Naomi Norquay, Toronto 298–302
Helen O'Connor, Surrey, British Columbia 363–364
Monica Oldham, Victoria 352–353
Martin O'Malley, Toronto 200–202
Pat O'Neil, Sydney, Nova Scotia 41–42
Mark O'Neill, Vancouver 317
J.P. Onion, Ottawa 229
Alice Page, Pakenham, Ontario 319
Liz Parslow, North Vancouver 138–139
Cleo Paskal, Tokyo 237–248
Susan Patterson-O'Neil, Cobden, Ontario 113
Lillian Pedersen, Redvers, Saskatchewan 361
Sarah M.J. Pelley, Lunenburg County 285–286
Julie Pithers, Winnipeg 107–108
Patricia Post, Vancouver 317–318

James C. Potter, Brampton, Ontario 140
Paula Price, Vancouver 338
Roma Quapp, Ottawa 230
Sue Redford, Prince George, British Columbia 280–282
Tony Rees, Calgary 49–50
Arthur Reid, Toronto 369–370
Jean Reinhardt, Leader, Saskatchewan 285
Michael Ridout, Toronto 374
Jill Cooper Robinson, Halifax 202–205
Bev Robson, Vancouver 150–151
Sam Roddan, Surrey, British Columbia 322–324
Dorothy P. Rogers, Comox, British Columbia 50–51
Otte Rosenkrantz, London, Ontario 371–372
Monny Rutabagas, Victoria 351–352
John W. Sabean, Pickering, Ontario 256–258
Lachlan Salmond, Victoria 129–130
Fred Schenkel, Creston, British Columbia 232
Sander Schimmelpenninck, Oakville, Ontario 226
Tom Scholte, Toronto 341–342
Eleanore Schönmaier, Ketch Harbour, Nova Scotia 342–343
Derek Scrivener, Surrey, British Columbia 140–143
D. Eleanor Scully, Waterloo, Ontario 347–348
Lion J. Sharzer, Aylmer, Quebec 57–61
Marion Sherwin, Baltimore, Ontario 164–167
Elva Skuce, Ottawa 367–368
Jean Smith, Toronto 373
Guida Sparehawk, Charlottetown 147–150
Bill Sparks, Oliver, British Columbia 378–379
Ted Spencer, Appin, Ontario 227–228